WHEN THE GRASS WAS TALLER

When the Grass Was Taller

Autobiography and the Experience of Childhood

RICHARD N. COE

Yale University Press

New Haven and London

Designed by James J. Johnson
and set in Zapf International Roman.
Printed in the United States of America by
Edwards Brothers Inc., Ann Arbor, Michigan.

Library of Congress Cataloging in Publication Data

Coe, Richard N.
   When the grass was taller.

   Includes index.
   1. Authors—Biography—Youth—History and criticism.
2. Autobiography.   I. Title.
PN452.C57   1984   808'.06692   84–3517
ISBN 0–300–03210–2

*The paper in this book meets the guidelines for permanence
and durability of the Committee on Production Guidelines
for Book Longevity of the Council on Library Resources.*

10   9   8   7   6   5   4   3   2   1

for
Terence,
Dominic,
and Laura-Julia . . .
for whom the grass is still deliciously tall

In childhood, everything was different.
Everything was more vivid—the sun brighter,
the smell of the fields sharper, the thunder
was louder, the rain more abundant and
the grass taller.
—Konstantin Paustovsky

*. . . belle très lumineuse sur les talus la jeune
mère femme à robe claire l'enfant disparaît
dans l'herbe trop odorante à souhait c'est le
matin et le vent est liqueur.*
—Paul Chamberland

The June grass, amongst which I stood,
was taller than I was, and I wept. I had
never been so close to grass before. It
towered above me and all around me, each blade
tattooed with tiger-skins of sunlight. It
was knife-edged, dark and a wicked green, thick
as a forest and alive with grasshoppers that
chirped and chattered and leapt through the
air like monkeys.
—Laurie Lee

Impression d'été, de grand soleil, de nature et
de terreur délicieuse à me trouver seul
au milieu de hautes herbes de juin qui
dépassaient mon front.
—Pierre Loti

From the terrace down to the lane there
lead . . . four steps: to the right . . . grass;
to the left . . . grass; venture down—you
will be lost.
—Andrei Bely

Contents

Preface

This study is an attempt to identify, define, and analyze a specific variant of autobiography which, over the past hundred and fifty years, has slowly developed to the point where it may now be considered as an autonomous literary genre: the "Autobiography of Childhood and Adolescence." The Germans had coined a single word—*Jugenderinnerungen*—to denote the form as early as the end of the eighteenth century; and the French, a generation later, were beginning to refer to their *Souvenirs d'enfance*. But, for some strange reason, the English critical idiom has produced no equivalent. "Childhood Reminiscences" sounds impossibly Victorian; "Autobiography of Childhood and Adolescence" is just clumsy. Consequently, throughout the present essay, the genre will be referred to simply as "the Childhood."

In its original conception, this essay was intended to be a straightforward exploration in the domain of comparative literature—an attempt to discover what distinctions, and what similarities, might be discerned in the narratives of childhood experience, as that experience was recreated in literary form by writers from different cultural groups. However, as the material accumulated, it became clear that at least three other intrusive and unforeseen factors must be taken into account.

In the first place, it rapidly emerged that the standard equipment of literary criticism would be inadequate to cope unaided with the problems involved. Jung and Freud, Caillois and Bataille, no less than Frazer and Huizinga, have proved to be as essential to my purposes as any of the more standard literary authorities. This broadening of the field is something I welcome, for it is my profound conviction that the function of the literary critic is not merely to dwell within the confinement of the text but to show how that same text illuminates the wider and more speculative problems posed by the human condition. Digressions, therefore, into philosophy, psychology, anthropology, and sociology have become inevitable, as have others into fields with which I am less familiar, such as cognitive development, psycholinguistics, and prereflexive memory. The present study, therefore, while it remains rooted in the analysis of a specific literary manifestation, nonetheless attempts to embrace a broader spectrum of human experience.

The second problem encountered was that of triviality. By adult standards, the experience of the child—especially the very young child—is necessarily trivial. Its concerns are not those of the greater world, but exclusively those of its own tiny and unimportant section of it. The writer who attempts to use as his subject matter the inferior manifestations of human experience is liable to become implicated in them. In the nineteenth century, when a Flaubert or a Baudelaire portrayed the moral turpitude and degradation of the society around him, he himself was accused of participating in, and propagating, those same infamous immoralities. Western literary criticism would seem, temporarily at least, to have graduated beyond that stage of identifying the creator with his creation. Nonetheless, there is a lingering risk that to write a novel about boredom *may* be to write a boring novel (see, however, Etienne de Sénancour's *Obermann*), that to write a novel about futility may be to write a futile novel (see, however, William Gerhardie's *Futility*)—and that to write a critical study of triviality may be to write trivial criticism.

The fact remains, however, that "triviality" is of the very essence of the childhood experience, and that any attempt to circumvent this basic truth would be to distort the evidence. The skill (or lack of it) in the writer who undertakes to recreate his child-self lies precisely in the manner in which he, or she, conveys to the reader the supreme significance of the unspeakably, the absurdly trivial; in consequence, I have taken courage and devoted an entire chapter ("Inventories of a Small World") to those minutiae of child-delight or torment that are frankly inadmissible in the domain of "serious" literature—the quality of ants' eggs suitable for the feeding of goldfish, or the patterns on the wings of butterflies, or the miraculous names and wrappings of long-vanished sweetmeats. The reader who is averse to such undignified probing among the litter of miscellaneous junk which constitutes an essential element of the child's world should perhaps be advised to skip this chapter—but not without reflecting that there may have been a time in his own past existence when the glittering, transparent miracles of Fox's Glacier Mints were prized more highly than the diamonds which they so closely resembled.

The third problem encountered is, however, the most serious one. In the course of my investigation, what emerged beyond all question was the fact that the experience of childhood—at least in the minds of those poets who, over the last century and a half, have begun to analyze the autonomous existence of their former selves—is "magical." If ever there was a term, to any critic brought up in the tradition of Taine and Sainte-Beuve, of Leavis and

Lukács, of Michel Foucault and George Steiner, which is wholly unwarrant-
able and unacceptable, it is that: "magical" . . .

>   The Soul that rises with us, our life's Star,
>   Hath had elsewhere its setting,
>   And cometh from afar:
>   Not in entire forgetfulness,
>   And not in utter nakedness,
>   But trailing clouds of glory do we come
>   From God, who is our home.

"O là là là *là LÀ!*," as Eugène Ionesco once commented in public on a similarly
unseasonable proposition. Yet the fact remains that all the evidence tends to
accumulate in this direction. If the conclusions appear to be irrational, then I
accept the Jungian argument that the irrational needs, not to be explained
away, but simply to be explained.

   In consequence, I have structured the present study, not in terms of a
currently predominant Cartesianism, which sets out the theoretical proposition first of all and then adduces the supportive evidence, but rather more in
accordance with my own inveterate skeptical and empirical method of argument: first, to formulate a question ("What are the common characteristics of
childhood, as interpreted in the perspective of literary autobiography?"); second, to assemble the evidence; and *then* to propose a tentative theory to explain
that evidence. (It is the principle of the detective story, that last refuge of the
empirical method.) The theory and the explanation (both very tentative) are
given, not at the beginning of this study, but at the end, in chapter 7, "*Puer
Ludens:* An Excursion into Theory." However, like a number of contemporary
novels, this study has no absolute order. The reader who prefers to have his
theory served up first may effectively begin with chapter 7 and read the whole
study, if not exactly in reverse order, at least beginning with the conclusion and
following up with the supportive evidence.

   As a comparatist, I have had to resign myself to my limitations as a
linguist, and I have confined my attention to those Childhoods written in the
major languages of European origin—English, French, German, Russian, Italian, and Spanish. I have, in other words, made no significant use in my
argument of any text that I was unable to consult in the original, with the
exception of a small number of texts written in the first instance in Irish or
Yiddish by bilingual authors.

   A very considerable part of the eight years' work involved in completing
this study lay in locating the texts on which it was based—the majority of them
well outside the canons of recognized "literary classics," but not, for that
reason, without literary merit. Many of them, in fact, might be acknowledged
as "classics" were it not for the fact that the genre to which they belong has
hitherto been perceived as anomalous. Moreover, given the very considerable

number of texts involved—some six hundred—I have made no attempt to refer to each one individually but have preferred to concentrate on following a line of argument, using the richest and most appropriate texts as illustrations. That these are frequently the *same* texts at different stages of the argument is neither accident nor oversight. The "great" Childhood is the one which reveals, through the very subtlety and complexity of its awareness, the implications of the use of this particular literary form; and the "great" poets of the Childhood are not necessarily the great names of literary history. Sometimes they are— Gide, Gorky, Joyce, Stendhal, Tolstoy—but with equal frequency, they are not. Sergei Aksakov, Andrei Bely, Paul Chamberland, Francis Jammes, Maxine Hong Kingston, James Kirkup, Hal Porter, Kathleen Raine, Henry Handel Richardson, Thomas Wolfe—all these have written great Childhoods, whereas often more universally acclaimed writers have failed lamentably. The Childhood is not merely an autonomous genre; it is an art in itself.

Acknowledgments

I should like first of all to acknowledge my gratitude to the people of Australia, for it is to them, on many different levels, that this book owes its existence.

Distant inspiration—students in Brisbane who told me that they were so happy as children, they "couldn't bear to grow up." Half a dozen years later, a first encounter with *The Road to Gundagai*, followed by the discovery, one golden evening, of No. 4 Grace Street, Malvern, unchanged in the minutest particular from the house described so hatingly-lovingly by Graham McInnes in that unforgettable account of his childhood. Shortly afterward, a first reading of *I Can Jump Puddles* . . . and, at a Christmas party held in the torrid heat under the gum trees of Clem and Nina Christesen's property at Eltham, outside Melbourne, a conversation with Alan Marshall himself. The idea was born.

And four years later came an invitation from the Humanities Research Centre at the Australian National University in Canberra to spend five months there, just writing . . . and talking . . . and writing. Without question, it was under the inspiration of Dr. Ian Donaldson, the enlightened director of that most enlightened of all research centers, that the present book began to take shape. To him, and to all his colleagues, my thanks.

Nearer home, I would like to thank my wife Ada for all her physical and intellectual foot-slogging around the shelves labeled "Autobiography" in Municipal, Further-Educational, and other miscellaneous libraries, and to apologize to her if, occasionally, the sheer weight of the day's "catch" which she brought home in the evening left me appalled rather than delighted. To her also (since she is a graduate in psychology and educational theory as well as literature) my gratitude for stopping me from talking too much nonsense about matters that I do not fully understand.

In particular fields, I would like to acknowledge my debt to Mr. Cedric May of the University of Birmingham, England, to Dr. Thomas Tausky of the University of Western Ontario, and to Professor David Smith and his colleagues in the University of Toronto for their consistent helpfulness in my efforts to locate Canadian specimens of the Childhood; and to Dr. Livio Dobrez of the Australian National University, for sharing with me his profound knowledge of contemporary Australian writing. Further, my acquaintance with the Childhoods of the Third World would have remained sadly inadequate without the enthusiastic cooperation of those two experts on contemporary African and exiled-African literature—Anglophone and Francophone respectively—Professors Bruce and Adèle King.

Finally, I would like to express my thanks to the University of Warwick, to the Canadian Commonwealth Universities' Federation, and to the University of California, Davis, for the help and encouragement that they have given, whether in terms of sabbatical leave, research fellowships, travel grants, or simply in terms of Inter-Library Loan facilities. Without such encouragement, it is unlikely that the present study would have come into existence.

In the following text, quotations, save for the occasional illustration in verse, are given in English. The translations are my own, except where otherwise indicated.

R. N. C.

Introduction:
The Discovery of Childhood

In the sun born over and over,
   I ran my heedless ways,
   My wishes raced through the house high hay
And nothing I cared, at my sky blue trades, that time allows
In all his tuneful turning so few and such morning songs
   Before the children green and golden
      Follow him out of grace.
                              —Dylan Thomas, "Fern Hill"

The Childhood is not just a "standard" autobiography which has failed or else been left uncompleted because the writer has run out of time, enthusiasm, or inspiration. It has a purpose of its own: it is an independent genre, with its own internal laws, conventions, and structures. "Standard" autobiography is the writer's attempt to tell the story of his life in a manner as factually accurate, and yet as significant, as possible; to reveal from the inside that personality and those motivations which his contemporaries hitherto have known and judged (or misjudged) only from the outside. Accuracy is his taskmaster; he is a responsible adult writing for other responsible adults about yet a third responsible adult: himself. Writer, reader, and subject share a common code, live in an identical dimension of rationality and understanding. What is significant to the one will normally be significant to the others. Between Self and Others there is no necessary barrier, beyond the inevitable obstacle of language.

By contrast, in the Childhood there is no such common ground of automatically shared preconceptions and presuppositions. The former self-as-child is as alien to the adult writer as to the adult reader. The child sees differently, reasons differently, reacts differently. An *alternative* world has to be created and made convincing. The experience of childhood, as every major observer from Jean-Jacques Rousseau to Jean Piaget has striven to demonstrate, is something vastly, *qualitatively* different from adult experience, and therefore cannot be reconstituted simply by accurate narration. Moreover, in relation to the child-self, what *is* accuracy? The adult-self, recalling an event which transformed its awareness at the age of six, may subsequently reconstruct this event wrongly; but it is often in the very wrongness of the unverifiable recollection that its significance lies. Childhood constitutes an alternative dimension, which cannot be conveyed by the utilitarian logic of the responsible adult. Not "accuracy" but "truth"—an inner, symbolic truth—becomes the only acceptable criterion. It is not surprising, therefore, to find that the majority of significant Childhoods have been written by poets, or at least by writers who have seriously attempted to write poetry.

In 1961, contributing a very brief introduction to Clifford Dyment's *The Railway Game*, Vivian de Sola Pinto observed that "the two most vital and interesting forms of English imaginative prose in the mid twentieth century are the new historical novel and the new poetic autobiography." The "new poetic autobiography" is a rather vague phrase, but a few lines later Professor Pinto becomes more precise:

> The ancestry of the new poetic autobiography is not . . . easy to trace. I suspect that it owes something to Proust and a great deal to Joyce's *Portrait of the Artist as a Young Man* and the autobiographical part of the writings of D. H. Lawrence, especially *Sons and Lovers*. An early example of this sort of writing was Dylan Thomas' *Portrait of the Artist as a Young Dog*. The form may be said to have reached its maturity in James Kirkup's *The Only Child* and *Sorrows, Passions and Alarms* and Laurie Lee's *Cider with Rosie*.[1]

This, to the best of my knowledge, is the first use in modern criticism of the term "*poetic* autobiography"; and it is highly significant that the examples given consist entirely of Childhoods. On the other hand, the progression from *A la recherche du temps perdu*, by way of the *Portrait of the Artist as a Young Man* and the *Portrait of the Artist as a Young Dog*, to *The Only Child* emphasizes what is perhaps the major difficulty encountered in any attempt to analyze the genre—namely, that the borderline between fact and poetry or fiction is virtually impossible to determine. Where the criterion of narrative veracity is the poet's "truth" rather than the historian's "accuracy," how is it possible to establish whether a narrative of that strange, alternative dimension of childhood experience is, or is not, "autobiographical"?

I

Fair warning. None of these sketches is wholly true. None is entirely untrue.
                                    —Robert Luther Duffus, *Williamstown Branch*

In the last analysis, the Childhood is an ideal form, destined never to be fully

---

1. Clifford Dyment, *The Railway Game* (London, 1962). Professor Pinto's introduction is dated May 1961. For a rather different interpretation of the notion of "poetic autobiography," see William C. Spengemann, *The Forms of Autobiography* (New Haven, 1980), especially pp. xvi–xvii, 110–65.

realized: the ideal being to tell a total truth about a previous self which, in reality, can never be more than half-remembered.[2] Ideally, it should have no "style"; it should be "not literature, but a sort of documentary."[3] The classic Childhood is one in which the writer conscientiously tries to approach as closely as possible to this ideal, producing an unstudied prose-narrative in the first person singular, in uninterrupted chronological sequence (probably authenticated by photographs from the family album), with dates and facts precisely adduced in their proper places and with a minimum of improvisation—restraints which often compel the greater novelists or poets to fall well below their best: witness John Masefield or Jules Supervielle, Henry James or Theodore Dreiser. This "classic" approach is frequently the accompaniment of dullness and mediocrity; nonetheless, it constitutes the basic material out of which the more memorable masterpieces are fashioned, and it would be unwise to neglect it. By contrast, the true poet reorganizes and refashions accuracy in the direction of truth—to the embarrassment of the critic, who is faced with the uncomfortable task of deciding what is autobiography and what is something else.

From the outset, therefore, the "rules of the game"[4] impose a certain degree of compromise between fact and fiction. The truth, in its totality and immediacy, is out of reach forever. At best, it can be reevoked through art in a new form, conjured up by way of symbols, images, and impressions, and endowed retrospectively with a pattern and a significance which it can rarely, if ever, have possessed at the time, when the later-circumscribed facticity of the past was dissolved into the shapeless and elusive fluidity of the present.

Moreover, argues the current doyen of studies in the field, Philippe Lejeune, *all* autobiography—but most of all the autobiography of childhood—rests on an act of faith. Given the text alone, the reader has no means whatsoever of determining whether what he reads is the product of memory or of imagination. In the eighteenth century, when the novel was striving to free itself from the imputation of vain fantasy and improbable romance, it frequently had recourse to the forms of fictitious autobiography, in order to endow itself with the weight of authority. "I do hereby give notice to all booksellers and translators whatsoever," wrote Sir Richard Steele in *The Tatler* (No. 84, 22 October 1709), "that the word *Memoir* is French for a novel." By a

2. *Half Remembered* is in fact the title of a Childhood by Peter Davison (New York, 1973).

3. Georges Simenon, *Je me souviens* (1945; reprinted in *Œuvres complètes*, ed. Gilbert Sigaux, Paris, 1968), 17:15. Concerning the attempt of one of the earliest authors of a Childhood to "write without style," see my essay, "Stendhal, Rousseau and the Search for Self," in *Australian Journal of French Studies* 16 (1979): 27–47.

4. One of the major Childhoods of this century uses this concept in its title: Michel Leiris's *La Règle du jeu* (4 vols., 1948–76).

neat reversal, the twentieth-century writer, searching for a different kind of authenticity, based on freedom from the encumbering autocracy of trivial and uninteresting fact, tends ever more often to entitle his work a novel even when, most palpably, it is in every significant aspect based on his own lived and remembered experience.

If we abide, then, by the strictest rules of literary interpretation, we are forced to rely on the good faith of the author himself. If he states in so many words, "The story which I am telling is that of my own childhood," we may, provisionally at least, take him at his word. Conversely, in the absence of any such positive affirmation, we must assume that the text in front of us is a fiction and treat it for what it undoubtedly is in any case: a particular sub-species of the novel. This is what Philippe Lejeune calls the "autobiographical pact" between writer and reader, and he excludes from his own analysis any text which does not specifically make this claim. It is no part of the critic's role, he maintains, to take upon himself the undignified postures of a Sherlock Holmes, down upon the carpet on hands and knees detecting traces of self-revelation and self-confession where none is claimed. "If an author does not state of his own volition that his text is an Autobiography, then we have no call to be more royalist than the king."[5] The thesis is tempting; it is convenient; and it is a useful corrective to critics of the Freudian school, who are all too willing to discover personal confessions, conscious or subconscious, in virtually every line a writer sees fit to publish. But for our purposes the *pacte autobiographi-que*, in its strict interpretation, is too rigorous. It excludes too many master-pieces in the genre. In the Childhood, the borderline between autobiography and fiction is admittedly nebulous; nonetheless, it is not impossible, save in comparatively rare cases, to establish its whereabouts.

In defense of Lejeune's rigorism, it must be emphasized that his analysis refers to autobiography as a whole, rather than to the autobiography of child-hood alone; and it is, of course, far more unusual for the adult, moving as he does among realms of verifiable fact, to disguise or fictionalize his identity than it is for the writer recreating a child who is in any case a being alien to his present self. There is no need, therefore, to relegate Anatole France, say, or Thomas Wolfe, Marcel Proust, and Jules Renard irrevocably to the domains of fiction because they called their recreated selves respectively Pierre Nozières, or Eugene Gant, or Marcel, or simply *Poil-de-carotte*. Anatole France, in partic-ular, is quite explicit about his reasons for assuming an alias, and they con-

5. Philippe Lejeune, *L'Autobiographie en France* (Paris, 1971), 24–25; see also *Le Pacte autobiographique* (Paris, 1975), especially pp. 13–46. Frank Baines, in his *Look towards the Sea* (London, 1958), fulfills the requirements of the "pact" in the most straightforward manner of all, by declaring on the dust jacket of the book: "Librarians may like to note that it can be kept on the shelf labelled 'Autobiography.'"

stitute an important statement about one of the basic assumptions underlying the present study:

> For my part, I was by no means ill-pleased to alter, in these pages, both my name and my background. By doing so, I acquired a much wider freedom to talk about myself, to indulge in self-accusation, self-praise, self-pity, self-complacency, and self-castigation at leisure. . . . This fictitious name did not disguise me; but it did signal my intention not to appear.
>
> This disguise has enabled me to conceal the gaps in my recollection, which is very faulty, and to compound the wrongs of memory with the rights of imagination. I have been able to invent concatenations of circumstance to supply the place of those which eluded me . . . ; but I am persuaded that no man ever told lies with a deeper concern for the truth.[6]

It was Jean Cocteau who coined the famous expression: "Il faut mentir pour être vrai" ["Lies are essential if one is to tell the truth"]; and his own Childhood provides a perfect example of the poet's particular form of autobiographical license in action. In reality, Cocteau's father died while he was still young and he was brought up by an intrusively possessive mother. In *Le Livre blanc* (1928) the situation is reversed: he is a motherless child, brought up by an aggressively masculine father; and this belligerent masculinity imposed on him at an early age is interpreted as being the source of his later homosexuality. Perhaps, in some obscure, negative way, it was; at all events, the *essential* elements of his adolescence—his discovery of this same homosexuality, his desperate quest for "normality," his religious crises interwoven with escapades among the sailors of Toulon—all these are as authentic and as impassioned a "confession" as anything in Jean-Jacques Rousseau or in Michel Leiris.

By contrast, if the autobiographical element, however memorable, provides merely a background, while the essential structure of action or of psychological development is drawn from other sources, then we may regretfully assign the work to the domain of fiction. Such is the case with Alain-Fournier's *Le Grand Meaulnes* (1913), or with Barry Hines's *A Kestrel for a Knave* (1968); with Charles Dickens's *David Copperfield* (1849–50) or with D. H. Lawrence's *Sons and Lovers* (1913); with Henry Roth's *Call It Sleep* (1934) or with Patricia Blondal's *A Candle to Light the Sun* (1960). *David Copperfield* provides an interesting test case. The immortal Mr. Micawber may be, indeed in all proba-

---

6. Anatole France, *La Vie en fleur* (Paris, 1922), 344–45. Clive James, in his *Unreliable Memoirs* (London, 1980), offers a neatly paradoxical formulation: "Most first novels are disguised autobiographies. This autobiography is a disguised novel." Cf. also Lord Dunsany, in his introduction to Mary Hamilton's *Green and Gold* (London, 1948): "The only thing that prevents this book from being a beautiful novel is that is has no plot" (p. 7).

bility *is*, a portrait of Dickens's own father, but so transformed, so profoundly assimilated into a totally alien structure that the autobiographical sources of inspiration are merely irrelevant. Mr. Micawber works on the level of fiction, and specifically, exclusively on that level. Even among what we shall discover to be a crowded gallery of eccentric, inefficient, and perennially bankrupt fathers, his proportions remain too gargantuan to be fitted into the domain of factuality.

In this borderline area between fact and fiction, Mr. Micawber is a personage well worth considering, not only in himself, but as he relates to the structure of the novel. Anthony Powell, in his own autobiographical *Infants of the Spring*, attempts to analyze the difference between the way a writer handles characters drawn "directly" from real life and characters adapted to the requirements of fiction. As a novelist himself—indeed, as a far better novelist than autobiographer—he is particularly well qualified to analyze the process of transmutation:

> Most novelists draw their characters and scenes in some degree from real life. . . . On the other hand, the images that present themselves to the mind of any novelist of more than amateur talent take an entirely different form when the same writer attempts to describe "real people" known to him; the former are altogether more complex, freewheeling, wide-ranging.
>
> There are no doubt exceptions to this rule, especially minor figures in the background to certain novels, drawn directly from life, but playing little or no part in the development of the narrative. . . . The smallest individual change made by a novelist to suit the story's convenience means, in truth, that all genuine dependence on the original model ceases—in contrast with traits (possibly inconvenient from a fictional point of view) that must unavoidably be chronicled about a "real" person in Memoirs or Autobiography. (London, 1976, pp. 52–53)

What must be deduced from this is that the character in the novel is, to a larger extent than is generally recognized, determined by the plot. He has to *act*; and his inner being is existentially defined by his outward action. He is transformed in the light of what he has to *do*; and what he does, in the novel, is only in the rarest of circumstances what he does in real life. By contrast, autobiography has no plot—at best a pattern, but a pattern which affects exclusively the narrator-subject, not the characters who surround him. They will not have to act; and although they will necessarily be transformed to a certain degree by the very fact of passing through the artist's mind and vision, there is nothing that need be added to the original. The autobiographer may *combine* existing material in patterns which were not those of recorded reality, but he may not *add*, "not even [as Erich Kästner so graphically legislates] a mouse."

If we apply this criterion—"plot" and "action," as opposed to "pattern" and simply "existing"—to any of the borderline cases where the attribution to novel or to autobiography is uncertain, the issue will normally resolve itself. In some instances—typically Valentin Kataev's *Lonely White Sail* (1936)—the line of demarcation will indeed become so clear that one can affirm without hesitation that *these* scenes are imagined while *those* are authentically remembered. In addition, however, there are two criteria which, while by no means absolute in themselves, provide useful corroborative evidence. The first of these is the use, to any significant extent, of dialogue. "The ways in which [this book] is not true will be immediately apparent," writes Arthur Calder-Marshall in his introduction to *The Magic of My Youth* (1951): "Lengthy conversations are not remembered verbatim over a quarter of a century." Beverley Nichols, in *Father Figure* (1972), notes conscientiously that the only conversations he has recorded are either those "which I heard not once but a hundred times" or those which were "impressed on a youthful mind in a very high state of nervous tension." Even more emphatically, Robert de Roque-brune, in his *Testament de mon enfance* (1958), avers that he can truthfully record only two words spoken during the whole of his childhood—an unforgettable instant when his mother stated "It's *tomorrow!*" although neither he nor she could subsequently determine what was due to happen after that fateful interval. This does not alter the fact that some impressive Childhoods are written almost entirely in dialogue—Peter Abrahams's *Tell Freedom* (1954), for instance—without therefore necessarily becoming incredible as the record of a certain "truth of memory"; yet, in others, scraps of dialogue introduced for realistic effect merely have the irritating consequence of obscuring the authentic truth of the child's underlying reactions.[7]

A second method for detecting a significant element of fictionalization in a text, without reference to external evidence, explores the concentration of the time-scale. By definition, the Childhood is an extended form, carrying the self from first consciousness to full maturity over an allotted span (normally) of some fifteen to eighteen years. Very occasionally this time-span can be abbreviated for purely internal reasons: because one section of the experience, typically in wartime or revolutionary situations, was so intense that the whole process of maturation was speeded up to a quite abnormal extent;[8] because, for sociohistorical, mythological, agricultural, or other reasons, the cyclical pattern of the year takes precedence over the linear chronology of development;[9] or, finally, because the writer wishes to analyze the formation of one

7. See, for example, Valerie Avery, *London Morning* (London, 1964), 8–13.

8. For example, Janina David, *A Touch of Earth*, 1966; Joseph Joffo, *Un sac de billes*, 1973; Jerzy Kosinsky, *The Painted Bird*, 1965; Frank O'Connor, *An Only Child*, 1961.

9. There is a classic instance of this structure in Gladys Carroll's *Only Fifty Years Ago* (Boston, 1962), which consists of twelve chapters, each titled with the month of the year and illustrated with appropriate items from *Leavitt's Farmer's Almanack* for the year 1910. For other instances, see Anne Treneer, *School House in the Wind* (1944); Robert Thomas Allen, *When Toronto Was for*

isolated element in his identity.[10] But in the majority of cases, the condensation in time reveals an attempt at a compromise between the retrospectively apprehended pattern of autobiography and the preconceived plot of the novel. This compromise may serve simply to emphasize a pattern which, otherwise, might not emerge with sufficient clarity; alternatively, it may be a concession to the reader, providing the tighter structure, the controlled sequences of suspense and resolution in the expected and time-honored traditions of fiction, which are absent in the comparative shapelessness and uneventfulness of lived experience. Most commonly, it is the period of adolescence—often corresponding to the main formative years at school—which can be thus isolated with the least interference from purely fictional elements: Robert Musil's *Young Törless*, for instance, and Thomas Hughes's *Tom Brown's Schooldays*, Henry Handel Richardson's *The Getting of Wisdom*, Rudyard Kipling's *Stalky & Co.*, Gilbert Cesbron's *Notre prison est un royaume*, and so forth. Nonetheless, the fact remains that in all of these, the novelistic element of *action* as opposed to *being* is significant; and the characters (including the self), trapped in a fast-moving sequence of incidents, are to a greater or lesser extent reshaped accordingly.

This rather lengthy excursion, anticipating as it does points which will be made in detail later, is necessary in order to explain why certain texts which, to a greater or lesser degree, fictionalize the childhood experience, have been included, while others have been debarred from the present study. By and large, the greater the writer, the more intense is the experience of childhood recreated, and the greater the need, in consequence, to refashion it in terms of poetic, or permanent, significance. To have confined this study to those writers who specifically make the "pacte autobiographique" would have meant excluding some of the most famous examples; on the other hand, no fictions, however poetic, have been admitted unless they satisfy certain clear and rigid criteria of autobiographical authenticity.

Having reached this point, it seems advisable to offer a formal definition of the Childhood. The genre, as I shall be discussing it, may be described as *an extended piece of writing, a conscious, deliberately executed literary artifact, usually in prose* (and thus intimately related to the novel) *but not excluding occasional experiments in verse,*[11] *in which the most substantial portion of the*

Kids (1961); Aleksei Tolstoy, *Nikita's Childhood* (1919–22); Antonine Maillet, *On a mangé la dune* (1962). The "cycle of the year" formula is particularly effective in Childhoods written for a juvenile readership: cf. Louisa May Alcott's *Little Women* (1868–69), or the first half of L. M. Montgomery's *Anne of Green Gables* (1925).

10. For example, Andrei Bely, *Kotik Letaev* (1915–16); Eugène Ionesco, *Découvertes* (1969).

11. I exclude (save for purposes of occasional illustration) short, detached lyrics and similar pieces, such as Thomas Hood's "I Remember, I Remember," Wordsworth's "Ode on the Intimations of Immortality," Victor Hugo's "A propos d'Horace," Rimbaud's "Enfance," or Louis MacNeice's "Autobiography." I also exclude the short story, save where a group of these may be held to constitute a coherent cycle.

material is directly autobiographical, and whose structure reflects step by step the development of the writer's self; beginning often, but not invariably, with the first light of consciousness, and concluding, quite specifically, with the attainment of a precise degree of maturity. The last element in the definition is among the most essential. The formal literary structure is complete exactly at the point at which the immature self of childhood is conscious of its transformation into the mature self of the adult who is the narrator of the earlier experiences.

There will be no need to underline the fact that the Childhood, considered as a literary form, is closely allied to a number of other recognized genres. It has, obviously, direct affinities with the *Bildungsroman;* between the two, however, there is a fundamental difference. The *Bildungsroman* relates the development or "formation" [*Bildung*] of the hero (who may, or may not, be identifiable with the author) from the point of his first full awareness of himself as an individual to a concluding point of his final and positive integration into the society of which he is a member. The Childhood, by contrast, narrates the development of the hero (who specifically *is* to be identified with the author) from a point of nonawareness to a point of total awareness of himself as an individual, and particularly as a writer and as a *poet*, who will produce, as evidence of his mature poet-identity, the Childhood which he has written.[12] Compare this with the hero of the *Bildungsroman*, who will (as it were) use the account which he has written of his later formative years as evidence that he is at last a worthy member of a sophisticated and articulate community. The *Bildungsroman (Wilhelm Meister, Der Grüne Heinrich)* subordinates the self (ultimately) to the judgment of the greater world; the Childhood imposes its own standards and, in the last analysis, judges and frequently condemns the world in terms of the self.

The Childhood is also related, although perhaps less obviously had it not been for the imperious presence of Wordsworth's *Prelude*, to the epic. It has (as Wordsworth instinctively realized) the epic dimension. It covers a wide span of time and a broad canvas of events, with a hero or heroine who starts out on a journey, who undergoes innumerable experiences which ultimately will form his or her definitive character, and who finally returns more or less safely to haven, from which resting-point he or she will shortly embark again on a still greater, still unfinished odyssey, the most momentous of all journeys, the epic of adult life. At the same time, however, it is related to the "Confession," insofar as the overriding concern is one with an exact and absolute truth, and further, in that normally the element of imagination or fantasy is restricted to a subordinate role—namely, that of making the factual and unadorned report effective as a consciously contrived piece of literature. And it

12. While "poetic" autobiography is not necessarily produced by poets, in the case of the Childhood this does happen with remarkable frequency. See the conclusion to the present study.

is worthwhile adding that, in contrast to writings *about* children, the Childhood is very rarely sentimental.

II

It may be assumed on good grounds that seeing and hearing have a different quality for infants than for grown-ups, and that they are more aesthetic and less intellectual in the first years of life. . . . Most of the members of the human race have lost the capacity to be poets, painters or musicians.

—Eric Berne, *Games People Play*

If the Childhood has been slow to gain recognition as an independent literary form, it may also be said that the discovery of childhood itself came late to Western civilization.

Our ancestors, by and large, would seem to have had very little time for children—no more for themselves in retrospect than for those whom they had produced. The wealthy handed them over to servants and tutors; the less wealthy farmed them out to peasant women in the comparatively healthy countryside, away from the endemic infections of the towns, for all their infant years, accepting them back into the family only when the first signs of controlled adult behavior were manifest. And the poor, overwhelmed with the hardships of staying alive, could only wait impatiently for them to grow up and contribute to the maintenance of the household.

The whole pattern of life, moreover, was simpler. In medieval Europe, as in the larger part of present-day Africa, the complexities of child psychology represented a luxury in which society could scarcely afford to indulge. The boys followed the father and learned the father's skills, just as Climbié, on the Ivory Coast in the twentieth century, "learns his trade as a man" in the company and by the example of his uncle N'Dabian;[13] the girls stayed with the mother and prepared, from their earliest years, to become mothers in their turn. A child with "complexes" was simply a misfit, unlikely to survive; even today, in West Africa, an "Oedipus complex" is a virtually meaningless term— something that was invented by Sigmund Freud solely in order to explain certain quirks of behavior encountered among the pampered Viennese bourgeoisie of his time. In Nigeria, in Senegal or in Dahomey, both child and adult have more urgent matters to attend to.

This sociologically based impatience with children was reinforced, in Europe, by religious and philosophical attitudes. Christ's wonder at the inspired innocence of children found few to echo it before the generation of Blake and Wordsworth. Instead, attitudes were fashioned rather by St. Paul and St.

13. Bernard Dadié, *Climbié* [1953], in *Légendes et poèmes* (Paris, 1973), 99.

Augustine—by St. Paul, who saw the thoughts and feelings of the years preceding manhood as mere irrelevance, to be discarded along with hopscotch, tag, and knucklebones once the serious burdens of manhood were assumed; even more by St. Augustine, to whom the child appeared as a monster of egoism and evil temper, "conceived in iniquity," carried and nourished sinfully in the womb, manifesting its presence in the world from the outset by fury, violence, jealousy and impurity, and heralding its future adult state by its overmastering urge to tyrannize and enslave all those with whom it came in contact. "Then where, my God, where, O Lord, where or when was I, Your servant, innocent?" Even more radically than St. Paul, St. Augustine disowned his beginnings. Himself as he had been, as a child, was long since dead; himself-as-a-child was simply not-himself; it was the absolute negation of everything that later he was to become. "What concern have I now with a time of which I can recall no trace?" he asked, having, a few lines earlier, summed up even more categorically: "I am loth, indeed, to count it as part of the life I lead in this world."[14]

And, for the better part of fourteen hundred years, generation after generation accepted the view of the austere North African bishop.

The current of rationalism which began to flow in Europe during the Renaissance, gathering strength throughout the seventeenth and eighteenth centuries, also played its part in devaluing the experience of childhood. Reason—an essentially adult faculty, not wholly unrelated to St. Augustine's concept of the Divine Grace, which was granted only at maturity—was not only supreme: it was unique and it was absolute. It was independent of the mere contingency of phenomena. "I think, therefore I am," asserted Descartes, thereby maintaining that the forms of pure rationality preceded all apprehension of sensually perceptible reality. "Before anyone had ever drawn a circle," reiterated Montesquieu, "its radii were already equal."[15] God Himself was subject to the laws of reason; and reason alone was sufficient to prove His existence. And if God Himself, the Prime Mover, the Divine Watchmaker, could in no way set in motion the mechanism of the universe, save within a context of rationality, the child likewise could expect to be evaluated only in terms of his reasonableness—or lack of it. That which was not "reasonable" was "imaginary": fantastic, monstrous, chimerical, untrue. Insofar as the child was irrational, it was inhuman. Only in its *promise* of humanity—that is, its potential of rationality, its eventual educability—was it in any way a subject worthy of interest, study, and attention. It was the misshapen larva

14. St. Augustine, *The Confessions*, trans. F. J. Sheed (London, 1944), 7–8. See also pp. 5–6.
15. Montesquieu, *Esprit des lois* [1748]: "Dire qu'il n'y a rien de juste ni d'injuste que ce qu'ordonnent ou défendent les loix positives, c'est dire qu'avant qu'on n'eût tracé de cercle, tous les rayons n'étaient pas égaux" (Bk. I, ch. i).

from which, in the fullness of time, the butterfly might perhaps be expected to emerge.

This concept is deeply rooted in the educational theory and practice of the period, and particularly of France in the seventeenth century. The structure of the mind of the child, argued Malebranche, is identical with the structure of the mind of the adult; the only significant difference between the two is that the mind of the child has insufficient data to work on.[16] The educator, therefore, has two tasks: first, to supply the facts, the experience of the world, the *data* which are lacking; and second, to inculcate, by the uncompromising rationality of his own pedagogic method, an awareness in the child's mind of its own rational potential, which awareness will enable it to respond to the arguments advanced.

Only very gradually did a different concept of education—and, together with it, of the very structure of the child's mind—begin to evolve. John Locke's *Treatise on Education*, the logical outcome of the empirical philosophy expounded in his *Essay Concerning Human Understanding* (1690), was published in 1693, and its influence was destined gradually to increase over the following half-century. Locke argued basically that *all* ideas—including the notion of rationality itself—had to be acquired in the first instance through sensual contact with the outside world; and that therefore it was absurd to teach through a principle of abstract reasoning—still worse, to punish a child for reasoning badly—when effectively the mind could only begin to assimilate knowledge by way of the senses.

By the 1730s, this idea was gaining ground rapidly. Various obscure but adventurous educational theorists—Louis Dumas, Pypoulain-Delaunay, or that elusive pedagogue turned utopian socialist whom we know by the name of Morelly[17]—were beginning to argue that the educator could only succeed by appealing first and foremost to his pupil's sense-mechanism; and further, that he could only awaken true intellectual interest by providing in the first instances experiences which were pleasurable. By 1740, the "play-teaching method" was born, and with it, a principle of fundamental and far-reaching importance, namely, that the mind of the child was *different* in structure from that of the adult, and therefore would respond only to stimuli adapted to its own autonomous character. This, in its narrow field, was the kind of specula-

16. "Les plus petits enfants ont de la raison aussi bien que les hommes faits, quoiqu'ils n'aient pas d'expérience." Nicolas Malebranche, *De la recherche de la vérité* [1674–75], ed. Geneviève Rodis-Lewis, 3 vols. (Paris, 1962), 1:138.

17. For details of these innovations, see my essay, "The Idea of 'Natural Order' in French Educational Theory, 1600–1760," *British Journal of Educational Studies* 5 (May 1957): 144–58. The "elusive pedagogue turned utopian socialist," after baffling scholars for the better part of two and one-half centuries, has finally been identified. See G. Antonetti, "Etienne-Gabriel Morelly: l'homme et sa famille," in *Revue d'histoire littéraire de la France* 83(1983): 390–403.

tion which, a generation later, was to act so powerfully on Jean-Jacques Rousseau and to inspire the total revolution that he was to bring about in the concept of childhood experience.

If, however, to the generations preceding that of Rousseau, the child was of no significance to the philosopher until he had started to develop the adult faculty of reason, similarly he was of no interest to the man of letters until he had acquired at least the beginnings of an adult sensibility. The readers of romances and novels—predominantly women, from the Renaissance to the early nineteenth century—demanded a love-interest; and neither hero nor heroine could command attention for more than an introductory chapter or two, until they were old enough to be stirred, emotionally and physically, by the opposite sex. Moll Flanders requires no more than ten pages to advance from the moment of her appearance in the world to the experience, "at the age of seventeen or eighteen," of her first passionate kiss; Robert Bage's Hermsprong reaches a similar state of maturity by the top of page five. Tom Jones, for reasons inherent in the structure of the novel, takes rather longer to emerge from short breeches; but the Chevalier Des Grieux, like his successor, the Chevalier de Faublas, and no less than the melancholy Werther, dismisses his early years as summarily as possible, extracting from them only sufficient material to justify, or to contrast with, his more mature adventures. Benjamin Constant's Adolphe does dwell significantly, if briefly, on his early education and on his relationship with his father—but *Adolphe* belongs already to the nineteenth century; and if the whole of *Tristram Shandy* is contained within the space between the hero's conception and his emergence from diapers, we learn in effect rather less about his own personal "life and opinions" after his emergence from his mother's womb than we do concerning the nine months which preceded that notable event. For every significant novelist of the seventeenth or eighteenth centuries, the true awakening of the sensibility is assumed to begin at the age of seventeen or thereabouts. Exceptionally, Chérubin, in the *Marriage of Figaro*, is younger; nonetheless, it is still his emerging love for the Countess which justifies his presence in the play; and Beaumarchais was well aware of the fact that he was departing from tradition.

What is true of the novel and of the drama is also true of autobiography, although here the "maturity" is sometimes spiritual or artistic rather than sexual or emotional. The early fifteenth-century mystic, Margery Kempe, begins the story of her spiritual life at the age of twenty, with the occasion of her marriage; Benvenuto Cellini (perhaps the first truly modern autobiographer) spends no more than a few pages on his family and apprenticeship, and plunges into the narrative proper only at the point where his craftsmanship is assured. Giacomo Casanova, notoriously, wastes little time on the years before he was able to embark on his innumerable erotic adventures; and, generally speaking, the same principle applies to the countless authors of memoirs who people the years between the English Civil War and the aftermath of the Napoleonic adventure: De Retz, Sir Kenelm Digby, Bassompierre, Barras, Marmont, and so forth.

There is, of course, an important distinction to be drawn between memoirs and autobiography. In memoirs, the writer is, as a *character*, essentially negative, or at best neutral. It is not he himself, considered as a unique and autonomous identity, who is important; it is the acts which he performs and their consequences, or it is the other people—frequently greater or more conspicuous than himself—whom he meets, with whom he has dealings. The self who narrates is first and foremost an eye which observes, an ear which records, or an agent by which things happen. Sometimes the personality of the writer is strong enough to break through, to impose itself in spite of the greater significance of the events which attended his occupancy of high positions, as is the case with Winston Churchill or with Charles de Gaulle. But this identity *as such* never dominates the work as a whole; and the archetypal volume of memoirs is perhaps Beverley Nichols's *Twenty-Five* (1926), in which we encounter Masefield and Chesterton, Dame Nellie Melba and Sir William Orpen, Horatio Bottomley and Seymour Hicks, Baldwin, Churchill, Bridges, Yeats, King-Somebody-of-Greece, and a couple of dozen other notorieties, but learn not a single thing about the author himself, save (unintentionally) that he was perhaps a self-assured and conceited young man. The supreme irony of *Twenty-Five* as an illustration of the memoir is that, many years later, this same Beverley Nichols wrote also an autobiography (*Father Figure*, 1972), in which he reveals, behind the bland, semi-anonymous figure of the President of the Oxford Union, the desperate and unhappy child three times attempting to murder his unloved, ponderously alcoholic father.

By contrast to the memoir, in the autobiography it is the writer himself who is the center of interest. Occasionally, other well-known personalities may fleetingly be observed, but they are never permitted to dominate the scene. They are allowed to intrude because in one way or another they were important to the writer or influenced his development; or because their interests were parallel with his own; or because of a simple accident or kinship or intellectual affinity. If Benvenuto Cellini refers to Michelangelo Buonarroti, it is not because he wants to paint for the reader an objective portrait of the "sublime genius" of Italian Renaissance sculpture, but because Michelangelo, as a fellow-professional, expressed interest in certain aspects of Cellini's technique.[18] If Pascal Jardin mentions Marshal Pétain and Pierre Laval, it is because they happened to be colleagues of his father.[19] The memorialist is a

18. Benvenuto Cellini, *Vita* [1558–66], trans. George Bull, *Autobiography* (New York, 1956; reprint 1973), 83.

19. Pascal Jardin, *La Guerre à neuf ans* (Paris, 1971), 142, 164–65.

historian, with the objectivity of outlook that every true historian must possess; the autobiographer is a solipsist, an individualist, a poet above all, whose truth, like that of the poet, is essentially independent of the evidence of facts.[20]

In consequence, in the great libraries of the world, there are significantly fewer volumes of true autobiography than of memoirs. If this isolated self is to be transmuted into something durably significant, it needs to possess a vitality and an originality which is very far from common; and it needs further to be spurred on, either by the imperious urge to impart a message or to reveal a truth which may not be allowed to vanish, or else by a dose of vanity so strong that never for one instant can the author doubt that his own existence, in all its intimate and unmomentous detail, is supremely meaningful to the world at large. And even in the latter case, vanity alone will not produce a readable autobiography; the artist or the poet must at some point intervene to transform the trivial into the universal. In no variety of autobiography is this truer than it is in the case of the child. For the child, by definition, has done nothing of importance in the world; his thoughts are not (or not yet) those of the philosopher, his language is not (or not yet) that of the poet; his schooldays will tend, in all essentials, to be remarkably similar to those of others; and those who surround him are not normally Prime Ministers or Academicians, but simply cousins and nannies and aunts, figures unknown to the mass of mankind, unless *he* is able to bring them to life. Even where the contrary is true, where by chance the child *is* in contact with figures who are household names, it reduces them relentlessly to its own level. Charles Darwin, for Gwen Raverat, was merely "Grandfather"; Voltaire, for Florian, was "Great-Great-Uncle"; while for Svetlana Alliluyeva, that nightmare figure of the Great Terror, Andrei Zhdanov, was primarily the father of the boy she fell in love with, and Joseph Stalin himself, just . . . "Father."

As literature, then, the self-portrait of the artist as a child has to be one of a being whose significance resides, not in his achievements, but rather in the unique qualities of his particular and individual *in*significance. And this sense of the significance of the apparently insignificant self, who has accomplished nothing, invented nothing, created nothing, can be appreciated only in a comparatively democratic social and cultural climate—whether in the spiritual democracy which constituted the vision of Christ, or in the sociopolitical democracies whose cornerstones were laid by Jean-Jacques Rousseau and the French Revolution. In feudal, hierarchical, or tribal societies, even the individual adult, let alone the child, derives his significance in the majority of

---

20. In making this distinction between autobiography and memoirs, I accept the more rigorous definition proposed by Philippe Lejeune in his *Autobiographie en France* (pp. 15–23), rather than the somewhat laxer one suggested by Roy Pascal in his *Design and Truth in Autobiography* (Cambridge, Mass., 1960), 5–8.

instances not from his own qualities, still less from his own "uniqueness" as an identity, but rather from his family, his class, his totem, or the deeds of his remoter ancestors. In societies of this type, it is logically impossible that the child should figure as a subject of literature; it could not do so in the past, nor can it today in those communities where the clan structure still predominates. The cultures which have produced the greatest flowering of Childhood literature are those which, in one way or another, are or have been inspired with an ideal of democracy and of equality: France and England, North America and Australia, the emergent Third World, and—perhaps paradoxically—Russia.

Two further factors may have contributed to the neglect of childhood experience in earlier generations. The first of these was the high incidence of infant mortality. When it could be reckoned that roughly seven out of every ten children born alive would die before they reached the age of maturity, the amount of emotional capital which the adult could afford to invest in the child was negligible. The child, as such, was a nonperson, until it had demonstrated, by its powers of survival into later adolescence, that it could properly take its place in the new generation of the community. The Freudian notion that the infant contains in embryo the total personality of the adult was not only unfamiliar, but inconceivable, to any century earlier than the seventeenth. The "typical" child, as Philippe Ariès has convincingly demonstrated, was the *dead* child.

This devastating rate of infant mortality began to decline, slowly at first, and then spectacularly, from the later years of the eighteenth century;[21] nor is it any coincidence that Rousseau's discovery of the autonomous identity of the child corresponds exactly in time with the great medical breakthrough. Throughout the nineteenth century, despite a momentary setback caused by the quasi-genocidal effects of the Industrial Revolution, the survival chances of the child continued to improve; and exactly parallel with these, the general emotional and intellectual interest of adults in the phenomenon of childhood increased, and have continued to increase down to the present day.

But the same period that witnessed these immense advances in medical skills also saw another significant change: the acceleration of mobility generated by the rapid advancement of transport. The regular stagecoach services introduced in the eighteenth century, the Napoleonic structure of inter-European communications, the highway toll system in England,[22] the coming of

21. Arab physicians had developed a technique of inoculation against smallpox, which was introduced into Europe, amidst much controversy, circa 1720. Edward Jenner's revolutionary discovery of vaccination and of the fundamental principles of immunology dates from 1796. Ignaz Semmelweis's almost equally important research on childbed fever was carried out between 1840 and 1860.

22. See descriptions by William Cobbett in his *Rural Rides* (1830) and by Benjamin Constant in his *Cahier rouge* (written ca. 1811). See also the remarkable details of Joseph Mitchell's

the railways, the motorcar, and the airplane—even the intervention of wars, persecutions, and exiles—have made it easier to conceive of childhood as a separate, autonomous state of being. The child who was born, grew up, lived, and died in the same village or hamlet was less able to distance his adult from his immature self than the child who, having passed his early years on some remote farm, estate, or sheep-station unidentifiable from the atlas, came later to roam among the great cities and capitals of the world. Even the childhood experience itself becomes more vivid when it contains not one, but two clearly distinct modes of being: the one commonplace and familiar, compounded of home and school and street-corner and garden; the other abnormal and ecstatic, a "summer-holiday self," moving in a magic dimension, far away amid the dunes and the forests, the towering grasses and the multicolored panoply of butterflies and unfamiliar birds. Mobility is of the very essence of the Childhood.

III

Children live more in pictures, in broken effects, in unaccountable impulses that lend an unmeasured significance to odd trifles to the exclusion of momentous facts, than in story. This alone prevents the harmonious fluency of biography in an honest account of our childhood.
—Hannah Lynch, *Autobiography of a Child*

The writer whose inspiration later furnished the first notion of the Childhood genre was St. Augustine, the inventor and indeed the first master of the autobiographical form as such.[23] Although this may appear paradoxical at first sight, in view of his contemptuous attitude toward the characteristics of childhood, it is not so in fact; for out of this very contempt there spring—since the childhood he is considering is his own—certain absolutely fundamental queries and preoccupations which will be echoed again and again, after a gap of some fourteen hundred years, by writers of our own time.[24]

---

political tour of the North and Midlands of England in 1817, which are given by E. P. Thompson in his *Making of the English Working Classes*, rev. ed. (New York, 1968), p. 716, note 3.

23. It is not the purpose of this study to trace the history or to discuss the theory of autobiography as such, but only certain aspects of one particular branch of it. For a wider survey, the reader is directed above all to William C. Spengemann's admirable "Bibliographical Essay" in his *Forms of Autobiography*, pp. 170–245, and to Philippe Lejeune's bibliography in his *Pacte autobiographique*, pp. 344–54. I am myself particularly indebted to Lejeune (see also his *Autobiographie en France*, and his *Je est un autre*, 1980); also to the much earlier, but remarkably dense and penetrating study by Roy Pascal, *Design and Truth in Autobiography* (1960).

24. Significantly, there was a strong renewal of interest in the *Confessions* of St. Augustine in the middle years of the nineteenth century, at precisely the time when the Childhood was beginning to emerge as a significant literary form. During the whole of the eighteenth century, in France, the *Confessions* had been granted only two translations; but I have traced no less than nine in the period 1831–84.

The *Confessions* (A.D. 399) are basically an account of Augustine's conversion to Christianity, and of his subsequent pilgrimage in search of spiritual truth. The definitive conversion—a conversion to a specific form of Christianized Neoplatonism as preached by that powerful Church administrator, Bishop Ambrose of Milan—took place only when Augustine had reached his thirty-second year; but it had been preceded by a number of other conversions—including one to the Manichaean doctrine—of which the first, the so-called "conversion to Philosophy" occurred as a result of his reading Cicero's *Hortensius* in A.D. 373, when he was nineteen. Only the first forty-odd pages of the *Confessions* recount the events which occurred before his first conversion; nonetheless, so vivid is the account that these few pages stamp the book indelibly as the prototype of a Childhood in the mind of the modern reader.

Throughout this section, there is an extraordinary ring of modernity—in Augustine's criticism of his parents and of their "conformist" values, in his dislike of "the drudgery of learning a foreign language," and in his later revolt against the "falsities of literature" in favor of a more practical and "relevant" program of education; in his account of his discovery of and initiation into the excitements of sex at the age of sixteen, culminating in the archetypal act of sacrilege which consisted in making love "actually within the walls of Your Church and during the very celebration of Your Mysteries"—a gesture of defiance against the conventions which no more than a handful of his successors have had the courage to imitate.[25] His passion for and involvement in theater is, as we shall see, one of the most recurrent features of the Childhood; yet most revealing of all is his description of the street-corner gang of delinquents to which he belonged and of the petty thefts and vandalisms in which they engaged, and through which they displayed their ill-formulated adolescent rebelliousness. Augustine's analysis of the psychological motivation of this gang has, making allowance for the language, the ring of a probation officer's tape-recorded transcript:

> I would not have done it alone. Perhaps then, what I really loved was the companionship of those with whom I did it. . . . I would not have committed that theft alone; my pleasure in it was not what I stole, but that I stole; yet I would not have enjoyed doing it, I would not have done it, alone. O friendship unfriendly, greediness to do damage for the mere sport and jest of it, desire for another's loss with no gain to the self or vengeance to be satisfied! Someone cries: "Come on, let's do it"—and we should be ashamed to be ashamed. (pp. 28–29)

Augustine's confession, however, was not made in private to some social

25. Jean-Jacques Bouchard and Jean Genet (seemingly) among others. Roger Peyrefitte's novel, *Les Clés de Saint-Pierre* (1955) is memorable for a very moving description of this type of experience.

worker or police psychiatrist specializing in juvenile delinquency, but in public, to God and to his own flock, to the members—often highly critical of their pastor—of his own diocese. There is, in the *Confessions*, an element of self-castigation, a deliberate exposure of the most shameful secrets, which will awaken echoes, not only in the two Jean-Jacques—Bouchard and Rousseau—but in a whole host of contemporaries, from Michel Leiris to Philip Roth, from Jean Genet to Violette Leduc, from André Gide to Michael Baldwin. From the very outset, at least one of the functions of the Childhood, that of masochistic self-denunciation, is affirmed.

Augustine's contemporaries, and the great Fathers of the Church who succeeded him, were more interested in his theology than in his intimate personal life. Some twelve centuries were to elapse before any further "Confession" with even a hint of similar frankness was to emerge. It is in the Renaissance that the autobiographical mode begins to establish itself, achieving its first masterpiece in the *Memoirs* (1558–66) of Benvenuto Cellini; nonetheless, the self was gradually stirring into consciousness during a hundred years or more before that notable event. François Villon, writing his *Grand testament* as early as 1461, embodies in it a certain element of confession, but it is fairly unspecific, at least about his earlier, adolescent failings and weaknesses—he tells how he dodged school, for instance (stanza xxvi), and he sketches in the feelings of general rebelliousness inspired by his poverty (stanza xxxiv), but gives little or nothing by way of detail. Moreover, the confession element is weakened by the poet's all-pervading religious optimism—the conviction that, whatever he has done, whatever sins he may have committed, the mercy of God will redeem his soul at last:

> Je suys pecheur, je le sçai bien;
> Pourtant Dieu ne veult pas ma mort,
> Mais convertisse et vive en bien.   (stanza xiv)

[I am a sinner, that I know well; yet God does not desire my death, but rather that I should repent and live in righteousness.]

Similarly, Montaigne's *Essais* contain a number of scattered and isolated references to childhood experience, but only the famous essay on education ("De l'Institution des enfans," 1580) uses early personal reminiscence to any significant extent, and then only in the concluding sections. Montaigne's account of his father's theories of education, and of the manner in which he reorganized his entire household so that the boy heard nothing but Latin spoken all day throughout his preschool years, is of course well known, as is his confession of his own laziness as a scholar, and his denunciation of the "horror and cruelty" of the teaching methods employed in schools at that time.[26] Less

26. Montaigne, "De l'institution des enfans," *Essais* (I, xxvi) ed. Alfred Thibaudet (Paris, 1946), especially pp. 176–77.

often quoted is his enthusiastic praise for a great headmaster, André de Gouvéa, Principal of the Collège de Guyenne in Bordeaux from 1534 to 1547—the first significant headmaster figure whom we encounter, and "incomparably the greatest Principal in France"; or his delight, at the age of twelve, in amateur dramatics, his account of his own ability as an actor, and his advice in consequence that drama should form part of the curriculum of all children striving after a liberal education. But beyond this, Montaigne, whose researches into his adult personality revolutionized the whole European concept of the self, tells us remarkably little about his immature experience.

It is in some ways paradoxical that Villon and Montaigne, who, together with Petrarch, may be considered as the founders of subjective individualism in European literature, should reveal so little of their earlier selves. But, in addition to the reasons given above for the virtually total neglect of childhood in the Renaissance, there is the fact that both writers, in their very different ways, were essentially moralists; and the moralist is concerned primarily with *adult* responsibilities. Montaigne's interest lies in trying to understand himself as he *is*, rather than as he was; his self-observation is direct and immediate, not retrospective. And Villon likewise uses the truancies of his childhood only to comment on the infinitely more dangerous truancies of his manhood: "Had I behaved better in my schooldays, then should I not now lead the life I do."

> Bien sçay, se j'eusse estudié
> Ou du temps de ma jeunesse folle,
> Et a bonnes meurs dedié,
> J'eusse maison et couche molle!
> Mais quoy? je fuyoye l'escolle,
> Comme faict le mauvays enfant.   (stanza xxvi)

[I am well aware that, had I studied in the time of my mad youth, and devoted myself to good conduct, I should now have owned a house and a soft bed! But what happened? I played truant from school, like the bad child I was.]

For Villon, childhood is a state, not a development; there is no slow process of maturation from the child to the adult, followed by a further evolution from the man of action to the philosopher. The still medieval moralist in Villon sees only the melancholy contrast between youth and old age, only the passage of time and the disappearance of those *gracieux gallants* "Si bien chantans, si bien parlans" (stanza xxix), of whom nothing remains but the memory.

But if Villon and Montaigne are moralists, their two most notable French successors in the seventeenth century are anything but. Given the climate of general neglect of, and disdain for, childhood which prevailed in the period, these two contemporaries of Descartes, the intriguer Jean-Jacques Bouchard and the poet-dramatist Tristan l'Hermite, stand apart as being so exceptional that it might be hard to account for their existence, did we not recall that their exact contemporaries in England included the Metaphysical poets, and among them Henry Vaughan and Thomas Traherne. So perhaps it would seem that, very fragmentarily and deep beneath the surface of the European consciousness, the first awakenings of a new sensibility were occurring.[27]

Bouchard, who was born in 1606, who was educated at the Collège de Calvy ("La Petite Sorbonne") in Paris, and who later became a Doctor of Civil and Canon Law with hopes of a Bishopric, found himself by the age of twenty-five afflicted with sexual impotence. And so, in the year 1634 or thereabouts, he sat down at his desk, trying to work out for himself on paper why this had happened. The result was the *Confessions*, the first forty-odd pages of which constitute one of the most extraordinary feats of quasi-Freudian self-analysis ever achieved before the rise of modern psychological theory.

Bouchard's impotence was of the kind later to be analyzed by Stendhal in his famous essay on the sexual "fiasco"[28]—the phenomenon which arises when the emotional and physical excitement of anticipation reach such a pitch of intensity that, faced with the moment of realization, the turmoil of the mind and senses precludes any physical response at all. In order to understand how this had come about Bouchard went back to his childhood: to his father— a successful apothecary—whom he despised and feared; to his mother, whom he hated more than any other being in this world; and to his desire to murder both of them. He alludes to them throughout the *Confessions*, with consciously aggressive symbolism, as "Agamemnon" and "Clytemnestra," and to himself throughout in the third person as "Orestes." If he is a satisfactory pupil at school, it is because he has only one goal: to take service with some notable figure and so escape from that woman who, when he was twenty-three, was still treating him contemptuously as her "slave."

Incubated in this hotbed of distorted family relationships, Bouchard embarked early on a course clearly destined to lead to almost every conceivable form of complex and neurosis. By the age of eight, he tells us, he was already having full sexual relationships with a large number of little girls, his sister's friends, although it was only some three or four years later that he learned anything of the implications of what he was doing. This premature promiscuity was succeeded by an affair with a girl whom he calls Alisbée (= Isabelle), whose power to induce sexual frustration in an adolescent male would appear to have been unrivaled. Bouchard's portrait of this virgin, who welcomed all forms of sexual attention, including "heavy petting," titillating her lover for hours on end to the point of total exhaustion yet never allowing him to

27. This is supported by Philippe Ariès, who concludes from his study of the figure of the child in painting: "C'est au XVIIe siècle que les portraits d'enfants seuls deviennent nombreux et banaux." *L'Enfant et la vie familiale en France sous l'Ancien Régime* (Paris, 1960), 38.

28. See Stendhal, *Œuvres complètes*, ed. Vittorio Del Litto and Ernest Abravanel (Geneva, n.d.), 4:277–83.

come to her, is a masterpiece, both of psychological observation and of self-appraisal:

That thing alone excepted, she welcomed conversation upon the most intimate of topics, and allowed herself to be touched upon every one of the most sensitive parts of her body indifferently, with little or no resistance: spending the entire duration of the night for the space of a whole month together with Orestes, while he, for his part, vouchsafed her no sign of desiring from her any other thing, save those liberties only, which she permitted him.[29]

Not surprisingly, this mixture of libertinage and frustration, combined on the one hand with an extreme sensitivity (to music, for instance), on the other with the sordid and violent licentiousness practiced at the Collège de Calvy,[30] served as prelude to an adolescence whose multifarious sexual brutalities are described in a language hardly less devastating than that used by Jean Genet in recalling his boyhood at the Reform School of Mettray. From solitary masturbation with the help of elaborate sex aids—"cunts and pricks made out of wax . . . pockets made out of skin with the fur turned inwards [etc.] . . . and always in front of a good fire, should that prove possible, the pleasure in this circumstance being doubled,"—through brutal mass orgies with his schoolmates, to an intense and enduring homosexual love affair carried on simultaneously with two of his companions, Bouthillier and Bellièvre. Even the present-day pornographic film industry might find difficulty in depicting all the adolescent experiences which this unhappy lawyer was setting down on paper for his own private exercise in psychoanalysis in the year 1634.

From the age of thirteen to that of eighteen, he recalls, he never failed to have an ejaculation twice a day, and "the more often, three or four times," the only exception being "the four great Church Festivals of the year"; and, as a bonus, he maintained regular relations with a chambermaid called Angélique, whose peculiarity it was always to claim to be asleep while making love, although Bouchard himself confesses that she always seemed to manage to sleep "in the most inviting positions imaginable . . . knees tucked up beneath her, head on the ground and her arse stuck up in the air"—which somnolent posture he fully knew how to appreciate. From all of which, he concludes, with dispassionate objectivity, that his present impotence results most likely from an overindulgence in sexual activity without respite between the ages of eight and twenty-three, and not from any inherent physiological defect.

29. Jean-Jacques Bouchard, *Les Confessions de Jean-Jacques Bouchard, Parisien, suivies de son voyage de Paris à Rome en 1630* [?1634], ed. Alcide Bonneau (Paris, 1881), 22.

30. Aldous Huxley, in *The Devils of Loudun* (1952), takes Bouchard's experience as the archetypal illustration of the ferocious brutality of French seventeenth-century educational institutions.

There is little that is of serious literary value in Bouchard: he was neither a poet nor a stylist, simply an introspective lawyer trying to understand his own predicament. His "confession" is literally what it claims to be: an unvarnished statement of the facts. And if its structure is complex, with three themes inextricably interwoven—his hatred of his parents, his experience of warfare in the sexual jungle of adolescence, and his frustrating love affair with Alisbée—it is not through artifice, but rather because it reflects the complexity of causes underlying any profound neurosis. In this, Bouchard was unique, and was destined to remain so for some two centuries or more. For his *Confession* is not, as was the case with Saint Augustine and as was later to be the case (at least in part) with Jean-Jacques Rousseau, an exercise in self-castigation, but rather an honest and extraordinarily lucid attempt to discover a truth about himself—a truth hidden in the past which, scientifically analyzed, would explain something about the self at the moment of writing.

By contrast with the morbid introspection of Jean-Jacques Bouchard, Tristan l'Hermite's *Page disgracié*[31] is a positive carnival of adolescence and adventure. Written in 1642, when he was approaching middle age, he tells briefly of his early childhood, of his pleasant but ineffectual father, and of his upbringing by that vigorous and impressive personality, his grandmother Denise de Saint-Prest. But the substance of the narrative begins when, at the age of twelve or thirteen, he is attached as page and companion to Henri de Bourbon, Duc de Verneuil (1601–82), who was his exact contemporary; and the central episodes concern his adventures and experiences in England in the middle years of the reign of King James I. The narrative concludes with Tristan's return to the court of France at the age of eighteen or nineteen, now a fully mature young man having behind him the experience, not only of love and adventure in foreign lands, but of death, of war, of the plague, and of many of the other calamities of life.

Doubts have been cast now and then upon the authenticity of the *Page disgracié*. Admittedly, it is episodic, and many of the episodes have about them the ring of the picaresque. Unfortunately, moreover, we have no other source which gives the biography of Tristan's early years, so there is no way to check the facts.[32] On the other hand, the life of a well-born young man in the seventeenth century undoubtedly *was* more adventurous than that of a middle-class adolescent in the twentieth; furthermore, the Childhood tends necessarily to be episodic, since striking incidents are, by and large, those which

31. Tristan l'Hermite, *Le Page disgracié* [1643], ed. Marcel Arland (Paris, 1946). This was intended as the first part of an autobiographical trilogy; but the failure of the writer to get beyond the completed childhood experience is characteristic.

32. See F.-V. Fournel, *La Littérature indépendante et les écrivains oubliés* (Paris, 1862), 245; M. Bernardin, *Un Précurseur de Racine: Tristan l'Hermite, Sieur du Solier* (1895; reprint Geneva, 1967, 43–83, especially p. 45 and notes).

memory isolates and recalls. Unquestionably, Tristan is a writer of very considerable talent, and he has calculated his effects very carefully: almost as carefully, perhaps, as a James Joyce or an André Gide. Against this, however, there is the significant fact that Tristan not only *claims* to be telling the truth, but justifies himself against accusations of egoism and vanity by reference to that most unimpeachably sincere and authentic of seekers after the truth of self, Michel de Montaigne (p. 49); and the more significant fact that certain passages have about them an involuntary ring of truth in the most unexpected places. For instance, we may well take with a grain of salt the episode in which the Page meets with the man who claims to possess the Philosopher's Stone (p. 96). But his struggles, on first arriving in London, with an English phrase book—"a small volume, printed in London, which instructed me in the manner of asking for all those things that I might require" (p. 111)—are recounted with the plain simplicity of fact; and above all, the supreme self-confidence with which, at the age of fifteen, perhaps, or sixteen, he starts teaching literature, instead of merely the elements of the French language, to the young English girl for whom he has been engaged as tutor, leads us straight into the presence of an archetypal character, of whose reality there can be no question. The Page imposes himself as authentically today as he did some 350 years ago, and we recognize without a moment's hesitation the voice of the precocious young French intellectual, supremely secure in his own culture, instructing the unlettered Anglo-Saxon in the subtleties and refinements of literary expression. Here, "somewhere in England" in the Year of Grace 1617, we already have the young *agrégé* attached to the Service Culturel of the French Embassy in London, lecturing to a W.E.A. evening class in Huddersfield . . . Michel Butor addressing the University Wives' Club in Melbourne . . . Jean Genet, in 1936, explicating *Le Bateau ivre* to the seventeen-year-old daughter of a gynecologist in Brno.[33] *This* is authentic; it cannot be anything else.

But *Le Page disgracié* is much more than a sparkling autobiographical portrait of adolescence; even making allowance for what may be a considerable element of fiction, it is in fact the first Childhood whose inner structure approximates to that which we have defined as being characteristic of this particular literary form—a structure in which the succession of episodes presented by the text reflects more or less exactly the sequence of past experience. It opens with the serenity of early childhood; it continues with the adolescent adventures and experiments in the progressive discovery of the self; and it concludes with a final return to haven, with the hero-narrator ready to begin life as a mature being. It has none of the solemnity of the confession; and yet, beneath the lightheartedness, an element of confession is nonetheless

33. This information on Jean Genet is based on unpublished correspondence in the possession of the author.

present. Tristan presents himself, not so much in the guise of a hero as in that of an anti-hero, like the "Francion" of his contemporary Charles Sorel. Half the time his plans fail, his intrigues come to nothing, his grandiose projects founder on the rocks of his inexperience. And out of this anti-heroic element (which is perhaps the most important contribution made by the picaresque novel to the development of the Childhood genre) Tristan develops an inner structure that gives the work a tautness which none of his predecessors had so much as glimpsed. It is not merely that Tristan the adult *judges* Tristan the child at the same time as he recreates his thoughts and gestures; it is rather that the self that knows itself to be a true, even a considerable, poet is deliberately set in counterpoise to that earlier self that embodied the incompetence, suffered the immaturity, and endured the embarrassments of the child. This inner tension, free almost for the first time of guilt or self-reproach, is destined to be the foundation of many of the greatest achievements in the genre. It is the dynamic force necessary to translate the arbitrary and frequently trivial experiences of childhood into a coherent form of literary expression.

Neither Bouchard, whose *Confessions* were in fact not published until 1881, nor Tristan, whose work, within a decade, was consigned to the shadows by the glitter and brilliance of French classicism, had any immediate influence on the further development of the genre. Both might have been dismissed as mere cultural accidents, were it not for the fact that, across the Channel, the poets later known as the Metaphysicals were similarly experiencing and expressing a new awareness of the self-as-child. Indeed, Thomas Traherne (b. 1637) was probably experiencing the immortal vision of the *Infant-Ey*—that intimation of paradise wherein "the corn was orient and immortal wheat which never should be reaped nor ever was sown"—exactly in that narrow span of years between the writing of Bouchard's *Confessions* and Tristan's *Page*.

Taken together with the evidence of the figure painters of the time,[34] the simultaneous appearance of Bouchard, Tristan, and the English Metaphysicals would seem to suggest quite clearly that the first stage of a new child-conscious culture was beginning to emerge in Europe in the middle decades of the seventeenth century. Yet the French and English reflections on childhood are not merely parallel, but at the same time contrasting; and this very contrast gives us an insight into the evolution of attitudes. John Donne, Henry Vaughan, and Thomas Traherne are incomparably greater poets than Jean-Jacques Bouchard or even Tristan l'Hermite; yet, in one important respect, the French—and in particular, Bouchard—are more "advanced." Bouchard may be crude and unpolished; yet this very crudeness is the product

34. See Philippe Ariès, *L'Enfant et la vie familiale*, pp. 35–41.

of an authentic spontaneity which is lacking elsewhere among his contemporaries. More than any of his predecessors, moreover, he is concerned to trace the origins of his adult sexual neuroses back into the trivial and half-forgotten, mindless tribulations of an earlier self: in other words, he envisages the relationship between his former and his present selves as one of a continuous process of evolution. In contrast, Traherne sees his earlier self as a state of being not merely detached from, but irrevocably destroyed by, the mutations of adolescence. His childhood, like that of Villon, was a *state*, not a process. It was a domain of blessedness; as such, its frontiers were fixed, rigidly and immutably, forever. In a curious way Vaughan, Traherne,[35] and their successors in the English tradition, Thomas Hood, William Blake, and the Wordsworth of the *Ode on the Intimations of Immortality*, reflect—albeit in reverse-image—the Cartesian view of the child. For Descartes and Malebranche, the child was a failed adult. For Vaughan and Traherne, the adult was a failed child. Neither perspective could in any way comprehend the process of transition. In this, as in so much else, it was left to Jean-Jacques Rousseau to resolve the dilemmas of his predecessors. *Emile* (1762) saw the child as *distinct* from the adult; the *Confessions* (1764–70) saw the child as *continuous with* the adult. And the fact that it was the same adult contemplating the singularities of the same child in both books, brought about a major revolution in European cultural attitudes.

Emile is, in its intention, simply a treatise on education. As such, its view of the child is neutral and dispassionate: it directs the attention of its reader to the child as an object of study. But what distinguishes *Emile* from all previous treatises on education is the care which Rousseau takes to analyze the characteristics of the child-mind before proceeding to elaborate on the techniques by which that mind may be formed. Rousseau's originality and impact lie, perhaps not in his discovery, but at least in his vehement and rhetorical assertion, that the mind of the child is *not* merely an inefficient prototype of the mind of the adult, but something quite independent and autonomous, with its own structures, its own ecstasies, its own miseries, and above all, its own value. Ultimately, the child may be "perfected" into the man, but this is not the immediate aim of the educator; his first purpose must be to perfect the child *as a child*. "In the man, it is the man who must be considered, and in the child, the child," exclaims Rousseau. "In children, we must allow childhood to come to its own fulfilment."[36] And, in the course of the same brilliant analysis, he argues:

35. For a detailed analysis of Traherne's *Infant-Ey*, see below, pp. 255–58.
36. Jean-Jacques Rousseau, *Emile* [1762], ed. B. Gagnebin and M. Raymond (Paris, 1969), 303, 324.

> Nature requires that children should be children before they become adults. . . .
> Childhood has its own way of looking at things, its own way of thinking, its own way of
> feeling; nothing could be more stupid than to try and replace *this* way by our way. . . .
> We can never hope to put ourselves in the place of children; we cannot share their ideas,
> we can only lend them ours. (pp. 319, 434)

Not only, however, is the structure of the child's mind autonomous and, in all important respects, inaccessible to the normal adult; it has also its own *value*, which is as high, if not in some respects higher, than that of the fully grown man. Man's highest faculty is his reason, but to the child, this is irrelevant. "If children understood reason, they would have no need to be educated" (p. 317). Anticipating Baudelaire, Rousseau argues that the child's fundamentally *irrational* modes of being—instinct, sensual awareness, above all fantasy and imagination—are the very stuff of which poetry is made, and, therefore, that the child's experience is richer, profounder, more varied and, in the broadest sense, more *poetic*, than that of the "finished being" who, by comparison, is limited, impoverished, and confined to that dreary routine of sterility which consists in never seeing anything save that which actually exists (p. 418). To be a poet, a man must return to his own childhood. Indeed, as our evidence will suggest, virtually every man, in the act of contemplating himself as a child, has the chance, however fleetingly, to be touched by poetry.

This, though, is only a small part of Rousseau's highly complex argument in *Emile*; and, from the point of view of his theory of education, it would be misleading to take it in isolation, since, in spite of all, Rousseau believed that the ultimate object of the educator was to produce the rational adult, whatever might be the danger of "corruption" which all education implies. But, from the point of view of the *experience* of childhood, the idea that every being possessed, in the memory he retained of his own earlier self, the living substance of poetry was the revelation that had been awaited, it would seem, for centuries—a truth which even Thomas Traherne, with his specific religious and moral preoccupations, had not wholly been able to grasp. In its own way, *Emile* has a curious and rather unexpected part to play in the elaboration of the modern ideal of democracy: every citizen in the Ideal City is potentially, in that once he was a child, the equal of that highest manifestation of human genius: a poet.

Emile differs from the later *Confessions* not merely in perspective but also in attitude. In *Emile*, Rousseau had been concerned to show that the child was fundamentally different from the adult; between the two existences lay a gap which no effort of rational understanding could wholly bridge. In the *Confessions*, while the awareness of the gap is still present, Rousseau nonetheless tries to do exactly the opposite: to show that there *is* an element of continuity from one state to the other, an intangible but nevertheless real and permanent

identity, an intrinsic "Self" linking child and man. The man—poet, mas-
ochist, God-seeker, champion of social justice, what you will—is ultimately
explicable in terms of the experience of the child:

> Retracing in this manner the first stirrings of my sentient being, I can discover
> elements which, for all that not infrequently they appear incompatible, have nonethe-
> less, in the course of time, combined together, so as to produce a single, strong, uniform,
> and simple effect; and I can discern others which, in appearance identical, have,
> through particular concatenations of circumstance, formed such different combina-
> tions that one might never conceive that there was any relationship between them.[37]

Many passages of self-analysis in the *Confessions* reveal similarities with
those of Montaigne; but Rousseau is constantly doing what the author of the
Essais attempts so rarely: namely, to trace the history of his present state of
being back to its origins in that "other existence" of childhood. The implications of this for the future of the genre are twofold. In the first place, having
shown in *Emile* that the worlds of childhood and of maturity are autonomous,
and the gap between them unbridgeable, he now suggests that the one and
only possible way to span this formidable abyss lies through the adult's memory of his own self-as-child. Second, by stressing the opposition between autonomy and continuity, he introduces a further important element of dynamic
tension essential to the structure of the Childhood as a literary form. The
tension in Tristan springs from the contrast between the competence of the
adult and the incompetence of the child; that in Rousseau lies in the awareness
of an identity which both is and is not continuous from child to man.

The density and richness of the *Confessions* is such that in them we can find
nearly all the significant characteristics which will later prove to be inseparable from the genre. But at this point, there are only two other features which
require comment. First, and quite simply, Rousseau's object is not (or not
only), as it was for St. Augustine, an exercise in contrition in the eyes of God
and men; nor is it, as it was for Jean-Jacques Bouchard, primarily an exercise in
self-understanding. Rousseau belongs to the Enlightenment, to the first age of
modern scientific thought; consequently the aim of this particular "confession" is not so much self-castigation, or even self-revelation, but rather the
setting out of a series of exactly observed scientific data about the behavior
patterns of *one* human being, which data may serve subsequently as material
for the development of scientific knowledge. His life history, he observes in the
preface, is a work both "unique" and "useful," and as such "may serve as a
primary piece of evidence, a standard of comparison in the study of man,
which study assuredly has not yet even been started" (1:39). In other words,

37. Jean-Jacques Rousseau, *Les Confessions* [written 1764–70], ed. Michel Launay (Paris,
1968), 1:39.

Rousseau is perhaps the first to envisage using *his* truth as material for the elaboration of *a* truth: the truth of the yet unborn science of psychology.[38]

And second, if, as we have argued earlier, one of the most serious impediments to the development of the genre as a form of *literature* lay in the fact that the average reader considered the child or adolescent uninteresting until he or she was mature enough to react in some degree—physically or emotionally—to the opposite sex, Rousseau virtually destroyed this barrier. Effectively, he pushed the origins of significant sexual experience right back into childhood; at the same time, by revealing the way in which his own sexual experience at the hands (literally!) of Mademoiselle Lambercier—the encounter which is the true starting point of the narrative—determined his entire sexual development as an adult, he advanced the initial point of reader-involvement in the fortunes of the hero (conventionally situated in later adolescence) by some ten years. When *Les Confessions* was first published—and indeed subsequently—it was this detailed analysis of his own "abnormal" sexual inclinations which at once shocked and fascinated his readers: his account of the discovery of his own preadolescent tendency to masochism and of its consequences was startling evidence that "childhood" was not merely a sub- or prehuman state, but a stage of life which could be filled with quasi-adult experiences so intense that even the grown man found difficulty in recording them.

Historical evidence suggests that Rousseau was about eleven when he had his bottom smacked by Mademoiselle Lambercier (herself at that time about thirty years old)—an event which awakened in him "that bizarre taste, ever persisting, and increasing to the point of depravity, even of madness" (*Confessions*, 1:53), which destroyed his normal adult sexual life and which drove him ever more deeply into those masturbatory fantasies that enabled him "to dispose, so to speak, at my fancy, of the entirety of the fair sex" (1:147). But the interesting fact is that he back-dates the occurrence by some three years:

Who would believe that this childish punishment, undergone *when I was eight years old* at the hands of a woman of thirty, should have determined my tastes, my passions, indeed my very self for the remainder of my life? (1:53; my italics)

These three years are absolutely vital. Whether he deviated from historical fact consciously or subconsciously, by locating the origins of adult experience, not in a period which might just be considered premature adolescence, but in one which is undeniably that of childhood, Rousseau definitively forced the

38. This "scientific" approach will rapidly become one of the commonplaces of the genre. In the introduction to *Monsieur Nicolas* [1796], Restif de la Bretonne asserts: "Ce n'est pas ma vie que je fais; c'est l'histoire d'un homme. . . . Ce ne sont même pas mes *Confessions* que je fais; ce sont *les Ressorts du coeur humain* que je dévoile. Disparaisse, Nicolas-Edmé, et que l'homme seul demeure!" Ed. J.-J. Pauvert (Paris, 1969), 1:xli.

barrier between the child and the adult. Furthermore, he emphasized the significance of this new departure by tracing the consequences of this "child-ishly" trivial episode throughout all the years that followed, through his temptation toward, and rejection of, homosexuality and through his exhibitionism—

I used to roam abroad in search of dark passages, of hidden lurking-places where, at a distance, I might expose myself to persons of the opposite sex in that state which I longed in vain for the occasion to adopt while actually in their company. (1:127–28)

—to the final and persistent frustration of nearly all his later sexual relationships, since he dare not declare, nor were his mistresses able to guess, what it was that in fact he really wanted.

The child, then, for Rousseau, both is and is not the adult. It *is*, in that the most significant of adult experiences can be shown to have their origins in childhood; it *is not*, in that only the adult can judge and evaluate those experiences. It is a kind of phenomenonological relationship, not unlike the Sartrian theory of perception: the child provides the material, without which the adult mind cannot function; but the adult mind alone creates definition and significance in the otherwise formless and meaningless experiences of childhood. With Rousseau, the values are created, the pattern of interpretation is established. The child is the "en-soi"; the adult is the "pour-soi"; both together constitute the "self."

Although the full text of *Les Confessions* was not published until 1782, some four years after Rousseau's death, its effect was instantaneous and enduring. "There exist but two models for my undertaking," wrote Restif de la Bretonne in the introduction to *Monsieur Nicolas* in 1796, "the *Confessions* of the Bishop of Hippo and those of the Citizen of Geneva" (1 : xli). "Dare I even consider a comparison terrifying by its very absurdity with the masterpiece of this great writer?" asked Stendhal in 1835, having *Les Confessions* unceasingly in mind as he worked frantically through the nights of Civitavecchia on his own *Vie de Henry Brulard*.[39] Nonetheless, fully half a century was to elapse before the Childhood succeeded finally in establishing itself as a self-conscious, deliberate literary form. Rousseau had extended beyond all previous measure the place allotted to childhood and adolescence in his autobiography; from a purely formal point of view, however, *Les Confessions* still does not conform to the basic structural law of the Childhood proper: namely, that the text should conclude with the attainment of its author's maturity. The years which separate *Les Confessions* from the *Vie de Henry Brulard* are rich in autobiographical writing; but, with only a very limited number of exceptions,

39. Stendhal, *Vie de Henry Brulard*, in *Œuvres complètes*, ed. Vittorio Del Litto and Ernest Abravanel (Geneva, 1968), 21:63.

the pattern followed is that of Rousseau. Restif's *Monsieur Nicolas*, Chateaubriand's *Mémoires d'outre-tombe*, Goethe's *Dichtung und Wahrheit*, even Wordsworth's *Prelude*, all have roughly the same outline: somewhere between one-sixth and one-quarter of the autobiography devoted to preadult experience, but no clear or emphatic dividing line between the self-that-was and the self-that-is. These four works have but one notable characteristic in common: their extraordinary length. It is also worth observing that, whereas Rousseau spent a mere six years writing, rewriting and revising *Les Confessions*, Goethe, Chateaubriand, and Wordsworth all spent the better part of half a century struggling with successive versions of their earlier selves. Two factors would seem to be involved here: the gradual assimilation of autobiography to the dimensions of the epic, and the beginnings of an attempt to wrestle with what will, eventually, prove to be the basic problem of the Childhood—the accuracy of memory, and the constantly changing relationship between the self who writes and the self who is remembered.

For some years, on either side of the turn of the century, the Childhood can be seen in the throes of an extraordinary turmoil of flux, experiment, and seemingly directionless effervescence. On the one hand, Jean-Pierre Claris de Florian's *Mémoires d'un jeune Espagnol* (1807) harks back to the picaresque and to the adventures of Tristan; on the other, Benjamin Constant's *Cahier rouge* (1811), together with Thomas de Quincey's *Confessions of an English Opium Eater* (first version, 1821–22) and the "Collège de Vendôme" episodes of Honoré de Balzac's *Louis Lambert* (1832), give a foretaste of that historically conscious naturalism which is destined to become characteristic of the genre in the later years of the century. In the same year that saw the publication of *Louis Lambert*—1832, seemingly a key year in the development of this aspect of the European cultural consciousness, since it also saw the first publication of *Dichtung und Wahrheit*—two other singular and by no means negligible figures, the French "godfather of the Romantic movement," Charles Nodier, with his *Mémoires de Maxime Odin*, and the popular Swiss illustrator and essayist Rodolphe Töpffer, in his *Bibliothèque de mon oncle*,[40] began to explore that borderland between childhood reminiscence and pure fantasy which was later to become the special province of writers such as Kenneth Grahame, Colette, or Valentin Kataev.

Out of this chaos, which was finally resolved in 1835 when Stendhal, in the *Vie de Henry Brulard*, created the first fully perfected example of a Childhood, four figures, or groups of figures, emerge with particular clarity, each having something specific to contribute to the eventual elaboration of the genre—a

---

40. Tolstoy quotes *La Bibliothèque de mon oncle* in the same breath as Rousseau's *Confessions* as one of the sources of inspiration for his own epoch-making *Childhood*. This same year, 1832, also saw the first publication of Robert Brown's *Memoir of Robert Blincoe*.

genre which, whatever its inherent qualities or defects, is symptomatic of the attainment of a new stage of development in the European cultural consciousness. The first of these is that cumbrous, crude, and enigmatic creature, Restif de la Bretonne.

Seriously underrated by the traditionalist literary critics of the nineteenth century for his lack of polish and finesse, Restif is in grave danger of being overrated by those of our own time for the very same reason. His greatest achievement, perhaps, is his *Nuits de Paris* (1788)—one of the first attempts, along with Arthur Young's *Travels in France* (1792) and Louis-Sébastien Mercier's *Tableau de Paris* (1781), at day-to-day, factual, sociological *reportage:* journalism, in fact, of the highest class, and destined in the long run to point the way, in one direction to Cobbett, Mayhew, and Durkheim, in another to Balzac, Stendhal, and Dickens. In contrast with the *Nuits de Paris*, however, Restif's two major experiments with autobiography, *La Vie de mon père* (1779) and *Monsieur Nicolas* (1796–97), appear disconcertingly conventional; or rather, both combine traditionalism and originality in such a way that the originality is often lost. On the surface, *La Vie de mon père* has little to distinguish it from the innumerable other quasi-autobiographical novels of the period, such as Louvet de Couvray's *Aventures du Chevalier de Faublas;* while *Monsieur Nicolas*, despite the pretentious claims of its introduction, has more in common with the *Memoirs* of Giacomo Casanova than it has with Rousseau's *Confessions*. It is shapeless, meandering, clumsy, episodic, and artificial. Restif, in fact, is a classic example of the autobiographer's inability to shake himself free of a novelistic convention—a failure which is all the more striking when that convention is a poor one.

Nonetheless, both *La Vie de mon père* and *Monsieur Nicolas* have their particular contribution to make. *La Vie de mon père* is the first example of what we may call the "indirect approach" to the Childhood—the reconstruction of the writer's child-self, not through direct reminiscence, but by way of a previous generation. Although Restif himself probably did not realize the fact, by embarking on a biography of his own father he was making what we can now see to be a heroic attempt to tackle one of the basic problems inherent in the genre: the total absence of confirmatory evidence in support of whatever arbitrary recollections the adult poet may chance to retain of his former existence. To mold and fashion the formlessness of the unremembered self in terms of the authentic, factually verifiable biography of a father or a mother is not exactly, perhaps, "confirmatory evidence"; nevertheless, it offers a framework in which that self may be apprehended and, in a sense, understood, inasmuch as it may be felt to be predetermined: "*they* were like this, and therefore *I* was like that." At all events, it is a technique exploited by many later poets of the Childhood: by Colette, for instance, in *La Maison de Claudine* (1922), or Marguerite Yourcenar in *Souvenirs pieux* (1974); by V. S. Naipaul in

A House for Mr. Biswas (1961), or Judith Wright in *The Generations of Men* (1959).

Similarly, although it may at first glance appear to owe more to its author's industry than to his ingenuity,[41] and to bear much the same relationship to the truth of experience as the paintings of his contemporary Jean-Baptiste Greuze bear to the truth of nature, *Monsieur Nicolas* is not without importance in our particular context. It is a wildly uneven work and has provoked wildly uneven judgments. Schiller admired it, and Paul Valéry ranked it above Rousseau's *Confessions;* the learned Quérard, on the other hand, referred to it as "a tissue of inanities." If Restif's style had lived up to his subject matter, instead of remaining anchored in the timid prurience of a Crébillon *fils,* he might have changed the face of literature. As it is, he stays relegated among the "precursors" of this or that, and not always among the most honored. Undoubtedly, *Monsieur Nicolas* may be taken as heralding the Childhood as "roman-fleuve," as the first of those interminable, many-volumed, shapeless, and self-indulgent effusions later to be perpetrated by George Sand, Marcel Jouhandeau, Augustus Hare, Osbert Sitwell, Leonard Woolf, Compton MacKenzie, Henry Williamson, and Sofiya Pregel'. In compensation, however, there are details of a notable originality. There is no equivalent elsewhere, for instance, of the detailed account of eighteenth-century children's games, with their accompanying chants and rhymes[42]—an account which seems to anticipate the Opies' *Lore and Language of Schoolchildren* or Norman Douglas's *London Street-Games.* Nor, in earlier Childhoods, do we find so accurate a reproduction of local dialects. But these qualities, real though they are, scarcely suffice to redeem the whole. By and large, *Monsieur Nicolas* must be ranked as a curiosity, that is, as a failure. It fails because of its rambling and garrulous formlessness; it fails because of its lack of love, or anger, or involvement; it fails because it is superficial in the unique way which characterizes the eighteenth-century rationalist when faced with the irrational; and it fails finally because there is no real tension, either between the adult-self and the child-self, or between the child-self and the world about it. Nicolas-Edmé Restif de la Bretonne contemplates his former state of being, it would seem, with a mindless and irritating complacency.

Meanwhile, in Germany where, under the influence of Christoph Martin Wieland's *Agathon* (1766–67), the pattern of the *Bildungsroman* was slowly evolving, two further pioneers of the Childhood, of a temperament very different from that of the exuberant and undisciplined Restif, were experimenting

41. The original edition of *Monsieur Nicolas* comprised seventeen volumes totaling 4,854 pages. Restif was a professional compositor, and set, printed, and published the work himself.

42. *Monsieur Nicolas,* 1:61–67. Philippe Ariès, in his well-informed chapter, "Petite contribution à l'histoire des jeux" (*L'Enfant,* 56–101), does not mention any earlier (literary) source of similar material.

with a form which was decidedly more controlled, and with material much closer to the commonplace triviality of normal childhood experience. The first of these, Johann Heinrich Jung, who liked to call himself Jung-Stilling, published the three volumes of his early reminiscences, *Heinrich Stillings Jugend*, *Heinrich Stillings Jünglingsjahre*, and *Heinrich Stillings Wanderschaft*, between 1777 and 1778—significantly, at a date when *Les Confessions* was still unknown outside those comparatively small literary circles in France and England amongst whose members parts of Rousseau's work had circulated in manuscript.

The fact that Jung-Stilling had not read *Les Confessions* was perhaps one of his greatest advantages, for it enabled him to present his former child-self in his own terms, without constant backward glances over his shoulder to ascertain whether he was following correctly in the footsteps of the Master. The result is one of the most original Childhoods of the eighteenth century; for once, at least, Rousseau's obsessive sexuality is almost completely absent.

For the first time, in the "Heinrich Stilling" narrative, we can observe the characteristic structure of a later period—the trilogy of "Childhood, Boyhood, Youth"—fully developed.[43] It begins with the earliest memories; it concludes with the attainment of a slightly delayed maturity after the seemingly inevitable series of wanderings which are so typical of the *Bildungsroman* proper, but which also reflect aspects of the society of the time in Germany.[44] Within this firmly established outer framework all manner of disparate material is included—intercalated folktales, religious discussions, even the occasional lyric or ballad, much as we find them in Goethe's *Wilhelm Meister* or in Heine's *Harzreise*—but all the while the account of the narrator's progress toward maturity continues steadily through time, the overall structure solid enough to contain any quantity of potentially disruptive episodes and to discipline them into submission.

There are a number of other ways in which Jung-Stilling's originality can be seen as pointing directly toward later developments in the genre. To begin with, in contrast to the more conventional wanderings of the third volume, the account of Stilling's early boyhood is set in an atmosphere of trivial, day-to-day intimacy unknown among earlier writers. For the first time we have the authentic *small* world of the young child: the close if uncomfortable rela-

---

43. Many years later, in 1804, Jung-Stilling added a fourth section: a "Retrospect." This afterthought in no way disturbs the essential unity of the first three volumes; it merely shows that Jung-Stilling was to a large extent unaware of the formal completeness of his earlier achievement.

44. The guild system in the eighteenth century was still stronger in Germany than elsewhere in Europe; and thus the journeyman stage following apprenticeship was still a familiar experience. Moreover, German university students retained until well into the present century much of the peripatetic habits of their medieval predecessors.

tionship with the father, the obsession with the dead mother, the minute pricks and torments of family life magnified into catastrophes, the ecstasies extracted from occurrences which adults take for granted. For the first time also we get a sensation of the wonder—the "magic"—which suddenly overwhelms the child for no ascertainable reason, the wonder, for instance, which envelops him at sunrise on the mountain track leading from Tiefenbach to Zellberg, and which leaves him "like one intoxicated."[45] Indeed, the imperious reason that prompted Jung-Stilling to write this Childhood was his need to recapture the sensation of such sublime experiences before they were lost for ever. And it is significant that it is at moments such as these, when the grip of the "magic" is at its strongest, that his prose gives way to poetry. Jung-Stilling was aware, in a way in which Rousseau was not, that there are certain experiences in childhood which defeat the prosaic, rational language of the adult. They belong to another dimension, another mode of being altogether.[46]

Karl Philipp Moritz's *Anton Reiser* (1785–90) is of necessity slightly less original than are the reminiscences of Jung-Stilling, if only because it was written a few years later. It follows much the same pattern as the earlier work, and reveals many of the same preoccupations; but if the conventional "wanderer" element is built into the very title of the book,[47] the subtitle, "A Psychological Novel" is very much more unexpected. It may in fact prove to be the first use of that now familiar term. The work's significance is difficult to estimate, but it resides perhaps in this: that whereas Rousseau, Florian, Restif, Chateaubriand were all too well aware of themselves as unique and exceptional adults, Moritz was not. He was not a genius, and he knew it. He was a friend of Goethe, but that, perhaps, was the extent of his ambitions. For the rest, he was a successful, reasonably competent academic with a special interest in the new and fashionable discipline of aesthetics. Consequently, whereas Rousseau and others were preoccupied above all by the *man*, and by

45. Heinrich Jung-Stilling, *Lebensgeschichte*, ed. Karl Otto Conrady (Hamburg, 1969), 90. For a more detailed analysis of the "magic" of the childhood experience, see below, chapter 3.

46. It could be argued that Thomas Traherne had a similar awareness, but for Traherne, it was the *totality* of experience which was "magical," not merely isolated episodes. Moreover, the vision belonged only to *infancy*; it was destroyed by childhood proper. Jung-Stilling is more typical, in that his "moments of ecstasy" recur spasmodically right through to adolescence, and so suggest, not merely the memory of a prenatal condition of the soul, but a transcendental dimension inherent in childhood itself.

47. "Reiser" = "Traveler." "Anton Reiser" is Moritz's symbolic name for himself. That the "novel" is in fact straight autobiography is made explicit by Moritz in his preface to the second part, where he states that he feels obliged to explain "that what, for reasons which may easily be guessed, I have called a *psychological novel* is in reality a *biography*, and is perhaps the nearest possible approach to the true and faithful representation of a human life, even down to its most insignificant trivialities, that anyone could manage." Karl Philipp Moritz, *Werke*, ed. Jürgen Jahn (Berlin und Weimar, 1973), 2:115.

the way in which he evolved from the child, Moritz, decidedly less obsessed
with his adult role, was able to concentrate more effectively on the earlier
stages of his existence. "I am writing the history of a Man," proclaims Restif.
Quietly, but effectively, Moritz replies: "I am writing the history of an Adolescent." The "psychology" of the title is that of the later stages of immaturity;
what happens beyond that is irrelevant.[48]

This, probably, is the factor which enables "Anton Reiser" to circumscribe
the time-scale of his narrative even more rigidly than does Heinrich Stilling. It
begins with his "earliest memories"; it ends when, at the age of twenty, he is
forced to admit the failure of his attempt to break out and become an actor,
and so returns, dutifully but unenthusiastically, to resume his second year of
university studies. It is not, in any picaresque sense, an enthralling story; but it
is a very neat one. And at this stage of development in the Childhood, the
neatness is all.

One of the forgotten revolutions brought about by the new middle classes
of the eighteenth century was the institution of privacy. Earlier generations
had lived out their lives largely in public—a fact which is clearly reflected in
the majority of Childhoods written before the French Revolution. To the children of those years, the highroad rather than the nursery, the Court rather
than the kitchen, was the center of their lives. From this point of view, the
Bildungsroman, with its stress on the Wanderjahre rather than on the home,
must appear to be rooted very much in the past. Insofar as Jung-Stilling and
Moritz see their earliest years bounded by the framework of a narrow family
intimacy, it is they, rather than Restif or even Rousseau, who are the prophets
of the coming age. But there are problems. A childhood passed within the
narrow compass of home and family may be cozy and comforting; but unquestionably, considered as the material of literature, it is liable to be unrewarding. What was required was something to replace the picaresque, some
new epic or heroic dimension, capable of transmuting the cozy into the sublime, the banal into the portentous, the trivial into the significant. And this
new dimension—the Epic of Insignificance—was what, each in his own way,
both William Wordsworth and Johann Wolfgang von Goethe attempted to
realize.

To Wordsworth perhaps may be credited the first full realization that the
progress from the earliest dawning of consciousness to the full attainment of
maturity—embracing the initial discoveries of love, death, poetry, and rebellion (or, in his own particular case, the French Revolution)—was subject
matter so vast and so momentous that its only true and fitting literary form

---

48. For this reason, the "continuation," *Erinnerungen aus den zehn letzten Lebensjahren
meines Freundes Anton Reiser* (1794) by Moritz's companion Karl Friedrich Klischnig, seems
particularly inappropriate.

must be the epic. And, having made this discovery, he attempted to realize it, quite literally, in the fourteen books of *The Prelude* (1798–1805), from the very first awareness, not even of self, but of that self's surroundings—"O Derwent! winding among grassy holms / Where I was looking on, a babe in arms"[49]— to his return from France at the age of twenty-two and his unwilling readaptation to English life after the failure of his dream of liberty.

The vision was tremendous; and Wordsworth was a very great poet. Yet it is perhaps not by chance that—with the half-exception of Elizabeth Barrett Browning's *Aurora Leigh* (1856)—the poem had no imitators. This may in part be due to the fact that Wordsworth delayed publication until over half a century after he had written the early drafts, by which time (1849) the poetical idiom which he had employed seemed already to belong to an earlier generation. But it is probably due, far more immediately, to weaknesses inherent in the very structure of the work itself. *The Prelude* contains numerous passages of splendid poetry, but they remain isolated passages. The conception of the poem as a whole, considering what it was intended to be, *an epic of progress towards maturity*, is unbalanced and uneven. The normal period of childhood and adolescence, from the age of two to seventeen, is covered scintillatingly but all too rapidly in the first two books. These are followed by four rather shapeless books on the Cambridge years, whose loose structure is held together by the more meditative Book 5. Next comes a book on London, accompanied by a meditation, "Retrospect: Love of Nature Leading to Love of Man" (Book 8). There follow then three vivid books on the French experience, two final meditative sections, and the conclusion. The point is that while the poem may hold together as a *spiritual* autobiography (four out of the fourteen books are purely meditative), this is not what it sets out to be. It proposes itself as an *epic*—that is, as the narrative of a progressive action—and as such, it proceeds at wildly varying speeds, by fits and starts.

It may seem absurd to talk of *The Prelude* as a failure; yet, considered from our own limited point of view, which is that of the history of the Childhood considered as a form of literature, it is so. And perhaps the real reason is this: the autobiography of childhood is necessarily compounded of trivialities, and indeed Wordsworth accepts this; it forms part of his Lockeian philosophy. For Locke, as for Wordsworth, nothing is essentially "trivial." *All* experience is significant, all eventually adds up to the totality of the completed being:

> How strange, that all
> The terrors, pains and early miseries,
> Regrets, vexations, lassitudes interfused
> Within my mind, should e'er have borne a part,

49. William Wordsworth, *The Prelude* [1850], in *Selected Poetry*, ed. Mark Van Doren (New York, 1950), Book 1, ll. 275–76. Subsequent references, to book and lines, appear in the text.

> And that a needful part, in making up
> The calm existence that is mine, when I
> Am worthy of myself.   (1:344–50)

All trivialities, in fact, are essential to the ultimate harmony. And yet the inescapable fact remains that trivialities, even the most "needful" among them, remain ineluctably trivial; consequently, neither the epic form nor the Wordsworthian diction can handle them. Wordsworth has difficulty enough in calling a spade a spade, let alone a potty a potty. His childhood was a paradise, and perhaps (since he was a poet) not even a lost one; yet, among the primary ingredients of this paradise were momentous trivialities such as family games of noughts-and-crosses beside the fire on a winter's evening . . . and William Wordsworth, the great poet, is forced to admit defeat:

> We schemed and puzzled, head opposed to head
> In strife too humble to be named in verse.   (1:512–13)

In strife too humble to be named in verse—this is the key.[50] His philosophy, his whole plan, demanded trivialities; his form, his language rejected them. His poetry established a distance between the vision and the object viewed; it was molded to the form and order of towering mountain ranges, whether in nature or in the mind. Faced with the disordered and messy proximity of the ordinary—the jumble at the back of the toy cupboard, the unwashed dishes in the sink—he was reduced to triteness, sentimentality . . . or silence. His domain was of the essential, not yet of the existential.

The Prelude, then, worked simultaneously in two diametrically opposite directions. On the one hand, it revealed that there *was* an epic dimension to childhood experience; on the other, it demonstrated (misleadingly, as the event was to prove) that although the full intensity of that experience might be the especial prerogative of poets, poetry as such was not the proper vehicle for its expression. Or at least, not nineteenth-century poetry. Throughout virtually the whole of that century, the Childhood was destined to evolve in terms of prose.

Like Wordsworth, Goethe also had an epic conception of his material. But he was perhaps too experienced to make the mistake of trying to embody it in a poetic form. By using prose, he left himself free to wrestle with other problems, and although he never actually completed a major work strictly within the "rules," as bit by bit they are emerging, his threefold contribution to the definition of the genre was of inestimable importance. For, in their time, who,

---

50. We can observe the same problems, both in Lamartine, and in his Russian contemporary Nikolai Nekrasov, when they attempt to use the conventional verse-forms of the period to discuss their childhood.

outside Germany, read Jung-Stilling or Karl Philipp Moritz? Whereas the very least of Goethe's works was assured of an international audience.

Goethe attempted two things simultaneously: a "straight" autobiography, *Dichtung und Wahrheit* (1811–31), and a novel (which might have been, but which categorically was *not*, autobiographical), *Wilhelm Meisters Lehrjahre* (1777–1829). Both occupied him on and off for decades, the former for twenty years, the latter for over fifty. As time went by, he began to distinguish more clearly between the roles of autobiographical elements in each. In fact, the first of his contributions was to estimate the advantages and the disadvantages of each literary form in relation to the handling of autobiographical material.

His second and most notable contribution is made through *Wilhelm Meister*, which, although it is a novel—in Goethe's case, *because* it was a novel, and as such enjoyed greater freedom from the awkward tyranny of fact— established what henceforward would come to be recognized as the basic literary structure of the genre. Although (like all other *Bildungsromane*) *Wilhelm Meister* begins at the point where the classic Childhood finishes— namely, at the point where Wilhelm is old enough to leave home and set out on his travels—it is nonetheless conceived, for the first time with absolute lucidity, as the account of the development of a human personality from a clear point of departure to an equally clear conclusion. Having this inner structure so comprehensively in mind, Goethe was able, likewise for the first time, to regulate the tempo of the text exactly in accordance with the inner development of his hero, so that the "completeness" of his Wilhelm and the "completion" of the novel coincided absolutely, and were indeed inseparable the one from the other. Here was the advantage of having a starting point already located in maturity: there was no temptation to rush through the early years; every episode, every stage of development, was equally important. Gone now are the Wordsworthian jerks, the sudden changes of tempo, the abrupt contractions and equally abrupt expansions of the material. There is a steadiness of pace and rhythm which, once again, corresponds to the steadiness and predictability with which the human being *does* develop, slowly, in the context of the ineluctable passage of the years, moving toward the final configuration of the self. So compelling was Goethe's imagination that, in Germany and for the rest of the nineteenth century, the Childhood was destined to be assimilated into the *Bildungsroman*.

Finally, however, there was also *Dichtung und Wahrheit*—"Poetry and Truth," a title so rich in implications that, had Goethe himself not used it, one of his successors inevitably must have done so. It is strange that it would seem to have been left for Goethe to formulate that problem which, almost without exception, was to torment his successors, yet which seems to have left his predecessors singularly indifferent. What, in fact, *is* the relationship between the "truth" of the lived experience and the "truth" of that same experience transposed into literature—transmuted into "poetry"? Having formulated the question, Goethe's answer is relatively simple: "Truth" and "Poetry" (which is but the imaginative interpretation of Truth) are inextricably interwoven; to the poet, neither is conceivable without the other. But this, as we shall see, is not an answer that will satisfy every questing intellect—least of all the French intellect, with its insatiable appetite for metaphysico-linguistic conumdrums.

It would seem, then, that round about the year 1835 the Childhood—that is, the "Autobiography of Childhood and Adolescence," or alternatively the "Souvenirs d'enfance et de jeunesse"—begins to crystallize as a clearly defined literary form. For the moment, in defiance of the authority of Wordsworth and Goethe, its center of gravity will remain in France. Why this should be so is not clear, except insofar as the culture of France tended to combine a passion for the exact analysis of human behavior with a very high degree of sophistication. And the Childhood is a genre which presupposes a sophisticated culture. It is inconceivable among primitives; even in the contemporary Third World, it emerges only in imitation of culturally more advanced models. It demands a sense of form, and the intellectual ability to adapt the ill-balanced and misshapen material of experience to the harmony of literary expression without overmuch distortion of the original truth. It requires a grasp of the epic dimension, and the severe discipline of a controlled rhythm. It needs the quick-wittedness to seize on the significance of the apparently trivial and to intuit the role that the minutest of incidents can play in the formation of a human destiny. It demands self-knowledge; it demands also the most delicately graded sense of values relating the individual to the community. It reflects, not necessarily but nevertheless frequently, a loss of belief in God. It is certainly favored by that state of mind engendered by Romanticism, though to recognize this is not to assert that it was engendered by the Romantic movement.[51] Above all, it requires the touch of the poet, who is able to sense the portentous significance of an ant crawling on a leaf held in a child's hand and to convey that experience to the reader. And so it is not entirely surprising that it is only during the last century or so that the Childhood should finally have come into existence as a genre in its own right.

51. It is a common misapprehension that the Childhood is a direct product of the Romantic sensibility. In point of fact, the majority of the Romantic poets were unable to make the distinction between the reality of their child-selves and the sentimentalized-idealized image of childhood innocence. With rare exceptions, those who succeeded in doing so (Stendhal, Michelet, even Wordsworth, Chateaubriand, and Nerval) were not published until the second half of the century.

1   Tales of Innocence and Experience

When I was a child, I spake as a child, I understood as a child, I thought as a child: but when I became a man I put away childish things.

—1 Corinthians 13

Le génie, c'est l'enfance retrouvée à volonté.

—Baudelaire

All true autobiography is assertion: *"This* is what I was; *that* is what I did." But in the autobiography of childhood, the mode of assertion, more often than not, is secondary to the mode of interrogation: *"How* did I come to be like that? *Why* was I impelled to do this?" In essence, the Childhood is a quest, a search for understanding; its primary motivation is intellectual rather than emotional; and behind the assertion of the uniqueness of self there tends to lurk the nagging doubt whether that past, that alien self had any substance, or value, or even ascertainable reality whatsoever. In this, the Childhood—certainly in some of its more recent manifestations—rejoins that literature of incurable metaphysical *angoisse* which characterizes the twentieth century. "We're on earth," as Samuel Beckett's Hamm remarks to Clov. "There's no cure for that."

Yet if there *is* any value in childhood experience, it lies in the fact that this experience is unique. Again, all autobiography is an assertion of uniqueness. The writer, by fixing immutably on the printed page the essence of that being who was and is himself, is in some degree reaffirming the Christian doctrine of the soul of man, and making a belated snatch after some crumb of that sweet immortality once promised to the faithful, but now fading into the realms of fairy tale.

But the uniqueness of the child is more absolute, more imperious than that of the adult. Later aspects of a human life are tarnished, as it were, and therefore stripped of some essential part of this quality of uniqueness, by being shared with others: by being documented. Records are kept, indexed, micro-filed, computerized. Facts can be checked. Whether he likes it or not, all too much of the life of modern man is public property. Admittedly, this too is immortality after a fashion, but an enforced one—an anonymous, faceless life after death, having more in common, perhaps, with hell or purgatory than with heaven.

Only one part of life remains secret and intact, unknown to any other being in the world, beyond the reach of the computer: childhood. "There is only oneself who is oneself," observes Flora Groult; "this certainly suffices *a priori* to endow with value the most commonplace of existences."[1] The theme is developed with infinitely greater sensitivity and depth by Hal Porter as he recalls the house that, once upon a time, used to be known as No. 36 Bellair Street, Kensington. Not Kensington, London; but Kensington, Melbourne:

> Of this house, of what takes place within it until I am six, I alone can tell. That is, perhaps, why I must tell. No one but I will know if a lie be told, therefore I must try for the truth which is the blood and breath and nerves of the elaborate and unimportant facts.[2]

The uniqueness of the experience is reinforced by the uniqueness—and hence the imperious and frightening responsibility—of being able to *tell* about the experience. No. 36 Bellair Street was neither a beautiful nor a noble house. It was Australian suburbia at its bleakest, dreariest, and dustiest. Once, however, it was alive. All those others who knew that life are dead, and have left no record. Unless that record is set down now, before it is too late, then silence and darkness will descend for all eternity; and where once there was something, henceforward there will be just . . . nothing.

It is not so much the annihilation of the self as the annihilation of life, of color and movement, of feeling, form, and thought, that is unbearable, indeed inconceivable, to the poet . . . which is why he is a poet. There is nothing cozily nostalgic about *The Watcher on the Cast-Iron Balcony*. Hal Porter is driven by an overwhelming, almost obsessive need to preserve from oblivion that which was, because, in all the aeons of eternity, it can never be again. Nor is he alone in this. In fact, as an initial generalization about what it is that compels a writer to record these early reminiscences, we may observe that, unless the motivation for doing so is extremely powerful, the result is almost certain to be commonplace. The Childhood is not something to be tossed off unthinkingly in an idle moment.

An analysis of some of the more compelling of these motivations forms the substance of the present chapter.

Whether the writer avows it or not, it is the primitive urge toward personal immortality which informs the vast majority of autobiographical writings. Clearly, this is one of the commonest and most powerful of all motivations for

---

1. "Il n'y a que soi qui soit soi." Flora Groult, *Mémoires de moi* (Paris, 1975), 8.
2. Hal Porter, *The Watcher on the Cast-Iron Balcony* (London, 1963), 10.

the re-creation of the child-self. And the converse is also true: that by and large, writers who retain a strong religious faith feel little need to secure this particular form of "survival-substitute." In the present century at least, Childhoods which reveal that their authors still adhere to any orthodox form of Christianity can be counted almost on one's fingers.[3]

In this sense religious belief, or the lack of it, forms an integral part of those particular preoccupations which inspire and inform the Childhood genre. Nothing could more clearly illustrate this than the number of Childhoods which are motivated by the urge to discover and understand the process by which the pure and unsullied religious faith of infancy has come gradually, in the course of adolescence, to be lost. In many cases, of course, the defection takes place incidentally, almost unnoticed: among Catholics, as the writer's developing intellect detects the irrationalities of dogma, and perhaps also the hypocrisies of the *bien-pensants;* among Protestants, as likely as not, out of sheer frustration and boredom with the church services. On the other hand, since the majority of the greater authors of Childhoods are also poets, as such they are necessarily suffused by some form of otherness—some degree of transcendental awareness of another dimension of experience, whether in art, in nature, in language, or in the very mystery of being in the world. In cases such as these, the religious experience is very real and very essential, and so the break with the simple faith of childhood is an overwhelming catastrophe.

The classic example of this in the nineteenth century was Ernest Renan; indeed his *Souvenirs d'enfance et de jeunesse* (1883) were inspired primarily by the urgent need which he felt to explain both to himself and to others how it was that he had come at last to reject the great Catholic tradition of his childhood in Brittany in favor of the historical positivism with which his name is associated. In Renan's case, the disillusionment was wholly intellectual. There was no disgust with the hypocrisy of unworthy priests; nor was there any serious degree of philosophical doubt concerning the basic tenets of doctrine. In many ways, Renan, like so many others, remained something of a mystic to the end. It was simply that, as a *historian,* he found himself forced to conclude that the Biblical narratives revealed nothing that was not susceptible to a purely human interpretation. This conclusion took him six years to reach—years when he was at the Petit Séminaire de Saint-Sulpice in Paris, nominally studying for the priesthood. "I needed to make my way through the entire corpus of German Biblical exegesis," he recalls. "I needed six whole years of meditation and of incessant labor before I was enabled to perceive

---

3. Perhaps unexpectedly, the majority of these are English: Richard Church, *Over the Bridge* (1955); Graham Greene, *A Sort of Life* (1971); C. S. Lewis, *Surprised by Joy* (1955); John Raynor, *A Westminster Childhood* (1973); Evelyn Waugh, *A Little Learning* (1964), and one or two others. Jewis or Islamic Childhoods fall into a different category.

that my teachers were not infallible."[4] And when, finally and publicly, he broke with the Church—a break which marks the conclusion of his Childhood—he did so with impressive dignity and gentleness:

> Catholicism: I loved it once, I respect it still; but having reached the conclusion that it was intellectually unacceptable, I broke with it; it was no more than fairness on both sides. (p. 165)

The severe and dispassionate objectivity of Renan's account of his loss of faith—for all that, evidently, it caused him unbearable heart-searching and subsequently changed the whole course of his life—is somewhat less than typical. A more characteristic example of the process by which a childhood faith, inadequately explained or justified, crumbles away beneath the questioning of the intelligent adolescent is that recorded by Gwen Raverat. In fact, the sections of *Period Piece* (1952) that deal with this archetypal crisis reveal a sequence which must be familiar to thousands if not to millions of Protestant children the world over. In the beginning was the simple (if rather unusual) image of God the father:

> God had a smooth, oval face, with no hair and no beard and no ears. I imagine that he was descended, not, as most Gods are, from Father Christmas, but rather from the Sun Insurance Office sign.[5]

Then came the first and (from the child's point of view) the most sinister of all metaphysico-theological booby traps: the child is told by its parents to pray for something that it wants. Gwen Raverat took this literally and crawled under the nursery table "to pray that the dancing-mistress might be dead before we got to dancing-class" (p. 210). The prayer did not succeed, which meant that God was either indifferent or incompetent; on the other hand, if it *had* been granted, the outcome would have been still worse: "That He should have done such a thing at my request would have destroyed my respect for Him once and for all" (p. 212).

This second verdict shows the child developing into the adolescent with its own moral standards and ideals. In a sense, Gwen Raverat makes better use of the potentialities of the Childhood than does Renan, for she gives us step by step the reasoning process by which a ten-year-old child reaches a major conclusion, whereas Renan, of necessity, is unable to take us in similar detail through a six-year study of Biblical exegesis. To Gwen Raverat, the inevitable consequence of what had gone before was that prayer now seemed to be "an immoral proceeding"—a self-seeking, egotistical, bargaining relationship with God, as opposed to that ideal and selfless ecstasy of adoration which

---

4. Ernest Renan, *Souvenirs d'enfance et de jeunesse* (1883; Paris, 1960), 26.
5. Gwen Raverat, *Period Piece* (London, 1952), 213.

Calvin and Jansen and every metaphysically minded adolescent at heart desires.

Whereupon came pat the revelation from another ten-year-old, her cousin Frances, that "it wasn't done to believe in Christianity any more" (p. 219). This was the beginning of liberation, but also of a more conscious critical attitude. The nonsensicality of standard religious instruction, the "supreme bore" of church going, now became active fermenting agents of revolt. Boredom, in the case of Gwen Raverat, seems to have been particularly intense. Church was "an active torment, not a passive one, and I just raged and seethed with impatience all through the service" (p. 223). The service in this case happened to be in the great Chapel of King's College, Cambridge; but, given the already-existing context of anger and rebellion, the beauty of the architecture and of the music merely aggravated the situation:

> I couldn't bear the music there. . . . I simply hated the unfair, juicy way in which the organ notes oozed round inside the roof and sapped your vitals, and made you want to cry about nothing at all . . . the kind of emotional appeal which I find most antipathetic of all. (p. 223)

What is most characteristic of all in the Protestant child, and thus of major significance in the motivation of the Childhood, is the reiterated sense of shock: the idealism of adolescence confronted with the pedestrian ritual of day-to-day conventional religious practice. "They told you God was a spirit; and then they spoilt it by doing all sorts of mumbo-jumbo, which could not possibly have anything to do with a God who was a spirit. This shocked me unspeakably; for I was very high-minded and pure in those days; not to say arrogant" (p. 221). Nor is this reaction confined to the Protestant child: for if the "last straw" for Gwen Raverat came when "Onward, Christian Soldiers" was sung as prelude to a school hockey match, it was no less of a "last straw" for the Catholic Robert Byrne to have to participate in basketball team prayers and halftime *Ave Marias* when Saint Procopius' High School played against Dubuque Central.[6] "Believing what you can't believe is a kind of exercise which some people like. Others don't. I don't. This is, however, the religious temperament" (Raverat, p. 221).

However tempered it may be by humor and satire, there is a deep, impassioned anger behind these outbursts. Given different social conditions, as in French Canada for instance, they may determine the transformation of the Childhood into a kind of revolutionary manifesto. "I stride forward now amid the ruins of God which are the world," thunders Paul Chamberland, the most nihilistic of ex-believers; and Juliette Adam, by the age of fourteen, was glory-

---

6. Robert Byrne, *Memories of a Non-Jewish Childhood* (1970; reprint, Scarborough, Ont., 1972), 82.

ing in her descendance from Saint-Just, the scourge of the faithful.[7] Because
the Childhood evolved and came to fruition in a prolonged period of religious
crisis, the anguish of a failed faith is rarely absent from the narrative of the
past self. These problems represent something a great deal more serious than
the archetypal adolescent protest against accepted values. They are as powerful among the genteel boarders of the Presbyterian Ladies' College in Melbourne in the 1880s as they are among the slum-dwellers of Montréal in the
1940s. They are of the very essence of the genre; they are part of its raison
d'être.

For instance, the dawning disbelief in the efficacy of prayer experienced by
Gwen Raverat in the high intellectual circles of Cambridge finds its exact
counterpart in the disillusionment of "Laura Rambotham," the alter ego of the
novelist Henry Handel Richardson, some sixteen thousand miles away in Victoria, Australia. A major episode in *The Getting of Wisdom* (1910) occurs when
Laura, in a characteristic mood of late-adolescent religiosexual hypertension,
"a spurt of intense religious fervour," discovers at last a real need for "suc-
cour," to help her pass her examinations. At the height of her fanaticism,
recalls Henry Handel Richardson, she "made a kind of pact with God, in which
His aid at the present juncture guaranteed her convinced, unswerving alle-
giance." By a freak of chance, she saw one of the examination papers in
advance, prepared a rapid crib, and passed. However, when the crisis was
over, she "reflected on the part God had played in the business. And then, it
must be admitted, she found it a sorry one."

He had given her the option of this way, throwing it open to her and then standing
back and watching to see what she would do, without so much as raising an eyelid to
influence her decision. In fact, the more she pondered over it, the more inclined she
grew to think that it had been a kind of snare on the part of God, to trap her afresh into
sin, and thus to prolong her dependence on Him after her crying need was past. But, if
this were true, if He had done this, then He must *like* people to remain miserable
sinners, so that He might have them always crawling to His feet. . . . She could not go
on loving and worshipping a God who was capable of double dealing; who could
behave in such a "mean, Jewy fashion."[8]

In both these cases—each in its own way extremely characteristic of the
Protestant Childhood—the loss of faith is a major episode in the adolescent's
existence, and the urge to explain it one of the compelling motivations. On the
other hand, the primary reaction is not one of spiritual torture, self-doubt, and
anguish, but rather a sense of dazed disbelief, followed by anger, in the
crudity, stupidity, and plain ineptitude of standard religious instruction. The

7. Paul Chamberland, *L'Inavouable* (Montréal, 1967), 34–35. Juliette Adam, *Le Roman de
mon enfance et de ma jeunesse* (Paris, 1902), 88.
8. Henry Handel Richardson, *The Getting of Wisdom* (1910; reprint, London, 1970), 227–28.

betrayal, in a sense, was social rather than spiritual; and the rebellion, not so much against God as against the inane reasoning of adults. It is the implacable judgment of the exceptional mind leveled against complacent mediocrity. In the majority of cases, our children—the future poets—are a great deal more intelligent than the adults who once encompassed and "guided" them; and the crass, unimaginative incompetence employed by these adults to introduce the child to what will, for the rest of its life, be of supreme importance—the sense of something greater than self—will appear in retrospect as wholly unforgivable. The resulting atheism is, at bottom, a refusal to perpetuate human, rather than to condone divine, stupidity. By contrast, however, unquestionably the two greatest Childhoods which deal with a loss of faith—the one Protestant, the other Catholic—are profound spiritual tragedies.

The childhood faith revealed by Edmund Gosse in his *Father and Son* (1907) bears little resemblance to the conventional Anglicanism of a Gwen Raverat; nonetheless, it epitomizes the Protestant pattern which we have outlined. The tragedy of Philip Henry Gosse, F.R.S., geneticist, marine biologist, father of Edmund and, unhappily, a member of the Sect of the Plymouth Brethren, lay in the fact that he was a scientist, and consequently, that his approach to religion was basically rationalistic. As a result, the main feature of Edmund Gosse's revolt against the religion so drastically and tyrannically imposed upon him during his childhood was that it followed a direction exactly opposite to most of his contemporaries. Gwen Raverat, Henry Handel Richardson, and innumerable others of their generation were carrying the banner of humanist rationalism in defiance of the irrationalism of conventional religion; by contrast, and in a different intellectual climate, a Rimbaud, a Claudel, a Gerard Manley Hopkins were driven to the irrationalism of faith (whether in God or Satan, no matter) as a refuge against the rationalistic intolerance, the "scientism" or state-indoctrinated atheism, of their time. Gosse got the worst of both worlds: victim of a remorselessly rationalistic religion (expressed in terms of narrow-minded intolerance, dogmatic argument, and the literal interpretation of the harsher passages in the Old Testament), for him there was no escape, either from rationalism into religion, nor yet from religion into rationalism. He could find relief only in the imaginative richness of an irrational and belligerently *pagan* art and culture.

Many of Gosse's earlier childhood uncertainties were identical with those of other Protestant children: the puzzle of the failure of prayer, and the "great, blind anger" awakened in his soul after the death of his mother when he was seven. Nonetheless, during the years which followed this loss, he reached a kind of working compromise between the normal unecstatic activities of the small boy and the dogmatic religious severities dictated by his father. The crisis came when, in late adolescence, his own religious sensibility began to develop—the wide, inquiring, idealistic sensitivity of the maturing poet. For a

while, in spite of some repressed criticism, the faith of the father and the faith
of the son still coincided. But then came the moment of confrontation. Old
Philip Gosse, "who had nothing of the mystic or the visionary about him,"
argued that, by a purely scientific and rational interpretation of the evidence
contained in the Bible, the date preordained for the end of the world could be
foreknown. The date arrived, and, in equal ecstasy, father and son awaited its
coming:

> This was the highest moment of my religious life, the apex of my striving after
> holiness. I waited a while, watching; and then I felt a faint shame at the theatrical
> attitude I had adopted, although I was alone. Still I gazed, and still I hoped. Then a little
> breeze sprang up, and the branches danced. Sounds began to arise from the road
> beneath me. Presently the colour deepened, the evening came on. From far below there
> rose to me the chatter of the boys coming home. The tea-bell rang—last word of prose
> to shatter my mystical poetry. "The Lord has not come, the Lord will never come," I
> muttered, and in my heart the artificial edifice of extravagant faith began to totter and
> crumble.[9]

This crisis effectively constitutes the end of the Gosse's Childhood. In
general, the hold of Protestantism over the inquiring adolescent mind is
weaker than that of Catholicism; Gosse is one of the few Protestant children of
modern times for whom the loss of faith constituted a veritable spiritual
overthrow.[10] The heights of exaltation had been so great that the fall was
irremediable. The potential mystic became one of the most outspoken enemies and critics of religion. The idealist found Christianity too lamentably
human and commonplace. His "journey" was a repetition, in miniature, of the
career of Julian the Apostate. Such was the paradoxical outcome when, in the
extreme forms of evangelical Protestantism current at the end of the nineteenth century, the domains of rationalism and religion became confused.

Gosse's dilemma belongs to a particular culture at a particular period in
time; that of James Joyce, as recreated in his *Portrait of the Artist as a Young
Man* (1914–16) resumes that of young Catholics the world over. A fact which
emerges from a study of the Childhood genre is the extent to which the
Catholic experience—and in particular the experience of a Catholic school—
differs from its Protestant equivalent. In the Catholic context, personal re-

9. Edmund Gosse, *Father and Son* (1907; reprint, Harmondsworth, 1973), 207.

10. Other characteristic Protestant Childhoods which conclude with a loss of faith include
those of Samuel Butler (*The Way of All Flesh*, 1903) and of W. H. Hudson (*Far Away and Long
Ago*, 1918). Butler, Gosse, and Hudson, it should be observed, all belonged to that generation
which was most profoundly affected by the publication of Darwin's *Origin of Species* (1859).
Slightly later comes Forrest Reid's *Apostate* (1926), the curious feature of which is that Reid's
revolt against Christianity in favor of a return to a pagan cult of sensual beauty appears to have
been purely instinctual and, unlike the same rebellion in Gosse, to have been based on no clear
process of reasoning.

ligious ecstasies, doubts, and confessions are much more public than they are in a Protestant atmosphere. Teaching performed by men or women who have taken holy vows, together with the general decor, the crucifixes, the shrines, the statuettes—all these oblige the child to live in a constant awareness of the religious dimension. The rhythm of the natural year, like that of the academic year, is counterbalanced by the rhythm of the religious calendar. The obligation to confess with regularity gives the Catholic child a constant sense of moral guilt—nagging frequently to the point of obsession—from which his Protestant rival at the school across the road is often free. And finally, the timing of that great spiritual climax, the First Communion, to coincide with the disturbances of adolescence,[11] combined with the sensuality and symbolism of the rites, the mysterious poetry of sonorous Latin, and the omnipresent femininity of the Blessed Virgin—all these tend to make adolescence for the Catholic child a period of intense emotional "unrest" (Joyce uses the word repeatedly), in which religious fervor, sexual yearnings and guilt complexes, starry-eyed idealism, and even political hatreds and enthusiasms become inextricably intermingled. The danger—from the Church's point of view—is that the magnitude of the climax is such that anticlimax must almost inevitably follow, as is indeed the case with Michel Leiris, and innumerable others:

I made what people refer to as an "ardent" First Communion. I lived in expectation of a miracle, a fabulous revelation at the instant when the Host should melt in my mouth. . . . In this expectation I was atrociously disappointed, as indeed I was in my fears (albeit scarcely more so than I was to be later, on the occasion of my initiation into the act of love). Repeating to myself: "So *that's* all it is" and holding out no more hopes of a miracle, I soon ceased to practise, shortly afterwards I ceased to believe, nor have I ever reverted.[12]

The *Portrait of the Artist as a Young Man* is not only one of the finest, but also one of the most carefully structured of all Childhoods, and since the narrator's loss of faith (or rather, of faiths) constitutes its major theme, nothing happens so offhandedly as with Leiris. In the *Portrait* we have the archetypal narrative of the Catholic adolescent's loss of faith: Joyce takes us step by step through the anguished dilemmas of the poet torn between the instinctive knowledge that he *is* a poet only because he is aware of some dimension transcending the limitations of the mortal self, and the unacceptable obligation to accede to the imperious demands of a divinity requiring him to make a

---

11. Traditionally, the Catholic ceremony of First Communion took place at the age of fifteen or thereabouts, as does the Protestant ceremony of Confirmation. During the present century, however, the tradition has been established of administering First Communion at a very much earlier age, between five and seven years. Such early communions, from our evidence, leave no impression whatsoever; the Childhoods record the rite only when it is performed in adolescence.

12. Michel Leiris, *L'Age d'homme* (1922; rev. ed., Paris, 1972), 91.

free sacrifice of his own freedom. In the aftermath of the first open conflict between the human and the divine ("God," armed with hell-fire)—a conflict symbolized by Stephen Dedalus's "fall" to the prostitute in the pink gown—it seems as though the end might come quickly:

A cold, lucid indifference reigned in his soul. . . . Devotion had gone by the board. What did it avail to pray, when he knew that his soul lusted after its own destruction . . . ? His pride in his own sin, his loveless awe of God, told him that the offence was too grievous to be atoned for in whole or in part by a false homage to the All-Seeing and All-Knowing.[13]

But the "All-Seeing and All-Knowing" is not so easily outwitted. After the "fall" come the three sermons of the Retreat, followed by a new climax: the confession, which in its turn is succeeded (Dedalus is now sixteen) by a prolonged period of such intense spiritual fervor that the Director is led to believe that he has a genuine religious vocation. He invites Stephen to join the order. And it is this challenge, actually to commit himself to the religious life, that precipitates the final crisis. In a magnificent piece of writing, which draws together all the major themes in the book, Joyce analyzes Dedalus's reasons for refusal, of which the ultimate one is the sudden realization of his own identity: he belongs, not to God, but to himself.

He was destined to learn his own wisdom apart from others or to learn the wisdom of others himself wandering among the snares of the world.
The snares of the world were the ways of Sin. He would fall. (p. 162)

However this is still not quite the end; and Joyce reverts to the problem in the concluding pages of the book, with the account of conversations between Stephen Dedalus, now a university student, and his colleague Cranly. But in this latter section, the argument is far more abstract and intellectual, revolving around the nature of "Truth"; consequently, it is perhaps less characteristically Catholic than are the earlier episodes. The end now at last *is* reached, and Dedalus, on the exact threshold between immaturity and maturity, rejects the very notion of categoric belief: not only because his reason finds it unbelievable; not only because, to the subtle sensibility of the poet, it seems crude; but above all because he fears to be untrue to himself by pretending to certain knowledge where all he really has is uncertainty. For Joyce, as perhaps for the majority of poets who have passed through this experience, truth to one's own doubt is ultimately closer to faith than faith undoubting. *A Portrait of the Artist* is the epitome of the Childhood which uses the personal experience of a failure of faith to assert a faith more powerful than anything asserted by

13. James Joyce, *A Portrait of the Artist as a Young Man* (1916; reprint, Harmondsworth, 1969), 103–04.

the Church. What in appearance is a faith rejected is in effect a deeper faith matured.

In the immensely complex texture of *A Portrait of the Artist*, the various themes, symbols, and motifs are so closely interwoven that it is virtually impossible to analyze one without alluding to others. In Stephen Dedalus's rejection of the faith of his childhood and adolescence, the dawning sense of his own true identity, both as a human being and as a poet, and the consequent need for total freedom in which this identity may be allowed to mature and flourish, play at least as big if not a bigger part than rational doubt. And certainly, among the more powerful urges which motivate such a degree of introspective research into the past as we find in the Childhood, the quest for a sense of true identity is paramount.

Almost without exception, the man or woman who, later in life, returns in imagination to revisit and re-create a past childhood was, in that childhood, a solitary, an alienated, an exceptional child. Not necessarily lonely, but, in all essential ways, conscious of being alone:

I read the other day in *Mon coeur mis à nu* a comment which I can readily apply to myself: *"Feeling of solitude, from my childhood onwards, in spite of my family and, above all, in the midst of my friends—feeling of a destiny composed of everlasting solitude, notwithstanding a most eager delight in life and in pleasure."*

There were days when in truth I felt myself possessed by an eternal loneliness; lonely had I been ever since my childhood, all through my adolescence—or alone, perhaps, rather than lonely, but the effect on me was the same either way, and I used to imagine that I could hear my own lonely footsteps echoing in me and around me, echoing far ahead into the empty caverns of the future.[14]

This is the voice of Maurice Sachs, the French Jew later exterminated by the Nazis, a voice recorded almost at random from among the four or five hundred more in the literature of childhood who echo it. Solitude in Russia—"I did not make friends with other children and found their presence tiresome"[15]—and solitude in South Wales:

I was a lonely nightwalker and a steady stander-at-corners. I liked to walk through the wet town after midnight . . . alone and alive on the glistening tramlines in dead and empty High Street.[16]

Solitude in Buenos Aires—"I was a solitary little boy in my rambles about the streets"[17]—and solitude in Fez:

14. Maurice Sachs, *Le Sabbat* (1946; reprint, Paris, 1960), 141–42. *Mon coeur mis à nu* is the title that Baudelaire gave to his private diaries; the quotation is from section xii.

15. Sergei Aksakov, *Detskiye gody Bagrova-vnuka* [1858], in *Sobraniye Sochineniy*, ed. S. Mashinsky (Moscow, 1955), 1:392.

16. Dylan Thomas, *Portrait of the Artist as a Young Dog* (1940; reprint, London, 1956), 65.

17. W. H. Hudson, *Far Away and Long Ago* (London, 1918), 133.

I dream of my solitude and I feel the whole burden of it. My solitude does not date from yesterday. . . . I was neither happy nor unhappy. I was just a solitary child.[18]

Solitude: the solitude of the child who, sooner or later, will grow into the adult describing his own solitude is perhaps the most universal of all characteristics of the Childhood. It may be that solitude is common to all the children of men. But certainly the child who is destined to be a poet or a writer is exceptional in the first instance, and therefore alienated willy-nilly from the average run of predestined research chemists and electrical engineers, pineapple growers or airport controllers. And if this sense of overwhelming isolation prevails even among happy and integrated children, how much more is it accentuated by unhappiness—by family quarrels, lawsuits, or divorces—or simply by the consciousness of being alien, of being different and so somehow *wrong:* of being Jewish, or Black, or Québécois; of being a Cape-coloured boy in Johannesburg (Peter Abrahams, *Tell Freedom*, 1954), or a Yiddish-speaking six-year-old in Western Australia (Judah Waten, *Alien Son*, 1952), or a Chinese girl in the "ghost-haunted" wildernesses of San Francisco (Jade Snow Wong, *Fifth Chinese Daughter* [1945], 1968; Maxine Hong Kingston, *Memories of a Girlhood among Ghosts*, 1976).

Clearly, the two phenomena—the sense of aloneness and the sense of an individual identity—are not unrelated; it is also possible that both are comparatively recent in origin, and thus may contribute, however indirectly, to the rise of the Childhood as a genre. What is clear, however, is that the obsessive preoccupation with the ultimate nature of the self does not go back much beyond the early years of the nineteenth century. Even Rousseau begins his *Confessions*, not with fragmentary flashes of awareness, but with a self already fully conscious and fully fashioned, equipped with self-knowledge, memory, and language. He takes as his starting point himself at the age of six: "That is the age from which I can date the uninterrupted awareness of my own being" (1:46). Earlier than this, he claims, he can remember nothing. Like the seed of the dragon's teeth, he springs into being fully armed with the knowledge of his own uniqueness.

Rousseau's dating of his consciousness could be a straightforward observation, a historical fact; equally, it could be a literary convention, a way of eliminating the arbitrary, the incomplete, and the trivial; or it could even be the statement of a philosophical proposition: man *is* only when his consciousness-as-self is established on a firm and permanent basis. Blaise Pascal's awkward questioning of the very foundations of identity was unfashionable in the eighteenth century, and the contemporaries of Voltaire needed at least a basis of certainty in the self if they were to cast doubt on all the other assumptions by which their fathers had lived.

18. Ahmed Séfrioui, *La Boîte à merveilles* (Paris, 1954), 7–9.

But the children of the twentieth century have no such self-confident assurance. Rarely—very rarely—the awareness of the self comes early and remains unshaken and unshakeable, to the extent that the individual is virtually complete in everything that is essential by the age of ten or twelve, having begun to intuit his identity from the time that he began to speak or even earlier. Such seems to have been the case with John Raynor; and there is sufficient evidence elsewhere of this kind of existential/ontological precocity to allow us to take him at his word:

> As I stood there [at the age of two, having his coat put on], impatiently suffering my arms to be guided into the sleeves, I suddenly knew that I was me, and no-one else. My separate identity was profoundly and startlingly clear; hitherto, I had given myself no conscious thought whatsoever. Now I saw myself detachedly, standing looking out of the window, putting my coat on, filled with secret power and glee, because I was me, and nobody—no-one at all—could stop me being me.[19]

Sometimes, by contrast—if we may trust the authenticity of Jean-Paul Sartre, a feat which requires a far greater exercise in the suspension of disbelief than to credit the authenticity of John Raynor—an entire childhood and half an adolescence can be consumed in the absence of any identity whatsoever. Sartre portrays himself, with a kind of grim delight, as a total void: a nonbeing, serving only to be filled with the words, the gestures, and the attitudes of others. Just as a Jew is "a man whom *Other People* call a Jew,"[20] so a child is a being whom *adults* call a child. At bottom, there is a sort of Rousseauesque logic in this: it implies not only that the child's world is autonomous, but that it can only be defined falsely, in terms of the adult perspective. But characteristically, Sartre inverts the proposition. It is not that the adult defines in contrast to himself, and in defining, distorts and misconceives the child; it is rather that the child, from the child's own unformulable point of view, *is* the adult's misconception. The child is a sort of total *pour-soi:* having no awareness of its own identity, it "is what it is not." And so, Sartre tells us, *while still a child*, he saw himself as "a child," looking at himself, in total lucidity, not with his own eyes, but with the eyes of those who surrounded him. "I was a child, that monster which they manufactured out of their regrets."[21] Being a void, a nonidentity, he could become anything: he could not merely imagine, but *become* a horde of tribesmen armed with assegais (*Les Mots*, p. 58); in church, he could *become* a statue of model piety (p. 18); he could even, with infinite, carefully modulated variations, manage to *become* a child. Every moment of his day, whether alone or in company, was spent in playacting, in

19. John Raynor, *A Westminster Childhood* (London, 1973), 6.
20. Jean-Paul Sartre, *Réflexions sur la question juive* (1944; reprint, Paris, 1954), 83.
21. Jean-Paul Sartre, *Les Mots* (Paris, 1964), 66.

being something other than himself. And then suddenly, one unforgettable day, by mistake, he found himself acting the part of himself. "I was horribly natural. I have never got over the shock" (p. 89).

These are splendid intellectual acrobatics—happily rare within the genre —but they ring false from beginning to end, since whether or not they represent a genuine effort at self-analysis, they are vitiated through and through by a kind of deliberately transparent hypocrisy. The very similar verdict concerning himself which is formulated by Jean Genet in the *Journal du voleur*— himself as a child without identity who consequently *becomes* what others call him (in the event, a thief)—is the self-torturing confession of a deeply experienced inner reality, whose basic authenticity, even if retrospectively constituted, is only increased by the poetic symbolism which envelops it. But with Sartre, the principal objective (even if never openly avowed) is not to confess but to discredit the ethical, religious, and social values of his prosperous, Protestant, perhaps self-satisfied *bon-bourgeois* grandfather. He admits to self-satisfaction and hypocrisy as a child, as betrayed in a photograph of him at the age of five:

> I am pink-complexioned with fair, curly hair, my cheeks are chubby and my eyes shine with amiable deference towards the Established Order; my mouth is puffed out with hypocritical arrogance; I know my own worth. (*Les Mots*, p. 19)

Yet the "confession" of his own smugness is overlaid by a new layer of ideological smugness in the act of confession itself, which is scarcely less disagreeable.

But Raynor and Sartre represent the extremes: between the identity effortlessly achieved on the one hand, and the identity felt as a void never to be positively circumscribed on the other, there comes the range of children and adolescents for whom the realization of an identity represented a struggle, often a fierce one, but who in the end came to know themselves as having a full, real, and positive existence in the world.

The factors which contribute to—or which, alternatively, threaten to destroy—this sense of identity are manifold. Frequently, the certainty of "being oneself and nobody else" emerges out of a strong feeling of resentment at being cast by adults for a given role, at being labeled as a certain *kind* of being which some inner sense affirms is not the "real" self. Thus Clara Malraux experiences a sudden, clamorous upsurge of anger when, hidden beneath the dining-room table, she overhears her father declare that he does not believe in individual immortality, but likes to think that we survive in and through our children. To the child Clara, this is absolutely intolerable. She is *herself*; she is not a mere "receptacle" for someone else's life after death. "Everything in me was unique, that I knew for certain," she protests. "What was there that could shackle me to this man, of whom I could see nothing save his polished shoes?"[22] There are

22. Clara Malraux, *Apprendre à vivre* (Paris, 1963), 25. Clara Malraux, as a child, was Clara Goldschmidt, heir to a Jewish background which deeply affects her apprehension of the world.

many variants of this attitude, particularly among children brought up in families with a strong sense of continuity and tradition. In these circumstances, the self is not a puzzle or a problem; it is a certainty, the one absolute certainty to oppose against every form of dynastic or metaphysical coercion, however benevolent. Jean Genet's surrender of his self to others is much more the exception than the rule. Far more typical is the attitude of Alan Marshall, the Australian boy from the Western District of Victoria, crippled at the age of five by infantile paralysis, and forced to go through childhood on crutches. Other people, even other children, saw him as a cripple, and called him to his face a cripple—so frequently, indeed, that in the end he was forced to concede that he must fit this description. Yet another part of him knew that this description was false; something *about* him suggested the cripple, but his "true" self, his ultimate identity, was anything but infirm. And so, in place of Genet's nonidentity, we have Alan Marshall constituting for himself a dual identity, a positive self and a negative self, both undeniably real, yet of decidedly unequal value. There was his self-as-he-was, his mind, his true and innermost being; and against this, there was his self-as-others-saw-him, a self which ultimately took on symbolic form as "the Other Boy," the incarnation of his own weakness, against whom he needed constantly to be on guard:

> The Other Boy was always with me. He was my shadow-self, weak and full of complaints, afraid and apprehensive, always pleading with me to consider him, always seeking to restrain me for his own selfish interests. . . . He wore my body and walked on crutches. I strode apart from him on legs as strong as trees.[23]

However, the supreme security of "knowing myself to be *Me*" can on occasion be destroyed, even by factors that seem insignificant—a nickname bestowed without the reason for it being understood (Mary McCarthy, *Memories of a Catholic Girlhood*, 1957); a child forced by a domineering mother to take his stepfather's instead of his real father's surname (Graham McInnes, *The Road to Gundagai*, 1965); or even a baptismal name disliked, felt to be "wrong," and thus resented. On the face of it, there is nothing horrific in being formally christened Ethel Florence Lindesay Richardson. Yet the child concerned suffered from it to the point of anguish; the name was actively destructive, hostile to her own identity. All the effort of which she was capable was directed at being *different* from the sort of girl she imagined the name suggested, and yet which she knew she was not. As soon as possible, she began to give herself her "real" names, names as far removed as possible from those which appeared on that hated certificate of baptism; and one set of these she finally adopted, being known to us as Henry Handel Richardson. But even this was not enough. Somehow there was the whole of a childhood passed under the shadow of this disrupted identity to be exorcised; and so "Henry Handel

---

23. Alan Marshall, *I Can Jump Puddles* (Melbourne, 1955), 134.

Richardson," reliving her own schooldays in *The Getting of Wisdom* (1910), deliberately saddled her revisited self with names even more antipathetic than her own had been: Laura Tweedle Rambotham.

There are, however, two writers, Stendhal and Hal Porter, for whom the problem of identity presents itself in such obsessive form that in many ways it constitutes the core of their respective Childhoods. For the earlier of these, Stendhal, the writing of the *Vie de Henry Brulard* (1835) was a significant event, not only in his personal life, but in the evolution of his career as one of the world's greatest novelists. From the outset, he had had only one basic subject: himself; but this self was something of an enigma—it was in essence a duality, his immature self as perhaps once he was, judged, described, and ironically commented upon by his mature self as a writer. The difficulty here—or what Stendhal seems to have felt as a difficulty—was that, since so many elements of his immature self, of the young Marie-Henri Beyle, were still present in the maturity of the man called Stendhal, it was not always possible to keep the two clearly separate. In Octave de Malivert, and above all in Julien Sorel,[24] where the immaturity predominates, what is missing is a truly mature character in which Stendhal can incarnate the reality of his self at the age of fifty or thereabouts; the only way in which he can approach it is through the specific literary device of permitting himself as author to comment directly on the thoughts and actions of his characters. In his third novel, *Lucien Leuwen* (1834–35), he made for the first time an attempt to set a mature and an immature self side by side: M. Leuwen *père* and his son Lucien. But M. Leuwen *père*, although a most memorable character, is essentially a failure. Whatever he is, he is *not* a true embodiment of Stendhal's maturity—or of *any* deeply realized maturity—and so his creator, possibly in despair, killed him off and left the novel unfinished. Immediately afterwards he embarked on the *Vie de Henry Brulard*, consciously or unconsciously determined to establish the difference between his immature and his mature identities, and to understand the process by which the one evolved into the other. He never published the *Vie*, possibly because he could not envisage finding a reader to whom he dared confide so much of himself; nonetheless, from his own point of view, this extraordinarily careful and profound exploration of the nature of his true identity seems to have proved effective, and in his final masterpiece, *La Chartreuse de Parme*, beside the immaturity of Fabrice, he was able to set one of the greatest creations of literature: the maturity of Count Mosca.

Like Pascal, like Samuel Beckett, Stendhal expresses the urgency of this quest for an elusive and unnamable identity in a series of questions. "What *is* this character of mine?" he asks; and again "What eye can contemplate itself?"[25] The *Vie de Henry Brulard* is completely different from Rousseau's

24. The heroes, respectively, of *Armance* (1826) and *Le Rouge et le noir* (1831).
25. Stendhal, *Œuvres*, 21:4; see also 20:9.

Confessions in that it is a work, not of self-revelation, but of self-discovery. Rousseau, as we have seen, knows what he is before he starts to tell the reader; Stendhal begins to discover what he is *in the process of writing*. Significantly— and unlike a Goethe, a Chateaubriand, a Wordsworth—he writes at tremendous speed: "223 pages in 23 days," he notes in the margin of his manuscript when just over halfway through (21:27n1). Indeed, among the earliest of his discoveries was that, once he started writing, his subconscious mind would release floods of hoarded material that his conscious mind was unaware of having retained—and that writing at absolutely top speed was a means of circumventing the normal processes of conscious thought and thus of liberating the subconscious. It is the first example we have of a kind of Proustian "total recall" in action: the writing at times seems almost (in the Surrealist sense of the term) "automatic": "Ideas rush by me at a gallop, and vanish unless I grasp at them. Frequent nervous jerks in my hand" (21:9n1).

Not only is the mature Stendhal discovering both his immature self and something of the reality of his maturity in the process of writing, but characteristically, he is at the same time constantly standing back and, in yet another manifestation of his own self, *watching* himself make the discoveries. "20 January 1836—I am making truly immense discoveries about myself as I write these Memoirs" (21:169) he comments, not in the margin, but actually in the text itself, and after some six hundred pages of manuscript at that. It is this awareness of having a multitude of identities, all positive, all interfused and continuous, and yet at the same time separate and distinguishable, that makes *Henry Brulard* one of the richest and most fascinating of all our Childhoods, and, in its very complexity, one of the most modern. "Know thyself," said the Ancients; "Know thyself," echoed Freud—each presupposing a self which is ultimately knowable. But the deeper Stendhal delves into the mystery of his identity, the more his self divides and ramifies, until it seems almost as though each year, each episode, reveals the presence of a different identity, each more impalpable than the last. The only conclusion is that no conclusion can be reached. "In the last analysis, dear Reader," he observes, not with disillusionment, but merely stating an objective fact, "I do not know who I am: good or wicked, sharp-witted or dull" (21:122). However, he notes elsewhere with incurable optimism: "It may be that I shall perceive the truth at the age of sixty-five, if I get there" (21:4). Stendhal died suddenly, in 1842, at the age of fifty-nine; but the most important of his truths he had already discovered some six years earlier: namely, that the ultimate reality of the self may be intuited, and that the process by which it evolves from earlier forms can in memory be traced; but that by no method of rational analysis can it ever be said to be *known*.

Stendhal wrote with deliberate simplicity about a truth felt to be bafflingly complex; for him, simplicity was the one tool or weapon by which the complexity might be reduced to its component elements and thus comprehended.

Hal Porter, writing somewhat over a century later, tackles a similar complexity of material by the opposite method: the richness and the complexity of his language, the intricate patterns of his ideas and images, are carefully contrived so as to reflect the complexity of his material and, as it were, to make it comprehensible by illustrating it in its own terms. Porter accepts from the outset the multiplicity of his self: himself being, himself watching himself be, and then again himself watching himself watching:

> I watch myself closely. It is hardly necessary. I have been watching myself, by this time, for too long, since the days of the cast-iron balcony. I have watched myself watching the small suburban creature, the uninnocent good boy. (*The Watcher on the Cast-Iron Balcony*, p. 20)

The key concept here is that of "uninnocence." The child not only watches himself, he also watches others, and, by watching others, he gradually becomes, in one particular way, not more, but less of himself. Bit by bit, in fact, he ceases to be "himself"; he becomes a poet. A poet (or any writer) is a being who lives, not in himself, but in and through others; even when, as in the case of the *Watcher*, the other is his own previous self—or, for that matter, his self here and now. "Je est un autre."

The concept that the self in the act of writing constitutes yet another identity is, by and large, a postexistentialist notion; we do not find it, for instance, in Stendhal, or even in Proust. On the other hand, Stendhal *is* very much concerned with the process by which the child becomes the writer, and Stendhal also uses (for the first time in French) the word "egotism" to express (and in a sense to apologize for) his constant preoccupation with the problems of his own identity. Taking these two ideas together, Porter gives them a highly individual twist of his own which, combined with an idea derived from St. Augustine, forms another controlling element in the structure of his narrative.

The child, for Porter, comes into the world with an identity which, while being wholly unselfconscious and unrealized, is nevertheless absolute. It is separate, distinct from every other identity in the world; and as such, it is a total solipsism, an absolute "egotism"—the sort of egotism that St. Augustine condemns as the root of evil and of original sin in the child: "Where, O Lord, where or when was I, Your servant, *innocent*?" For Porter, then, for so long as the child retains without question the unbreached security of its own identity, it is *un*innocent, or, to use Porter's phrase, in a state of "non-innocence." It can even, in its early stages, be the watcher of its own non-innocence, without flawing its unselfconsciousness—without being aware of itself even as a dual identity, watcher and watched. But gradually, as the watcher watches others, so that their otherness becomes, temporarily or permanently, part of himself—these others becoming "as it were, uniforms to be worn by the several creatures I am splitting into" (p. 151)—the secure and perfect egotism of the child is progressively shattered: the others intrude more and more insistently; or rather, the self—now a poet, a writer—dissolves into the selves of others, leaving his own an empty shell. This is the diametrical opposite of "egotism"; and since egotism was "non-innocence," then the second state is one of "innocence"—an odd, paradoxical, and fascinating conception which is of the very essence of Porter's understanding of the *Bildung* of the human being from infancy to maturity. In this context he recalls an episode when (he then being ten years old) his mother met a nun who had once taught her at school, and they started singing together the old songs they once had practiced:

> It is my first recallable experience of un-self-consciousness. This correctly supposes developing self-consciousness in me. . . . 1921 is the last year, for many years, of my early poise, and is, therefore, part of the design of me, the last year of unflawed non-innocence. I am soon to begin that long, tempting and often shocking journey through the experiences of others which is, year by year, to wear the soles of non-innocence thinner and thinner.
>
> I should, ultimately, die innocent, if I live long enough to wear down, to have wrenched from me, to lose in a half-dream, to give wantonly away, the supply of non-innocence I brought on to earth with me. (p. 115)

This neat, Oscar Wilde-like reversal of the Blake-hallowed concept of Innocence giving way to Experience does not leave the impression of being contrived; it is simply that Hal Porter starts, not from identity as *realized* by consciousness, but from the given fact of identity as the sine qua non of human existence. The child *is*. This is the inescapable starting point; its realization of the fact is secondary. And the later awareness, the awareness of others as well as the self, undermines the undiluted egotism of pure being-in-itself. In the end, Porter seems to be arguing, the poet achieves the kind of void of personal identity which Sartre sees as the beginning—save only that there is always that impersonal being, the Watcher, who stands, God-like, faceless, and objective, observing everything that is—an identity absorbing all other identities, yet offering only pure existence as the attribute by which it may be defined.

Both Stendhal and Hal Porter are excellent instances of what we described earlier as one of the essential elements of structure in the Childhood genre: the tension which arises, on the one hand, from the sense of continuity from past to present, thus enabling the adult to *explain* his present self in terms of his childhood experience; and, on the other, from the sense of difference, of discontinuity, which makes it possible for the adult to *judge* his past self as though it were that of another. "I am so utterly different from what I was twenty years ago," remarks Stendhal, "that I have the impression of making discoveries about somebody completely different" (21:273n1); and yet it is the identical Stendhal who, only a few days earlier, had written:

> In 1793, that is forty-two years ago, I was accustomed to proceed in my pursuit of

happiness exactly as I do today; in other, more familiar terms: my character then was absolutely the same as it is now. (20:164)

Perhaps the most revealing of all Childhoods—certainly the most memorable—are those in which this double standard is consciously maintained, each side of the argument being given its full weight. André Gide's *Si le grain ne meurt* (1926) accepts this duality and converts it into a highly artificial but effective structural device. In all of Part 1—essentially his childhood and early adolescence—the point of view is emphatically adult: Gide, at the moment of writing, fully understands his own identity; all that interests him lies in trying to comprehend the process by which this identity was perfected. Thus he judges his childhood accordingly, noting with approval every movement of his earlier self which foreshadowed the definitive version, and flatly rejecting everything in the child which did not appear to lead clearly to the end product, not merely as irrelevant, but actually as false, "a lie." Only the complete adult, Gide maintains, can understand the child; without this assessment, the child can be nothing but an untruth, since no act, no thought even, can be evaluated accurately, save in terms of its consequences, and these, to the child itself, will necessarily be unknown.[26] Every child-judgment is therefore, necessarily, a false judgment; every child-act, a false act (a non-act masquerading as an act), unless its consequences give it significance and therefore—in the fullest sense—Truth. Yet then, suddenly, in Part 2, Gide completely alters his point of view:

> The facts, which it is now incumbent upon me to narrate, the upheavals of my emotions and intellect, I am resolved to present in that same light in which they appeared to me originally, concealing to some extent the judgment which later I was to pass upon them.[27]

The effect is startling, even dramatic; nonetheless, the reader is aware of the contrivance, and of the reasons underlying it—Gide's hesitation at that point in time to pass judgment upon his own late-discovered homosexuality— and the result is something less convincing, all in all, than in those writers, such as Andrei Bely, where child-experience and adult lucidity are interwoven without fuss or comment from the first page to the last.

Si le grain ne meurt provides a good instance of a Childhood in which the need to establish an identity is so strong that it dictates the whole structure of the narrative. But there are more extreme cases than that of Gide. The compelling temptation, of course, is to adduce external evidence, arguing in effect: "It

26. This retrospective determination of the meaning of the act by its unforeseeable consequences is one of the dominating themes of Gide's strange novel (or "sotie"), *Les Caves du Vatican*.

27. André Gide, *Si le grain ne meurt* (Paris, 1926; rev. ed., 1955, 1966), 249.

is not merely *I* who declare that I was such-and-such as a child . . . look! I can prove it!" Thus Mary McCarthy, in her *Memories of a Catholic Girlhood* (1957), follows each section of reminiscence with pages of scholarly footnotes, in which she corrects, explains, or confirms the impressions her memory had retained with the (possibly tongue-in-cheek) ardor of a Ph.D. candidate offering a thesis on *The Early Life of Mary McCarthy*. Or, in one of the strangest of all Childhoods, Georges Perec's *W ou le souvenir d'enfance* (1975)—a *texte* (there is no other word for it) which combines fact, parody, pedantry, and novelistic experimentation in about equal proportions—the simple statement "I was born on 7 March 1936" is elaborated not only by the evidence of a birth certificate duly and properly produced in confirmation, but by details of the appearance and origin of that certificate, whose accuracy is balanced only by their conscientious irrelevance:

> In point of fact, this declaration, made in accordance with the provisions of Art. 3 of the Law of 10 Aug. 1927, was furnished and signed by my father several months later, to be precise on the 17th day of August 1936, in the presence of the Registrar of Births and Deaths for the XXth *Arrondissement*. I have in my possession a duly certified copy of this entry, typed out in purple ink, on a card dated 23 Sept. 1942.[28]

At the other end of the scale, we can find Childhoods in which the quest for identity is impelled by pressures which, while purely psychological in themselves, are external rather than internal. There is the case, for instance, of Christopher Robin Milne (*The Enchanted Places*, 1974), who had the misfortune to be immortalized at the age of six by his father, A. A. Milne, and to become known to countless millions the world over as "Christopher Robin." Here, the identity of the child was fixed, virtually forever, by the rare talents of a great artist; and the comparatively unmemorable, but nonetheless frustrated ex-six-year-old is faced with the Herculean task of somehow rescuing his mature identity and detaching it from the unforgettable pseudo-identity which his father had created for him. It is sad, but perhaps not wholly unexpected, to find that "Christopher Robin" can only recover his liberty by revealing some of the weaker sides of the man who, without his permission, had "created" him and fixed his identity immutably as the companion of Pooh Bear, Piglet, Tigger, and Eeyore. Equally, it is fascinating to learn that "Eeyore's Gloomy Place" may have had something in common with A. A. Milne's own study, and that Eeyore himself could be conceived as an allegorical figure of his creator.[29] Even if they constitute extreme cases, however, both Milne and Perec serve to confirm the general observation that the need to establish an identity, in one way or another, is one of the most compelling

28. Georges Perec, *W ou le souvenir d'enfance* (Paris, 1975), 32.
29. Christopher Robin Milne, *The Enchanted Places* (London, 1974), 131.

motives for writing a Childhood. And, as we have argued, a Childhood written without a compelling motivation of one kind or another is not likely to be a memorable piece of literature.

Among the other powerful drives which inspire the writing of this particular form of autobiography is, predictably, the desire to recapture something of a paradise which has been lost, or partially lost, forever. *Farewell Happy Fields* is, in this respect, an archetypal title, picked out by Kathleen Raine from Book 1 of *Paradise Lost:* "Farewell happy fields / where joy for ever dwells."

However, save in one particular context which we shall examine later, mere nostalgia is rare. As a motivation, nostalgia alone is perhaps too feeble, too undynamic an emotion; it can also tend toward sentimentality, and sentimentality, it would seem, must weaken the resolve to write still further, for it is a surprising fact that scarcely one among the six-hundred-odd examples which constitute our material can seriously be accused of sentimentality. Most of them—even the feebler specimens—are written with too much urgency and have something far too important to express to waste time and mental energy on mere nostalgic sentimentalizing. Colette, who at times comes near to it, has too nice a sense of style, too strong a feeling for classical discipline to indulge in anything like a real wallow; Erich Kästner is saved by his sense of humor, just as Fred Archer is (almost) saved by the consciousness of his role as a social historian; and Graham McInnes is rescued by the baffling complexities of his obsessive love-hate relationship, both with Australia and with his own mother, the terrifying Angela Thirkell. Where nostalgia is strong, it is frequently when the background elements of childhood—the hills, the gardens full of blackcurrants and strawberries, the sunsets—are still accessible to the adult and still as redolent of paradise . . . only the beloved figures that once peopled them have vanished.

The vision of paradise lost, then, only becomes truly powerful as a motivation when it is given life and intensity by some other force, when it is something more positive than mere regret or homesickness for the unattainable—in fact, when it is felt as the source of something supremely valuable or significant in the present. It is because the adult Eugène Ionesco is obsessed with the idea of death that the time which, as a child between the years of eight and ten, he spent in the village of La Chapelle Anthenaise now seems like paradise: not because that area of the French countryside was in itself particularly beautiful, but because the whole experience was rendered luminous by the absence of any awareness of time or mortality. It was not merely a state of physical security or psychological well-being, but a purely "magical," mysterious, even mystic glimpse of a world wholly other, wholly surprising, in which—we find again and again—the characteristic themes which are later worked out in Ionesco's poetry and plays have their source. For him, as for

Thomas Traherne, to live as a child was to live, in the fully religious sense, in a state of grace:

> Childhood is the world of the miraculous or of the supernatural. It is as though the entire creation had surged up suddenly, all luminous, out of the night, new-minted, fresh-fashioned and wholly astonishing. Childhood ceases at the moment when things cease to astonish.[30]

One recalls immediately the vision of the "radiant city" in *Tueur sans gages*, and Bérenger's ability to retain his sense of wonder, his perpetual astonishment which leaves him so vulnerable in the face of happenings which others, snug in their rhinoceros armor of indifferent familiarity, take for granted. Eternal radiance eternally renewed is the essence of Ionesco's vision of paradise; and it is a paradise whose loss can be borne only if the rest of life is spent in trying to recover it: "What I am seeking to regain is Paradise. How else can one live, if not in the mode of the Garden of Eden?" (p. 122; "Comment vivre, sinon édéniquement?").

Although the language is very different, reflecting some influence from Jung and his concept of a subconscious heritage of myth, the general picture is basically similar in *Farewell Happy Fields*. For Kathleen Raine, the paradise of childhood is significant, not so much as a personal experience, but rather "as part of the Fable we know; Paradise and the Fall"—and as such belongs to our common cultural inheritance, not as a cause of impotent regret, but as "a refuge, a source of wisdom and poetry, inexhaustible to this day."[31] It is because the mind of man retains in its subconscious depths these memories of paradise that the individual childhood becomes momentous; they are the link which the seemingly isolated being maintains with forces and experiences far greater and nobler than itself. In particular, this "communal" memory of paradise, reflected through individual experience, is the ultimate source of the idea of Beauty; without such memories, the singers would be silent for all eternity:

> What is all the art and poetry of the world but the record of remembered Paradise and the lament of our exile? We tell one another, we remind one another, we seek ever to re-create, here on earth, what we saw and knew once, elsewhere and for ever. (p. 8)

Both Kathleen Raine and Eugène Ionesco are highly characteristic in their handling of the *paradis perdu* motivation: the lost paradise of childhood only serves as a primary source of inspiration when it is clearly felt as something more than human—when it is allied, in fact, with the underlying mystery of

---

30. Eugène Ionesco, *Journal en miettes* (Paris, 1967), 64–65. See also p. 31, and my essay "On Being Very, *Very* Surprised . . . Eugène Ionesco and the Vision of Childhood," in *The Dream and the Play: Ionesco's Theatrical Quest*, ed. Moshe Lazar (Malibu, Ca., 1982), 1–19.

31. Kathleen Raine, *Farewell Happy Fields* (London, 1973), 7.

poetry and the deep mysticism of the poet. Not that other writers do not have their nostalgias and their sweet regrets; but all too often these are swamped by other memories—memories of fears and terrors, of nightmares, and of the dark staircases, corridors, and broom cupboards which, in the days before electric lighting, made the young child's life a perpetual torment.[32] The horror of one evil and menacing corner to be crept past every night, with an irrepressible shudder of dread, can outweigh the bliss of years of security and love.

There is, however, as we mentioned earlier, one special context in which mere nostalgia can intensify to the point of becoming a genuine source of inspiration: it is not so much that the child itself, now an adult, has forever outgrown the splendors of the past, but rather that civilization and "progress" have annihilated, perhaps totally and irretrievably, an ancient way of life and replaced it with something crude, rootless, and modern. This is more than nostalgia; it is nostalgia shot through with bitterness, resentment, and disgust. Not merely—once upon a time—did the grass *seem* taller, the flowers and butterflies brighter, the birds noisier; it is a fact that there *was* once more grass and less concrete, that the wild flowers and the butterflies had not yet been reduced to rarity by weedkillers and insecticides, and that, only a few years ago, for instance, the birds still thronged within a short tram-ride of the city-centre of South Shields (James Kirkup, *The Only Child*, 1957). This is what we might call, perhaps, "black" nostalgia: far from being sentimental, it is an outburst of despair or protest against the wanton murder of countryside, village, and even town, a lament for the deliberate destruction of beauty. Even Ilford, that dismal desert of subtopia, was once a place of indescribable beauty, before the tide of the housing estates advanced and drowned it:

> The unreal and the mean had moved like a nightmare into a place that had seemed as enduring as seed-time and harvest, summer and winter, day and night.
>
> To say I grieved is needless; but besides grief there had already begun to grow in me an indignation and disgust and outrage and misanthropy; bitterly, but not with childhood's innocent grief, I lamented the usurpation of the beautiful by the mean, the meaningless and the vulgar. . . . That transformation which I was to watch, day by day, week by week, month by month in that doomed countryside has left its desolation upon me. Never have I become reconciled. (Kathleen Raine, *Farewell Happy Fields*, p. 98)

Inevitably, the frustrated anger felt by Kathleen Raine is encountered more and more frequently as the pace of change increases; since the first bomb fell on Hiroshima, it has become one of the predominant themes of the genre. Its intensity, of course, varies from culture to culture, but less so than one might

32. The earlier child's modern counterpart can have little or no conception of this ordeal; as a virtually universal childhood memory (at least in northern Europe), the dreaded "fear of the dark" vanishes almost completely in poets born after 1920.

expect. The note is most strident in England, where the destruction of an inherited culture has been most devastating; strident also in Africa, where traditional ways of life have been overthrown with unprecedented violence. It is less intense in the West Indies, the United States, and South America, where traditionalism is comparatively weak and where "progress" may still be considered beneficial; but it reappears again in Canada and Australia, where a pioneer culture has been shattered in the course of a few decades and left a people uncertain either of their past or of their future. The only country where the motif is practically nonexistent is Russia where, before 1917, change occurred so slowly as to remain almost unnoticed, whereas after 1917 it may be deemed, to say the least, impolitic for a writer to lament over-loudly the way of life that reigned before the Soviets.

But if this motif is most clearly discernible in recent writings, the fact is that the origins of the Childhood as a genre coincided from the outset with a major period of upheaval, with the French Revolution and the Industrial Revolution each in its own way hard at work destroying the past; and so, although muted, this same note of frustration and anger can be detected from the beginning. As early as 1811, Chateaubriand, in the *Mémoires d'outre-tombe*, could describe the idyll of life as it once was in his grandmother's household at Plancoët, when he was seven years old, in terms which served to emphasize the "graciousness" of pre-Revolutionary existence as opposed to the onset of nineteenth-century philistinism and selfishness: "In those days, old age was a matter for veneration; now it is nought but a burden."[33] The same sense of instability, which commercial and industrial progress was thrusting into the secure heart of English rural traditionalism, becomes one of the major themes of *The Mill on the Floss*. It is strange, in a way, to think that George Eliot's diatribe against the desecration of the ancient, mellow brick houses of St. Oggs by "incongruous new-fashioned smartness" and "plate-glass in shop-windows," innovations which gave the whole place "the air of a town that sprang up yesterday,"[34] dates from 1859; yet this was, of course, already the age of Brunel, of the steel-mill, the steamship, and the railways—those same railways, as Edmund Gosse records, which were bringing hordes of "trippers" to the seacoasts to destroy forever the wealth of marine life which once had surrounded the British Isles:

All this is long over and done with. The ring of living beauty drawn about our shores was a very fragile one. . . . These rock-basins . . . exist no longer, they are profaned and emptied and vulgarized. An army of "collectors" has passed over them, and ravaged every corner of them. The fairy paradise has been violated. (*Father and Son*, p. 97).

33. Chateaubriand, *Mémoires d'outre-tombe* [published 1848–50], ed. Levaillant and Moulinier (Paris, 1962) 1:23.

34. George Eliot, *The Mill on the Floss* [1860], ed. Gordon Haight (Oxford, 1980), 121.

This is very far from mere nostalgia: it is a tragic fact, and a fact stated by a trained, objective scholar who was himself the son of a renowned marine biologist who had opened the gates, as it were, to the "army of collectors." And, albeit to a lesser degree, there is a depressing amount of genuine socioeconomic observation interwoven with the pure poetry of childhood in what may be considered a classic of the nostalgic approach: Laurie Lee's *Cider with Rosie* (1959). *Cider with Rosie* is the account—perhaps retrospectively tinted in brighter colors than reality might justify—of a way of life, and, at the end, in a few unemphatic paragraphs, of the manner in which that way of life was totally destroyed in the course of a single decade. It is an impressive little summary: the coming of the car, the motorcycle, and the charabanc; the opening up of broader worlds and the shortening of distances; the death of the age-old twin hierarchy of Squire and Parson; the invasion by "fragmentation, free thought and new excitements" (p. 269); the crumbling away of an ancient and immutable security. "I belonged to that generation which saw, by chance, the end of a thousand years' life."[35] There is a gentleness in Laurie Lee which is very different from the cold, implacable anger of Kathleen Raine, but at bottom the message is the same: something has been destroyed, wantonly destroyed. A richness has gone out of life which can never quite be replaced:

> Time squared itself, and the village shrank, and distances crept nearer. The sun and the moon, which once rose from our hill, rose from London now in the East. . . . The horses had died, few people kept pigs anymore, but spent their spare time buried in engines. The flutes and cornets, the gramophones with horns, the wind-harps were thrown away—now wireless aerials searched the electric sky for the music of the Savoy Orpheans. Old men in the pubs sang, "As I Walked Out," then walked out and never came back. (p. 279)

Perhaps it is too easy to allow oneself to become depressed by the reiteration of this picture of loss, impoverishment, and destruction, which echoes from almost every part of the globe save from those which are ruled by an unremittingly "progressivist" and optimistic ideology.[36] By no means was all that has been destroyed valuable, or even tolerable, as we can discover, for instance, from Flora Thompson's monumental sociohistorical *Childhood*, *Lark Rise to Candleford* (1939–44). Moreover, some part at least of George Eliot's "incongruous new-fashioned smartness" may seem to us today as part of a beloved tradition, rich already with a hundred and twenty years' existence, and due at any time now to come under the wing of the Society for the

---

35. Laurie Lee, *Cider with Rosie* (London, 1959), 279.

36. Both Claude Lévi-Strauss, in *Tristes Tropiques*, and Michel Leiris, in *L'Afrique fantôme* (to name only the most celebrated writers in this field) emphasize the same theme: the total annihilation of immemorial ways of life (in South America and Central Africa respectively) by the forces of "progress."

Preservation of Ancient Monuments. Nonetheless, the unanimity of the chorus of protesting voices is disturbing; and it is difficult to avoid the feelings that, in England at least, the child of the future may inhabit a rather more arid paradise than that of earlier generations.

Few childhoods, even among the most sordid and the most degrading, are entirely without *some* experience of paradise; in fact, the more dreary and oppressive generally the atmosphere in which the child lives, the greater the intensity with which isolated episodes will stand out, illuminated with a brilliance scarcely of this world: instants which are truly sublime, and destined to color the rest of a life. Such experiences are often totally arbitrary and wholly inexplicable: Jean Genet, incarnated in the child Culafroy, suddenly starts dancing in a white labyrinth of drying sheets, and the world of poetry is born in that instant;[37] Davie, a ten-year-old in the shabby, dead, unlovely Melbourne suburb of Maribyrnong, is dazzled by a "sunburst of happiness" while paddling on a kero-tin canoe across the stagnant and polluted waters of Moonee Ponds Creek:

Just then . . . I first saw what I was and what I loved best about being alive. . . . I saw a great beauty in the draggled slope ahead, the bumpy clefts where shale showed yellow, and the thrusting, tangled box. My happiness ran out in all directions, over the bumpy water, up, up to the grey cloud beyond the bridge, the great knots of it, watery, weepy at the edges, moving slowly across the sky, slowly like we were, coming apart a bit, so that through it there came these gleams of the light beyond, so still and sure, reaching down to touch the box thorn and streaming out, up there, far beyond the cloud, to shine on the towers, towers of the New Jerusalem, Jerusalem the Golden with milk and honey bless'd.[38]

If a young, present-day Australian can have a vision of the New Jerusalem on Moonee Ponds Creek, then indeed no child in the world need feel so underprivileged as to be excluded wholly from paradise. The fact remains, however, that in many cases the urgent need to exorcise a childhood which was *not* paradise, but rather uninterrupted hell, constitutes the overriding motivation.

Poverty alone, it would seem, is rarely if ever sufficient to make a child feel in hell—not even in the case of Helen Forrester who, together with all her family, almost died of starvation during the Great Depression (*Twopence to Cross the Mersey*, 1974). Indeed, one of the richest, and most blissful of all accounts is that of James Kirkup (*The Only Child; Sorrows, Passions and Alarms*) whose father was an unemployed joiner and whose home was in the

37. Jean Genet, *Notre Dame des Fleurs* [1944], in *Œuvres complètes* (Paris, 1951), 2:80–81.
38. R. D. Burns, *Early Promise* (Sydney, 1975), 25–26.

blackened, cobble-streeted slums of Tyneside during that same depression. The truly unhappy child (save in certain very special cases)[39] is made so by the people, not by the circumstances, that surround it: the drunken or sadistic father, the domineering mother, the narrow-minded and intolerant family, the brutal schoolmaster, the cold indifference of the orphanage, the fears engendered by violence or passions (racial or religious, for instance) no more than half-understood. Politics as such rarely influence the child one way or another, except when some extreme event offers the possibility of unexpected adventures or a break from the routine and monotony of home and school;[40] but when politics intrude their dissensions into the family itself, then the child is the first to suffer. Moreover, while a description of paradise is not in itself enough to constitute the material and motivation of a successful Childhood, the description of hell is. The unhappy child can fill a book with its unhappiness; every happening, every judgment even, is distorted by remembered misery. Little or nothing else is of significance, until the suffering has been cried aloud.

Occasionally it would seem that the very obsessive quality of this kind of unhappiness can lead to slightly facile or poorly controlled writing: the adult, one feels, is still so livid with anger that he can make little or no attempt to understand either himself or those who oppressed him.[41] But such cases, on the whole, are rare. The catalogue of truly significant writers whose childhoods were rendered intolerable, whether by sheer boredom, oppression, brainwashing or out-and-out sadism, is impressive: Svetlana Alliluyeva and Marguerite Audoux; Hervé Bazin and Robert Blincoe; Drieu la Rochelle and Jean Genet and Edmund Gosse; Mary McCarthy and Claire Martin and Robert Musil; Philip Roth and Jean-Paul Sartre; Jules Vallès and Pierre Vallières and D. I. Yakir, to name only some from among the many. Even Gide, Joyce, and Stendhal would not have willingly relived the majority of their earlier experiences.

In part, of course, this high proportion of unhappiness can be ascribed to a phenomenon noted earlier: namely, that the children with whom we are concerned are by definition exceptional, and consequently lonely and alienated. But in many cases, circumstances further conspired to increase this sense of alienation to intolerable proportions. Michel Leiris, at the age of six, had his tonsils extracted without an anesthetic (L'Age d'homme, pp. 111–12); this appalling experience left him prey to sheer terror for the rest of his childhood

---

39. See my essay "Childhood in the Shadows," *Comparison* 13:3–67.

40. See, for instance, Valentin Kataev's (highly romanticized) adventures in *The Lonely White Sail* (*Belyeyet parus odinokiy*, 1936).

41. For example, J. R. Ackerley, *My Father and Myself* (1968); A. S. Jasper, *A Hoxton Childhood* (1969); Beverley Nichols, *Father Figure* (1972); Ernest Raymond, *The Story of My Days* (1968).

and led eventually to an attempted suicide and to prolonged mental disorder. Marguerite Audoux would probably have lived a perfectly "normal" life, had not her mother's death, her father's disappearance, and her neighbors' cruel indifference confined her to a mid-nineteenth-century French orphanage. But perhaps the three most unforgettable and at the same time most revealing experiences of hell are to be found in the Childhoods of Maxim Gorky, Juliette Adam, and Hervé Bazin.

Maxim Gorky's *Childhood* (*Detstvo*, 1913) is narrated with studied naturalistic simplicity and a minimum of comment. The brutal facts are allowed to speak for themselves. Losing his father at an early age, virtually deserted by his mother,[42] the boy Gorky was brought up in the household of his grandfather, owner of a small dye-works in Nizhni-Novgorod. In this family, with its numerous grown-up sons and daughters-in-law, all the ignorance, boorishness, stupidity, drunkenness, malevolence, dishonesty, and animality of the unformed, uncultured Russian petty-capitalist class of pre-Revolutionary days is not merely embodied, but endowed with a kind of tragic grandeur which perhaps owes something to *King Lear*. In no intimate sense does Gorky write about himself. With dispassionate objectivity, he observes. He observes the imbecile depravity of the creatures about him and he observes their actions as they affect himself; he leaves the reader to make his own deductions. In a rather curious way, these pages might almost be classed as memoirs rather than as autobiography proper. "It is not about myself I am writing," he notes early on, "but about the stifling and horrifying surroundings in which the ordinary Russian lived—and still lives to this day."[43]

To the adult Gorky, his own childhood seemed something "inexpressibly strange—almost unbelievable." Beginning within a week of his arrival in Nizhni-Novgorod, when his grandfather beat him until he lost consciousness and was seriously ill for several days, and reaching a climax a few years later when he burst in upon a new stepfather who was kicking his mother in the breasts, and attempted to stab him with a bread-knife, the whole narrative is an uninterrupted saga of sadistic bestiality, not stopping short at manslaughter and even murder. One figure alone emerges with a touch of humanity: his grandmother, one of the great figures in Russian literature. But in the end she too died, and Maxim, at the age of fourteen, was left to face the world on his own. For better or for worse, his childhood was over.

What is noticeably absent from Gorky's tale is any suspicion of self-pity. Anger, yes; and also some degree of pity for his torturers, since he sees them,

42. For a more detailed analysis of the mother-figure in Gorky's *Childhood*, see my essay "Mother Russia and the Russian Mother," in the *Proceedings of the Leeds Philosophical and Literary Society* 19 (1984), part 6, in press.

43. Maxim Gorky, *Detstvo* [1913], in *Sobraniye Sochinenii* (Moscow, 1951), 13:19; trans. Margaret Wettlin, rev. Jessie Coulson, *Childhood* (London, 1961), 18.

not so much as individually responsible, but rather as the products and victims of the society in which they lived, the ramshackle rottenness of czarist Russia. There seems to be little doubt about the authenticity of Gorky's narrative; yet his reason for writing it at all is oddly impersonal. There is evil to be exorcised; but it is something far more serious than the evil of his own remembered unhappiness: it is the evil that oppresses the whole of Russia, of which his own experience was merely a symptom. Nor is he unaware of this motivation:

> Sometimes when I recall the abominations of that barbarous Russian life I ask myself whether it is worth while to speak of them. And, with renewed conviction, I answer—yes, it is; for they are the vicious, tenacious truth, which has not been exterminated to this very day. They represent a truth which must be exposed to its roots and torn out of our grim and shameful life—torn out of the very soul and memory of man. (*Detstvo*, 13:185; trans., 302)

Gorky's Childhood, in fact, is among the first of those which may be called ideological in inspiration.

By contrast, Juliette Adam's *Roman de mon enfance et de ma jeunesse* (1902) paints the portrait of a far more sophisticated variety of hell. In later life well known as a political hostess and as a minor figure behind the machinations of the Third Republic in France, as a child Juliette was the victim not so much of brutality as of other people's neuroses; and these neuroses themselves were inseparable from the violent political agitations which finally exploded in 1848. If Gorky's narrative is a saga of brutality, Juliette Adam's is one of insecurity. Her mother, jealous almost to the point of insanity at the role which anyone else at all might play in her life, sulked furiously at Juliette's birth to prove to the world how badly her husband was treating her, and refused to have anything to do with the infant. Consequently, Juliette's grandmother (her mother's mother) arranged for her to be kidnapped. The mother retaliated, and Juliette's infancy was a long series of kidnappings and counterkidnappings. Abandoned turn and turn about by father, mother, and grandmother, each of whom was ferociously opposed to the others' political convictions, she was like a shuttlecock tossed relentlessly backward and forward between contending factions, Jacobin and Legitimist, Socialist and Republican.[44] Furthermore, Juliette's mother stood high in the crowded ranks of French *mères dénaturées:* if we are to believe the later Juliette (and there is no reason to disbelieve her), "ma mère" was callous, cruel, sadistic, and vindictive to her own daughter. There is all the physical barbarity of Gorky's experience, but there is an additional refinement of deliberate mental torture—as in the central episode: at the age of eight, Juliette is riding home after dark on a

---

44. For an analysis of the political pressures acting on Juliette Adam in her childhood, see below, chapter 6.

donkey behind her mother; the latter deliberately whips up the animal so that the child falls off, and leaves her alone, terrified and covered in blood, in the silence of the night.

> I crashed onto a heap of stones. The fall had stunned me. I was bleeding, the blood was in my eyes, I couldn't see. I called out for mother, but I knew that she was no longer there. . . . She had vanished on purpose, so as to punish me. I was convinced that she had forsaken me, then and there, all alone, covered with blood. . . .
> I started to run, as fast as I could. My mother was waiting for me. The blood that was streaming down my face left her unmoved. She hauled me up by my belt, without even getting down off the donkey, which she had remounted. . . .
> When I recall my distress during those unforgettable minutes, I can still sense the shock, so deeply was my whole being convulsed. (pp. 118–20)

Without belonging to the domain of great literature, Juliette Adam's Childhood gives us an unforgettable portrait of the hell of insecurity in a child's life. And, once again, the *modernity* of the *Roman de mon enfance* is surprising. Juliette Adam's analysis of her mother's repressions and neuroses are a pre-Freudian case history, while her experiences in 1848, when she was not quite twelve years old, seem to anticipate those of thousands of *lycéennes* in the feverish ferments that agitated France exactly one hundred and twenty years later. Her insecurity, her lack of any sense of direction, the hodgepodge of conflicting and ill-digested propaganda in her mind, her bourgeois background, and her rebellious idealism in favor of "workers" who, to her, were no more than the abstractions of high-flown theory—all this seems to belong to the twentieth rather than the nineteenth century. Hers is the first wholly *politicized* account of a childhood of which we have a record.

Finally, in this category of the childhood in hell, we may take Hervé Bazin, whose *Vipère au poing* (1948) is the story of the persecution of a family of children (himself and his two brothers) by their own mother *for no ascertainable reason whatsoever*. It is a narrative of unexplained but unrelenting hatred on both sides: a "Greek tragedy"—or *farce-tragique*—in which the doom of the Atrides is reenacted in the lives of three small boys after the First World War. Many mothers, according to our evidence, are disliked, feared, or despised; but none is hated with such an obsessive, all-pervasive, murderous hatred as the lady who is referred to, never as Mother, let alone as *maman*, but progressively as "Mme Rézeau," "Madame-Mère" (an allusion to the formal title which Napoleon bestowed upon Madame Bonaparte senior), and finally as "Folcoche." "Folcoche" is an appropriately Soviet-like contraction of the two words *folle cochonne*, the crazy sow, which in the course of time is abbreviated even further to the two symbolic letters "V.F."—"Vengeance on Folcoche"—scratched and chiseled by the children on every tree and wall in the garden, on every door and window in the house, and on every missal and exercise book in the schoolroom:

V.F. . . . V.F. . . . V.F. . . . Meaning Vengeance on Folcoche! Vengeance on Folcoche! . . . . Oh no, Mother-mine, those letters were not, as it was sometimes suggested
to you, simple mnemonics to help us learn our verbs—our *Verbes Français*—never to
forget to learn our V-for-Verbs F-for-French! Oh no, Mother-mine, there is only one
French Verb which means anything hereabouts, the verb *haïr*, the verb *to hate*, and we
know how to decline it, *that* verb, impeccably, in every tense known to the grammar
book: I hate you, you hate me, he hated her, we will hate each other (reflexive), you had
hated each other (pluperfect reflexive), they (past *very* definite) HATED. V.F. . . .
V.F. . . . V.F. . . . V.F. . . .[45]

Bazin is unique in that his loathing and contempt for his mother were so
intense that not only did they motivate his Childhood—the same can be said of
Jules Vallès—but they launched him on his whole career as a novelist. Yet here
again, unlike the case of Juliette Adam, there were no outside pressures to
excuse or justify the transmutation of a childhood into a foretaste of the
Inferno. The Bazin (or "Rézeau") family was well-off; there were no parental
quarrels or separations, no wars or revolutions, no religious or racial dissensions to destroy the harmony and happiness that the child had every right to
expect. There was simply the character—arbitrary, unjustified, inexplicable—of one human being: the mother who, cuddled by her son after a two-
year absence, simply *kicked* him away. "Man," argues Jean-Paul Sartre, "is a
gratuitous passion" ("une passion inutile"). *Vipère au poing*, alone among our
Childhoods, presents evil as a thing-in-itself, as a kind of categorical imperative. It is the magic of childhood in reverse image: a metaphysical absolute,
but of evil rather than good. The one thing the child cannot do is to advise its
parents to consult a psychiatrist. Fortunately so, perhaps. For the psychiatrist,
in all probability, would have "explained" Madame Rézeau's hatred of her
children as a Medea complex and recommended her for treatment by elec-
trotherapy, in consequence of which, her son might never have become the
novelist whom we know. There would appear to be something to be said for
the unhappy childhood.

Concerning one final primary motivation which may impel a writer to
revisit his childhood, the desire for confession, something has been said already. Originally spiritual and religious in nature—a burning desire to attain
to a state of purity in the eyes of God through a public avowal of secret sins—
this motive weakened necessarily with the decline of faith in the eighteenth
century, although it can still be strongly felt in Tolstoy, even degenerating at
times (particularly in the later sections of *Childhood, Boyhood, and Youth*)
into a kind of masochistic self-flagellation.

From Rousseau onward, however, where the confession element is present

45. Hervé Bazin, *Vipère au poing* (1948; Paris, 1976), 89.

at all, its spiritual content tends to be replaced by a narrative of sexual devia-tions. This presents the modern writer with a number of problems, and above all with a weakened or vitiated motivation for his writing. In the first place, whereas the confession of sins may be held to imply a genuine and imperative desire for forgiveness, accompanied by a resolve to live a better life, the confes-sion of, say, homosexuality can hardly be held to portend anything more significant than a plea for social toleration. In the second place, the true confession, which involves a determination to tell a total and uncompromising truth about the innermost self, becomes suspect in the case of the sexual confession, where there must always be some hint of an urge to titillate, excite, or shock the reader. And finally, there is the awkward fact that what *might* have shocked, angered, or disgusted the reader at the time when Gide was writing *Si le grain ne meurt* or Cocteau *Le livre blanc* can hardly be held to do so any more. Instead of being humiliated, outlawed, or classed as a social pariah by all those whose opinion matters, the writer is liable to achieve nothing more humiliating than a best-seller, as happened in the case of *Portnoy's Complaint*, *La Bâtarde*, and (to Jean Genet's genuine distress) *Notre-Dame des Fleurs*.

In the days of Jean-Jacques Bouchard, the desire for confession could be considered a genuine and compelling motivation for the writing of a Child-hood; this is no longer true. The permissive age has not left the child with much that is worth confessing, with still less that it is difficult or humiliating to confess. It is not that, in our own time, there are *no* opinions which are held to be sacrilegious, *no* actions which may be deemed infamous; but the taboos have altered and the sacred cows are of a different breed. They are social and political, rather than moral. An adult might feel some embarrassment in publicly acknowledging that he is violently anti-Semitic, loathes Blacks, doesn't give a tinker's curse for the environment, is never happier than when engaged in harassing females, and believes in treating the workers with the contempt that they deserve—but none of these is an issue likely to be of much concern to a child. From the child's point of view, the new permissiveness began in the later 1950s (cf. Raymond Queneau's *Zazie dans le métro*, pub-lished in 1959); and it is no coincidence that the last attempt to argue for the "intimate confession" as a serious motivation for the writing of a Childhood was that proposed by Michel Leiris in his introduction to the new edition of *L'Age d'homme*, written in 1946: "De la Littérature considérée comme une tauromachie."

"Literature Considered as a Form of Bullfighting": the title is a splendid challenge, and the argument full of echoes of the then-popular Sartrian con-cept of "committed literature." When a bullfighter earns his applause, argues Leiris, it is because he has, quite literally, exposed himself to danger and to death. The "Real Presence" of death bestows more than nobility on the art, it elevates it to the domain of transcendental experience, to the plane of "the sacred."

Yet (continues the argument) the writer has far greater responsibilities than the bullfighter's. Bullfighting may be an art, but it is gratuitous; it entails no consequences. Whereas the writer bears on his shoulders the responsibility for the ideas, and hence for the development, of a whole society. The writer, then, has an obligation a thousand times stronger than that of the bullfighter to expose himself to danger—to *commit* himself to his words and to their consequences by risking death for them just as surely as the guerilla on the barricades. In fact, though, this is what never happens—at least in France. The writer remains comfortably in his desk-chair, and his words fly away from him, leaving no trace of responsibility behind. He may *protest* that he is committed; but his inviolate security in his desk-chair gives the lie to his boast.

And therefore, argues Leiris, the duty of the writer is to expose himself *personally*, "confessing publicly those failings, those acts of cowardice, of which he is most deeply ashamed," and for which he *must* be held personally responsible, thus setting his own security and comfort at risk in relation to the society he desires to serve. Only then will society truly respect him and listen to his words. Only thus will it be possible "to introduce be it but the shadow of a bull's horn into a work of literature" (p. 11).

This argument sounds plausible, but, in the last analysis, it is wholly specious. For if, on the one hand, the writer confesses to something really dangerous—willful murder, espionage, or high treason—his career as a writer is likely to be abruptly terminated; this is not bullfighting, but plain suicide. Whereas if he confesses to something more anodyne, he is ipso facto not in danger. The only compromise—as Leiris himself demonstrates in his various autobiographical writings, but particularly in *L'Age d'homme* itself— is to confess to sexual degradation and abnormality. But this is mere bad faith and self-deception. For while it may be difficult for the *writer* to confess in public his private and petty secrets, weaknesses, and forbidden ecstasies, the public reaction is liable to be far removed from that of the bull to the red rag. The last great writer positively to endure personal suffering on account of the abnormality of his sexual life was probably Oscar Wilde. And this simple fact may mean that, as a serious motivation for the writing of auto- biography—and above all, of the Childhood—the confession is dead.

We have attempted in this chapter to examine some of the more significant reasons that compel writers to revisit their own childhood, and to retrace the steps which once led them from innocence to experience—or, alternatively, from non-innocence to innocence. There is the lament for a faith which some- how, at some point (where, when, and above all, *why?*), evaporated—not necessarily a formal religious faith, but "faith" nonetheless, faith, perhaps, in a dimension of Otherness, once familiar, now (with the loss of faith) recuperable only with effort and anguish. There is the imperative search for an identity, for an understanding of the present self in terms of, and in contrast to, the self that was; there is nostalgia embittered and transformed by anger for a paradise not so much lost as willfully and wantonly desecrated and destroyed; there is the need to exorcise a past which was not paradise, but hell; and finally, there is the motive of confession, perchance with the hope of absolution.

All these motivations, with the exception of the last, the most problematic, serve specifically to inspire the Childhood rather than the more conventional patterns of autobiography; and it is significant that those writers who are strongly impelled by the confession motive, from St. Augustine by way of Jean-Jacques Rousseau to Marcel Proust and Michel Leiris, are precisely those who find it most difficult to establish a clear line of demarcation between their former and their present selves. The confession implies at least a strong element of continuity (a continuity of responsibility, if of nothing else) between child and adult; the other motivations rest on the notion of a *separation* between the two manifestations of the self. There are, perhaps, other, rather more complex motivations, some of which will be discussed in the next chapter: the quest for patterns and meanings in existence, and the striving toward integrity, authenticity, and the telling of an "absolute truth."

But above all else, in the present intellectual climate—the climate which Nathalie Sarraute has described as the "Era of Suspicion," one in which the reader is becoming ever more skeptical of fiction (that is, of the "permitted lie") and ever less willing to suspend his disbelief—autobiography has the advantage of being, not fiction, but fact. The *form* may be the work of the creative imagination; but the substance at least is *reportage*. Once falsehood is detected, autobiography fails. Hence the challenge of the Childhood. For, in adult autobiography, facts and falsehoods can be checked, verified, contested. But, in the Childhood, the entire responsibility lies with the poet. It is *his* truth, and he is on his own. The controls and the safeguards have vanished. He has his own key, he has come of age. And if he abuses his freedom, there is no one to condemn him but the worst of all his enemies: his own conscience.

2   Truth, Memory, and Artifice

Mein Freund, die Zeiten der Vergangenheit
Sind uns ein Buch mit sieben Siegeln.
Was ihr den Geist der Zeiten heisst,
Das ist im Grund der Herren eigner Geist,
In dem die Zeiten sich bespiegeln.
—Goethe, Faust

Every authentic account of childhood of necessity relies mainly upon memory—indeed, upon remote and uncertain areas of memory—as its primary source of material. In addition, this material is liable to consist largely of a vast, disordered, and inchoate accumulation of disconnected trivialities, whose residue of significance in the mind may bear little relation to any objective assessment of meaningfulness—a junk-pile of discarded or discardable bits and pieces which make heavy demands on the literary skill of the writer to fashion them into some valid, coherent, and well-proportioned shape. In this, the Childhood differs appreciably from related genres: from memoirs, in which frequently the hesitancies of memory can be checked and corrected by reference to outside sources; and from the diary,[1] where "remembering" does not constitute a serious difficulty, and where the comparative formlessness of the whole is part of its attraction, since it embodies the spontaneity of immediate experience, the consequences of which are not known at the time of writing. Thus, of its very nature, the Childhood raises specific problems in an acute form: the reliability (or the arbitrary unreliability) of memory; the question of the validity of a purely subjective view of the truth, when there is no possibility of cross-checking; and the conflict between the

---

1. For obvious reasons, there are not many published diaries of authentic childhood experience. See, however, the anonymous *Diary of a Young Girl* (introduction by Sigmund Freud), the famous *Diary of Anne Frank*, and Christine Pawlowska's *Journal d'une jeune fille de quinze ans.* Queen Victoria's *Diaries*, which begin at the age of thirteen, are also interesting. Girls, it would seem, write more publishable diaries than do boys.

raw material of unplanned, haphazardly accumulated experience and the structural requirements of literary form.

To write *about* himself as a child, the writer must have ceased to *be* a child. Whatever elements of continuity may be traced between child and adult, from this point of view at least the childhood must be felt to have ended once and for all. This, incidentally, is another of the attractions of the Childhood as an exercise in introspection: it enables the writer to do for one part of his life that which he can never achieve with the whole of it: to see himself living through a complete experience in time, an experience that evolves in a series of logically necessary steps from start to finish, and therefore is potentially endowed with a discernible pattern and the possibility of comprehensible meaning. To grasp a significant pattern in the past may perhaps represent the only way to intuit a pattern—and therefore a meaning—in the apparently patternless present.

This sense of completeness is essential to the genre, both thematically, in the sense that the writer sees himself and fashions his material with the conclusion clearly envisaged from the first sentence, and also structurally, in that the work itself, as a literary artifact, comes to a full close at the point at which the adventure of childhood is felt to have reached its termination. The ending may be comparatively simple and clear-cut: a death (most frequently of mother or grandmother); leaving home, getting the first job, breaking with the family; leaving school, going to university, graduating; engagement or marriage; going off to war or military service; losing faith or discovering a vocation; publishing the first book or writing the first poem. All these are archetypal. Occasionally there are more idiosyncratic experiences which, however, mark the end no less categorically. Drieu la Rochelle, for instance, at the age of sixteen, visited Oxford and discovered in the splendid physique and robust health of the games-playing undergraduates an ideal of "manliness," as opposed to the "decadence" and "flabbiness" of Third Republic France, that eventually was to drive him straight into the arms of fascism:

> Sixteen. Should I not conclude that my life stopped when I was sixteen? Was it not already drying up in its very springs? What is the point of pursuing this tale any further: it is not destined to be edifying.[2]

And, as a neat contrast, we find Kathleen Raine (*Farewell Happy Fields*, p. 171) having done with her past self and assuming the full freedom of her maturity as a direct result of having crossed the Channel in the opposite direction.

Not infrequently, we encounter Childhoods which have a "double" ending: a clear-cut climax at the age of twelve or thirteen, followed by a long, dull, unspeakably painful period of adolescence; and then the gradual buildup to a second, definitive climax some six or seven years after the first. Such was the

---

2. Pierre Drieu la Rochelle, *Etat civil* (Paris, 1921), 177.

case with James Kirkup, Abel Hermant (*Confession d'un enfant d'hier*, 1903), and, even more emphatically, John Raynor (*A Westminster Childhood*, 1973). Alternatively, the dénouement may be experienced as a complex, interlocking series of experiences, each one of which, thought of in isolation from the rest, *could* seem conclusive, and yet each of which needs to be seen in terms of all the others for the cumulative effect to become irrevocable. For W. H. Hudson, the symbol of the end was his fifteenth birthday:

> Fifteen years old! This was indeed the most memorable day of my life, for on that evening I began to think about myself, and my thoughts were strange and unhappy thoughts to me—what I was, what I was in the world for, what I wanted, what destiny was going to make of me! . . . It was as though I had only just become conscious; I doubt that I had ever been fully-conscious before.[3]

Nonetheless, Hudson's dividing line between childhood and maturity would probably not have assumed its full weight of symbolism had it not been surrounded by a constellation of other significant events: his father's financial ruin; his own brushes with death, first from typhus and shortly after from rheumatic fever; the death of his mother; his loss of religious faith; and his first encounter with Darwinism. But in any case, whether the circumstances are simple or complex, the outcome is the same: the writer is faced with the problem—and the exhilaration—of recreating, through the forms of literary imagination, a completed experience in the past, and of reshaping it first and foremost in terms of its own completeness. So powerful is this relationship between form and content that in many cases the pattern establishes itself subconsciously. More than one writer had decided that his Childhood was simply to be the first volume of a standard autobiography, only to find that, once the "full close" of maturity had been sounded, he was unable to write anything further; and so the "subsequent volumes," confidently announced at the end of the presumed volume 1, were destined never to materialize. Tristan l'Hermite does it; Jean Genet does it; Stendhal does it. As so often is the case, it is Stendhal who provides the classic example. When, on 26 March 1836, a letter arrived on his desk in the French consulate in Civitavecchia, announcing that he had been granted leave to spend three months in Paris, he scribbled in the margin of his manuscript "on this account the present work is inter-rupted" . . . and scholars ever since have classified the *Vie de Henry Brulard* among the novelist's "unfinished" works. But a careful examination of the text shows quite clearly that it *was* finished; that all along, Stendhal had never thought beyond that point of his life—the discovery of that Italy which was to transform the immature Henri Beyle into the writer Stendhal—where the *Vie de Henry Brulard* does indeed end. His instinctive sense of form was so strong

3. W. H. Hudson, *Far Away and Long Ago* (London, 1918), 292.

that *some* part of his mind knew that there was nothing more to be added—
even though his conscious intellect remained content with the theory of the
"interruption," and liked to imagine that there might have been a continuation.[4] Stendhal had created in the *Vie de Henry Brulard*, without ever being
consciously aware of the fact, the first perfect and unflawed specimen of that
literary form which we have called the Childhood.

It follows, then, that the laws governing the internal structure of the genre
will be, in two important respects at least, closer to those of the novel than to
those of autobiography proper.[5] In the first place, the Childhood, like the
traditional novel, is clearly structured with a beginning, a middle, and an end,
and, as in the Aristotelian ideal of tragedy, the end is implicit in the beginning.
In the second place, the balance between literal and symbolic truth is shifted
in the direction of the latter. Incidents are given weight in the straight autobiography according to their *factual* significance; in the Childhood, more
often than not, according to their emotional, imaginative, or metaphysical
significance. Details therefore may be adjusted and emphasized in such a way
as to bring out their full import to the child *as a child*, rather than as a future
writer. This adaptation of the literal facts so as to achieve a surer delineation of
the past self is particularly apparent in the handling of the family. Tolstoy
invents for his "Nikolai" the mother whom he ought to have known, but never
did; Proust's "Marcel" directs against his father most of the neurotic resentment that the writer himself felt towards his mother; Jules Vallès states that
his alter ego, "Jacques Vingtras," was the first-born child of his parents'
marriage and thereafter leaves the reader with the impression that he was an
only child—whereas in fact Vallès was the third of seven; and so on. As a
general rule, these deviations from factual reality are used not to disguise the
truth, but to emphasize it—to make it clearer, sharper, more meaningful. *A la
recherche du temps perdu*, it has been argued, is not so much the story as the
allegory of Proust's own life history. The same might be said of most significant Childhoods. "Stalky & Co.," at the United Services College, have the
adventures that Kipling and his companions *ought* to have had. The fact that,
in the spoilsport judgment of historical research, they didn't, is, in a sense,

    4. For an elaboration of this argument, see my article "Stendhal, Rousseau and the Search
for Self," in *Australian Journal of French Studies* 16 (1979): 27–47.
    5. This is clearly brought out in the case of those writers who have given both a (semific-
tionalized) Childhood and a "straight" autobiography: Rudyard Kipling, for instance (cf. *Stalky
& Co.*, 1899, with *Something of Myself*, 1937); Henry Handel Richardson, (cf. *The Getting of
Wisdom*, 1910, with *Myself When Young*, 1948); Valentin Kataev (cf. *The Lonely White Sail*, 1936,
with *A Mosaic of Life*, 1976). In all these instances, the later "straight" autobiography leaves
what is virtually a blank for the period of time covered by the earlier work: the material has
already been used.

irrelevant. The poet of the Childhood is concerned not so much with *the* truth, as with *his* truth.[6]

Virtually without exception, our writers are concerned first and foremost with telling a truth about themselves which shall be as complete, as authentic, and as absolute as possible. "My narrative has no justification save that it is true," observes André Gide categorically at the very outset of *Si le grain ne meurt* (p. 10); and from across the Channel comes the echoing voice of Edmund Gosse: "This book is nothing if it is not a genuine slice of life" (*Father and Son*, p. 6). This utter single-mindedness of purpose can be discerned in every age and in every country. "My Page," declares seventeenth-century Tristan, "is the faithful copy of a lamentable original; it is as a picture shown in a mirror" (*Le Page disgracié*, p. 50). "Objectivity," echoes twentieth-century Eugène Ionesco, saying the same thing exactly, only in rather more difficult language, "means coinciding to perfection with one's own subjectivity, that is to say, never to tell lies, that is to say, never to tell (oneself) lies" (*Journal en Miettes*, p. 47). In New York: "I, Sholom Aleichem, the Writer, shall relate to you the true life-history of Sholom Aleichem, the Man";[7] and in Moscow: "This is a true story. It begins in the year 1893 in the South of Russia. . . ."[8]

> Pomo pero
> dime 'l vero

chanted the children in the village of Malo, not far out of Vicenza, much as an English child might sing

> Wet my thumb,
> Wipe it dry,
> Cut my throat
> If I tell a lie

—and Luigi Meneghello uses the title *Pomo pero*[9] to affirm, in terms binding upon the child itself, the veracity of his own childhood saga.

---

6. In all the Childhoods referred to in the last paragraph, the writer has "objectivized" and, in so doing, has clarified and in a way *structured* his own past self, by giving it a name different from, yet specifically related to, his own. "Jacques Vingtras" and "Henry Brulard" have the same initials respectively as Jules Vallès and Henri Beyle. "Nikolai" was Tolstoy's father's name and as such, by Russian tradition, his own patronymic. The "Beetle" of *Stalky & Co.* was Kipling's own nickname at school. There are numerous other examples. This careful choice of a "symbolic" name for the protagonist/self acts as a kind of signpost set up at the crossroads of fact and allegory.

7. Sholom Aleichem, *The Great Fair* [*Funem Yarid*, 1913–16] (London, 1958), 4.

8. Kornei Chukovsky, *The Silver Crest* [*Serebryaniy Gerb*,? 1963] (Oxford, 1977), "Preliminary Note."

9. "Apple, pear—Tell me the truth!" This classic "truth-test rhyme" gives the title of Luigi Meneghello, *Pomo pero* (Milan, 1974). The English parallel is quoted from the Opies' *Lore and Language of Schoolchildren*, p. 147.

But it is one thing to resolve, however cross-my-heart-earnestly, to tell the truth, the whole truth, and nothing but the truth; it is quite another matter to do so. Setting aside for the moment the whole question of the reliability (or otherwise) of memory, the Childhood writer is faced from the very outset by a further problem which is not only fundamental to the whole notion of "telling the truth about oneself," but is probably insoluble into the bargain—namely, what is the relationship, if any, between the truth of lived experience (sensual, emotional, above all *fluid*), and the truth of that same experience abstracted into language, fixed and fashioned immutably between the covers of a book?

For, to begin with, no writer can give the *whole* of his experience; in this sense, to write down a "total" truth is an impossibility. Even to describe a single room in *absolute* detail is beyond human power, for, in Kantian terms, the number of phenomena relating to any given thing-in-itself (*Ding-an-sich*) is infinite. Even a six-year-old child will have accumulated such a "baggage of memories" that not even a piece of writing as massive as *A la recherche du temps perdu* or Marcel Jouhandeau's *Mémorial* could hope to deal with all of them:

> The moment of unpacking at hand I am astounded by the size and complexity of this child's luggage. Even now, a middle-aged man, I cannot unpack all: I have not yet the skill to unlade what a happy, egocentric little boy skilfully jammed into invisible nothing. (Porter, *The Watcher on the Cast-Iron Balcony*, p. 10)

From the beginning, then, there is the inescapable condition that the material of memory must be selected, even where memory itself has not made a ferocious and arbitrary preselection; and as such, it must represent less than a total truth. Moreover, as Proust knew only too well, lived experience is fluid, a continuity in time, whereas what normal memory retains is merely a series of "still photographs," isolated the one from the other, often in irrational juxtaposition, and consequently with the one essential element which constituted their "reality" omitted altogether. Once immobilized in words on paper, they are further removed than ever from the truth which was originally inherent in them. "All thought," as the Russian poet Tyutchev noted, "*once expressed*, is a lie."

And it is a lie in more subtle and treacherous ways as well. "Ah! how hard it is to be true, with nothing but truth to serve at once for matter and for means," observes Georges Duhamel in a neat and memorable paradox.[10] Merely to *state* a truth, in this context of imperfectly recalled emotions, is not necessarily to *convey* a truth. Even where the writer uses the first-person singular for his narration, thus thrusting his own experience directly into his

10. Georges Duhamel, *Inventaire de l'abîme* (Paris, 1949), 109.

reader's consciousness, there is no guarantee that the "I" who wrote, say, in 1880 will have anything significantly in common with the "I" who reads a century later. The process of identification may be nothing more than a delusion, in which case the truth would be better served by using a third-person narrative, thus forcing the reader into a conscious awareness of the *differences* between himself and that alien other whose truth he is attempting to assess.

Moreover, a "literally" true fact will quite often destroy an equally (but not verifiably) true emotion. The "petit fait vrai" needs to be selected with extreme care, and essentially for its power as a symbol; not everything will do, and nothing is worse than a truth stated inappropriately. All too often, a literal truth will seem so out of place in a literary context that the effect can be devastating. The poet of the Childhood, even when he has factual evidence in support of his memory—diaries, photographs, and so forth—is usually better advised not to reveal it. Letters, for instance, if quoted at any length, breed tedium and unreadability to a remarkable degree—witness the monumental failure of Augustus Hare's *Story of My Life* (1896–1900), at least considered as literature; and much of Osbert Sitwell's *Left Hand, Right Hand* (1945–48) suffers from the same defect. Extracts from diaries make their presence felt as unmistakably as marionettes among a troupe of live actors; a single photograph can shatter once and for all a mental picture that may have taken a hundred pages or more to build up. Gwen Raverat—herself an artist—is intelligent enough to realize this:

> One of the difficulties in illustrating this book is that if I draw the people as they really were, they simply look impossible. Not quaint, or old-fashioned, or uncomfortable, or even ugly; but just simply impossible. (*Period Piece*, p. 258)

If this is true of realistic drawing, how much more is it true of the photograph. The photograph needs to be handled with even greater care than the diary. In fact, out of our six hundred texts, three alone gain rather than lose from the introduction of photographs. Mary McCarthy, in her *Memories of a Catholic Girlhood*, sets out her family photographs *in the manner of* an old family photograph album; and by this simple device, she achieves three things simultaneously. First, she gives the pattern of photographs on the album page the status of an independent artifact in its own right, not merely illustrating the literary text, but having an autonomous and legitimate existence parallel to it. In other terms, she acknowledges the fact that verbal structures and visual structures are absolutely distinct the one from the other, and cannot positively contribute to each other's truth unless the autonomy of each is recognized. Second, by introducing a certain element of pastiche into the presentation of the visual images, she modifies the crude immediacy of photographic realism, so that the photo stands at roughly the same distance from its subject as does the text itself. And third, she contrives that, while on the one hand the photographs illustrate the text, at the same time, and far more effectively, the text illuminates the photographs, so that an otherwise lifeless sequence of mechanical and unskilled visual representations comes alive with meaning and can be perceived to convey an independent narrative of its own.

The two other Childhoods which use photographic illustrations with similar success—Claude Jasmin's *La petite patrie* and Edna O'Brien's *Mother Ireland*[11]—serve only to confirm the principle that the relationship between photograph and text can only succeed when, in Gilbert's famous phrase addressed to Sullivan, it is "a meeting of master and master." Marc Barrière's dramatic and startling compositions based on Montréal slum tenements, like Fergus Bourke's equally memorable studies of rural and urban poverty in Ireland, follow the same method: they illustrate, not the text itself, but the atmosphere in which it evolves. In doing so, they add a new dimension to the whole, whereas even such a master of the art of photographic portraiture as Cecil Beaton achieves no greater success than does Miles Franklin with her selection of archetypal people and places looking "just simply impossible."[12] In the Childhood, the function of the photograph is not to confirm a truth, but to contribute to an illusion.

The same applies to overmuch realism in language. The language of childhood revisited is that of the adult. Perhaps by instinct, perhaps warned by the Awful Fate of Lewis Carroll's *Sylvie and Bruno*, scarcely one among our poets has fallen into the trap of carrying the search for literal truth to the point of reproducing the lisping (or whining) tones of the genuine child.[13] In fact, among the greater writers, the opposite would seem to be true: the younger the child, the more adult the language. Andrei Bely's *Kotik Letaev* (1915–16) begins when "Kotik" is three and ends when he is five, yet it is without question one of the most sophisticated of all Childhoods, the most rigorously intellectual in the handling of its material, and one of the most difficult to read. It takes an artist of the stature of James Joyce to risk the genuine tonality of childhood accents:

> He was baby tuckoo. The moocow came down the
> road where Betty Byrne lived: she sold lemon platt.

11. Claude Jasmin, *La Petite Patrie* (Montréal, 1972). Edna O'Brien, *Mother Ireland* (London, 1976; reprint, Harmondsworth, 1978); textual references are to the Penguin reprint, but the photographs should be studied in the original Weidenfeld & Nicolson edition.

12. Cecil Beaton, *My Bolivian Aunt* (London, 1971). Miles Franklin, *Childhood at Brindabella* (Sydney, 1963); in defense of Miles Franklin, it should be noted that *Childhood at Brindabella* was published posthumously, and there is no evidence that the photographs were of her own choosing.

13. Peter Coveney, in *The Image of Childhood* (Harmondsworth, 1967), quotes memorable monstrosities resulting from the attempt to incarnate the "innocence" of the child through the reproduction of its language. See especially p. 190 (quotations from Marie Corelli's *Boy*).

> *O, the wild rose blossoms*
> *On the little green place.*
He sang that song. That was his song.
> *O, the green wothe botheth.* (*Portrait of the Artist*, p. 7)

And even Joyce risks only some thirty lines at the opening of a three-hundred page narrative. Dedalus's "moocow" is not a reproduction, it is an *impression* of early childhood; and an impression is as much of over-literal reality as the genre can absorb.

The writer, in fact, is entirely on his own. "I have not consulted my mother or father in any way," notes James Kirkup (*The Only Child*, p. 11), similarly apprehensive of the intrusive materiality of raw fact as it may obtrude into the poetic dimension of memory. In his resolve to establish the truth of his earlier self, not only is factual corroborative evidence rarely available to him, but when it is, it will more often than not prove to be unusable. The Childhood, over and above everything else, is a form of *literature;* and as such it follows the inviolable laws that govern any purely literary text: the law of readability, and the law which decrees that the truth of the imagination shall take precedence over the truth of fact.

At best, the outcome is a compromise. Childhood revisited is childhood *re-created*, and re-created in terms of art. To return to Georges Duhamel: "The thought of an experienced artist," he observes, "invariably *deforms*" (*Inventaire de l'abîme*, p. 237). What is to be avoided, other than the telling of untruths motivated by *anything* other than the desire for an even greater degree of truth, is artistic embellishment for its own sake. From one point of view, the ideal might seem to be that kind of pared-down poverty of language which Samuel Beckett uses in some of his later writing—a neutral, toneless, colorless voice designed "to capture, in all its aridity, the ungraspable truth" (Duhamel, *Inventaire de l'abîme*, p. 238). But against this is the fact, on the one hand, that childhood is supremely rich in an abundance of sensual experiences which are anything but arid, and which wholly defeat any attempt to reduce them to the *sécheresse* of abstraction; and on the other, that most of the greater writers are poets, whose childhood is at the root of their poetry and of its essence, and for whom, therefore, the exercise of reducing that experience to the dry dust of its factuality is a nonsensical proposition.

A compromise, then, is essential; but it is precarious. Because of the special nature of their material, Childhood writers are particularly and acutely conscious of the gap between truth and poetry, and of the fact that, at bottom, all literature is a "variant on the permitted lie." Indeed, among the more perceptive of our children, this discovery itself constitutes one of the more traumatic experiences of adolescence. Tolstoy, commenting on a poem he wrote at the age of ten, observes that the need to rhyme and scan was already forcing him to say what he did not mean: "Why did I write that? Why have I told a lie? Of course, it's only poetry, still I ought not to have done it."[14] And Hal Porter, quoting some verses he wrote at the age of fourteen, echoes the Tolstoyan self-reproach almost word for word:

> God knows who the inferior Georgian poet is who serves as model for this piffle and these lies. . . . I write poems of lies which I think I mean, about dreams I do not have, and a desire I have not formulated.

Porter concludes even more emphatically than the great Russian: "The young, at this stage, do not really exist."[15]

It is this urgent need to escape from the toils of "literature," while still remaining embroiled in the literary act, that causes so many writers, even in the nineteenth century, to experiment with new, unfamiliar, and difficult forms. Stendhal's attempt at "speed-writing"—his deliberate refusal to correct his first draft—has already been commented upon. Jules Vallès develops a very strange technique, a sort of hour-by-hour and minute-by-minute commentary on the crisis which marked the end of his childhood.[16] Even the somewhat sedate Pierre Loti, as early as 1890, can be found exploring a technique for which the best modern term might be "abstract expressionism": the recurrent description, in visual, emotional, and spiritual contexts, of a simple, apparently meaningless phenomenon—a shaft of yellow sunlight. The result, he observes, is "virtually unintelligible"—and yet nonetheless justifiable: it is his attempt "to be absolutely true."[17] To employ a textual structure which cracks wide open the whole literary convention of an age seems in more than one case to be the only means by which truth and literature can be reconciled.

The truth, then, however ardently desired and earnestly sought, will of necessity be no more than relative. It will be relative to the fact and manner of writing; it will also be relative to whatever scale of values happens to be uppermost in the writer's mind on the day he sits down at his desk. "What at some other time I might have recalled, and called my story," remarks Kathleen Raine, "I cannot say; for we select, in retrospect, in the light of whatever self we may have become, and that self changes continually" (*Farewell Happy Fields*,

14. L. N. Tolstoy, *Detstvo* [1852], in *Sobraniye Sochineniya*, ed. S. P. Bychkov (Moscow, 1951–53), 1:48; trans. Aylmer Maude, *Childhood, Boyhood and Youth* (1930; reprint, Oxford, 1947), 63–64.

15. Hal Porter, *The Watcher on the Cast-Iron Balcony*, 169. The "inferior Georgian poet" strongly suggests the W. B. Yeats of *The Wind among the Reeds*. As an interesting contrast to Tolstoy and Porter, one may speculate on how far Marguerite Audoux's narrative in *Marie-Claire* (1910) is distorted by the severely "classical" form which she imposes on it.

16. Jules Vallès, *L'Enfant* (1879). On Vallès's style in *L'Enfant*, see Philippe Lejeune, "Vallès et la voix narrative," in *Littérature*, no. 23 (October 1976), 3–20.

17. Pierre Loti, *Le Roman d'un enfant* (1890; reprint, Paris, 1920), 29.

p. 5). Many writers evolve a sort of rule-of-thumb method for dealing with the problem—"rules" of the kind which are humorously formulated by Erich Kästner: "One may, indeed must, leave out a good deal; and one must not add anything, not even a mouse."[18]

As a working generalization, this seems fair enough; but what it leaves out of account (apart from whatever patterns the subconscious may impose upon the conscious mind) are those pressures exerted by intellectual fashion on the one hand and by ideology on the other. Here we are on uncertain ground, because, of course, we have no means of checking what the "absolute" truth may have been. But when one is aware of the fashion, or of the ideology, then one can sometimes pick out a kind of retrospective conformism which seems too good to be true. Goethe was writing his *Dichtung und Wahrheit* exactly at the time when the avant-garde of the Romantics was discovering the medieval, the Gothic, and the brand-new time-sense of living amidst history. And so the doubt is implanted: *did* the young Goethe, half a century earlier, really spend his boyhood wandering around Frankfurt, engrossed exclusively by its history and its medievalism? Or is it wishful thinking, a reinterpretation of a childhood which ought to have been in terms of the preoccupations of the sexagenarian? Or, to take another instance, did Konstantin Paustovsky, in 1905, really turn out "to join the Students' brigade—to defend the Jews"?[19] Was Lt. Col. Karavayev's cooperative store in Bryansk really burnt down "by rival shopkeepers"? It is possible. To judge by the conditions of that time in Russia described in other Childhoods, it is only too probable. And yet, what is worrying is the way in which Paustovsky, with monotonous regularity, behaves with ideological rectitude. What is missing is the moment which finds him doing something embarrassingly but reassuringly *wrong*.

To the simpler minds, the resolve to tell an "absolute" truth presents no problem—yet, as we have seen, the problems are there, and they are anything but easy to resolve. Hence, many of the more serious writers have preferred the form of the novel to that of autobiography, since, while this does not solve the problems, at least it sets them in a different perspective. To write the story of *another* child—and more especially, to write in the third person—does not commit the writer to the detailed and factual exactitude demanded if he should choose to write about himself directly. The "autobiographical novel of childhood" (the *roman de l'enfance*, or the *enfance romantisée*) permits adjustments to that precarious balance between literal and symbolic truth that is so difficult to maintain in the autobiography pure and simple: the literal truth

18. Erich Kästner, *Als ich ein kleiner Junge war* [1957], in *Gesammelte Schriften* (Zurich, n.d.), 6:154.
19. Konstantin Paustovsky, *Povest' o zhizni* (1946–64; reprint, Moscow, 1966), 1:149; trans. Manya Harari and Michael Duncan, *Story of a Life* (London, 1964), 1:126.

being recalled and recorded where it presents no problem, or sacrificed where it would interfere with something more important. In exceptional cases, the two can even run side by side, sections of fiction and of autobiography alternating in the same piece of writing.[20] But at least the novelist has this most marked advantage: when his memory fails him, he is at liberty to conceal the fact. He can omit or invent; he is not forever obliged to confess. And this is important, for nowhere does memory play so important a role as in the Childhood; and the already insoluble problem of incarnating in literary form a "Truth" which is conceived as "Absolute" is desperately complicated by the fallibility of human memory.

The simplest solution to the problem of memory is obviously that of Proust. A cup of lime-flower tea, a *madeleine:* and an entire, hitherto forgotten sequence of childhood experiences is relived, by "total recall," in its original flow of time. The *madeleine* episode is probably the most famous single incident in the whole of our literature of childhood; but the question which arises concerns its authenticity. Did Proust really have this experience more or less as he describes it? Or did he have only some part of it, some intimation of what it might have been, and subsequently use his creative imagination to emphasize its momentousness and to increase its metaphysical significance?

The occurrence on which Proust based the *madeleine* episode of *A la recherche du temps perdu* took place in Paris, possibly on New Year's Day of the year 1909. Returning home late at night, he asked his cook-housekeeper, Céline Cottin (later one of the many models used in the creation of "Françoise") to bring him a cup of tea with a piece of dry toast. He dipped a finger of toast in the tea, placed it in his mouth, and was rewarded by a "recall," intense but by no means "total," of the garden of his great-uncle Louis Weil at Auteuil, and of his grandfather Nathé Weil who, back in the 1880s, had been in the habit of giving his grandson a rusk soaked in tea when the boy visited him in his bedroom on summer mornings. In 1909, although he found the tea-and-toast phenomenon interesting and pleasurable, he was very far from being aware of all its potential implications. His mind at the time was concerned with the meaning of art and the functioning of the creative processes, and he was becoming convinced that art had nothing to do with intellect, but grew by some form of intuition out of the profound and "real" self of the artist. The problem was to locate this intangible real self; and in that moment of partial involuntary memory Proust believed that he might have had suggested to him a mechanism by which the elusive reality could be held and mastered. It is highly probable that, shortly before the tea-and-toast episode, he had had

20. See James Agee, *A Death in the Family* (1957) or Valentin Kataev, *Lonely White Sail* (1936) as typical examples.

other experiences of this kind of recall (some of which he was later to use in *A la recherche*), without being able to analyze their significance; but, by New Year's Day 1909, his thinking had developed to a point at which the "recall mechanism" began to fit neatly into a pattern. It was *an intuitive apprehension of an ultimate reality*—whether of the self or other aspects of the world—*dissociated from time*. The object or being which could be apprehended only in time was not its "true" self: truth was that which was outside time, that which had "pure Existence"; and only such truth was the material of art.

This was the essence of the ideas which he noted down shortly afterward in the draft of a preface to the book he was working on at the time, *Contre Sainte-Beuve*.[21] In a sense, it was not the phenomenon of memory which interested Proust at this stage, since "memory" as such is inseparable from time, and what Proust was searching for was a reality *outside* time: that past which *is* the "intimate essence of our Selves" (*Contre Sainte-Beuve*, p. 215), and which is just as surely part of immediate reality as is the present. On the other hand, Proust had earlier reflected at length on the problem of memory as such; and sooner or later the two trains of thought were bound to come together. When they did, he began to sketch out *A la recherche*. In other words, the *madeleine* episode is not so much a starting point as a conclusion: the conclusion of a long and complex process of thinking about time and (quite separately) memory; only when that conclusion had been formulated could the novel as we know it be born.

The most striking confirmation of this can be found in *Jean Santeuil*. From many points of view, *Jean Santeuil*, on which Proust had worked on and off between 1895 and 1899, may be considered as a primitive version of his later masterpiece; yet significantly, the phenomenon of memory plays virtually no part in it, and such memory processes as are described and analyzed are very different from those set in motion by the *madeleine*. In a section headed "In the Mountains, Recollections of the Sea," Proust/Jean is on holiday among the high hills, which he detests, when a particular sunset "reminds" him of Brittany and of the sea, which he adores. This produces an immediate, but again by no means "total," recall of an *isolated* experience: "Instantly, Jean saw himself on the track leading to La Forêt."[22] Proust states specifically that this flash of immediate association lasted only for a second, but that it inspired a degree of emotion and nostalgia powerful enough to make Jean reflect on what his memory had shown him, and gradually to reconstruct a picture of what was probably happening "now" at this other place hundreds of miles away: the fishing boats would be coming back into harbor ("Oh! could I but be there to

21. Marcel Proust, *Contre Sainte-Beuve*, ed. Pierre Clarac and Yves Sandre (Paris, 1971), 211–18.

22. Marcel Proust, *Jean Santeuil*, ed. Pierre Clarac and Yves Sandre (Paris, 1971), 388.

behold them")—and bit by bit he built up the whole scene: "And whilst he imagined the sails moving past one after the other, he could see the dazzle of the waters little by little losing its fire" (p. 388).

This is a very far cry indeed from the *madeleine* episode: after the first flash of association, all the emphasis is placed on the *gradual* buildup of the total picture, and it is the intensity of the emotion generated which is the most important theme. The same is basically true of another episode in *Jean Santeuil* involving memory, included in a section entitled "Recollections of the Channel from the Shores of the Baltic." Here, Jean is at The Hague and, looking at the North Sea, he realizes that, just a few miles down the coast, the same sea laps the beach at Ostend, where he used to play as a child. By association, his memory veers to yet another beach, this time on the Baltic, where, on the only occasion when he visited it, the form of the waves had "recalled" to him the waves on the beach at Dieppe. In this section, the associative interaction of recalls is more intricate; furthermore, the experience is accompanied by a degree of philosophical reflection; but, in sharp contrast to Marcel's reflections on savoring the *madeleine*, these comments are of sadness and of melancholy. Because the waves remind him of the waves at Dieppe but in fact are not those same waves, he feels an overpowering sense of alienation, as though in a human face he had thought to recognize a friend, and had encountered only the cold stare of a stranger:

> Thus in that growing dusk he was beset by this melancholy impression, more melancholy, perhaps, than that of not recognizing things familiar: an impression and a melancholy compounded, in part, of the recognition of things in fact unfamiliar; but above all, of our own failure to be recognized by things which we know perfectly well, of sensing them to become estranged. (p. 393)

The only other section of *Jean Santeuil* relating directly to memory is a short, detached fragment in which a piano played by M. Sandre recalls, by its tone, the piano in his grandfather's house, at which he used to play in his adolescence. This is rather closer to the *madeleine* episode, but still a very long way from it. Again, the stress is on the instantaneity of the flash, the effort required to develop it, and the absence of any continuitive sequence in time. In fact, the real interest of the passage lies in the imagery of the subconscious which accompanies it—the image of a photograph album seldom opened:

> The photographic record of all that had been filed away in the archives of his memory, archives so extensive that, for the larger part, he would never go and look at them, unless some chance should cause them to be opened up again, such as had been the case with the false note struck by the pianist that evening. (pp. 897–98)

A few years after *Jean Santeuil*, however, Proust published in *La Renaissance Latine* an article entitled "Sur la lecture" ["On Reading"], later republished as "Journées de Lecture" ["Reading Days"], and originally destined to stand as preface to his own translation of Ruskin's *Sesame and Lilies*. It is an odd piece of work to stand at the head of a book devoted to the praise of reading, for, if anything, it is an attack on all that is normally sought and appreciated in that art. Proust's argument is that the real value of reading lies in the perusal of poor, superficial books, because, our deeper attention thus being insufficiently held by the pages, the surroundings among which we are performing the reading act will stamp themselves on the subconscious part of the mind; years later we need only reopen that same volume for all those forgotten surroundings to spring magically back into life. To illustrate this notion, he describes how recently he had reopened *Le Capitaine Fracasse*, and on the instant had been granted a complete recall of a day in his grandfather's house, one summer holiday, when he had idly wasted long hours reading for the first time Théophile Gautier's trivial tale of theater life. And in the twenty-odd pages of this description, he gives us what is in fact a first, but already unforgettable, version of Combray.

The interest of this essay is that, to a limited extent, the recall involves a movement in time: the day passes from early morning until late at night, while the inhabitants of the house go about their business. The instantaneous flash has been replaced by a continuous flow. But this apparent similarity with *A la recherche* is in fact misleading, for the catalytic agent which produces the recall is itself an extended operation in time. The time spent rereading the book corresponds to the time spent reading it originally, and thus to the general time-flow of the past recalled; whereas the *madeleine* is an instantaneous phenomenon out of which a protracted reliving in time of past reality will be born. And it is precisely the fact of an instantaneous experience giving rise to a time-flow which is of the utmost consequence: for the time-flow thus produced must of necessity be different from "normal" time. It will be, in effect, not "le temps mathématique," but "la durée."[23]

In addition, the movements of people described in "On Reading" are simplified, stylized almost: people coming in to lunch, eating, getting up from the table, going out into the garden. All the detail is reserved for *static* objects: the elaborate white lace tablecloth, Brown's photograph of Botticelli's *Primavera* on the wall, and so on. It is more an illusion of movement recalled than a reality. And in many ways the same is true of the projected preface to *Contre Sainte-Beuve*, which grew directly out of that tea and toast on New Year's Day. There is certainly an *impression* of time recreated in movement, but it is really no more than an impression. The wording seems almost deliberately vague:

23. "Mathematical time" and "duration"—Bergson's terms, which he uses to distinguish between time as an external, measurable factor, and time as an internal, nonmeasurable sensation.

"the summers . . . with their mornings, bringing along in their wake the procession, the ceaseless assault of the happy hours." Again, the telling detail is reserved for the static elements in the picture: it was the garden, "with its forgotten walks, which was depicted in my mind, with its endless rows of circular beds, and with all its flowers"; it was "the shadow which lay that day over the canal where my gondola lay awaiting me" (*Contre Sainte-Beuve*, pp. 212–13). Nonetheless, compared with *Jean Santeuil*, what both "On Reading" and the projected preface have in common is the new feeling of delirious happiness with which Proust is invaded at the moment of recall, and it is this emotion, rather than the melancholy of *Jean Santeuil*, which will be transmitted to the episode of the *madeleine*.

We can see then how Proust gradually developed his thought over the years toward its culmination: the totality of a childhood revisited in a single instant of infinite timelessness. Undoubtedly, two of the essential elements of the *madeleine*-recall are genuinely part of Proust's own experience: a comparatively static, but impressive recall—a minutely detailed "still photograph"— of a room, say, or a garden exact in every tiny particular; and with it, the feeling of joy that accompanied the experience. But the third and vital element—the continuous flow of time accompanying the visual image—would seem to have been no more than vaguely intuited. And so we may conclude, perhaps, that the narrative of the *madeleine*, already transposed from reality into fiction, is also in its very essence a compound of autobiography and art— or rather, in this instance, of autobiography and philosophical speculation. It is Proust the metaphysician who completes the picture of what was only partially experienced by Proust the man.

Yet perhaps even this is not quite exact. The essential part of the experience for Proust—the occasion of the "delicious pleasure" which accompanied it— was the awareness, not so much of a continuity relived in time past, but rather, simply, of time abolished altogether. And it is this intuition of the possibility of grasping an essence of self independent of time which gives Proust his place of significance among post-religious philosophers. It is an intuition of potential immortality, of a transcendental dimension of being wholly divorced from the discredited dogmas of revealed Christianity. And it is precisely this transcendental quality which gives the vision its importance:

> In an instant, it had reduced the vicissitudes of life to a mere matter of indifference, its brevity to an illusion, operating in the same manner as does love, by filling me with a precious essence: or rather, this essence was not *in* me, it *was* me. I had ceased to feel myself mediocre, contingent, mortal.[24]

So, then, the autobiographical basis of the *madeleine* episode contains

24. Marcel Proust, *A la recherche du temps perdu* [1913–27], ed. Pierre Clarac and André Ferré (Paris, rev. ed., 1968), 1:45.

three elements: the transcendental intuition of time abolished, the joy—a mystic's certainty of immortality—accompanying it, and the sensory flash-back to a moment of past experience revealed in all its multifarious detail. Where the artist steps in is, in the first place, to evoke Bergson's concept of *la durée* in order to *explain* the intuitive sense of the suppression of time; and in the second, to ascribe the remainder of the events in time portrayed in the novel to the original moment of recall. It is very possible that Proust's creative method resembled that of Stendhal: the act of writing itself contributing to the retrieval of forgotten material from the storehouse of the subconscious. It is more than probable that he summoned his conscious, intellectual memory into play a good deal more than he was prepared to admit. What does not appear to be credible, from this assessment of the evidence, is that the whole of *A la recherche,* or even the whole of the Combray section which inaugurates it, with its incessant movement of innumerable characters through time and space over a period of years, should have emerged in a single flash of spon-taneous revelation from the *madeleine.*

Childhood writers

This is not to deny that the phenomenon of total recall exists. Other writers, both before and after Proust, have had similar experiences. Chateaubriand, listening to a song thrush in the topmost branches of a birch tree, was instantly "carried back into the past" (*Mémoires d'outre-tombe,* 1:76), as was Pierre Loti by the sight of a snail-track running across a book left carelessly lying in the garden (*Le Roman d'un enfant,* pp. 168–69), and Graham McInnes by the smell of Irish stew (*The Road to Gundagai,* p. 54). For Marcel Jouhandeau, the experience represented immediate and incontrovert-ible evidence of "le sacré," that is, of direct contact with a supernatural or transcendental, but not necessarily agreeable, dimension of existence; it was a "conveying-away" of the soul.[25] By contrast, for the more pragmatical James Kirkup, it was simply evidence of that well-trained and well-practiced faculty of memory "that I was born with and that I have cultivated and carefully exercised as I would any other gift" (*Sorrows, Passions and Alarms,* p. 12). More interestingly, for Hal Porter—unusual in that his total recall includes an objective picture of himself, the Watcher, constantly present at the center—it is evidence of a kind of existential continuum of reality: the object, to have significant and defined existence, has first to be perceived, but once perceived, will continue to retain that precise degree of existence and significance for all the time that the mind which had originally created them (and which they themselves helped to mold) continues in this life:

> It rains. He sits, neat as a story-book boy, on the colonial sofa in the living-room. He watches the drops on the pane. For how long? For a little while? To this moment; he sits there watching to this very moment. (*Watcher on the Cast-Iron Balcony,* p. 24)

25. Marcel Jouhandeau, *Mémorial* (Paris, 1948–72), 1:11.

For Porter, total recall presents no problem and very little exhilaration. It is a fact of life. If the mind, by whatever process of Sartrian *néantisation*, creates, then it must continue, willy-nilly, to live by and with what it has created. And that is that.

Besides these, however, there are two writers whose total recall is so vivid that it is not inappropriate to set their experience against that of Proust. The first of these is the naturalist W. H. Hudson, born and brought up in Argentina, the son of an English father and an American mother, and one of the most gifted nature writers of his time. It is this childhood in the Argentine which he describes in *Far Away and Long Ago* (1918); and at the outset he evokes in detail the total recall which prompted him to write the book. The occurrence took place, in all probability, in November 1914; he had just returned to England in an acute state of depression, and then he fell seriously ill:

> On the second day of my illness, during an interval of comparative ease, I fell into recollections of my childhood, and at once I had that far, that forgotten past with me again as I had never previously had it. It was not like that mental condition, known to most persons, when some sight or sound or, more frequently, the perfume of some flower, associated with our early life, restores the past suddenly and so vividly that it is almost an illusion. That is an intensely emotional condition, and vanishes as quickly as it comes. This was different. . . . What happiness it would be, I thought . . . , if this vision would continue. It was not to be expected: nevertheless, it did not vanish, and on the second day I set myself to try and save it from the oblivion which would presently cover it again. (pp. 3–4)

By comparison with Proust, Hudson is a refreshingly naive writer, and this account carries an aura of credibility. It is at once so similar and so dissimilar to the episode of the *madeleine* that it may serve to shed some light on the latter.

The chief elements in common are the sense of joyous happiness which accompanies the "vision" (although Hudson, scientist and disciple of Darwin as he is, carefully avoids any metaphysical speculation, merely commenting on the remarkable scope and retentive ability of the subconscious mind), and his conviction that what was revealed to him *was* a continuum: "a wonderfully clear *and continuous* vision of the past" (emphasis added). What exactly this means is not clear, since Hudson does not elaborate or explore the implications; nonetheless, if there *is* evidence of continuity in time in Proust's experience, then Hudson might well be invoked to support it.

On the other hand, Hudson specifically dissociates the origins of his experience from the kind whose archetype is the *madeleine:* the instantaneous but fleeting recall, "known to most persons," produced by a single moment of evocative sensation. That which triggered the experience in Hudson's case was a state of mind induced by illness: that is, a special condition, in which the control of conscious mind over subconscious is weakened, and which has in itself an element of continuity—in the event, a sense of heightened psychological awareness persisting, albeit gradually weakening, over several days and even weeks. The analogy, then, is closer to Proust's reading of *Le Capitaine Fracasse* than to any of his moments of instantaneous revelation. Unlike Proust, who wrote *A la recherche* over a period of some twelve years following the tea-and-toast episode, Hudson completed a first draft of *Far Away and Long Ago* within six weeks; consequently he was, in all essentials, writing down the vision while it was still with him. This was certainly not the case with Proust. So what the combined and contrasted experience of Proust and Hudson might seem to suggest is that there are two clearly distinct varieties of total-recall: the one instantaneous, and "known to most persons"; the other, a state of mind which is comparatively persistent, but also much rarer. Insofar as memory in a time-continuum can be envisaged at all, it belongs to the latter category. In other words, and in defiance of all Proustian-Bergsonian metaphysics, a past time-continuum in memory cannot exist independently of a parallel, albeit condensed, time-continuum in the present act of remembering.

The second writer whose experience merits comparison with that of Proust is the composer John Raynor. Hudson's experience took place in 1914; therefore it can be reasonably assumed that he had no knowledge of *A la recherche*. Raynor's occurred in 1940, but if, as is quite probable, he by then knew Proust's novel, he makes absolutely no use of it. In fact, his reaction to the phenomenon is as far removed from Proust's as it is possible to conceive.

On the day in question, he came to the church of Haresfield (between Stroud and Gloucester) which he had known as a child, and, from the base of the church tower, looked up at the clock. Then

such a sense of the past, with its power, its glory and its fear, seized me, that I was unable to move, and could only crouch there, with my back prickling, motionless, hypnotised; knowing that time and space were no more than names coined by man to protect himself from the unchanging, which he could not long look upon, and live. For I was this same small boy of five who had done the same thing so many years before; and the collapse and the annihilation of the years was terrifying in its beauty, and beautiful in its terror. (*A Westminster Childhood*, pp. 59–60)

This is a completely different experience of the "collapse of time" from that of *A la recherche*—one no longer wrapped up in the cozy rationalizations of the humanistic Bergson, but felt as the direct encounter with a dimension beyond all human imagination. It was "eternity nakedly revealed," and as such terrifying. The instant of recall relates only to another, identical instant; there is no trace of a continuum. In fact, more logical than Proust, Raynor realizes that, given a total timelessness, *continuity* is a nonsensical concept. For Proust, the need for continuity is imperative, for only in terms of a continuum can he know that his past self is one with his present self, both together forming the "pure" incarnation of his reality. And, to justify this continuum, he is forced to invoke the concept of *la durée*, which allows for a kind of cumulative development outside the normal boundaries of time. For Raynor, where there is no time, there can be no continuity; and so there are two selves, forever dissociated from each other: himself as he is now, and "the ghost of a forlorn little boy who had wanted no more than to play with me a game harmless to himself, but terrible and dangerous to me" (p. 60). Halfway between the visions of a mystic and the conundrums of science-fiction, Raynor's experience again helps to shed light on Proust's and to set it in a truer perspective; for Proust, by the time he comes to incarnate himself as Marcel, is working on the material of the original experience in two ways at once: he is employing his novelist's imagination to magnify it, so that it may serve as starting point and framework for his gargantuan work, and (unlike Raynor) he is employing his rationalizing metaphysic to rid it of its potential terror and to reduce it to manageable dimensions.

Even Proust, however, makes no attempt to recall events which took place before his seventh year. He does not try to struggle with the haphazard and inconsequent memories of very early childhood. As with Rousseau, this suggests perhaps an arbitrary simplification of the problem; it provides a tidy, uncluttered starting point, one which may even be granted some (dubious) philosophical significance. "I think that it is the Gnostics who believe that the soul is born when we are seven years old," writes Richard Church; and his own seventh birthday happening to fall in the year 1900, he finds his recollections of this memorable year sufficiently impressive to enable him at least to flirt with the notion: "I am inclined, from my own experience, to believe this dogma, and I base my belief on the events of that wonderful year, the first of the new century."[26]

There is obviously something tempting in the magical number seven, and a whole group of writers—De Quincey and Chateaubriand, Michel Leiris and Julian Fane among others—favor this neat and uncomplicated point of departure. However, to do so to some extent begs the question, since psychologists generally agree that the most important formative events take place before the child is five; and comparatively few individuals really seem to find it impossible to remember anything at all before their seventh birthday. Indeed, one of the more fascinating problems of the genre is that of the first memory.

---

26. Richard Church, *Over the Bridge* (London, 1955), 66. In general, the "new-century" year 1900 leaves more impression in the minds of French than of English children, possibly because it was also associated with the great *Exposition Internationale* of that same year: cf. the comtesse de Pange, *Comment j'ai vu Paris 1900* (1962). In English Childhoods, the year 1900 tends to be overshadowed by the Diamond Jubilee of 1897.

The first memory is obviously significant from many different points of view. It also presents a number of difficulties as soon as we attempt to analyze and interpret this significance. To begin with, while the clear majority of our poets situate their earliest recollections at approximately the age of three (from the psychologist's, as well as from the Wittgensteinian philosopher's, point of view this is to be expected, since it corresponds to the average age at which the child learns to speak with some fluency), some place it much later, others considerably earlier. Camara Laye observes that the "first memory" episode with which *L'Enfant noir* opens, when his family found him playing with a small but exceedingly dangerous snake, occurred when he was at least five and probably six.[27] "I have even met people who say that they recall nothing that happened before the age of ten," notes Philip Hope-Wallace, "whereas *I* say I can remember my christening."[28] Samuel Beckett, it is rumored, claims to remember being born, and to dislike the recollection very thoroughly. Pretensions to *very* early recollections (prelinguistic memories) of course raise special problems of their own, but even the average is surrounded by uncertainties. Bruno Vercier, currently one of the most knowledgeable critics of autobiographical literature in France, has even suggested in a light-hearted article that the quest for the earliest flash of recollection has something in common with the quest for an Olympic gold medal, each writer vying with the other to push it further and further back toward infancy.[29]

However, even if a memory can, with reasonable accuracy, be situated at the age of three, what is its status—trivial or significant—in relation to that exposé of an "absolute truth" which is the aim of the genre? Archetypally, the first memory is a clear picture, like a still photograph, entirely without context and surrounded by mists: "magic-lantern slides," as Clara Malraux calls them, slithering about confusedly one on top of the other; "at one moment everything is blurred, then suddenly the image becomes clear."[30] Certainly, it is the detached visual image which predominates, very often the image of a step or staircase, a door or window, and above all the awareness of one room leading to another:

> Passages, rooms, corridors, rising up toward me in the first moment of consciousness, transfer me into the most ancient era of life: into the cave period. . . . I experience the cave period; I experience the life of the catacombs; I experience

27. Camara Laye, *L'Enfant noir* (Paris, 1953); trans. James Kirkup and Ernest Jones, *The African Child* (New York, 1979).

28. In *The Guardian*, 13 January 1976, p. 12.

29. Bruno Vercier, "Le Mythe du premier souvenir," in *Revue d'histoire littéraire de la France* 75:1027–40.

30. Clara Malraux, *Apprendre à vivre* (Paris, 1963), 53.

. . . Egypt beneath the Pyramids: we live in the body of the Sphinx; rooms, corridors are voids of the bones of the Sphinx's body.[31]

But the other senses also have their place. The sense of smell, which is extremely active at a later age and frequently contributes to an instantaneous recall, does not appear to be particularly acute in very early childhood; but the sense of taste comes into play from the beginning—"I recall the salt, I recall the salt, which the yellow nurse had to wipe about the corner of my eyes"[32]—and, albeit more rarely, the sense of touch: "I apprehended the world through the skin of these hands which take their shape from whatever object they are allowed to approach" (Clara Malraux, *Apprendre à vivre*, p. 11).

Nothing, it would seem, is too arbitrary or too trivial to constitute an earliest recollection. This is particularly the case where the recall involves one sense only—hearing, for instance, the words of the Lord's Prayer mingled with the bidding from the bridge-table in the next room: "For Thine is the Kingdom, the Power and the Glory. Forever and Ever. Amen. One No Trump. Two Diamonds."[33] By contrast, there is a different category of first recollection which is more generalized, less specifically a primary sense-response—the impression left by a serious illness, by a flood or fire, or by a death in the family:

> Just before Christmas (this I know is a memory
> For no one ever spoke of it) the baby quietly
> Disgorged a lot of blood, and was taken away.[34]

It has been suggested that, at least in instances such as these, the choice of the recollection is by no means arbitrary, but has been carefully selected by the subconscious mind from among innumerable other possibilities as being specifically relevant to the shaping of the subsequent identity: a fully meaningful event which relates so intimately to a whole personality that it comes to be felt as the symbolic starting point of consciousness. Obviously this is the case with Proust's memory of the goodnight kiss which his mother refused him, but in Proust, as we have seen, there is a good deal of literary artifice. Both interpretations—arbitrary chance or symbolic selection—would seem to be legitimate, for it could be argued that even the most meaningless of recollected trivialities is symbolic of *something*. It depends perhaps more on the critic than on the writer, and on the way in which he understands the meaning, if any, of life and

---

31. Andrei Bely, *Kotik Letaev* (1915–16; reprint, Chicago, 1966), 8. Trans. Gerald Janacek, *Kotik Letaev* (Ann Arbor, 1971), 21.

32. Saint-John Perse, *Pour fêter une enfance* [1910], in *Œuvres* (Paris, 1972), 24.

33. Donald Horne, *The Education of Young Donald* (1967; reprint, Harmondsworth, 1975), 3.

34. D. J. Enright, *The Terrible Shears* (London, 1973), 11.

the mechanisms of self-awareness. All in all, however, the evidence is strong in favor of arbitrariness; where the symbolism is unmistakable, one may suspect the shaping influence of the mature artist's sense of values and of form.

"This I *know* is a memory," writes D. J. Enright in the lines quoted above—but this again is a problem. Are the very young child's memories truly his own, or is the adult recalling what he was told while still a child? And even if there is at the bottom of all a "true" memory, does the adult still have a *direct* memory of the original event, or is he remembering that event subsequently re-remembered on countless occasions through the following years? Here again, it seems to be a matter of philosophy rather than of psychology, since we lack all means of objective verification. Some writers argue, as Enright argues, that at least on the first question, the authenticity of the reaction can be tested, for no one had ever spoken about the event Enright recalled. Miles Franklin employed a kind of Socratic dialectic to prove to her parents that she had worn a red flannel nightgown on the night when, at the age of ten months, she had slept with her father in the end room at Bobilla. Their reaction to the "memory" was contemptuous disbelief:

> Mother dismissed this as a notion. Father had no skill as a nursemaid. "You never slept with your father in all your life."
> "Yes, I did. I remember Father carrying me along the veranda. The wind blew the candle-flame to one side, and it was cold, and I did not like it."
> "A nice pair you and your father would be in the end room."[35]

Bit by bit, however, Miles Franklin forced her parents to admit that there *had* been one occasion when what she remembered must actually have occurred, and claims that thus she had proved the authenticity of her own recollection. But there is still, of course, room for doubt. Miles Franklin was writing in her extreme old age, so that the comparatively recent memory of her conversation with her mother dated back perhaps some fifty years; furthermore, there is still the possibility that the episode had been alluded to, perhaps by her late father, on some occasion while she was still a fairly young child, and that both parents had subsequently forgotten all about it, precisely because it was so trivial to them. Certainly, among all the problems concerning the accuracy of memory which the Childhood raises, that of the authenticity of very early recollections is among the most challenging.

The red flannel nightgown episode from *Childhood at Brindabella*, moreover, involves us in a further and even trickier question: that of prelinguistic memory. Miles Franklin states categorically that she was ten months old at the time of her adventure in the cold corridor leading to the end room in the newly-built Bobilla homestead, and that she could recall it through a variety of

35. Miles Franklin, *Childhood at Brindabella* (Sydney, 1963), 1–2.

sense impressions—the sound of the wind, the feel of the draft, the sight of the bending candle-flame. However, many (but by no means all) modern psychologists would deny that *any* recollection is possible before language exists to concretize a sensation in the clear and permanent conceptual form of words: "Worum man nicht sprechen kann, darüber muss man schweigen." The writers may *enjoy* themselves, believing that they can recall events from the days before they could talk, but their delight lies in the enjoyment of a delusion.

Again, we are in very difficult territory. For, while there is a fair amount of evidence on the side of the psychologists (although less, perhaps, than there appeared to be twenty years ago), the poet's conviction that he *can* remember pure sensation without conceptualization through language is very difficult to demonstrate, since, even to begin the demonstration, he must use language to conceptualize the sensation, and thus destroy his own argument (see below, chapter 7). On the other hand, the absolute conviction with which a number of Childhood writers *do* insist on the fact that they possess this peculiar attribute of memory is impressive.

Abel Hermant and John Raynor both claim to have clear memories which go back to the age of two or earlier. Henry Handel Richardson recalls an aunt bewailing the death of her baby, an event which occurred when she was one year old, and, revealingly, she associates it with the Childhood's archetypal vision of doors, steps, and interconnecting rooms: "Still more striking was the fact that the doorway leading down two steps into the next room had no door to it, was just an empty space."[36] All three of these are classic examples of the phenomenon, in that they simply accept it as a fact, without seriously inquiring into its psychological or philosophical implications. To them, we may add two others, not so much for the reason that they are exceptional, as because they illustrate what would appear to be a general trend: namely, that the human individual who is most intimately aware of his earliest, prelinguistic self is the one who is destined to become a poet. Both James Kirkup and Andrei Bely are primarily poets. In *The Only Child*, James Kirkup's recollection of life at the age of two or earlier is not only strangely vivid—the front door, "which was quite different from all the other front doors of the street" (pp. 11–12), the boot-scraper behind which he hid his treasures, the smell of his pram, his terror on being taken to the pantomime, from which he was removed screaming—but is of particular interest in that, without any pretense at theorizing, merely by "the exercise of his faculties," he claims to be able to recall in detail at least one episode which occurred before he could talk (a moment when his pram, unattended, began to run away downhill, with him in it, and he was rescued by passersby). Kirkup claims not only to recall the mood of strange-

---

36. Henry Handel Richardson, *Myself When Young* (London, 1948), 7. Cf. also Anatole France, *Le Petit Pierre* (Paris, 1918), 21–22.

ness and fear, but actually to remember a sequence of thought and emotions: his sense of frustration at wanting to tell the strangers where to take the pram, at knowing clearly that is was *possible* to communicate through speech, and yet failing to make himself understood:

> There was a feeling of dreadful impotence at not being able to tell them who I was or where I had come from. Even at that age I felt utterly exasperated by human obtuseness, and had only scorn for fatuous, baby-talk questions. I started to weep, not because I was frightened, but because these well-meaning folks all seemed so stupid, so inadequate. (*The Only Child*, pp. 13–14)

With what degree of emphasis a modern psychologist would throw this out of court as evidence would depend largely on the school in which he had been trained. Within the context of any purely *rationalistic* analysis of the human mind and its workings, it could well seem improbable. On the other hand, it is undeniably true that babies from six to eighteen months old can quite clearly conceive an intention of what they want to do, and equally clearly express their violent frustration at their failure to do it. So the question again is one of memory. If it can be demonstrated that the mind can *receive* an impression directly through the senses and the emotions, but *retain* it only when it has been conceptualized through language, then these intriguing pages can be summarily dismissed as fantasy. But unless and until this is proved, we cannot wholly reject the notion that the poet may have access to realms of experience unclassified by the psychologist, and that it is precisely for this reason that he is a poet. We shall return to this later.

Andrei Bely—who makes no claim to absolute veracity, and whose *Kotik Letaev* is presented as a symbolist/surrealist prose-poem rather than as auto-biography [37]—is unique for a different reason: his attempt to *reconstruct* imaginatively the experience of a world without language, and to re-create the gradual transition to a world dominated by linguistic conceptualization. Kotik is on the edge of his third birthday when we enter his world: the moment of the first intimations of consciousness, of the first awareness of identity giving meaning to all that hitherto had been meaningless. And in its early stages, the conflict between the self and the totality-minus-self (one is again strongly tempted to use the Sartrian terms *pour-soi* and *en-soi*) is both disturbing and painful:

> The first conscious moment of mine is—a dot; it penetrates the meaninglessness; and—expanding, it becomes a sphere, but this sphere—disintegrates; meaningless-ness, penetrating it, tears it apart. (*Kotik Letaev*, p. 7; trans., p. 16)

---

37. "Kotik" = Kitten, Bely's nickname when he was very small. "Letaev" substitutes the Slavonic root *let* ("to fly," symbol of the vision of poetry), for his true surname, which was Bugaev. See above, note 6.

In spite of (or because of?) its adult language, this is clearly a picture of
the emergence of consciousness which would be more acceptable to the conventional psychologist than would Kirkup's. Nonetheless, Bely's imagination
(or *could* it be memory?) takes him further: into an intuition of prelinguistic
consciousness, when, having no language to conceptualize objects outside
himself, his self was indistinguishable from these objects. A corridor *is* "his
own skin":

> It moved along with me; turn around—it squeezes out from behind through a hole;
> ahead, it opens through to the light; the little passageways, corridors and alleys are
> subsequently known to me; too well known even: and this is "I"; and this is "I." . . .
> Rooms are—parts of the body. . . .(p. 7; trans., p. 16).

Then, with the dawning of language/consciousness, the "skin" is shed "like a
snake's." There is something in common here with Proust's (and Genet's)
experience, when, in certain situations, the self, which is a *néant*, a void, can
become the objects which surround it—a wardrobe, a dustbin. But here the
experience is reversed—and is frightening: "the sensations were horrible,"
notes Kotik. Objects—rooms, corridors—which *had* been comfortably part of
the self now take on a hostile and impenetrable existence of their own: "Out
fell lands born of blackness . . . it is the black-birth of land" (p. 16). Kotik is
lost now in a world from which he is alienated. His self is a burden of
intolerable loneliness, separate from all that is not-self. "All lies outside of me:
it buzzes, lives,—outside of me; and it is incomprehensible" (p. 112). The
impenetrability and incomprehensibility of the world of "not-I" culminate in
the encounter—deep in the grass head-high—with a hen—as "contingent"
and as "superfluous" as the tree roots that incarnate the *angoisse* of man's
alienation in *La Nausée:*

> Chicken . . . this is . . . this is . . . something: crested and feathered, it clucks, it
> pecks, it bristles; it doesn't change because of the conditions of my consciousness: a
> "chicken" is impenetrable; in addition to this, she is absolutely distinct to me; and—
> she is sparklingly clear to me in the incomprehensibilities of her *bristling, pecked* life.[38]

How far this represents Bely's genuinely remembered experience is, of
course, impossible to tell, but the fact remains that *Kotik Letaev* constitutes an
extraordinary attempt by a great poet to reconstruct by intuition the prelinguistic world of the child. It is the more impressive since, at the time of

---

38. *Kotik Letaev*, p. 38; trans., p. 112. Bely's idiosyncratic punctuation is an integral part of
his text, and is very difficult to transcribe into English, particularly since he makes deliberate
and skillful use of the Russian convention of leaving out the present tense of the verb *to be*, and
replacing it in print by a dash. Thus "This bird is a chicken" becomes "This bird—chicken." The
ambiguity of the child's relationship, both with itself and with the outside world, is consistently
emphasized by this use of the dash.

writing the book (1915), Bely had come under an influence which he was later to discard: that of Rudolf Steiner. Yet Steiner's vaguely mystic belief in a life before birth, of which the child still bore memories, so that a memory of childhood was "a memory of a memory," while it still colors certain pages of *Kotik Letaev*, does not seriously detract from the quasi-existentialist rigor of Bely's deductions. This is essentially because Bely does not attempt to relate any *specific* imagery to the prebirth experience. For him, the "clouds of glory" which the child trails into the world are felt simply as a "rhythm," or as "the pulse-rhythm of a sparkle." They dictate the pattern of a memory, but they do not comprise that memory; they help perhaps to explain the poet's *emotional* attitude toward his childhood, but they are not *of* that childhood. They are "essential"—but ultimately expendable:

> The *memory of memory* is such; it is—a rhythm in which objectness is absent; dances, mimicry, gestures are—the opening of the shells of memory and a free passage into another world.
> The recollections of childhood years are—my dances; these dances are—flights into the never-having-been, and none-the-less essential. (*Kotiv Letaev*, p. 47; trans., p. 141)

There are a number of other writers (some of whom will be discussed in the next chapter) who harbor the conviction that we bring into the world with us memories of a previous existence.[39] "Unquestionably there dwell in the hidden folds of our flesh traces of all our history, and of the whole history of the world," observes Marcel Jouhandeau (*Mémorial*, 1:13)—but in the end, he makes little use of the notion. Yet (in spite of Rudolf Steiner) it is Bely, rather than Wordsworth, who stands as the archetypal childhood poet in the present century: the poet who proposes an argument rather than a vision, and supports it with a dialectic based (as likely as not) on structural linguistics, rather than with the effulgent imagery of Romanticism. "Mysticism," in the cruder sense, is almost wholly absent from the modern Childhood, even if "mystery" is not. *Mystery* invites the discovery of an explanation, or at least prompts the attempt to convey to others in rational terms a suprarational experience; *mysticism* presupposes a pattern of concepts and a terminology already worked out by someone else. Between the two, in the context of our Childhoods, there is all the difference in the world. Whatever mystery envelops the child-self, the experience never loses its individuality; it is too unique ever to be wholly subsumed into a preestablished ritual. The flowing robes of the prophet sit uneasily upon it; but the boiler-suit of the materialist or the lab coat of the

---

39. George Du Maurier's *Peter Ibbetson* (1891) is an interesting example of the fascination of the concept of "racial memory" in popular form in the later nineteenth century. The first fifty-odd pages of *Peter Ibbetson*, incidentally, are authentic childhood reminiscences.

scientist fit it little better. The child-poet has "intimations" of many things, but most of them more intangible than merely of "immortality." What is needed is a term which goes beyond the everyday, and yet commits the poet to nothing outside himself. So why not the child's own term: "magic"? For the moment it will do.

Total recall, prelinguistic memory, recollections of an earlier existence—these, once again, are the extreme cases. The average writer (where he shows concern about the problem at all) is merely concerned with the unaccountable gaps and disconcerted by the oblivion—by the weaknesses of memory as an instrument in the search for truth—its vagaries, its lapses, its exasperating failures. Sometimes, as with Simone de Beauvoir,[40] the child will forget unpleasant experiences, leaving it for the adult to rediscover them later, perhaps requiring the guidance of a psychiatrist to enable him or her to do so. Sometimes, as with Edmund Gosse, it is the rare moments of joy, or perhaps merely of normal existence, which vanish down the memory-hole. Sometimes, as is the case with Stendhal, *any* extreme form of emotion, whether a "divine happiness" or the "extreme perturbation" of a "poor persecuted little mite," is wholly beyond recall in detail. And sometimes the gaps are inexplicable, and the blanks among days, months, or years arbitrary and patternless. Frequently, there is a note of despair, for what is gone beyond recall is gone for ever. But, in writing a Childhood, the writer's task is to make the best job of the material which *has* remained to him; and to use the process of writing, if possible, to recapture a little more. We remember what we *need* to remember, argues D. J. Enright; and memory, "a shrewd and maybe shifty tradesman," supplies our needs:

> You know your business
> You know ours.
> You may deceive us a little,
> You prefer not to ruin us.   (*The Terrible Shears*, p. 63)

In writing, in seeking at all costs to tell a total truth, the need increases; and it seems to be the common experience that the "Shifty Tradesman" does his best to ensure a reasonable continuance of supply.

40. Simone de Beauvoir, *Mémoires d'une jeune fille rangée* (Paris, 1958), 20–21.

3   Myth, Meaning, and Magic

Il y a la réalité et il y a les rêves; et puis il y a une seconde réalité.
—André Gide, *Si le grain ne meurt*

To many writers, the experience of recreating a previous self marks a crucial point in their adult lives. Concentrated reflection over a long period about a seemingly patternless past, followed by the need to shape that past into sentences and sequences which will be meaningful to a reader, has the effect of imposing patterns where seemingly none existed; these patterns in their turn suggest a *meaning* where before none had been apparent. "To write is to select," notes Jean Genet.[1] The complex process of making a selection from among the innumerable recollections preserved by memory—which in any case has already made its own selection from among the infinite multitude of lived experiences and sensations—*may* be interpreted simply as an inevitable series of distortions, and the result, as we saw in the last chapter, as something necessarily less than the total truth. However, it is tempting to draw the opposite conclusion, and to see the patterns that emerge from the act of writing as intrinsic to the experience itself, endowing it with coherent shape and significance, hidden at the time, but now unmistakably revealed. It is hard for us to accept the fact that our lives are merely superfluous, or that man, in Sartre's phrase, is no more than "a useless passion"; and in the present context of unbelief, even the most elusive glimpse of meaningfulness is enough to awaken veins of dormant transcendentalism in the most pragmatical of writers, let alone among the poets. Once a pattern becomes apparent, then man's life on earth can be felt to be no longer an accident, a mere coincidence of atoms, but rather something that has its share in some kind of cosmic destiny, responding to a will and a purpose greater than itself.

Although not referring directly to his childhood, T. S. Eliot summarizes

1. Jean Genet, *Pompes funèbres*, in *Œuvres complètes* (Paris, 1953), 3:10.

most effectively the process by which the exercise of memory reveals a whole range of potential significance:

> It seems, as one becomes older,
> That the past has another pattern, and ceases to be
> a mere sequence—
> Or even development.   (*The Dry Salvages*, ll. 85–87)[2]

Eliot, in fact, reverses what we may think of as the normal process of recall, in which an experience in the present will awaken slumbering memories clustering round a similar experience in the past, and in which "significance" is conjured up out of the juxtaposition of past and present. Eliot's sudden illumination lies in the unexpected discovery of a pattern of meaning; and once the *meaning* has become apparent, then the forgotten or half-forgotten past begins to come alive again, to emerge into the light of consciousness, not simply as remembered phenomena or even emotions, but as something already structured and meaningful—reality in another dimension:

> We had the experience but missed the meaning,
> And approach to the meaning restores the experience
> In a different form, beyond any meaning
> We can assign to happiness.   (ll. 93–96)

This awareness of "experience restored in a different form" is by no means uncommon; but to explain it in terms acceptable to the sophisticated intellect of the twentieth century is anything but simple. Freudian psychoanalytical theory is on the whole unhelpful, because, while it may reveal the importance of a forgotten childhood occurrence in relation to the adult, it does not illuminate the ultimate significance of the individual's life as a whole. Clara Malraux and Michel Leiris, among others, undertook their original researches into the past on the advice of their Freudian psychiatrists—and both declare themselves thoroughly dissatisfied with the result. Clara Malraux, in fact, was so fascinated by the intimate and wholly irrational world which she rediscovered that she was quite unable to bring herself to waste its glory and its richness on the systematized professional understanding of a "mere scientist."[3] Leiris, although confessing to a "broad credence accorded to Freudian psychology," rapidly found himself exploiting the techniques which he had learned during his sessions on the couch for thoroughly non-Freudian purposes of his own as a poet—purposes which involved constructing patterns infinitely more complex than the somewhat elementary, cause-and-effect mental structures envisaged

2. T. S. Eliot, *The Dry Salvages* (London, 1941), 10.
3. Clara Malraux, *Apprendre à vivre* (Paris, 1963), 28.

by the disciples of Freud.[4] Freudian psychology, concludes Leiris cynically, has one, and only one, overwhelming advantage: "It offers to each and every individual a convenient means to hoist himself up on to the plane of tragedy, by conceiving himself as a new Oedipus" (*L'Age d'homme*, pp. 16–17). Among our six-hundred-odd Childhoods, only one was written by a trained Freudian analyst; and in this one exception, Elizaveta Fen's *A Russian Childhood* (1961), once she has got out of her system a light scattering of predictable jargon to sprinkle over her infancy—for example, "My brother and my father both entered my world for the first time as frustrating agents, and they maintained these roles throughout my childhood"—she makes virtually no further use of the method.[5]

Freudian psychology, in fact, is irremediably one-dimensional; positivistic, rational, and utilitarian, it takes no account of that "second reality," as Gide terms it, which is the essence of childhood revisited, nor is it in any way concerned with intuited meanings and ultimate significances. For the poet, once he has caught a first glimpse of purpose or destiny in the patterns of the past, this meaningfulness demands to be situated in a context *outside* himself; otherwise it is futile. It must be felt to relate, if not to a transcendental dimension in the normal sense, then at least to other human beings and to other experiences: to a communal subconscious, perhaps, to an inheritance from past generations, to an all-embracing mythology revealed in dreams and symbols, more "real" than any real experience and more mysterious in its workings than any run-of-the-mill psychological determinism. T. S. Eliot's "past experience revived in the meaning" (1. 97) belongs to this category: It

> Is not the experience of one life only
> But of many generations—not forgetting
> Something that is probably quite ineffable:
> The backward look behind the assurance
> Of recorded history, the backward half-look
> Over the shoulder, towards the primitive terror.   (ll. 98–103)

Whether Eliot had any direct acquaintance with the works of Jung is debatable; but it is certain that, in the 1930s and even earlier, Jung's ideas, as well as those of Freud, were very much in the air in England, mainly as a result of discussion provoked by A. R. Orage in his influential periodical *The New Age*,[6] and it is highly probable that, through his work on *The Criterion*, Eliot

---

4. Michel Leiris, "De la littérature considérée comme une tauromachie," in *L'Age d'homme*, rev. ed. (Paris, 1972), 16. For his use of Freudian techniques in his poetry, see in particular the opening chapters of *Biffures* (Paris, 1948).

5. Elizaveta Fen, *A Russian Childhood* (London, 1961), 13. Elizaveta Fen received her training as a Freudian psychotherapist *subsequent* to her emigration from Russia.

6. On Orage's influence, see Paul Selver, *Orage and the New Age Circle* (1967). See also

had absorbed at least echoes of them. At all events it is clear that, if Jean-Jacques Rousseau is prophetic of much that will be found in Freud, the majority of the twentieth-century Childhoods reflect instead the type of psycho-philosophical preoccupations which are incarnated in the work of Jung.

Carl Gustav Jung, one-time disciple of Freud, later the focus of opposition to his former master, makes to psychology a contribution similar to that which Sartre makes to philosophy: namely, the insistence that a rational discipline should make room for the irrational. In effect, to place, as Sartre does, a void (*un néant*) in the heart of consciousness and at the very center of a rationalistic inquiry into the nature of identity and into the theory of perception is, as A. J. Ayer pointed out so gleefully in his famous review of *Being and Nothingness*,[7] not only to echo the arguments of the White King in *Alice Through The Looking-Glass* ("I see nobody on the road," said Alice. "I only wish I had such eyes," remarked the King. "To be able to see Nobody! And at that distance, too!"), but to open the door wide to all manner of metaphysical irrationalism, Beckettian "Otherness" and *Bald Prima-Donna* absurdism. In a different field of equally rationalistic speculation, Jung does much the same thing, although Jung is perhaps more aware of the delicate nature of the balance which he is holding:

> Psychological truth by no means excludes metaphysical truth, though psychology, as a science, has to hold aloof from all metaphysical assertions. Its subject is the psyche *and its contents*. Both are realities, because they work.[8]

In other words, the contents of the mind are as significant to the scientifically trained psychologist as the functioning of the mind; and if the mind—and in particular, the child-mind—contains irrational elements such as intimations of immortality, "magic," and preexistence, then these uncaused factors are deserving of as much serious consideration as the "positive" and traceable effect of "something nasty in the woodshed" seen at the age of two and subsequently relegated to the subconscious.

It is the very ambiguity of Jung's argument which explains the fascination he has exercised on the explorers of childhood. He rejects unconditionally John Locke's argument that the mind of the child at birth is blank, a *tabula rasa*,

---

Edwin Muir, *The Story and the Fable* (London, 1940), especially pp. 186–87. The very title which Muir gives to his own Childhood reflects the Jungian influence: the arbitrary sequence of facts and incidents (the "Story") on the one hand, and, parallel to it in a different dimension, the "Fable"—the subconscious pattern of dreams building up from a racial mythology and bestowing "meaning" upon the mere facticity of existence (pp. 191–94).

7. In *Horizon*, June 1945.

8. C. G. Jung, *Collected Works*, trans. R. C. F. Hull (London, 1956), vol. 5, pt. ii, p. 231 (emphasis added). The essay concerned, *Wandlungen und Symbole des Libido*, was originally published in 1912 and revised in 1952 under the title *Symbole der Wandlungen*.

and he likewise rejects the traditional Cartesian notion of innate ideas. Instead, he postulates a number of "specific inherited aptitudes," which are the "*a-priori* and formal conditions of apperception that are based on instinct."[9] The ambiguity arises when he attempts to define these "inherited aptitudes," for it soon becomes clear that they are much more than Lockeian faculties, operating with a greater or lesser degree of efficiency, or even than "inherited *possibilities* of ideas," but in fact are "pre-formed patterns," which reveal themselves in, and which respond to, certain universal archetypes and symbols, often, if not preponderantly, of a visual nature. In simplified terms, an awareness of myths and symbols is inherited by the individual from the culture-group to which he belongs; each child brings with it into the world instinctive memories of complex patterns that were formed by its ancestors long before it was born.

Jung, in fact, is a scientific psychologist with the courage consciously to use such terms as "the soul," "rebirth," and "supra-sensitive experience"—irrationalities which the blunter materialism of the nineteenth century would have rejected as uncompromisingly as A. J. Ayer rejected Sartre's *Néant*. That which is universally believed in, argues Jung, deserves serious consideration: not simply in order that it may be "explained away," but rather in order that it may be explained. And if the exploration involves concepts such as preexistence, Karma, or rebirth, the mere fact that these are unverifiable by means of scientific experiment does not necessarily invalidate them. Rebirth, for instance, is a phenomenon that much concerns the explorers of childhood; and "rebirth," avers Jung,

is an affirmation that must be counted among the primordial affirmations of mankind. These primordial affirmations are based on what I call archetypes. In view of the fact that all affirmations relating to the sphere of the suprasensual are, in the last analysis, invariably determined by archetypes, it is not surprising that a concurrence of affirmations concerning rebirth can be found among the most widely different peoples. There must be psychic events underlying these affirmations which it is the business of psychology to discuss—without entering into all the metaphysical and philosophical assumptions regarding their significance.[10]

As is often the case when the thought of a major scientist or philosopher obtrudes upon the world of literature, what is important is not the precise significance of the ideas in themselves, but the response which they evoke in minds not trained to that particular discipline, and the manner in which they work on the poetic imagination. In the case of Jung, the precisely defined and

9. *Collected Works*, trans. R. C. F. Hull (London, 1959), vol. 9, pt. i, p. 66. The essay concerned, *Die psychologischen Aspekte des Mutterarchetypus*, was originally published in 1938 and revised in 1954.

10. *Collected Works*, vol. 9, pt. i, pp. 116–17. *Die verschiedenen Aspekte der Wiedergeburt* was originally published in 1950.

circumscribed concept of the archetype appears to the poet as "scientific" evidence brought forward in support of what he or she had intuitively felt to be the case: namely, that the child entering this world carried with it memory patterns of a previous existence, and that these memory patterns in themselves constituted further evidence of a scale of values and significances which might subsequently serve to furnish a human life with a blueprint of preconceived purpose.

Within the structure of the Childhood, the problem of "fatality" emerges as clearly as it does from a study of *Oedipus Rex* or *Othello*. On the one hand, it is incontrovertible that what has happened, *has* happened: certain circumstances prevailing, certain decisions taken, have produced certain results, and there is no going back in time to change any one of them. In this purely deterministic, historical sense, any childhood revisited bears upon it the stigma of fatality; "fatality," argues the positivistically minded Georges Duhamel, resides in the *facts*:

> For the autobiographer . . . there are no unexpected twists of fate; there is nothing but the relentless succession of facts, at once inflexible and arbitrary, for life offers no compromises; life could not care less about sight-lines or lighting effects, about Good Taste or Rules. . . . He who tells the story of his life is the most oppressed of all slaves among storytellers. (*Inventaire de l'abîme*, p. 108)

Duhamel, however, is somewhat exceptional in his unflinching acceptance of the purely mechanistic operations of retrospective inevitability. *Destiny*, in its more commonly accepted sense, implies the action of an outside force or will capable of foreseeing the future, and of guiding its victims in a preestablished direction, with or without their cooperation. Tristan l'Hermite, along with most of his contemporaries, believed that his destiny was predetermined by the conjunction of the planets ("Mercury was distinctly well-disposed towards me, but the Sun far from favorable" [*Le Page disgracié*, p. 52]); and some three centuries later, James Kirkup, like Beckett's *Murphy*, reveals something of the nostalgia of modern man for this neat and simplifying act of surrender, "believing in the stars as some rationalists believe in God" (*Sorrows, Passions and Alarms*, p. 93). André Gide, by contrast, preferred to believe in the devil (*Si le grain ne meurt*, p. 249); and there is likewise a fair amount of Satanism in the universe of Marcel Jouhandeau.

In the last analysis, however, none of these solutions—not the devil, nor the stars, nor blind mechanical determinism—holds the key to the problem. The difficulty for the autobiographer, and above all for the autobiographer of childhood, lies in the conflict between an acute sense of individuality—and therefore of the purpose and meaning of that individuality, without which the child would never have become a writer—on the one hand, and on the other, the unalterable, and therefore "fatal" evidence of a factual past. Undoubtedly, there *is* a pattern; otherwise the Childhood, with its own intrinsic and necessary structure as a literary text, could never have been written. Where there is a pattern, there is at least a possibility of meaning; the question is whether that meaning is imposed—or rather, "created"—retrospectively out of material in itself arbitrary and meaningless, or whether it existed, unsuspected, from the beginning.

Jean Genet provides an extreme case of a writer who believes that, by the act of writing, he is not merely imposing on the past a pattern of his own devising, but actually creating meaning where none existed before, not only for himself, but for others. When Genet completed his first novel, *Notre-Dame des Fleurs*, in 1942, this was for him a momentous turning point. By writing— in the event, largely about himself—he was for the first time conquering his own emotions instead of being conquered by them: he was altering the pattern of his life, taking charge of his own destiny. And at the same time, by creating "characters," he himself became destiny in relation to them: he controlled their lives without allowing them to realize it, permitting them to imagine themselves free when they were in fact the slaves of his quite arbitrary will, and filling their hearts with anguish at the thought of those alternative possibilities which life might have offered, and how it could have been changed "by what it might also have been, but will not be, *because of me*" (*Notre-Dame des Fleurs*, 2:58).

What models Genet may have used for *Our Lady of the Flowers*, we do not know; in any case, in this novel, the autobiographical elements, although omnipresent, are nonetheless of comparatively minor importance. But in *Miracle de la rose* (1946), of which an important part recalls his experiences as an adolescent in the reform school of Mettray, the implications of the feeling that he has for himself as "Destiny" grow more complex. If those characters for whom he is God are modeled on real, living beings, and particularly on beings who, in the past, controlled *his* fate, then does he now retrospectively control theirs? Seemingly, yes. For, in the existentialist view, all significance is ultimately retrospective, so that, even if he allows them to act as in fact they acted in reality, during his own childhood, these same actions *now* serve a lucid and coherent purpose—*his* purpose—even though at the time they had no notion of it. *He* knows what they were doing and why, or what they were, better than they knew it themselves; and even if he distorts them, this very distortion "is also what they also are, though unaware of being it."[11] If "they"—the staff at Mettray—thought that they were controlling Genet's destiny, they were right—but only because, in the pattern of the book, Genet himself shows that it was necessary that they should do so. "They were writing my story." But at the same time, and without their knowing it, Genet, by allowing them to print their images indelibly on the imagination of a poet, was creating *their* signifi-

11. Jean Genet, *Miracle de la rose*, in *Œuvres complètes* (Paris, 1951), 2:349.

cance: a significance which they could not conceivably have possessed without his cooperation. "They were my characters. They understood nothing about Mettray. They were idiots" (p. 264).

For Genet, then, as for Sartre, the past *as such* has no significance, and can have no significance, because it has no reality. The past exists only insofar as it is still recallable in the present: it is a mode of present consciousness. And, as a mode of present consciousness, it necessarily takes its significance from the present. But since this retrospective significance is the only one it can possibly have, then it is neither gratuitous nor arbitrary. Where all meaning and all reality is an act of present creation, then that which is created here and now has a value which excludes all others. The structures and patterns which present consciousness creates in the past *are* the meaning of that past; without them, it does not have an alternative meaning; it is nothing.

Genet stands alone in pushing to its logical extreme this existentialist interpretation of a childhood. For him, the "Dichtung" *is* the "Wahrheit"; *poetry*, in Genet's highly idealistic interpretation of the concept, is enough to constitute a valid referential framework for the arbitrary facticity of *truth*. For most other writers, however, the Jungian theory of the preformation of early consciousness offers a more easily accessible means of establishing a meaningful frame of reference. It goes without saying that such intuitions of participation in a communal, ancestral, or mythological subconscious have occurred at all times and among all peoples from the beginnings of recorded history; Jung did not invent them, he simply gave them a new status, transferring them from the realm of legend, ritual, and religion to that of academic psychology. Tolstoy's Natasha, in *War and Peace* (Book 3, ch. 16), observes that "when you remember, remember, remember everything, you remember so far back that you remember what it was like before you were on this earth." Significantly, Bely uses this quotation as the epigraph to *Kotik Letaev*. But Bely was by no means alone in believing that full consciousness, in the individual, was preceded by a kind of dream-consciousness reaching back into the communal past of humanity, and emerging in the child in the form of myths, half-memories, and symbols. If this is the case, then the significance of the childhood experience is twofold: on the one hand, the child, through its inspired fantasies, is still able to participate more immediately than the average adult in the common, total past of the human race; and, on the other, the whole process of development from birth to maturity (which is the basic schema of the Childhood) can be apprehended clearly as one of individuation—the replacement of the communal dream-consciousness of preexistence by the more limited but more sharply defined and positive awareness of the adult self.

Variants of this quasi-mystical attitude are frequent. Richard Church, for instance, claims that as a young child he found that he had inherited quite specific memories of ancestral experience, and that, although born and brought up in a tiny house in Battersea, he "recognized" immediately the more spacious dimensions of an artist's studio in Chelsea "as something more familiar, more fitting" than those of his own home—the explanation being that his father, an illegitimate scion of the Russell family—the Dukes of Bedford—had been conceived of a maidservant in Woburn Abbey, and although the girl had subsequently been "settled" in London, and appropriately married off, the ancestral memories of the Stately Home persisted. "It was as though a self beyond myself" welcomed the tall doorways and the noble windows of that Chelsea studio, "recalling them as familiar to a way of life impossible to a Battersea-born child, but which I must have known."[12]

Possibly the most interesting variant of the theme of prenatal memory, however, is that of Kathleen Raine. Certainly it is more sophisticated than any other account, in that a conscious absorption of the tenets of Jungian psychology is combined with a Shakespearian (rather than Sophoclean or Racinian) concept of destiny. The first gives rise to the conviction that there are, hidden in the depths of childhood consciousness, traces of a communal heritage of memory, revealing itself in myths, archetypes, and symbols, and also that there are "inherited aptitudes" which will incline the course of life in one direction or another, and thus, in this sense, constitute a predestination. Against this, however, the "Shakespearian" concept asserts that what, even in this very limited sense, "predestines" the self *is* the self; and that the self is free to choose its own myths out of the abundance of humanity's experience— "First choose your Myth, then live it, was Jung's rule of life" (*Farewell Happy Fields*, p. 8)—so that in fact, between predestination and freedom there exists (as in Shakespeare) a most delicate balance. The patterns that emerge from the interaction of freedom and destiny will only be seen as meaningful in retrospect, when they are complete:

> If in the course of time we come a little into our own, we begin to see reflected in the seemingly fortuitous succession of events the inner pattern of our own nature, of what was predestined for us through what we are. Only when it has reflected that inner order can that which has befallen us be called our life. (p. 6)

For Kathleen Raine, the context which gives significance to an otherwise arbitrary-seeming sequence of events is at once inside and outside the self; even in childhood, the meaning lies in the perfection with which inner and outer worlds correspond. "It is a mark of the perfection of the wise to arrive at the place they should be, at the time they should be" (p. 7). At bottom, this is perhaps a religious—a profoundly Christian idea—one which is, in fact, very similar to the concept of destiny and of Grace which is the hallmark of the great dramas of Paul Claudel, *The Satin Slipper*, for instance, or *Meridian*. The

12. Richard Church, *Over the Bridge* (London, 1955), 5–9.

very idea of "perfection," and of the controlled interaction between freedom and destiny, leading in the end to an arrival at the "right" place at the "right" time—these are as much of mysticism as the modern mind can accept without feeling itself estranged. It is the "Other Reality," not of the saint, but of the poet.

In the preceding section, certain central experiences of childhood were described as "quasi-mystical." Perhaps (once again) *magical* would be a better word—or something halfway between the two, if it could be discovered. A loss of formal (churchgoing) faith is, as we have seen, one of the archetypal experiences of the Childhood, but in very few instances does the rejection of an orthodox religious attitude lead to any positive acceptance of materialism. More often than not, the repudiation of an official act of faith is felt as a liberation, giving the child or the adolescent at last the freedom to work out its *own* relationships with an instinctively realized transcendentality—or perhaps, more simply, to cope with the effect of experiences whose emotional impact was in direct proportion to their unpredictability. In perhaps the majority of instances, the supreme moments of childhood are irrational in origin; there is no obvious, logical explanation *why* they were so important.

In a significantly large number of cases, the supreme ecstasies of childhood arise out of contact with the inanimate—not with dolls or other toys which are simulations of known, living beings, not even (although this is encountered more frequently) with natural phenomena such as trees or sunsets—but with bricks or snowflakes or pebbles. To convey such experiences in all their intensity requires not only a high degree of artistic skill, but also an ability to encompass the object—tree or stone or apple—in the completeness of its reality, to reendow it with the magical powers which, for the child, it once possessed—magical not in the sense of wands and wizardry, but in the sense that pure existence in itself is magical and miraculous. To the child, a stone or a shaft of sunlight may contain all the joy and mystery of a world new-created; but to translate something of this experience in its original simplicity, avoiding at once sentimentality and overemphasis, would seem to require a special state of mind. The sheer, indescribable joy of the child is, in Ionesco's words, "a gift of Heaven, it is like the descent of Grace, unexplainable but evident, absolutely certain" (*Journal en miettes*, p. 161). Or, in different, Bergsonian terms, the child's contact with the outside world is essentially that of intuition rather than of reason: its need is "to establish contact with the so-called inanimates, whose intense animism [puts] the sluggish animism of most humans into the shade" (Raynor, *A Westminster Childhood*, p. 9). Some degree of pantheism inhabits the soul of almost every major re-creator of the childhood self.

What does emerge incontrovertibly is that there is a clear and persistent

distinction between the child—later the artist—who possesses an innate instinct for the "mystery" of life and the child who, for a number of years, may
live through a series of intense experiences within the framework of a "taught"
religion, only to abandon it in the long run. The innate instinct—often kept
secret as something too strange and precious, too inexpressible to be debased
by a clumsy translation into language—seems capable of infinite development from infancy through adolescence into maturity, never wholly losing its
power; the taught religion, perhaps aiming too high in the first place, leads
usually to disillusionment, unless its inner substance can somehow be absorbed into a more private, more personal form of mysticism. Joyce, Leiris,
Forrest Reid, and innumerable others reject their religions; James Kirkup
keeps something of his, because he can assimilate the authenticity of emotion
that lies hidden beneath the banality of the formulae. Even the hymn "There is
a Green Hill far away," sung by his Sunday-school class in procession on Palm
Sunday, "sent cold shivers down my spine and blurred my eyes with tears,"
although the actual verses themselves conveyed little or nothing. But if he
"sensed completely their sad acceptance and their tragedy," it was because the
mystery of the crucifixion was not all that alien to the more intimate mysteries
of his own private world—the mystery, for instance, of snowflakes:

> I would begin slowly to feel that the veils of snow were no longer falling: they were
> still, and I was rising, and the window and the table I sat at, and the whole heavy house
> were rising weightless with me. After the first shock of this optical illusion, I would
> often allow myself to drift into its smoothly-rising, unbroken rêveries. . . . I said it was
> like going to Heaven. Yet I kept to myself the conviction of the reality of that magical
> event. I knew it *had* happened to me. Everything became weightless. I was lifted out of
> myself, and the whole house became as unsubstantial as the snowy air outside. (*The
> Only Child*, pp. 164–65)

Kirkup's attitude toward that "magical event" is highly characteristic: he
accepts the irrational qualities of the experience as valuable in their own right
for the intensity of emotion which they generate, and perhaps as positive
intimations of a different reality; yet at the same time he never surrenders his
rational control. He can judge the experience to be based merely on an optical
illusion at the same time as he can cherish and savor its magicality. And this
duality is of the very nature of the artist; for the poet or the painter, out of an
irrational emotion, creates an irrational vision, which is "beauty," while all
the time using skills and techniques which reveal a high degree of critical and
rational control.

The typical progression, from a sense of magic in the very young child, to
an awareness of beauty, thence to a sense of the mystery of the beautiful, and
finally to a kind of pantheism, frequently with existential overtones, is already
analyzed in depth by Wordsworth in Book 2 of *The Prelude*; and in spite of

Wordsworth's romanticism, it is clear that many modern poets would not wholly disown him.

The child Wordsworth unaffectedly loves the countryside and the "incidental charms" of "rural objects." But, as he moves into adolescence, his interest in particular natural phenomena wanes, and he begins to seek a "communion" with Nature (now endowed with a capital *N*) "for her own sake"—"Nature" conceived as a totality, coequal with "this entire universe," and independent of any particular manifestation. The visible gods, in fact, have been transmuted into the Invisible God: the "One Great Mind." At this point, the poet discovers the possibility of the communion he was seeking, and his "visionary power" is born.

If Wordsworth had halted his analysis at this point, it would probably have seemed of little relevance to his less susceptible heirs in our own time. But the abiding interest of this passage lies in the fact that, while he is able "To feel the spirit of religious love / In which [he] walked with Nature," his submission to this pantheistic, mystic spirit of the world is never complete. He retains his own strong sense of individual identity, as a force separate from, and in some ways in opposition to, the greater force outside him. And if he acknowledges that Nature as a whole is more powerful than himself, at the same time he feels that his identity, his control, his "plastic power" is as strong, if not stronger, than Nature in her individual manifestations. In other words, faced with any individual natural phenomenon, he can simultaneously experience communion with a totality—which affords him a joy beyond expression—and yet dominate and control the particular manifestation, reducing it to the status of an image in his own mind, and then forcing it to yield to the imperatives of language and the structures of poetry. This, it would seem, is the sense of one of the key passages in Book 2:

> But let this
> Not be forgotten, that I still retained
> My first creative sensibility;
> That by the regular actions of the world
> My soul was unsubdued. My plastic power
> Abode with me; a forming hand, at times
> Rebellious, acting in a devious mood;
> A loyal spirit of his own, at war
> With general tendency, but, for the most,
> Subservient strictly to external things
> With which it communed. An auxiliar light
> Came from my mind, which on the setting sun
> Bestowed new splendour.   (Book 2, ll. 358–70)

This explanation of a duality—the sense of being possessed by, yet at the same time possessing and "forming" the experience—is more helpful to us in trying to understand the latent mysticism which haunts a majority of Childhoods than is the more exuberant pantheism of subsequent passages in Book 2, or even the careful juxtaposition of pantheism and rationalistic deism which is developed in Book 6. It is, in embryo, the mysticism of the existentialist, whose theories of "transphenomenal perception" and the "creative Void" are neither wholly rational nor wholly irrational. It is a mysticism which can appeal to characters as widely differing as Bernard Berenson, in his search for the origins of his vocation as an art-critic—

> I can remember [at the age of five]—I need not recall—that I climbed up a treestump and felt suddenly immersed in *It*-ness. I did not call it by that name. I had no need for words. *It* and I were one. . . . A revelation, a vision, a psychological equipoise, call it what you will, this experience has furnished me with a touchstone.[13]

—and Camara Laye, endeavoring to interpret and evaluate the superstitions and rituals of his West African childhood in terms acceptable to a modern French intellectual:

> The mute mystery of things, their how and why, predisposes you to silence. It is enough to call such things to mind and to become aware of their inscrutable mystery which leaves behind it a certain light in the eye.[14]

What the Childhood makes abundantly clear is that the rejection of formal religion has not led, as nineteenth-century positivism unquestioningly believed that it would, to a world devoid of mystery, but if anything to a world more obsessively mysterious than ever, since the abandoning of overfacile explanations has left man face to face with the ultimately inexplicable: the "facticity" of the world, the superfluousness of pure existence. Where once there were all-embracing "mysteries"—the Trinity, the Incarnation, the Resurrection, the Redemption—comfortingly remote from day-to-day existence, there are now innumerable and ever-present, intrusive mysteries: the unjustifiable, perhaps even hostile presence of the inanimate, whose impenetrability constitutes the ultimate defiance of human intelligence. The mind, it would seem, had far more chance of penetrating the mystery of God than of grasping the unfathomable reality of a pebble on the seashore, for God, it may be assumed, is at least Mind, whereas the pebble is not-Mind. To apprehend the reality of that which is not-Mind is the severest challenge which the human intellect can encounter; and if it can be met at all, it can only be, in Abel Hermant's phrase, "by intuition, in a manner which is simultaneously mysti-

13. Bernard Berenson, *Sketch for a Self-Portrait* (London, 1949), 21–22.
14. Camara Laye, *L'Enfant noir* (Paris, 1953); trans. James Kirkup and Ernest Jones, *The African Child* (New York, 1979), 53.

cal and positivistic."[15] The child has the intuition, to which it responds by a
sense of magic; but the poet does indeed have to discover a very delicate variety
of "mystical positivism" if he is to succeed in describing the intuitive experience in adult language.

Unless it is highly fictionalized, the autobiography of childhood is of necessity largely descriptive. There is, by and large, comparatively little scope for
narrative, still less for dialogue, while reflective or analytical passages must be
seen strictly as the contribution of the adult. The normal child—particularly
the young child—rarely lives through coherent sequences of adventures,[16]
unless they be of his own invention, the fantasy of his own mind:

> I had a plan of action worked out in case a Messerschmidt soared out of the sun on a
> strafing run. As the bullets kicked up a path along the ground towards me, I would
> jump behind a tree and throw up a clod of dirt as high as I could, hitting the pilot in the
> eyes and making the plane crash in a ball of flame followed by a civic reception in my
> honor at the Hotel Julian.[17]

Nor does he recall conversations. For a long time, indeed, he observes objects
more than people, and people only in proportion as they are remote from him,
and thus resemble objects. His own parents are frequently among the last to be
clearly visualized, retaining a blurred, mythical dimension, sometimes for
many years. The Childhood, then, must describe; and the world of its description has to be the child's world of intuition and magic, yet made accessible to
adults—a remarkably difficult task, one in which otherwise highly accomplished writers—a Jules Supervielle, a Colette, a Jean Guéhenno[18]—may
notoriously fail. Colette, in fact, is a particularly interesting example of failure.
The series of brilliant and charming vignettes of her childhood which she gives
in *La Maison de Claudine* (1922) and elsewhere are masterly instances of a
certain type of delicately nuanced poetic prose; yet they remain wholly adult
structures. Her imagination lacks that flexibility which would enable her to
reconstruct the vision of her younger self; and the faint condescension with
which she treats this self effectively destroys the last vestige of any authentic
sense of childhood.[19]

15. Abel Hermant, *Confession d'un enfant d'hier* (Paris, 1903), 50.

16. Exceptions are mainly to be found among accounts of childhoods spent in wartime or in
revolutionary situations: cf. Joseph Joffo, *Un sac de billes* (Paris, 1973); Janina David, *A Touch of
Earth* (London, 1966), etc.

17. Robert Byrne, *Memories of a Non-Jewish Childhood* (1970; reprint, Scarborough, Ont.,
1972), 10.

18. Jules Supervielle, *Boire à la source* (Paris, 1951); Colette, *La Maison de Claudine* (1922;
reprint, Paris, 1929); Jean Guéhenno, *Changer la vie* (Paris, 1961).

19. *La Maison de Claudine* is in fact the story of Colette's mother, and as such it belongs to
that category of Childhoods recreated *indirectly*. It is perhaps unfair, therefore, to criticize it by
standards applying to the more "classic" form of narrative.

"Children do not belong to the same epoch, to the same race, to the same
continent, as grown-ups"—unexpectedly, perhaps, the tough-minded and
cynical Drieu la Rochelle gets the point much better than the feminine and
intuitive Colette. "Armed through all their senses with strong powers of div-
ination," continues Drieu, "they hold converse with the whole universe in a
mystic language which they forget soon enough, and they live in virgin
lands."[20] Again, it is the mystery of immediate, *intuited* experience which has
to be conveyed: a kind of "being-in" or "being-with" [*être-avec*], to use a term
coined by Gabriel Marcel—phenomena of the outside world; a closeness verging on fusion, the self absorbing, or being absorbed by, the presence of the
inanimate; a sense of "being lost in *it*—whatever 'it' was."[21] And the overwhelming experience for the child, in nine cases out of ten, is the contact with
nature.

What is called for, then, and what has gradually been developed over the
past century, is a specialized technique of description—at once impressionistic and minutely factual—which transmits the intensity of the emotion
experienced by the child in its relation with a particular aspect of the world,
without necessarily situating that aspect in its "real" context or framework.
Given this very precise requirement, the "set piece" descriptions of the great
nineteenth-century prose writers were destined to prove inadequate. Tolstoy is
a case in point. Tolstoy is masterly in his descriptions of the natural world
from an *adult* point of view: one recalls Prince Andrei on the battlefield of
Austerlitz lying watching the clouds, or Levin in the fields reaping with his
peasants. But the objective of these descriptions is quite different from that
required by the Childhood. For Tolstoy, the very breadth and beauty of the
panorama which encircles the central figures constitutes in itself the message:
it is the individual in relation to Nature/God, the instant in relation to the
eternal, or the possessor in relation to the unpossessable that makes up the
problem which he and his characters are attempting to solve. But when it
comes to describing the world experienced by the child, the same technique
gives results which seem misplaced and artificial, as though the writer were
describing, not so much a real experience at all, but a painting—and an
emphatic, overdramatized painting at that, in the best tradition of Caspar
David Friedrich. Take the well-known storm scene from the opening pages of
Boyhood:

> But now the nearest cloud begins to obscure the sun, which peeps out for the last
> time, lights up the terribly gloomy part of the horizon, and disappears. Everything
> around suddenly changes and takes on a sombre aspect. Here the aspen grove begins to

20. Pierre Drieu la Rochelle, *Etat civil* (Paris, 1921), 69.
21. Eleanor Farjeon, *A Nursery in the Nineties* (London, 1935), 259. The similarity between
Eleanor Farjeon's experience and that of Bernard Berenson, quoted above, is striking.

quiver, its leaves turn a kind of dim whitish colour clearly outlined against the purple background of the cloud, and they rustle and turn about; the tops of the tall birches begin to sway and tufts of dry grass fly across the road. Martins and white-breasted swallows, as if intending to stop us, sweep round the *brichka* and fly under the very breasts of the horses; jackdaws with ruffled wings fly sideways to the wind, the flaps of the heavy apron we have fastened over ourselves begin to lift, let in gusts of damp wind and, blowing about, flap against the body of the *brichka*. The lightning seems to flash right into the *brichka*, blinds me, and lights up for an instant the grey cloth, its braiding, and Volodya's figure crouching in the corner. Just above my head at that very moment, a majestic peel sounds . . .[22]

—and so on, and so on, for some five pages. Considered as the authentic experience of childhood recalled, this style of description contains at once too little detail and too much. Or rather, it is the wrong *kind* of detail, unfocused, and seen from the wrong angle. Its structure is elaborate and highly contrived, reminding one above all of similar "storm scenes" in Beethoven's Sixth Symphony or in Rossini's *Barber of Seville*. The writer is not *in* the experience, he is above it, God-like, ostentatiously controlling its pattern and its effects. One child might have noted the angle of flight of the jackdaws, another, the texture of the upholstery in the *brichka*; no child—not even the young Marcel Proust —would recall the lot. Moreover, the switch from the previous use of past tense for the narrative to the present tense with which the description opens has the paradoxical effect, not of increasing the immediacy, but of emphasizing the artificiality. "Look how well I write," Tolstoy seems to be saying; not "this is what I felt."

In the extremely interesting foreword to *A House of Children* (1941)—a retrospective comment written some ten years after the publication of the original text—Joyce Cary makes a valiant attempt to analyze the problem in philosophical terms. For him, the impressions of early childhood contain two distinct elements: "pure sensation" and "visual context." These, he argues, are different both in origin and by nature, and therefore do not always correspond. "Pure sensation"—that which causes the experience to be remembered at all—is the result of direct collision with the outside world; in the last analysis, it is *in* the outside world, and, for a moment, the child *becomes* the sensation that the outside world arouses in it: his inner self is made one with the exterior phenomenon. The "feel" of this kind of "extradition of personality" is necessarily authentic; it can neither be invented, nor elaborated, nor reconstructed. It is "a kind of elated, solemn tension." It *is*. But it is not, in any literary or even everyday sense, a valid memory. "Pure sensation leaves no

22. L. N. Tolstoy, *Otrochestvo* [1854], in *Sobraniye Sochineniy*, ed. S. P. Bychkov (Moscow, 1951–53), 1:108; trans. Aylmer Maude, *Childhood, Boyhood and Youth* (1930; reprint, Oxford, 1947), 137–38.

recollection," noted Stendhal more than once in his *Diaries*;[23] and Joyce Cary is in effect making the same point. "The sensation that remains does not belong to the picture. It is confused and, as it were, inadequate even to itself." Even disregarding all the specialized preoccupations of the writer, the ordinary human being, in the urgency of his need to retain or recapture the inexpressible joy of certain "fearful and glorious" sensations of childhood, will reconstruct their visual context; and this reconstruction, involving innumerable degrees of elaboration, substitution, or distortion, is the work of the conscious mind alone. The "picture" may be wrong, argues Cary, but the "picture" is only the means to an end. The sensation alone is authentic; even the wrongness of the picture may be justified if it owes its existence to the need to retain, to delight in—eventually to transmit to others—the inexpressible, the magical effect of pure sensation:

And so I have only to give the fact, without comment, that even a small child records experience from both sides of its being, in its senses and in its imagination, which can remain separate and yet react upon each other.[24]

This quality of pure sensation, which Joyce Cary describes as "the fear and the glory," is another of the elements which would appear to lie at the roots of that which less analytically minded writers refer to simply as the "magic" of childhood. One incontrovertible fact which is emerging from our own analysis is that this platitude, "the magic of childhood," conceals a very real fact of experience, and also an equally real problem of literary expression. The fundamental difficulty confronting the poet of the Childhood is that of having to use the inherited language of literary description to convey, not the "picture," but the "pure sensation"—a sensation which, by definition, lies outside the range of conventional descriptive language.

"If there is a certain magic value which pertains to everything which once enchanted our childhood, not in vain shall we disturb the powers that lie asleep in the depths of our consciousness" (*Mémorial*, 2:76), writes Marcel Jouhandeau, a highly sophisticated practitioner of the art of the Childhood. But in the less sophisticated environments of Africa, the West Indies, India, and elsewhere in the Third World—and not only there—the notion that certain experiences of childhood are unquestionably magical is taken rather more literally. Repeatedly, we find the magic and the mystery of pure, inexplicable sensation, the "fear and the glory," incarnated in the encounter with creatures which, in the depths of some subconscious stratum of being, effectively symbolize the child's sense of terror in the face of this phenomenon. One

23. See my essay "Stendhal and the Art of Memory," in *Currents of Thought in French Literature: Essays in Memory of G. T. Clapton*, ed. J. C. Ireson (Oxford, 1965), 145–63.
24. Joyce Cary, *A House of Children* (1941; reprint, London, 1951), 7.

such creature, predictably, is the snake, but it was by no means predictable
how frequently the snake myth would recur embedded at the very heart of
authentically experienced Childhoods. That Camara Laye in the highlands of
French Guinea (*L'Enfant noir*) and Mulk-Rāj Anānd on the outskirts of
Peshawar[25] should have this particular experience, is not wholly unexpected—and yet, in Anānd's case more especially, the fact that snakes in India
are both common and recognized as dangerous by no means accounts for the
almost supernatural terror which one *particular* encounter inspired in him. It
is stranger to find virtually the identical experience recounted by W. H. Hudson
(*Far Away and Long Ago*, London, 1918); stranger still to discover it in the
otherwise casual and factual Thomas Wolfe. Anānd and Laye were fully accustomed to living familiarly with magic, myth, superstition—and snakes.
Wolfe was not. The raw American, whose father had been a second-generation immigrant to Asheville, North Carolina, and whose mother was a practical, avaricious property speculator and boardinghouse keeper, might seem
to be as far removed as any human one can imagine from mythical involvement in snake magic. Yet the strange encounter with the serpent is one of the
most memorable and most puzzling passages in the whole marvelous account
of his early life—or rather, of the life of "Eugene Gant":

> Still midget-near the live pelt of the earth, he saw many things that he kept in fearful
> secret, knowing that revelation would be punished with ridicule. One Saturday in
> Spring, he stopped with Max Isaacs above a deep pit in Central Avenue, where city
> workmen were patching a broken watermain. The clay walls of their pit were much
> higher than their heads; behind their huddled backs was a wide fissure, a window in
> the earth which opened on some dark, subterranean passage. And as the boys looked,
> they gripped each other suddenly, for past the fissure slid the flat head of an enormous
> serpent; passed, and was followed by a scaly body as thick as a man's; the monster slid
> endlessly on into the deep earth, and vanished behind the working and unwitting men.
> Shaken with fear, they talked about it then and later in hushed voices, but they never
> revealed it.[26]

This extraordinary episode (which, significantly, is introduced by another
"miraculous" experience—"the opening gates in him, the plunge of the tide,
the escape"—the experience simply of learning to read) embodies the essential problem of childhood and its transmutation into the wholly different
world of adult experience. The two worlds simply do not correspond. The
child lives "midget-near the live pelt of the earth," and its awareness of what
can exist there is consequently not only more intense, but utterly different
from the awareness of those whose eyes are situated six feet above it. As a

25. Mulk-Rāj Anānd, *Seven Summers* (1951; Delhi, 1972), 168.
26. Thomas Wolfe, *Look Homeward, Angel* (1929; reprint, New York, 1957), 71. I am making
allowance for the fact that Wolfe never claimed that his text was anything other than a novel.

result, the "truth" of that awareness is necessarily unverifiable by adult standards. Its truth lies wholly in the manner of its reporting. Wolfe grasps the nettle firmly in both hands: he juxtaposes the miraculous and the prosaic in the extremity of their contrast, without the hint of a qualm whether the reader will believe him or not. Having carefully avoided any Freudian or other escape routes into symbolism, he nonetheless suggests that the prosaic-miraculous reality of the serpent in some way corresponds with the equally prosaic and even more miraculous escape of learning to read. In the upshot, Wolfe's serpent is more credible than Tolstoy's storm.

In somewhat similar terms, albeit with slightly different conclusions, the Moroccan Ahmed Séfrioui confronts the same problem in his *Boîte à merveilles* (1954). Instead of monsters, Séfrioui's "box of miracles" contains nothing but utter trivialities: "glass marbles, copper rings, gilt-headed nails . . . etc."[27]— yet each of these speaks to him "with its own language," each is the inexplicable, irrational revelation of a dimension of reality which is *not* that of adult experience. Séfrioui, whose father, originally a mountain Berber, had settled as an artisan in the Arabized cultural ambiance of Fez, and who, himself, was later to experience the intellectual life of Paris in the heyday of postwar existentialism, explores a fascinating series of transmutations of the concept of magic, each in the last analysis representing an attempt to explain the same phenomenon: namely, that his contact as a child with the outside world was wholly different from his contact with the same world as an adult. Starting from a background of fairly primitive and superstitious magic (but what very young child doesn't?), in which the world could be apprehended as "a fabulous domain, a large-scale fairyland, wherein witches maintained familiar intercourse with invisible powers" (p. 9), Séfrioui felt at first that his treasures were magical inasmuch as they had the power, by "setting his senses in ecstasy," to place him in direct contact with that other world. Gradually, however, the interpretation veers toward the existential: the magic of the object lay in the inexplicable uniqueness of its very existence, the eternally elusive quality of its being as a thing-in-itself, its mystery (and therefore its beauty) as pure, contingent *Dasein*:

> There was, however, in that object an element which could be apprehended neither through the eyes, nor through the fingers, a mysterious and untranslatable beauty. It fascinated me. I sensed my failure to extract the fullest delight from it. I wept almost, feeling around me a strange, invisible something, impalpable, which with my tongue I could not savor, yet which had a taste nonetheless, and the power to intoxicate me. (p. 13)

For some such reason, as a child, must Antoine Roquentin have wept—or

---

27. Ahmed Séfrioui, *La Boîte à merveilles* (Paris, 1954), 14.

could it be that the adult bafflement which he records in *La Nausée* is simply the child's sense of the mysterious otherness of things, stripped now of its qualities of enchantment and innocence? At all events, Séfrioui, returning to earth after his excursions into the intellectual stratosphere of existentialism, found himself enriched with a new feeling for the magical significance of his treasures, and with a new language for conveying it. They were plain *things*; and yet . . . and yet they were the key to the world of ecstasy and dream. "Every single one of these objects spoke to me in its own tongue. *They* were my only friends" (p. 14). But (and Séfrioui is more aware of this than most) this gift of "sharing in the Mysteries of the Invisible" is not that of every child, but only of the child-poet. It is yet a further contribution to that prison-house of solitude, that sense of utter alienation, which sets the child who is destined to create through art and imagination apart from his fellows. "*I* longed for the Invisible to invite me to partake of its Mysteries. My little schoolfriends were quite content with the Visible" (p. 9). It is the mark of Cain.

So, if this magic, apprehended as a primary dimension of reality, is essential to the experience of the child in its contact with the world about it, it is not to be wondered at that traditional techniques for describing that world are liable to prove inadequate. In addition to its normal functions, language has to take on the roles both of incantation and of invocation. The reader has to be carried *beyond* the visible surface of nature to its inward reality, to the "miracle" of an existence in which, once upon a time, the child wholly participated. The question is not, what did that bottle-cap (or pendant, or pebble, or piece of glass) *look* like, but what did it *feel* like to be irradiated with its very essence, to be exposed, through the medium of its mundane existence, to the miraculous otherness of a dimension beyond language? And this is the problem which all the greater artists who have explored the domain of the Childhood have attempted, in their varying ways and with varying degrees of success, to solve. For each, as for Baudelaire, the essence of poetry lies in recapturing— somehow—the authentic, the magical vision of the child.

Given the nature of the problem—how to communicate through the conventional language of description the child's existential awareness of nature and of the world—it might have been expected that languages such as Russian and English which, in their poetic contexts, are evocative rather than precise, would have the advantage over languages such as French, where the role of sensory or irrational evocation is much reduced. In the event, however, this distinction proves meaningless. Each writer deals with the problem in his own way, overcoming whatever obstacles may arise out of his own culture or language, discovering his own route toward a solution. In comparing various literatures, one can discover tendencies, perhaps myths; never rules.

Moreover, most major writers, in the present century at least, appear to be very much aware of the problem; so, by taking a small but representative selection of texts from different cultural areas, we may begin to understand some of the ways in which language can be made to approach a task which is in itself virtually impossible: that is, to recreate, in terms of literature, an experience which, in its origin, was pure sensation—that is, pure "magic."

Perhaps the best-known and best-loved of all such descriptive passages is, once again, to be found in Proust: the vision of the hawthorn hedge ("le petit sentier des aubépines") from the *Combray* section of *Remembrance of Things Past.*[28]

Proust is not a landscape artist in the Tolstoyan sense, least of all in *Combray*. His immense universe is built up of innumerable fragments, minute particles minutely observed, then set in parallel and juxtaposed with other fragments—colors, sounds, scents and echoes—to form a brilliant mosaic whose overall artistry and pattern is apprehended only gradually through the shimmering clouds of detail. The hawthorn passage is a perfect example of the problem which Proust has set himself: to intuit the essential realities of the child-self, its world and experience, in such a way that language, as it were, becomes transparent, and the reader is made one with the immediate presence, in all its dimensions, of the flowering arcades of the hawthorn path. And, incautious as the assertion may appear, Proust, for all his mastery, fails, and perhaps even recognizes that he has failed. In his aim to extend his *apprehension* of the flowering mass through language into a total experience, he achieves a totality but somehow just misses the innermost secret of the experience.[29]

Proust introduces his subject indirectly: not through sight but through smell and (metaphorically) through sound. "I found the whole path throbbing [*tout bourdonnant*] with the fragrance of hawthorn-blossom." Immediately after this, he introduces the first of his major "extensions" of the experience—"The hedge resembled a series of chapels"—an extension which in itself contains a whole range of elements which can be explored as further extensions in their own right: religious experience, the Gothic mode, architectural patterns, the fragrance of incense, the spring festivals of the ecclesiastical calendar. As the sentence proceeds, each of these various elements begins to assume its own clear shape, but always intertwined with one or more of the others:

The hedge resembled a series of chapels, whose walls were no longer visible under the

28. In the following paragraphs concerning *A la recherche du temps perdu*, I have used the famous Scott-Moncrieff translation, *Remembrance of Things Past*, as a basis, modifying it as necessary when it seemed to lose too much of the meaning or the rhythm of Proust's original.

29. Many illustrated books on Proust—e.g., Léon Pierre-Quint, *L'Univers de Proust* (Souillac, 1959)—contain photographs of "le petit sentier des aubépines." Nothing is better calculated to destroy the magic of the Proustian vision.

mountain of flowers that were heaped upon their altars; while, underneath, the sun cast a square of light upon the ground, as though it had shone in upon them through a window; the scent that swept out over me from them was as rich and as circumscribed in its range, as though I had been standing before the Lady-altar, and the flowers, themselves adorned so, held out each its little bunch of glittering stamens with an air of inattention, fine, radiating "nerves" in the flamboyant style of architecture, like those which, in church, framed the stair to the rood-loft or closed the perpendicular tracery of the windows, but here spread out into pools of fleshy white, like strawberry beds in spring.[30]

At this point, and in spite of the fact that a new extension is beginning to be explored—that of exact scientific observation, in noting the botanical relationship between hawthorn and strawberry—Proust realizes that he has in fact failed to achieve his aim, which is not merely to *experience* the wonder of the blossom as a miracle, yet still as something other than himself, but rather to "be-with" that miracle, to apprehend it *from within*, and thus, in the ultimate sense, to "understand" it. Not intellectual effort, nor multiple sensual experience with all its overtones and extensions, nor even the almost metaphysical sensation of "being at one with the rhythm of the flowers"—none of these things allows him to break through the ultimate barrier: the barrier between self and not-self. And this is the final frustration. "They offered me an indefinite continuation of the same charm, in an inexhaustible profusion, but without letting me delve into it any more deeply." And so, anticipating the grievousness of the frustration, Proust tries another approach altogether. Turning aside from the hawthorns, he allows his mind to wander off towards other flowers, in the hope that eventually, by reverting suddenly to the hawthorns, he may be able, as it were, to take them unawares and, with a fresh, unsaturated mind, surprise them, catch them unprepared and vulnerable, and so forestall the secret of their being.

This experiment fails likewise. Obstinately, the gap between the flowers themselves and the sensations which they awaken in him remains. "The sentiment which they aroused in me remained obscure and vague, struggling and failing to free itself, to float across and become one with the flowers." Nowhere more clearly in all the literature of the Childhood is this ultimate problem of problems more meticulously explored. The flowers themselves, notes Proust ruefully, wouldn't help him; if he was going to achieve the miracle, the miracle had to be *his*.

Then his grandfather pointed out to him a solitary *pink* variant of the otherwise bridal-white blossom—and this immediately provided a new focal point: unique, uniquely exquisite, offering an approach to the mystery at the

30. Marcel Proust, *A la recherche du temps perdu*, ed. Pierre Clarac and André Ferré (Paris, 1968), 1:138.

heart of things because now the entire effort to break through the barrier could be concentrated on one single, minute point. Immediately, the religious imagery, which had vanished while Proust had turned away from the hawthorns, returns, but more specific now than ever, reinforced to give strength to the final effort. "It, too, was in holiday attire, for one of those days which are the only true holidays, the holy days of religion." It is the supreme moment; virtually the barrier is crossed: Marcel will "be-with" the solitary pink blossom, and so taste of and know the magic of that total fusion of experience and thing-experienced which is the ultimate wonder of childhood. And then something begins to go wrong. Into the magic and the mystery there begins to creep a sudden, grating note of vulgarity. Why, his nagging mind proceeds to ask, is pink a rarer, a more exquisite color than white? The answer is that pink is the color of things which he, Marcel, a child, likes to eat. Pink is "the color of some edible and delicious thing." Even worse, if a pink flower seems prettier than a white, this is no more than mindless conformism with the aesthetics of the village general stores, which work on the elementary principle of "penny plain tuppence colored." All colored comestibles were

of a superior quality, by the aesthetic standards of Combray, to the "plain," if one was to judge by the scale of prices at the stores in the Square, or at Camus', where the most expensive biscuits were those whose sugar was pink. And for my own part I set a higher value on cream cheese when it was pink, when I had been allowed to tinge it with crushed strawberries . . .

—and so, by progressive contamination of vulgarity, from the shop-counter to the holy altar in the house of God. The pink of the village biscuits is the identical pink which the same vulgar and uncultured *commerçante* who sells them will weave into the crude patterns of some overdecorated cloth or ornament for the village church. It was not the *commerçante*, however, who had created the pink blossom, "overloading the bush with these little rosettes too preciously pink in color, a provincial copy of courtly sophistication,"[31] but nature herself. In other words, the ultimate reality of the hawthorn is that it looks crude and artificial, but doesn't even have the excuse of being so. Nature is not merely imitating art; it is imitating bad art badly. The spell is broken. The barrier will not be crossed, was perhaps not even worth crossing. Was it rewarding to make all that effort to penetrate a reality composed of provinciality, childish greed, and the aesthetic standards of the *petite-bourgeoisie*? But the effort had already in part been made, and Proust was reluctant to waste it. So in the end he returns to his religious imagery, as it were to cast a cloak over the bitterness of his failure, but now there is something tongue-in-

31. Ibid, p. 140. Scott-Moncrieff gets a completely different sense from the passage at this point.

cheek about it. No longer the antique and mysterious "series of chapels" with their wondrous tracery of fan-vaulting, but rather the Greuze-like picture of a village maiden arrayed in the flamboyant finery of her first-communion gown, all decked out for the month of Mary: "thus it shone and smiled in its cool, rosy garments, a Catholic bush indeed, and altogether delightful."

Proust's account of his failure has a great ring of authenticity about it, although it is not clear whether it was the boy Marcel who was already too intellectually precocious still to have the gift of "projecting himself into nature,"[32] or whether it was the adult Proust who could not recapture the Bergson-type intuition of the world which the very young child, it may be suspected, to some extent shares with the animals. But two other features emerge from this analysis of the hawthorn passage: first, the value of an indirect, allusive approach to the problem through the fragmentation of rationalistic sentence structure—in fact, through the use of poetic prose. The phenomenon itself does not belong to the domain of purely rational experience; consequently the limpid lucidity of the classical text is ill-equipped to deal with it. And second, the significance of minute detail as the key to the child's apprehension of the mystery or the magic of the whole.

The child's world is a small world. Obvious as this statement may sound, it has implications which affect the literary reconstruction of that world, and which may not be so immediately apparent.[33] The child's world is confined to a few streets or to a few fields; it is a path down to the beach along which every fence and every stile is known intimately by name, and the names remain as incantations; it is a "private domain," a "little world apart";[34] a "small but very personal world, in which the names of streets were like the names of continents on a map of the world" (Kirkup, *Sorrows, Passions and Alarms*, p. 45). It can have overtones of Freudian suggestiveness, of longings for a return to the womb:

> I like small, confined places. . . . But small, dimly-lit places like the lavatory, the coal-house and the wash-house filled me with curious excitement and almost fevered happiness. . . . These small, enclosed places made me feel safe and secure, and seemed to release my imagination, as if the very essence of my personality had been captured and concentrated by their restrictions. (*Sorrows, Passions and Alarms*, pp. 28–29)

Or it can irradiate the subsequent years with a sense of rich and romantic adventure, as happens with Francis Jammes's childhood town of Tournay, whose topography remains engraved in his memory from earliest times,

---

32. The phrase is that of W. H. Hudson (*Far Away and Long Ago*, pp. 224–25), whom we again find following up the same problems as Proust.

33. See below, Chapter 6.

34. Anne Treneer, *School House in the Wind* (London, 1944), 42.

like some antique map, largely rubbed away, yet here and there brilliant, glittering—a map which some retired old sea-captain drags forth out of a chest, where it has lain for half a century.[35]

This feeling for the world of childhood as a fragmented map or chart, with certain details luminously clear, while the intervening areas remain obscure or blank, and all the lands beyond, a faceless and frightening terra incognita—this is something which is frequently encountered and which, indeed, has been skillfully exploited by writers *for* children, such as Arthur Ransome, A. A. Milne and J. R. R. Tolkien. In the present century of rapid transport, the gaps between the luminous areas may grow greater, but the mechanism of memory remains the same. Fredelle Bruser Maynard's inner topography, for instance, covers virtually the whole Province of Saskatchewan, together with a hunk of Manitoba, but its truly distinguishing feature, nonetheless, remains Woolworths!

Had I been asked to produce a Child's Own Geography, it would have gone something like this. Birch Hills, center. A long car ride away, Round Lake, where we waded in bathing dresses, and—farther still, Watrous, a beach for sick people. To the North, Prince Albert, its special distinction being Woolworth's, really a fifteen-cent store in those days. To the West, Battleford, where crazy people were locked up. And to the East, Winnipeg, the great city, grandparents, our people.[36]

What Proust understood in a way that Tolstoy (at least in *Boyhood*) did not, is that the child sees objects in isolated close-up, and that any description of childhood experience, if it is to appear authentic, must adopt a similar perspective. In the nineteenth century more especially, this passionate involvement in the minute detail of the natural world often crystallized for the child in the form of an obsessive interest in the natural sciences. Sea anemones and caterpillars, waterhens, wasps, and above all butterflies—one could piece together quite a fair encyclopedia of the natural world from the Childhoods of our collection. Sergei Aksakov watched birds, collected and pressed grasses, studied the ways of caterpillars—and the last thing he ever wrote in his long life was in fact an essay entitled "Butterfly Collecting: An Episode of College Life."[37] André Gide collected beetles, and from there extended his range to mantises, scorpions, and centipedes, confessing without shame that, had he not become a poet, he might easily have become an entomologist. Vladimir Nabokov conceived his "dominating single passion" for butterflies at the age of seven and, in retrospect, could see the trail of rare specimens in fact mark-

35. Francis Jammes, *De l'âge divin à l'âge ingrat* (Paris, 1921), 5.

36. Fredelle Bruser Maynard, *Raisins and Almonds* (Toronto, 1972), 22.

37. "Sobiraniye babochek," now included in Aksakov's *Vospominaniya*, in *Sobraniye Sochineniy*, ed. S. Mashinsky (Moscow, 1955), 2:5–214.

ing out the "pattern of meaning" of his life.[38] Edmund Gosse, under the guidance of his father, explored and classified the contents of rock-pools. Marcel Pagnol tells with sadistic but still scientifically accurate glee how he experimented in persuading ants to attack a mantis. Francis Jammes records as a "miracle" the discovery of Linnaeus, while, further back still, the twelve-year-old Charles Nodier spent the whole period of the Terror during the French Revolution in a state of "unalloyed bliss," constituting his own private museum of butterflies, shells, and birds' eggs, while at the same time intoxicating himself with the poetry of their names.[39]

Among all the paradise-lost archetypes of childhood experience, one of the most intensely felt is that of the child discovering the methods of science, and for the first time using these methods to observe and classify the world around him. Admittedly, the making of collections, over the period which separated Francis Bacon from Lord Rutherford, was one of the most characteristic features of European progressivism, and one which, at the same time, was accessible even to the child. But the most revealing feature of this obsession, as it is portrayed in the Childhoods of the time, is that the language used to describe the memory of these activities is virtually identical with that which we encounter among more modern writers whose interests are anything but scientific. In other words, for the pre-1914 child, the scientific approach to nature was something very much more than a duty imposed by the rationalistic spirit of the age; it was *his* direct and immediate experience of the "magic" which we have been trying to analyze, *his* intuition of pure poetry, *his* passage through the barrier of subjective experience toward "being-with" the thing experienced. When Vladimir Nabokov describes Richard South's *Butterflies of the British Isles* as "unforgettable and unfadingly magical" (*Speak, Memory*, p. 97), he is doing no more than to echo the phrases of his predecessors. "I felt new life in myself *and became a part of nature*," observed the far-from-mystical Aksakov;[40] while André Gide placed the "pure joy" of his observation of mantises and centipedes high above that ever afforded him later by books, music, or pictures (*Si le grain ne meurt*, p. 88). For Francis Jammes, collecting butterflies in the Allées de Molaàs "overwhelmed me with some inexplicable intimation of immortality" (*De l'âge divin à l'âge ingrat*, p. 50), while the day he spent examining the stamens and corollae of the common wood anemone remained throughout his life "an inexpressible sweetness in my memory."[41] A century or so earlier than Nabokov, Charles Nodier recalls

38. Vladimir Nabokov, *Speak, Memory* (London, 1967), especially pp. 94–110.

39. Charles Nodier, "Séraphine," in *Mémoires de Maxime Odin* [1832], reprinted in *Œuvres complètes* (Geneva, 1968), 10:32–44.

40. Sergei Aksakov, *Detskiye gody Bagrova-vnuka*, ed. S. Mashinsky (Moscow, 1955), 1:502; my italics.

41. Francis Jammes, *L'Amour, les muses et la chasse* (Paris, 1922), 45–46.

the moment when he first caught sight of *Carabus auronitens* as one consumed by an emotion so intense that it left "an eternal void" in his life ("Séraphine," p. 37), and a few pages later he uses the ecstatic religious terms "Grace" and "Mysteries" in his efforts to evoke the meaning which emanated from his lepidoptera—a fitting parallel for Kathleen Raine who conjures up the terminology of the Vedas and the Maya concept of Oriental mysticism to express her reaction to botanical specimens observed for the first time beneath the microscope. "I was a Berkeleyan," she concludes, "before I knew who Berkeley was" (*Farewell Happy Fields*, p. 117). Once again, however, it is the little-known but perceptive Abel Hermant who best resumes this escape from the self into the totality experienced by the nineteenth-century child through the scientific observation of the minute details of nature. In his garden, recalls Hermant, there grew a chestnut tree overshadowing a small pond:

> As yet, all I knew of life was disconnected: by observing [that tree] I learned to know a life that was organized. But since it was reflected in a pool of unclear water with a muddy bottom in which thousands upon thousands of rudimentary creatures assuredly were crawling, this combination of tree and pond struck me as a kind of microcosm, where all conceivable forms of being, the most diverse and the most extreme imaginable, had been collected together on purpose, so that the ultimate secret of the universe should be made accessible to the eyes of my childhood. Ah! how many uncountable hours did I spend in contemplation, in interrogation of this tree, whose knowledge was infinite! (*Confession d'un enfant d'hier*, p. 40)

The child's world is the world, not of mountains, but of molehills; primarily not of steppes and prairies, but quite specifically of gardens. To *name* a flower is already to half-penetrate the secret of its world. "This is watermint . . . this is wild mustard," said the new schoolteacher, Mademoiselle Côté, to her unlettered pupils in the bleak lands by Lake Winnipegosis; and thus she transformed their lives, lavishing on them "all those things that children long to know, the *names* of everything around them, the knowledge of which bestows possession."[42] Even Hans Carossa's otherwise dreary *Kindheit* comes suddenly ablaze as one by one he names the flowers in his garden,[43] much as the magical names *Jelängerjelieber*, *Stiefmütterchen*, and *Tausendguldenkraut* lend splendor to the melancholy pages of *Werther*. But this brings us back to our central problem: the technique of description exercised in a special context. How does the writer handle his vision of the small world of childhood, when by force of geographical circumstances, the most impressive feature of that world is its vastness, its lack of boundaries, its infinitude? Critics have, in a different context, identified a literature of "the Steppe, the

---

42. Gabrielle Roy, *La Petite Poule d'eau* (Paris, 1951), 89.
43. Hans Carossa, *Eine Kindheit* [1922], ed. Jethro Bithell (Oxford, 1942), 31.

Pampas and the Prairie." In the Childhood, however, it is rather the Steppe, the Pampas, and the Outback which exhibit features in common. The North American prairie and the Canadian wilderness produce different, less clearly identifiable, reactions.

If we take the child in a Russian context, these problems immediately become apparent; not so much in the urban setting of a Bely or a Gorky, nor even in that of Sergei Aksakov, whose early years were spent in the land of rivers and rolling hills between Kuybyshev and Orenburg, already close to the first foothills of the Ural Mountains, but very much so in the case of Konstantin Paustovsky, born and brought up in the flatlands of the Ukraine. Here, everything was vast: the plains, the forests, the fields of rye and buckwheat, the skies beneath which no railway journey seemed to take less than three days. Even in such a setting, of course, there is still plenty of scope for the same type of minutely observed detail as we have analyzed elsewhere:

> There were caterpillars on the pavements even in the Kreshchatik [in Kiev]. The wind swept fallen petals into drifts. Butterflies and maybugs flew in at the windows of the trams. Nightingales sang at night. The fluff off the poplars eddied on the flagstones like the surf of the Black Sea, and dandelions blossomed in the gutters.[44]

Yet this detailed description tends to focus on the cities or towns, and it is not the source of Paustovsky's major effects.

The magic, the fabulous quality of Paustovsky's world is achieved by breaking down the vastness, not so much into the details which compose it, as into the separate elements of the impressions which it causes: its luminosity, its color, its light and shadow, its abundance. Clouds with their different shapes and contours, "true Ukrainian clouds, lazy and magnificent" (*Povest' o zhizni*, 1:19; trans., 1:16) focus with precision the infinitude of the sky. Effects of pure light are caught in particular situations at precise and unrepeatable moments in time, immobilized, yet suggesting the boundless flood of luminosity to be apprehended beyond the narrow focus of vision. "The shadow of the train ran clattering over the fields," recalls the poet, "while the carriage was flooded with such a brilliant orange sunset that all you could see in our compartment was a fiery haze" (*Povest' o zhizni*, 1:97; trans., 1:83). The intensity of perfume likewise is used to suggest, not a Proustian "ultimate reality," but the horizonless abundance of the flowering buckwheat from which it emanates. In Paustovsky's landscapes, most of the nouns are in the plural; but this form is used with such artistry that it evokes, not the vague impersonality of imprecise or inadequate observation (as frequently happens in poor writing), but rather the infinite richness of the unseen land, and nearly

---

44. Konstantin Paustovsky, *Povest' o zhizni* (1946–64; reprint, Moscow, 1966), 1:80; trans. Manya Harari and Michael Duncan, *Story of a Life* (London, 1964), 1:69.

always some unique detail of observation will serve as focus to the whole, holding it firmly in place, and keeping it from disintegrating into generalities. Even the dreams and images which sometimes accompany the factual description prolong the rhythms, the vastness, and the abundance of the real world, yet will be held together by a detail almost surrealist in its unexpected urgency, in its suggestion of Delvaux or Magritte:

> I used to imagine a far-away country which I felt certain that I would some day visit. It was an undulating plain filled with grasses and flowers as far as the eye could reach. The towns and villages were submerged in vegetation, and *the coaches of the express trains which crossed this region had thick layers of pollen clinging to their sides.* (*Povest' o zhizni*, 1:43; trans., 1:38; my italics)

In Childhoods such as those of Konstantin Paustovsky or Sergei Aksakov, where the minute observation of detail is used, not so much to intuit the essence of a totality beyond the boundaries of the senses, but rather to focus the awareness of a vastness actually perceived, there is very little feeling of *paradis perdu*. It could be argued in Paustovsky's case that it would be politically unwise to portray even the birch forests and buckwheat fields of pre-Soviet Russia as a paradise *lost*. But, while there may be some truth in this, the real reason lies certainly deeper. Proust knew that his ecstasy beneath the canopies of hawthorn blossom could never be wholly recaptured. It had been an irrevocable instant in time; as the flowers withered, he himself grew older; and the sequences of years elapsing between one May-month and another had relegated both child and flower into an impenetrable past. But, on the vaster scale, the prairies, the mountains, the forests, and the skies endure—or at least seem to. One of the elements in the equation is comparatively stable. And so the instant of vision appears, not as a speck of light vanishing into the night of time, but rather as a point of departure. Mulk-Rāj Anānd knew that the hills of the Northwest Frontier, those "ladders of heaven, the bare copper-coloured and ochre-brown mountains which stretched to the dry river-bed" (*Seven Summers*, p. 231), would be with him as a real presence, as the "stable background" to all his later years; and indeed his first full awareness of them, standing in the Nowshera Cantonment, marks the end of his childhood. Similarly, Paustovsky knew that the basic features of the Russian landscape were unchanging and unchangeable, and that it was *his* Russia. The luminosity of the Ukrainian vault of heaven engendered another kind of luminosity: that of the poet.

"The world was certainly abundant in those days" (p. 231),—thus again Mulk-Rāj Anānd; yet abundance in itself is not sufficient to transform the child's world into the full glory of its fabulous otherness. There is abundance enough in the recollections of Henry James, abundance of groceries, of fruit above all, "bushels of peaches, peaches big and peaches small, peaches white and peaches yellow," in the bustling sidewalk markets of old New York:

> Above all, the public heaps of them, the high-piled receptacles at every turn, touched the street as with a sort of southern plenty; the note of the scattered and rejected fragments, the memory of the slippery skins and rinds and kernels with which the old dislocated flags were bestrown, is itself endeared to me and contributes a further pictorial grace.[45]

Yet there is something missing in the description. It has neither the monstrous opulence of Zola's *Ventre de Paris*, nor the delicate, Raphael-arabesque quality of Paustovsky's dandelions and caterpillars. It is, as it were, abundance for its own sake, a sort of heavy-handed affluence. It contributes a dutiful element to the backdrop ("a further pictorial grace"), and an occasion for nostalgic sentimentalizing: "Where is that fruitage now, where in particular are the peaches *d'antan*? Where the mounds of Isabella grapes and Seckel pears in the sticky sweetness of which our childhood seems to have been steeped?" (pp. 70–71). The tone, alas, is that of M. Robert de Roquebrune, or of Miss Mabel Lucy Atwell divested of her pre-Disney fantasy.

To be sensed as a vital factor in the poetry of childhood, the material concept of "abundance" needs, as it were, to be sublimated, to be granted a more aerial dimension. To return to Anānd: throughout his Childhood the theme of abundance runs like a distinguishing scarlet thread, but it is linked with two other themes, infinitude (symbolized by "The Road") and luminosity. The same three related ideas, moreover, can be traced in the majority of nonurban South American, Russian, Australian, and occasionally West Indian Childhoods.

Among these motifs, the essential magical experience is probably that of luminosity; if this is so, it would account for the otherwise strange fact that all three themes (except that of abundance in Henry James, as has just been noted) are virtually absent from Childhoods located in North America, where the landscapes may be similar, but the quality of light quite different. It is light—light, and with it color—which produces the unforgettable impressions in Saint-John Perse (Guadeloupe) and in W. H. Hudson (Argentina), in Valentin Kataev (Ukraine), and in virtually all the Australians—Randolph Stow above all, Hal Porter, and Alan Marshall, but even in the mainly urban experiences of David R. Burns, Donald Horne, Graham McInnes, or David Malouf. At the age of six, Hal Porter left Melbourne and was taken to live in Bairnsdale, a small, primitive, still-pioneering township, eastward near the lagoon-lakes of the Gippsland coast:

45. Henry James, *A Small Boy and Others* (New York, 1914), 71.

My first sight of Bairnsdale strikes me breathless and still and smaller. Space!
Infinity! Light! . . .

In Bairnsdale I feel myself let loose at the centre of an immeasurable sphere. Pure
light gushes and soars away from my minuteness in every direction, upwards and ever
upwards, inhabited by slicing swallows and creaking swans and stock-still hawks and
pin-prick larks; outwards to arch over northern mountains . . . ; outwards and east to
curve for a century of miles over the farthest eucalypts and their sumless tons of
glistening morocco leaves. (*Watcher on the Cast-Iron Balcony*, pp. 52–53)

Porter's prose (sometimes criticized for its overjeweled intricacy) is in fact
a kind of incantation: it is his way of translating into language the magic of the
experience. His unusual images—the "distant ring-barked gums" which
"wriggle in the heat-waves, and seem to melt like the bristles of a melting
hairbrush" (p. 174)—contribute to the same effect. But it is in Porter also that
the theme of abundance emerges with its fullest power, burgeoning with all its
ramifications as perhaps the most important symbol of the book. The "lavishness," the "copiousness" of Gippsland, with its "bees and butterflies and
blossoms and gusts of scent" (p. 63), is echoed in the "middle-class lavishness"
of the contents of his parents' meat-safe (p. 21); the fertility of the land, with
the "bees staggering drunk in the Madonna lilies" (p. 69), is paralleled in the
fertility (both physical and emotional) of the mother; the objects on his mother's dressing table multiply as rampantly as the "mirages resembling pools of
mica" on the midsummer streets (p. 16); and his own language is as rich, as
brilliant, and as uncontrollably, anarchically prolific as the land in which he
grew up. The boy is overwhelmed by the abundance of the world; the man will
give it back as the abundance of the poet.

This irrepressible, almost baroque exuberance of language and imagery
is, in *The Watcher on the Cast-Iron Balcony*, a skilled and deliberate technique—derived in part from Proust and Joyce, more directly, perhaps, from
Thomas Wolfe—for transmitting experiences which had the same qualities.
An equally deliberate and effective technique is that of Alan Marhsall in *I
Can Jump Puddles* (1955). Here, the impressions of luminosity, infinitude,
and abundance are carefully emphasized by being juxtaposed with others
from which these qualities are absent absolutely—the descent into the dead
crater of Mount Turalla, for instance, where

the earth was brown . . . all brown . . . the dark green of the ferns was swamped with
brown. The still, silent boulders were brown. We sat cut off from the bright sounds of
the living world that lay over the encircling rim and all the while we felt we were being
watched by something huge and unfriendly. (pp. 136–37)

The words *magic* and *magical* occur in Marshall with more than usual
frequency, if only because, after his emergence from the "dark night" of the
hospital ward, the world appeared to him with miraculous brightness. But, if

we look at the text closely, the elements which constitute the magic can be reduced to a limited number of categories.

In the serious literature of childhood, the cuddlier archetypes of infant delight—kittens, dolls, hamsters, teddy bears—play virtually no role whatsoever. In the confrontation with the world of otherness, they are irrelevant. Characteristically, Christopher Robin Milne is at pains to relegate the immortal archetypes which his father created—Kanga and Tigger, Eyore and Piglet—to the reality where they in fact belonged: "cuddlies," deliberately chosen *for* him by his parents, with a view to their eventual literary exploitation. Pussies and piggies are too human; they present no challenge, no metaphysical opposition. Perhaps one of the greatest sins against the child of the twentieth century is that committed by Walt Disney, who contrived to present almost *all* living creatures, from grasshoppers to elephants, as assimilable to the human state, as *cuddly*. Gerald Durrell (*My Family and Other Animals*, 1956) adds his own contribution to the anthropomorphic fallacy. Robert Thomas Allen, looking back to his Canadian childhood in the 1920s, makes the point:

> Our wild animals weren't like the wild animals of today. Today people see so few animals, and so many cartoons of animals talking and falling in love and playing pranks, and so many TV shows of chimpanzees cuddling up to Garry Moore, that they're beginning to think animals are just quaint little people who would really like to join our Home and School Club.[46]

The challenge to the intuition of the child (as to the contemporary metaphysician) is precisely that which *cannot* be assimilated to the human: centipede or stamen or sea anemone; pebble[47] or porcelain button or crystal peardrop fragment from a vanished chandelier. Dogs, birds, and horses may occupy a sort of halfway house, but only insofar as they are "homely." The magical—that is, the alienating—factor is beauty, and inasmuch as they are beautiful, they are unassimilable. In the subconscious aesthetic of childhood, the "beautiful" and the "cuddly" are diametrical opposites. The cuddly can be assumed or discarded at will; the beautiful imposes itself with the irrational violence of arbitrary fact. "My parents," notes Paustovsky, "thought of nature as an escape, a holiday." But not so for him. His love of it was "passionate and violent"; it was "a necessary condition of life" (*Povest' o zhizni*, 1:364; trans., 2:21). The resistant, unassimilable beauty of *things* is the child's most immediate, most incommunicable experience of the "sacred."

46. Robert T. Allen, *When Toronto Was For Kids* (Toronto, 1961), 91.
47. "The path in front of the veranda was made of large, round, water-worn pebbles from some sea-beach. . . . I *adored* those pebbles. I mean literally, *adored*; worshipped. This passion made me quite sick sometimes." Gwen Raverat, *Period Piece*, 141.

Sacred in their impenetrable barrier of sheer beauty there are, for Alan
Marshall, first and foremost, the birds: their notes, their colors, their movement—"Birds in flight affected me like music" (p. 101). The fairy-wrens, the
grey thrushes, the magpies (not the European squawkers, but one of the most
musical and haunting of all the sounds of the Australian Bush), the parrots,
the kookaburras, the Major Mitchell cockatoos . . . even the common domestic ducks. Marshall's description of ducks entering a pond is as vividly accurate
as Flaubert's description of a parrot walking sideways down the bannister of a
staircase:

> We both enjoyed watching the ducks with lowered breasts enter the water then
> glide out with the tiny wave of the pond slapping and rocking them. In the centre of the
> pond they stretched erect and flapped their wings then sat back in the water with a
> comfortable wiggle of their tails and bodies before searching for the water-creatures
> that inhabited the pond. (*I Can Jump Puddles*, p. 121)

The comparison with Flaubert here, however, is perhaps misleading.
Flaubert comes close to a novel of adolescence in his *Education sentimentale*;
nonetheless, in every page the writing is shot through not only with the
cynicism, but also with the mental viewpoint of the disillusioned adult. Alan
Marshall, by contrast, not only records as a child, but actually adopts the
child's angle of vision. This is a deliberate, contrived, but nevertheless extraordinarily effective stylistic artifice. When writing the book, he used to go out for
walks with his three-year-old granddaughter, keeping his head always exactly
on a level with her own.[48] The result (which has its parallel only in Bely's *Kotik
Letaev*) is that everything changes focus: the tops of the gum trees are higher
than the sky; the pebbles are larger than the rocks; and, while the grass is tall
as a jungle, its roots are even more magical than its summits:

> I began walking in the bush in the evenings so that I could smell the earth and the
> trees. I knelt among the moss and fern and pressed my face against the earth, breathing
> it into me. I dug among the roots of grass with my fingers, feeling an intense interest in
> the texture of the earth I was holding, the feel of it, the fine, hair-like roots it contained.
> It seemed magical to me, and I began to feel that my head was too far above it to
> appreciate to the fullest the grass and wild flowers and ferns and stones along the tracks
> I walked. (p. 101)

Alan Marshall is anything rather than an introspective philosopher—indeed, his buoyant, self-conscious and class-conscious optimism has led to *I
Can Jump Puddles* being made into a film in post-Dubchek Prague. But, by
virtue of his unique angle of vision, he achieves a coherent harmony between

48. Conversation with the author, Melbourne, December 1971.

the Childhood's small world and luminous infinitude—a harmony of incompatibles which, in other writers, is portrayed as a dichotomy. The moment when the private world of minutiae broadens out suddenly into the rhythmic and light-flooded world of limitless space is usually unforgettable, even traumatic, and is translated in the Childhood through recurrent archetypal episodes: the summer holiday; the first snowfall (replacement of detail by contour, of familiar color by the subtly variegated intensities of white); the first long journey; the first view of the sea (the latter, in the case of Pierre Loti for instance, an experience so overwhelming that it takes some four pages to describe[49] and may be said in some degree to have shaped his whole subsequent career). But in all cases, the intrinsic nature of these archetypal experiences is the same: in the instant when the impenetrable world of pebbles and petals is replaced by the even more impenetrable reality of seascape and cloudscape, the child senses another chance to "be-with" all that is not-self, to intuit the mystery of pure existence. Even when Proust has failed to "penetrate" [*approfondir*] the alien reality of the hawthorn blossom, he is himself "invaded" by the inexplicable *Dasein* of the inanimate on the wide-open heath above Martainville with its three wandering church steeples. And not all poets are as obstinately rationalistic as Proust.

Once more it is Kathleen Raine—existentialist, semimystic, woman, poet—who records the magic of the child's vision of the world most clearly, analyzing it in terms which not only carry conviction, but which shed light on all the other writers whom we have been discussing. For her, the talisman, the catalyst, the key to unlock the door in the barrier between self and not-self, was a spray of flowering currant; and so young was she that when she first became aware of it, and of its message, it was hanging over her pram:

> I looked up at the flowers with their minute perfect forms, their secret centres, with the delight of rapt knowledge. They were themselves that knowledge. Not discovery, but recognition; recollection; not as memory brings the past to the present but as something for ever present coming to itself. In the manifold, the innumerable I AM, each flower was its own *I am*. A bush burning green and rose in the light of day. . . . I lived in a world of flowers, minute but inexhaustible. . . . All were mine, whatever I saw was mine in the very act of being. To see was to know, to enter into total relationship with, to participate in the essential being of each *I am*. . . . The forms of nature are what they are, mean what they are, endlessly and for ever. (*Farewell Happy Fields*, pp. 12–13).

"L'*en-soi* est ce qu'il est." It is strange to find Sartre's prickly and abstract definition of the "in-itself" so strikingly apt to summarize what appears, from all our evidence, to be at the core of childhood recollected, the experience

---

49. Pierre Loti, *Le Roman d'un enfant* (1890; reprint, Paris, 1920), 16–19.

which lies at the root of those intimations, if not of immortality, at least of paradise, and to reside at the heart of the problem of description which faces the writer. The *pour-soi*, argues Sartre, *cannot* identify itself absolutely with the *en-soi*—only in "God" are subject and object fused into a single and unique totality: "Then shall I know even as also I am known." Or, apparently, in the child, when, through the agency of some talismanic object, blossom, bird, forest, or luminous infinitude of horizon, the barrier between self and not-self can be broken.

> I can be bounded in a nutshell,
> And yet count myself king of infinite space

—Hamlet's paradox exactly embodies the "magical" extremes of childhood.

4 Portrait of the Artist Surrounded by His Family and Friends

In the life of every child there are encountered certain irreducible facts. There is the fact—for Samuel Beckett, Violette Leduc, and others, the guilt, indeed the *sin*—of having been born. And of having, however regrettably, a mother. Perhaps, and putatively, a father. Of being dependent, ineffective and small:

> Can any very young child know anything of happiness? Does not every infant in the whole world share in a common sorrow—in the misery of having no other means of making itself understood, when it is in distress, than that of an irritating and un-differentiated wailing . . . ?
>
> And if the infant *does* get upset, is it not very likely because there is nothing in the world around it which is the right size for it? All the doors are always too high.[1]

There is the fact of having to rely, complacently or disgustedly, upon the ministrations of others, unchosen and uninvited. Of becoming emotionally attached to some, at least, of these others. Of apprehending the gullibility of aunts and the absurdity of uncles. Of growing up. Of willy-nilly being educated. Of being Awful. Of discovering the world and one's own body: its prowesses, its demands, and its fiascos. Of falling in love or soaring in lust—or vice versa, or both at once. Of dedicating one's existence to the Glory of God or to the Cause of the People . . . and of failing one's first-year examinations. And ultimately of realizing that one's existence has conformed, in the most regrettably tribal, or middle-class, or proletarian, or otherwise average human manner, to a certain number of archetypal patterns.

Necessarily, therefore, in every Childhood there will be encountered certain irreducible archetypes of experience or of situation. There will be

1. Jules Supervielle, *Boire à la source* (Paris, 1951), 22.

139

mothers, teachers, lovers; there will be schools and truancies and rebellions. Many, if not most, of these concern primarily the psychologist or the sociologist. But, from the point of view of the present study, archetypes and archetypal situations begin to assume significance specifically when they reveal something—as likely as not by their peculiar *deviation* from the norm— about the nature of that being who subsequently is destined to develop into a writer. And the first of these "deviations" is this: that the man or woman who, in later life, is destined to use his or her own childhood as the subject of literature, originates, in nine cases out of ten, from a family in which there is a strong element of emotional imbalance.

Indeed, from the wide range of Childhoods that we are considering, there emerges a pattern far too insistent to be attributed merely to chance. There is a father who is harsh, domineering, and tyrannical, or else, far more frequently, one who is dead, absent, weak, or—most characteristically of all—a failure. And there is a mother who is occasionally cruel and vicious, but more usually deeply beloved yet hopelessly inadequate—powerless against the world: subservient, superficial, or superstitious; pious, uneducated, or vulgar; frivolous or futile; and in one or two extreme cases half-witted. And finally there is a more marginal figure—grandfather or grandmother, aunt or cousin or nanny —who is to prove the major influence, for evil or for good, on the child's development. So dominant, seemingly, is this pattern that not infrequently, when a writer alters the facts of his childhood in such a way as to transform autobiography into novel, he alters them precisely in the direction of this archetypal autobiographical norm. George Eliot's father was a competent and successful estate-manager who eventually retired to a large house in Coventry; in *The Mill on the Floss*, Mr. Tulliver, powerful and authoritarian at the outset, is transformed by the end of the novel into a failure, one whose "disgrace" disrupts the whole course of his children's lives. Marcel Proust's father was one of the great nineteenth-century pioneers in the field of public health and quarantine regulations, while his mother was neurotic and demanding. In *A la recherche du temps perdu*, however, the novelist endows his "Marcel" with a mother so deeply beloved that the withholding of a single kiss subsequently colors the whole of his life, yet who is significantly ineffective in any positive sense, and with a father crudely uncomprehending and bitterly resented, who is deliberately robbed of all the achievements of the real-life original.

There could, of course, be a simplified, Freudian explanation: the child whose sensitivity is so highly developed that, in later years, he or she will become a poet may be expected to respond, consciously or subconsciously, to some variant, however muted, of the Oedipus complex. Stendhal was "in love with" his mother (who died when he was two months short of his eighth birthday), and all his life he felt like murdering his father; Beverley Nichols actually did attempt, on three separate but unsuccessful occasions, to murder Mr. Nichols, Senior, without, however, any particular desire, as far as we can deduce, to marry the latter's wife. But, like most Freudian formulae applied to literature, this seems to leave too much unaccounted for, if only because most writers are far too competent in the matter of introspection and self-analysis to overlook anything so obvious. So we are back with the pattern itself and with what might be deduced from it.

Archetypes are awkward. "In the beginning, one loves one's parents. Later, one judges them. Later still—sometimes—one forgives them": so runs the French aphorism. Six-hundred-odd examples of tyrannical or bankrupt fathers and of silly, beloved, and ineffectual mothers might fascinate the statistician, but would be infinitely boring to the student of literature. Orphans, who might have provided a standard against which to measure normally parented children, are sufficiently rare as to constitute uninformative exceptions. Nor even do the orphans, with the notable exception of Jean Genet, furnish the majority of the real *enfants terribles*, the court-case delinquents. Claude Brown (*Manchild in the Promised Land*, New York, 1965), child-thug and hoodlum in the cocaine-plagued wilderness of Harlem in the 1950s, owned both a father and a mother, both of the archetypal variety.

THE FATHER

Je les recherchais (les puissances du père—il est essentiel à l'intelligence de mon récit que vous sachiez que je n'eus pas de père; aussi, je l'ai imaginé multiple).
—Paul Chamberland, *L'Inavouable*

The Father is dead, or has completely vanished: this is the most mythical of all situations encountered among our Childhoods, and the one which perhaps suggests the clue for the interpretation of all the others. For the search for the literally missing father is only the extreme case; beneath all the more everyday accounts of paternal incompetence, bankruptcy, and failure there lies a recurrent nostalgia for the *ideal* father. Women no less than men seem to relive in their reminiscences this quest for an ideal.

Within the domain of reality, there are of course, in addition to the absentees, the brutes. Claire Martin, for instance, refers throughout to her father as a "Tiger." In one memorable episode she recalls her mother asking for housekeeping money just as "the Tiger" was setting out on a journey. The outcome was torment for the entire family. Nonetheless, as he was actually leaving, the mother attempted a reconciliation:

"You aren't going to refuse to shake hands, are you?"

His only reply was to strike at her proffered hand with a back-blow from his own, a blow fully worthy of the strength of which he was so proud. The tiny hand flew up with crushing force against the brick wall behind, and bruises began to show instantly. By evening, it was all swollen, huge and black, a horrible sight, that made one feel sick just to look at it. But Mother never uttered a single word of reproach.[2]

But—outside England and French Canada, which appear to have more than their fair share—the brutes are rare. The dead father, the absent father, the failed father: these are the archetypes, the subtly varied degrees of inadequacy which leave a void to be filled, an ideal somehow to be sought, a kind of quest which, consciously or subconsciously, provides one of the more powerful motivations for recreating the past.

Typically, Maxim Gorky's story begins with the scene of his mother keening over the dead body of his father in the cabin of a Volga River steamer, and all the subsequent events of his childhood stem from this initial loss. In a similar vein, Jean-Baptiste Sartre, a naval officer, died young, leaving his infant son, Jean-Paul, to the care of his widow and *her* father, the ponderous Charles Schweitzer, whose detested image dominates the narrative of *Les Mots*. "The death of Jean-Baptiste was the most influential factor in my life," records Jean-Paul at the very outset of his narrative; "it restored my mother to her chains, and it gave me the gift of liberty."[3] In some impressive passages of self-analysis, Sartre traces the development of his subsequent philosophy back to the sense of liberty that he acquired as a result of being fatherless. Yet if, on the one hand, he sneeringly congratulates his father for having disappeared in good time, accusing him of all the brutalities and oppressions which he *would* have perpetrated had he lived ("There is no such thing as a *good* father; that is the law" p. 11), at the same time the book is filled with resentment at his absence. If he, Jean-Paul, feels himself "inauthentic" and "superfluous," if, from his earliest childhood, he suffered from that profound psychological malaise with which he was later to endow his hero Antoine Roquentin, he attributes this to the total lack of any outside framework of rule and discipline, such as the father normally provides for his son's development. And since there was no given order, in terms of which he might be-what-he-was, he grew up being-for-others, conditioned exclusively by the need to appeal to their arbitrary whims and desires. "One obligation, and one only: to please; everything for outward show" (p. 22).

Beneath its display of somewhat contemptuous acerbity toward the grandparents who brought him up, there is one striking element of honesty and lucidity in *Les Mots*: Sartre's acknowledgment—and it must have been painful

2. Claire Martin, *Dans un gant de fer* (Ottawa, 1965–66), 1:76.

3. Jean-Paul Sartre, *Les Mots* (Paris, 1964), 11.

to make—that the philosophy of total authenticity and total responsibility to which he has given his name is perhaps at bottom no more than the rationalization of his own resentment at *not* being part of an established order. His freedom was not of his own choosing; he would rather not have had it. He would rather have belonged. And whereas, in *The Flies*, Orestes triumphantly assumes a liberty inherent in his very being, Sartre himself, looking back into the past, reveals himself to be closer to Orestes' sister Electra, *afraid* of a freedom which she had never asked for, which was thrust upon her by the irresponsible whim of another creature whom she would never be able to forgive.

A second Childhood which is wholly obsessed with the absence of the father is Fernando Arrabal's *Baal Babylone* (Paris, 1959). Arrabal was not quite four years old when, on 18 July 1936, the Spanish Civil War broke out. The evening before this, however, his father, a painter who belonged to a left-wing group in Melilla, the Spanish-Moroccan town where Arrabal was born, was dragged from his bed by Franquist agents, imprisoned, and eventually killed (or perhaps he committed suicide) some six years later, in January 1942. Obviously he had been betrayed by someone. The boy Fernando never saw him again, and his mother buried him in silence; his name was obliterated from the family records, his face from the family photograph albums. To the mother, *he*, the father, was the traitor: he had "betrayed" his family by indulging in the dangerous game of politics. To Fernando, *she*, the mother, was the traitor: she had "betrayed" his memory, she had robbed the son of his father—perhaps even it was she who had betrayed him in the first place to the police. As the years went by, the father grew for Arrabal into an obsessive myth, and he spent literally years searching for him—to be left only with the pipe he once had smoked.

Although the actual circumstances are entirely different, the intrinsic situation in *Baal Babylone* is similar to that in *Les Mots*: the God-figure, the lawgiver, is absent, and—so the mother maintains—through his own fault. It is Beckett's Hamm blaming God for not existing. And, just as in the case of Sartre it is the absence of the father which lies deep at the root of the subsequent philosophy and ethic, so in Arrabal, the father whom he scarcely remembered, who had "deserved" his own death and might be blamed for it, inspires not only the powerful and pathetic "Letters to His Mother" in *Baal Babylone*, but underlies much of the fury, the sadistic violence, and the beating of wings against the void which form the theme of most of his dramas.

In the light of these extreme cases the more commonplace archetype—that of the weak, failed, or unsatisfactory father—can be seen in its true significance. It would seem that, as the child grows up and begins to view more critically, if not more objectively, the hitherto uncriticized God-figure, this criticism must appear something in the nature of a sacrilege—the breaking of a taboo—unless there is evidence, from the behavior of the father himself, that such criticism is rationally justifiable. In consequence, while some fathers are failures from the outset—and these are usually portrayed with immense understanding and compassion, as is the case with Fredelle Bruser Maynard, or with V. S. Naipaul in his unforgettable delineation of "Mr Biswas"[4]—the majority meet with failure or reveal their weaknesses exactly at the point when the adolescent is ready to pass judgment on them. When in reality the collapse takes place at the wrong age, the result is frequently a modification in the Childhood; for example, Henry Handel Richardson's father died in a mental hospital when she was only eight, so that, in *The Getting of Wisdom*, "Laura" is seen as virtually fatherless, and the unfortunate Walter Lindesay Richardson, an incompetent doctor of Irish origins, receives only one mention in the book. By contrast, a virtually identical mental collapse in the father which occurs when the child is thirteen is commented on by Donald Horne in detail and with considerable harshness:

> For several years I had been resentful of him for his neglect of me; now I understood why he had acted as he did, but it was easy for the habit of resentment still to colour my attitude. . . . I began to cement my compassion over, although the sense of horror was indestructible.[5]

Given the rich and variegated gallery of fathers who, in one way or another, betray their weaknesses exactly at the moment when the child is ready to seize upon them, it is impossible not to see a fairly specific pattern emerging in terms both of human and of literary psychology: the collapsed image of the father, like the total absence of the father, is one of the traumatic shocks of childhood, and one which requires at some stage redress, exorcism, or, at the very least, explanation. The result is one further contributory motivation to the writing of the reminiscences. "O papa! pauvre con!" ("Oh Dad! Poor bugger!" *Journal en Miettes*, p. 205) exclaims Eugène Ionesco in one of his rare moments of compassion for the father who had deserted his mother, driving her to attempt suicide, who had joined the Fascists in Rumania, and who reappears symbolically and consistently in his son's dramas as the Inquisitor, the Dictator, or the Policeman. Moreover, until one starts to explore the literature of the Childhood, it is difficult to conceive in how many different ways it is possible for a father to forfeit his teenage child's esteem, love, or reverence, and in how many ways he can realize his vocation for failure. He can gamble wildly at cards and kiss the maidservants, or he can go further

4. Fredelle Bruser Maynard, *Raisins and Almonds* (Toronto, 1972). V. S. Naipaul, *A House for Mr Biswas* (London, 1961). My assumption that "Mr Biswas" is in essence a portrait of the novelist's father is based on personal communication.

5. Donald Horne, *The Education of Young Donald* (1967; Harmondsworth, 1975), 161.

and actually set up house with one of these desirable damsels, thereby deserting his family, or he can desert his family for no ascertainable reason whatsoever. He can be a bankrupt company-director too well-bred to understand the basic financing of mortgages, or an unemployed joiner caught in the Depression, or a foundryman on short time; he can be a small shopkeeper driven out of business by the chain stores, or a skilled craftsman deprived of his living by modern mass-production techniques. He can be an unsuccessful politician who loses his daughter's dowry, or a successful lumberjack who foolishly thinks that he might do better as a farmer. He can be a chronic liar, or a chronic absentee. He can be wildly eccentric—rebuilding his house by beginning at the bottom without first removing the top; bringing home 120 pairs of Dover soles from Billingsgate fish market "because they were so cheap," or meat in such quantities that it takes two pages to describe, or armfuls of red roses on an evening when there is no food in the house and no money to buy it. He can be obsessed by a passion for bicycles, or for junk, or, less captivatingly, for booze.[6] And again and again and again, he can lead his family into financial chaos, if not from being too trusting, then simply from being overconfident—whether the finances be on the grand scale of Mr. Aldrich's shipping business in New Orleans,[7] or on a smaller but no less disastrous one, as is the case when Mr. Séfrioui drops his handkerchief in the cloth market in Fez, and with it—tied inside it—*all* his capital.[8] In Judah Waten's father, perhaps, we find the archetype of archetypes. Destined by tradition, inclination, and temperament to be a scholar and a rabbi, he descends at length to the status of a Sydney "bottle-oh": "But bottle-dealing was bad, nobody bought bottles and no-one had any to sell. Times were hard."[9] Times were so hard indeed, and Judah's father so incompetent, such "a cripple when it came to the real job," as his mother put it, that, obeying the downward drag of circumstance, he became a horse-dealer, only to discover that

6. These illustrations of the "incompetent father" are taken (in order) from: L. N. Tolstoy (*Childhood, Boyhood and Youth*); Georges Duhamel (*Inventaire de l'abîme*); Saul Bellow (*The Adventures of Augie March*); Helen Forrester (*Twopence to Cross the Mersey*); James Kirkup (*The Only Child*); R. D. Burns (*Early Promise*); Louis-Ferdinand Céline (*Mort à crédit*) and Fredelle Bruser Maynard (*Raisins and Almonds*); Erich Kästner (*Als ich ein kleiner Junge war*) and Alan Marshall (*I Can Jump Puddles*); Colette (*La Maison de Claudine*); Helen Carmichael Dodge (*My Childhood in the Canadian Wilderness*, New York, 1961); D. J. Enright (*The Terrible Shears*); Jean-Pierre Florian (*Mémoires d'un jeune Espagnol*); Benjamin Constant (*Le Cahier rouge*) and Joyce Cary (*A House of Children*); Goethe (*Dichtung und Wahrheit*); Eleanor Farjeon (*A Nursery in the Nineties*); Robert Byrne (*Memories of a Non-Jewish Childhood*); Mary McCarthy (*Memories of a Catholic Girlhood*); Richard Church (*Over the Bridge*); Marcel Pagnol (*La Gloire de mon père*); A. S. Jasper (*A Hoxton Childhood*); and Beverley Nichols (*Father Figure*). The list could be extended almost indefinitely.

7. Thomas Bailey Aldrich, *The Story of a Bad Boy* (1869; reprint, Boston, 1894).

8. Ahmed Séfrioui, *La Boîte à merveilles* (Paris, 1954).

9. Judah Waten, *Alien Son* (Sydney, 1952), 156.

horses were less rewarding even than bottles. And then it was that his son Judah, thirteen years old, began *really* to observe him.

Judah Waten observed his father with at least a modicum of compassion. James Joyce did not. Joyce's ultimate verdict on his father is ruthless in its irony and its bitterness. Mr. Dedalus was, Joyce tells us,

a medical student, an oarsman, a tenor, an amateur actor, a shouting politician, a small landlord, a small investor, a drinker, a good fellow, a story-teller, somebody's secretary, something in a distillery, a tax-gatherer, a bankrupt and at present a praiser of his own past. (*Portrait of the Artist*, p. 241)

Against this, set Judah Waten's final verdict: "Evil fortune followed Father like a faithful hound" (p. 156). Taken together, the two conclusions epitomize the father-figure of the Childhood.

From this summary analysis there emerge quite incidentally two interesting facts. First, the authors of Childhoods who were nurtured in wealthy and cultured families—the Tolstoys and the Sitwells, the Gides and the Prousts, the Pascal Jardins and the Susanna Agnellis—are very much the exception rather than the rule. Even in the nineteenth century, the social average is no higher than a modestly comfortable middle class, or a semi-impoverished nobility. Country lawyers, struggling landowners, retired army officers on half-pay: these are the typical fathers who furnish the nineteenth-century background. And, from the 1880s onward, the average socioeconomic level drops rapidly. Butcher Jouhandeau, Army clerk Anānd, casual laborers Brown and Archer, furniture-remover Jasper, horse-breaker Marshall, Private Avery (deceased), together with a sempiternal leavening of primary-school teachers, shopkeepers, artisans, postmen, and other public employees—these in the twentieth century provide the starting point. Literature, far more than politics, is ruthlessly democratic.

The second fact which emerges is this: within the genre, the innate, Freudian rivalry between son and father is tempered by the fact that, in virtually every case, the father has been outdistanced by the son—or for that matter, by the daughter. The son has become a poet, a writer, whilst the father remained to the end inarticulate. If he lives on at all, it is thanks only to the greater talents of the child that he engendered. And so that child can afford, emotionally, to criticize (or patronize) its father. In those rare cases where the father—a Josef Stalin, a Philip Gosse, a Norman Lindsay, an A. A. Milne, or a Dr. André Proust—was unquestionably a great man in his own right, then the relationship becomes vastly more intricate, and the patronizing tones carry disquieting echoes of jealousy, resentment, or guilt. But, as a general rule, the author of a Childhood is aware, however subconsciously, that he or she has outdistanced the father, and so the portrait tends to remain comparatively simple. Nonetheless (at least in the case of the *son*) the possibility of rivalry was always there; the comparative simplicity of the portrait is the result of rivalry appeased by victory. In the case of the mother, the pattern of relationships is very different. Few writers, male or female, feel obliged to admit that, *as writers*, they have been outdistanced by their mothers (Graham McInnes is perhaps the unique exception); consequently, the satisfying simplifications which result from rivalry appeased are absent, and the figure of the mother assumes far greater complexity.

THE MOTHER

> *My mother wore a yellow dress;*
> *Gently, gently, gentleness.*
>
> —Louis MacNeice, "Autobiography"

When a boy quarrels with, or rebels against, his father, the estrangement appears often to be short-lived, unless it is accompanied by a complete breakdown in communication. By contrast, when a girl, in the process of growing up, comes into collision with her mother, the severing of the relationship is likely to be both acrimonious and enduring. Such, at least, is the evidence of the Childhoods.

That the small child should love its mother and her "adorable obscure miracles" (Duhamel, *Inventaire de l'abîme*, p. 82) calls neither for psychological nor for literary comment—save to note, perhaps, that the intensity of this early relationship is often understated, probably to avoid that almost inevitable lapse into sentimentality to which even the great Tolstoy half-succumbs in the early chapters of *Childhood*. What is remarkable, and what provides some of the most interesting psycholiterary portraits within the genre, is the manner in which the adolescent, as he becomes aware of the potentialities within himself which far outdistance the comprehension of the mother, retains nevertheless a rich affection for her, though at the same time lucidly observing and commenting upon her silliness, vulgarity, or empty-headed inadequacy.

Really vicious mothers are of course uncommon, although perhaps not quite so exceptional as might have been predicted, particularly in French or French-speaking communities. Few children, even in nineteenth-century orphanages, can have experienced the physical or psychological brutalities suffered at the hands of their respective mothers by Juliette Adam, Jean-Jacques Bouchard, Hervé Bazin, Jules Renard, or Jules Vallès. However, without resorting to the type of ferocious brutality described by Vallès or (in fiction) by Anne Hébert,[10] mothers can earn their children's dislike, even hatred, by subtler

---

10. Anne Hébert's epoch-making short story "Le Torrent" (1950), which concerns the revolt of a child against the domineering brutality of the mother, was hailed as a "proclamation" by the younger generation of revolutionaries in Québec Province in 1968. See my essay, "Childhood in the Shadows," in *Comparison*, no. 13 (Spring/Summer 1982), 3–67, especially pp. 15–18.

means. The archetypal mother is gentle to the point of futility, unassertive to the point of characterlessness; she is frequently driven to suicide or attempted suicide by the brutalities of the real world. When, by contrast, the mother is strong-willed, domineering, or aggressive, the relationship with the child appears to suffer. A. S. Jasper is almost unique in the love and admiration he bears toward his "Mum" with her "two arms that were like large legs of mutton" and her habit of suddenly picking up the shovel from the hearth and "clouting [his] father around the face."[11] More typical is the bitter resentment with which Gide reacts to the severe and somewhat unintelligent moral rigidity of his mother; or the way in which Eugene Gant "chokes with fury" at the very thought of Eliza Gant's money-grubbing avarice, her hoarding, her sordid but effective speculation in property, her boardinghouse keeping, "her slow speech, her endless reminiscences, her maddening lip-pursing" (Wolfe, *Look Homeward, Angel*, p. 112). Eliza Gant is the epitome of one type of well-hated mother: the mother whose offense against her poet-son is perhaps, above all, "her lack of magnificence in a magnificent world" (p. 128). Whatever was magical in Thomas Wolfe's childhood, it was clearly *not* his mother.

Many of the subtlest portraits of love-hate relationships between child and mother come from Russian literature, and exhibit a coherence and a continuity, whether of literary or of social tradition, so marked as to deserve a special study of their own.[12] Whatever the characteristics of the archetypal Russian mother may be—and they do not seem to be agreeable—she appears, in her relationships with her child, at least to explore depths of emotion which defend her against the silliness and the intellectual superficiality which so frequently characterize the mother-figure in other cultures. Even André Gide, whose mother sprang from a highly cultivated and well-established Huguenot background, is constantly bemoaning her lack of artistic sensibility: Madame Gide disapproved, for instance, of wild flowers growing on an old wall because they damaged the structure; she refused to take her son to a concert because she considered Chopin "unhealthy"; and her preferences in reading, he observes, ran to "the insipid and the elaborate."[13] But Madame Gide was a veritable paragon of serious moral and intellectual culture compared with the average. The catalogue of shabbiness and silliness is seemingly unending. Eleanor Farjeon's mother, an American née Margaret Jefferson, "hid from thunderstorms, and was one of the few women who really had hysterics at the sight of a mouse."[14] At one moment, she would be imposing a high level of moral rectitude; a moment later, she would be indulging in a display of abject

11. A. S. Jasper, *A Hoxton Childhood* (London, 1969), 25, 33.

12. See my essay "Mother Russia and the Russian Mother," in the *Proceedings of the Leeds Philosophical and Literary Society* 19 (1984), part 6, in press.

13. André Gide, *Si le grain ne meurt*, 64, 148, and 175.

14. Eleanor Farjeon, *A Nursery in the Nineties*, 247.

irrationalism which was "the prey of every superstition." Donald Horne remarks that conversation with his mother involved "hopping from one subject to the next as if we were playing hunt-the-slipper" (*The Education of Young Donald*, p. 35). Robin Eakin recalls that her mother "had never grasped the principle of accounting," and consequently the family was invariably in debt.[15] Going far back into the past, Chateaubriand is unequivocal in his assessment of his mother's character with her "noisy melancholy interrupted by sighs" and her general inability to cope:

> Orderly by nature, her children were brought up in disorder; essentially generous, she contrived to create an appearance of avarice; gentle at heart, she was always scolding: my Father was the terror of the servants, my Mother was the scourge. (*Mémoires d'outre-tombe*, 1:20)

A century and a half later, another American mother, this time of Huguenot extraction and née Maud du Puy, evokes the following comment from Gwen Raverat: "Education, like an unsuccessful vaccination, had not *taken* very well. . . . However, she got on perfectly well without it" (*Period Piece*, p. 17). Dorothy de Celincourt, wife of A. A. Milne and mother of Christopher Robin, was, according to the latter, well to the forefront of his father's mind when he made Rabbit say to Owl: "You and I have brains. The others have fluff" (*The Enchanted Places*, p. 107); and a few pages later he is still more categoric: "From time to time my Father and I used to wonder just what it was Dorothy *had* been taught. . . . Dorothy was *not* brainy" (p. 110). From Ernest Renan to J. R. Ackerley ("My poor, dear, scatterbrained Mother"),[16] from the bored mother of Clara Malraux—who in the end from sheer boredom committed suicide—to the "simple-minded," the "big, gentle, dilapidated, scrubbing and hugging" mother of Saul Bellow, to the chattering, sulky, obtuse, selfish, and shamingly strident mother of Ahmed Séfrioui—the gallery of nitwitted mamas is rich, varied, and of endless fascination. And the vast majority of them contrive to be deeply loved in spite of all.

Feminist critics might argue that the archetypal picture of the mother which emerges from these Childhoods is simply the portrait of a second-class citizen, a reflection of the social and educational disadvantages which have beset women for generations. But there may be a deeper reason behind the characteristic imbalance that haunts the parental background of so many of these writers. The poet—above all the great poet—needs two qualities if he is to succeed: a delicately nurtured sensibility attuned to every aspect of experience, and an iron intellectual self-discipline enabling him to master the intricacies of language, to translate his emotions into literature, and to overcome

15. Robin Eakin, *Aunts up the Cross* (London, 1965), 62.
16. Joe Randolph Ackerley, *My Father and Myself* (1968; Harmondsworth, 1971), 43.

that "sense of anguish that leaps at one from the empty white page." In the obscure field of genetic inheritance, the elements of this imbalance could well prove significant: if weakness and inadequacy are the consequences, as is often the case, of a sensibility ill-adapted to the pedestrian realities of everyday life, then either the incompetent father or the scatterbrained mother may provide that strain of immaterial unworldliness which is as essential to the poet as the discipline inherited from the other side, from the domineering dad, or the selfish, ambitious, vain, and impatient mum.

Occasionally, the very intensity of the mother-child relationship defeats the writer's purpose when he attempts to translate into literature the figure who meant so much to him for so long. He is *too* close, *too* deeply involved; or else, years later, mother and son have drifted apart, and present indifference transforms past emotion into an unreality, whose retelling can only be a mocking anachronism, a falsehood which, in spite of its alluring tragic irony, confounds the poet in his search for a truth about himself uniting past and present. Such is the case, for instance, with Pascal Jardin, in *La Guerre à neuf ans* (Paris, 1971):

> Where has she vanished to, my mother of those far-off days, what has become of her? I would like to talk about her. I can't manage it. When I started on this book, I imagined that my mother would be the very kingpin and pivot of it, that the whole narrative would revolve about her bright-shining presence. Why is it that I am grown silent about her? (p. 99)

The answer is that a "divorce" has taken place; with the passing years, both have turned in upon themselves instead of reaching out toward each other; and yet the memory of the previous relationship still remains too intense, too obsessive to permit objective, impartial judgment.

Pascal Jardin's case is perhaps not wholly atypical; yet few other writers whose mothers play little or no part in their early reminiscences express the dilemma so lucidly. By contrast, however, where objective judgment *does* prove possible, there emerge detailed character studies which are as finely textured and as convoluted as any in the more conventional field of the realist or psychological novel. Violette Leduc, Sergei Aksakov, Hal Porter, Camara Laye, Henry Handel Richardson, Thomas Wolfe—all these and many others have exploited the very difficulty which defeated Pascal Jardin: namely, the necessary fact of starting with an uncritical and purely subjective relationship with their major character, and gradually evolving toward a critical and objective assessment. And the process of evolution itself becomes a significant structural feature of the narrative.

To understand further how the evolution of a relationship can operate as a literary device within the limits of the genre, it may perhaps be rewarding to look more closely at a small group of examples: four quite distinct, yet clearly interrelated "Portraits of My Mother," each drawn from a different culture, each with its own tonality, yet all illustrating the same process at work.

Erich Kästner's *When I Was a Little Boy* (*Als ich ein kleiner Junge war*, 1957) is unusual, although by no means unique, among *serious* reminiscences in that its tone is fundamentally humorous. Yet the portrait of Ida Kästner which emerges through that atmosphere of amused and tolerant whimsicality is as devastating as anything recalled by Hervé Bazin or by Jules Renard. Ida Kästner belonged to the race of strong-willed, domineering mothers forced to compensate for the failings of a weak and unsuccessful husband. To Erich Kästner, she was "great," and the word is used without irony. As her husband's business as a saddler and harness-maker edged toward bankruptcy, she decided to learn a trade of her own:

> And when my mother decided on anything, no one dared to get in her way. No chance and no fate would be so presumptuous. Ida Kästner, who was already thirty-five, decided to take up a trade, and she took it up. Neither she nor fate batted an eyelid. The greatness of a human being does not depend on the size of his or her field of action.[17]

The gently mocking—or self-mocking—tone, so perfectly adapted to this stage of the narrative, continues unchanged. But beneath it, the character of the mother gradually deteriorates, and the relationship with her child begins to alter, so that the gentle mockery eventually appears to the reader as a kind of horrifying and ferocious irony. Her possessive, dictatorial character focuses more and more upon her child; she was determined to become "the perfect mother"; she was staking everything "like a frenzied gambler, on one single card—on me!" Kästner gives a hint or two, no more, of the strain that this single-minded purposefulness imposed upon its victim; and on the surface, at least, the relationship remains unaltered: "I truly loved that perfect mother; I loved her very much indeed." Because of this love, he cannot criticize her directly; *he* remains neutral, detached—it is the others who show us the reverse side of the medal, others who find her "cold, stern, haughty, domineering, intolerant, and egotistical." And because the world finds her utterly unlovable, and makes her feel it, so gradually she loses confidence, and becomes desperate. By the age of forty, she is a grotesque, self-pitying neurotic, "profoundly unhappy," observes Kästner, and constantly on the brink of despair. Not only does she repeatedly threaten or attempt suicide, but she uses these threats and these attempts as a kind of calculated torture to increase her domination over her son: "and when I came home from school, I used to find

---

17. Erich Kästner, *Als ich ein kleiner Junge war* [1957], in *Gesammelte Schriften* (Zurich, n.d.), 6:84.

those hurriedly scribbled notes lying on the kitchen table. 'I can't go on,' they said, or, 'don't look for me,' or 'Goodbye, my dear boy.'"

For just half a page, Kästner drops the veil of half-ironic objectivity, and describes his own anguish and frenzy as he used to scour the city for her, at each of the Elbe bridges expecting to see her body dragged from the river, and finally making his miserable way back to bed in the empty house half-fainting with exhaustion—only to wake up to find her sitting beside him saying cheerfully, "It's all right again now" (6:102–04). Immediately afterwards, the humorous, bantering tone returns. But now, of course, it has a different sense. It is not the tone of the wise man contemplating without bitterness the vanities of the world; it is the voice of the once-terrified child not daring to relive with too much immediacy those unforgotten moments of anguish, and trying desperately to understand—so as to avoid having to condemn—the mother who tortured him, and whom he nevertheless (once) loved. The final picture is of his mother's chronic incompetence as a cyclist, an incompetence deriving from the fact that she never learned to use the back-pedal brake. Here the tone is a neat parody of a Freudian case history:

To the above patient, Frau Ida K., there existed only an uphill course in life in general and cycling in particular. The opposite concept, the downhill course, was utterly foreign to the aims and nature of her inexhaustible ambition, which sought in her promising son a compensation for her own frustrations. Since Ida K. categorically rejected the downhill course and was therefore incapable of considering its consequences, she naturally lacked all understanding of the precautionary measures necessary. (6:143–44)

Kästner's skill lies (through most of the book) in allowing the reader to make his own deductions about Ida Kästner's character and to formulate his own condemnation. *When I Was a Little Boy*, he claims, is a story written *for* children. The style, in fact, is very carefully calculated to work on two levels: for the child to read and enjoy, for the adult to read and understand.

Hard against the picture drawn by Erich Kästner we may set for contrast a very different "Portrait of the Artist's Mother": the portrait painted by Mulk-Rāj Anānd in *Seven Summers* (1951). Again, it is a character study of great significance and complexity; and again (since Anānd is an Indian novelist using the English language), it is a portrait which has to work simultaneously on two levels—for readers with an English and for readers with an Indian cultural background. Its unusual characteristic is that it reverses the normal evolutionary pattern of the child-mother relationship, beginning with criticism, and culminating in admiration and love.

Unlike his father, who was a *babu*—an educated, English-speaking Indian, and a havildar-clerk in the British army administration—his mother was wholly uneducated, brought up in a remote Sikh village, coming from a "world of mud huts built on high plinths with verandas and courtyards" (p. 68), untouched by European civilization or even by any but the most rudimentary forms of Indian culture. Her ingrained ignorance is chronically aggravated, and only in the very end redeemed, by her "stubbornness" and her usually misdirected strength of will. She is absolutely incapable of introspection, judgment, reasoning, or self-criticism. She arranges a positively catastrophic marriage for her elder son Harish, and then blames the dreary, selfish, and unattractive bride for her own lamentable mistake, which ruins Harish's career. "She could not see how she was wrong," observes Anānd. "I also realised when I grew up by what devious and involved arguments she deceived herself into a feeling of righteousness" (pp. 58–59). She is pigheaded, narrow-minded, ill-tempered, prejudiced, and superstitious . . . superstitious above all, avid for all manner of "charms, tricks and magical potions," a predestined victim of priests, fakirs, and charlatans. Pantheistic at all times, in moments of crisis her pantheism explodes into "a kind of unbalanced henotheism." An altar in her room combines elements drawn from every religion—Christian, Hindu, Buddhist, Muslim—with which she has ever had contact, and, turn and turn about, each of these "minor tokens, images, symbols and signs of faith" is exalted temporarily to "the position of the Supreme God" (pp. 159–60).

And yet, as the years pass, it is these very defects which will prove to be her finest qualities. In the period immediately preceding the First World War, as the first murmurings of revolt against British imperialism began to make themselves heard, and as the first groups were formed to work for Indian independence, it was she, not the father, who took the lead. *He* was assimilated into Imperial India, semi-Westernized, his attitude toward the British compounded half of admiration, half of fear. When Bengali seditionists, protesting against the transfer of the capital from Calcutta to Delhi, placed a bomb in the Viceroy's palace; when Pathan tribesmen kidnapped the stationmaster of Rawalpindi and held him for ransom in defiance of the whole British Raj, it was the mother who publicly and fearlessly declared her joy in these enterprises and sowed in her son's mind the seeds of those ideas which, later, were to transform him into one of India's leading political writers. Her "revolutionary ardour" (p. 114) was anything but pure and rational; prejudice, superstition, and ignorance nourished it as they had nourished every other aspect of her life. But now, if only by accident, she was on the side of the angels—of the angels who make history. "What is so terrible about it?" she asks after the latest outrage:

"After all, they deserve what they get, these Angrez log, they have raised their heads to the skies! They have no religion, no shame. Look how they butchered the Sikhs. My father lost half his land because of their injustice when they rewarded the traitors. The eaters of their master." (p. 111)

Anānd's picture of the political situation in India between 1907 and 1914 (the "seven summers") is remarkably well-balanced; but in these particular episodes there is no doubt about the direction of his sympathies. Indeed, again with great skill, he has combined in the figure of the mother both the authentic and detailed realities of his own relationship with her, and a symbol of India itself, with its past in ignorance, poverty, and superstition, and its future in the stars. Narrow-minded she may have been, and "cowering in her submission to ready-made idols"; nonetheless, "I felt I should never love anybody as much as I loved her" (p. 158).

A third portrait of the mother which deserves special comment because of the way it is handled is that drawn by Judah Waten in *Alien Son* (1952).[18] Here again the conventional pattern is reversed: criticism (implied rather than stated) comes at the beginning; understanding, admiration, and love at the end. In fact, far more than in Anānd, the mother is the central figure of the book, but Waten's literary skill lies in concealing this centrality until the last few pages, so that it comes to the reader as a revelation. Immediately all the other events and incidents narrated are seen in a different light and, no longer a mere arbitrary sequence, acquire a pattern of structured significance.

The Waten family was desperately impoverished. They were Russian Jews, the victims of centuries of persecution, who, in the early years of the present century, emigrated to Australia in search of a better and freer life. That they were a long time in finding it was due in part to the Father's (archetypal) incompetence, but mainly to the mother's total negativity. She refused to learn English; she refused all contact with any beings other than similarly placed Russian Jews. She confronted every single aspect of Australian life with a blank and categorical rejection. "Ever since we had come to this country," comments Waten, "she had lived with her bags packed":

> This was no country for us. She saw nothing but sorrow ahead. We should lose everything we possessed: our customs, our traditions; we should be swallowed up in this strange, foreign land. (p. 1)

Knowing, as we do, that her son Judah was destined to become a major Australian poet and writer, we may see the portrait as carefully calculated: the mother is the enemy of the future, desperately trying to drag the child back into the stifling atmosphere of age-old superstitions and miseries, thwarting him by every means in her power. She is untidy, ragged, sulky; she gets a cruel pleasure from deflating the father in front of his own children, and from

18. Judah Waten was born in 1911. In *Alien Son*, he appears to have back-dated his experiences by some six to eight years; hence his description of the book as "a novel."

pouring cold water on his enthusiasms. She has a theory that "soap is good for the eyes" (p. 27), and tortures Judah remorselessly in consequence. She has all the makings of all the devouring, detested mothers of the Childhood.

And then, in the end, Waten fills out the picture. An illiterate Jewish girl in czarist Russia, constantly in hiding from the Black Hundreds, she had finally taught herself to read, and, in reading, had discovered the world of Russian idealism. Fired by this, she had joined a mission working among the victims of the cholera epidemic, and this had been the greatest, the most joyous episode of her whole life. When the missions were disbanded in the aftermath of the 1905 Revolution, she had returned to her old life, but now fired with the passionate ideals of Russian liberalism—the idealism of Tolstoy and of the *Narodniks*, the idealism which had driven Chekhov to work among the convicts of Sakhalin Island, the idealism which, a century earlier, had fired the wives of the Decembrists. Her rejection of Australia, of the new life and the new potential happiness, then, was not mere negativity, but the rejection of a land which was closed to idealism: the rejection of a culture possibly more materialistic than any other on earth. As in Anānd, the authentic mother merges into a symbol—a symbol of protest against the impenetrable granite bedrock of philistinism which, until the 1950s, was so characteristic of the Australian way of life, and which every significant Australian writer, artist, or intellectual has struggled to break through. The mother, in fact, serves to reveal the very purpose for which *Alien Son* was written.

A final mother-figure—again in an Australian setting, but in a totally different cultural context—is the portrait of Angela Thirkell painted by her son Graham McInnes in *The Road to Gundagai* (1965), one of the finest pieces of literary portraiture in the genre. Angela Thirkell was not only one of the supreme examples of the strong-willed, dominating mother, but also the representative of a great cultural tradition: her father was the famous classical scholar, J. W. Mackail, her grandfather was the painter Burne-Jones, and her more distant relatives included Rudyard Kipling and Stanley Baldwin; and her own portrait was painted by John Sargent. And she herself, of course, was a highly successful novelist; in fact, part of the narrative of *The Road to Gundagai* tells of her first determination to write, mainly to compensate for the loss of income suffered by the amiable but (archetypally) incompetent George Thirkell during the Depression.

Here again, the fascination and skill of the portrait lies in the various levels on which it works—in this case, three rather than two. There is the first, the "public" level. Angela Thirkell was a well-known personality in her own right, and no future biographer of hers could hope for a richer vein of information about her private life than that provided by *The Road to Gundagai*. Second, there is the "intimate" level—the authentic, emotional relationship between child and mother, particularly when that mother was, to put it mildly, eccentric, and when her own renown surpassed, and perhaps still surpasses, that of her sons. That relationship was anything but easy. For instance, having the nine-year-old Graham (and his brother Miles) at home for two whole months during the summer holidays was more than Angela could bear. In consequence, she composed "the famous document (in black type for work and in red type for play) and thumb-tacked it to the back of our bedroom door." The "document" began as follows:

7.30	Get up.
7.30– 8.00	Prepare breakfast.
8.00– 8.30	Eat breakfast.
8.30– 9.30	Wash up breakfast things, make beds, sweep and dust own room.
9.30–10.00	Play.
10.00–11.00	Do any shopping errands that may be required and bring goods home.
11.00–12.00	Study.
12.00–12.30	Play (or help Dad in garden).
12.30– 1.15	Lunch.
1.15– 1.45	Wash up lunch things.
1.45– 3.00	Rest QUIETLY [etc., etc.] (p. 90)

Even at the age of nine, Graham McInnes was at once fascinated and repelled by Angela; and it is this simultaneous reaction of fascination and repulsion which constitutes the third level—again symbolic, since the love-hate relationship with the mother, a relationship contemplated later with amused irony, embodies an identical love-hate relationship with Australia as a whole. On the one hand, the unbelievably repulsive ugliness of Australian suburbia; on the other, the equally unbelievable beauty of the Australian Bush. McInnes is too competent a writer to make labored comparisons; but the parallelism of ambiguous emotion is there for the reader to detect, and in fact constitutes the essential inner structure of the book.

If considerable space has been devoted to this study of the mother-figure, it is because it is the most difficult of all the recurrent archetypes of the genre to handle successfully in literary form. On the one hand, there is the temptation toward sentimentality; on the other, the danger of uninteresting obviousness. There is the problem of a constantly evolving relationship, at its most intense when it is unformulated, weakened by the very fact of becoming formulable; and there is the problem of reconciling the critical judgment of the adult with the uncritical emotion of the child. Finally, there is the virtual impossibility of objectivity, in a genre whose chief justification lies in attempting to tell a "total truth." The four mothers we have considered are, each in her own way, "strong" mothers, and therefore not wholly typical. But when the mother becomes a major character in the book, it is almost invariably because she has some element of strength, even when this is concealed. The more characteristic "weak" mother, however well-beloved, is usually—in literary terms—little more than a shadow in the background.

One other, minor, point emerges from this aspect of our study, and that is that the child, however complex, or passionate, or sexual it may be in its relations to the father, or mother, or both, has nothing but the most simplistic awareness of the relationship existing between its parents. Or rather, to all intents and purposes, there *is* no relationship between them, save that of living in the same house. Clara Malraux is virtually unique in noting that she "supposed" that her mother and father loved each other; but she only deduces this from the fact that they seemed to quarrel rather less than the parents of all her other schoolfriends (*Apprendre à vivre*, p. 30). A positive sexual relationship between its parents appears to be almost literally inconceivable to the child, or even to the adolescent. "Despite my own hunger, I recoiled at the thought of Mum and Dad having intercourse," recalls Robert Byrne in his *Memories of a Non-Jewish Childhood* (1970); "It was so undignified, and they were so respectable" (p. 53). The adolescent, in fact, would seem to be incapable of making any link between his or her own obsessive quest for sexual experience, and the parents' own fulfillment. Indeed the very idea of such a relationship (which necessarily exists, or at least existed, since the child itself resulted from it) seems to be the only remaining notion still capable of shocking the twentieth-century teenager. Eugene Gant is repelled even at the age of five when he sees his father "putting his arm stiffly" round his mother's waist:

Shame gathered in him in tangled clots, aching in his throat; he twisted his neck about convulsively, smiling desperately as he did later when he saw poor buffoons or mawkish scenes in the theatre. And he was never after able to see them touch each other without the same inchoate and choking humiliation. (Wolfe, *Look Homeward, Angel*, p. 53)

This, admittedly, is a matter for psychological rather than for literary investigation; but it is notable that the six-hundred-odd texts which form the substance of this study admit of not one exception.

THE OUTER CIRCLE

For we are his sisters and his cousins and his aunts . . .
                                                                    —W. S. Gilbert, *H. M. S. Pinafore*

Given the fact that the poets of childhood seem so frequently to spring from families in which one or the other of the parents is in some way unsatisfactory, it is not surprising that, repeatedly, we find that the major influence on the child's development—above all, in his development as an artist—was a figure outside the immediate nucleus of the family: a grandmother or grandfather, aunt or uncle (in one exceptional case, that of Ernest Renan, a sister); a revered schoolteacher or headmaster, or some still more marginal figure. And all of these contribute to the rich tapestry of archetypal figures which populate the literary recreation of childhood.

Grandmothers and grandfathers, of course, furnish some of the most memorable characters in the genre: Maxim Gorky's grandmother Kashirina; Stendhal's grandfather Gagnon; Jean-Paul Sartre's grandfather Charles Schweitzer; Violette Leduc's grandmother Fidéline. . . . There are, inevitably, a few detestable grandmothers—Sergei Aksakov has one, and Mary McCarthy's great-aunt Margaret Myers fulfills the same role—but they are rare. More characteristically, Drieu la Rochelle refers to his grandmother's influence on him as being "quasi-divine," for it was she who made him adventurous, who developed his appetite for danger and difficulty—who made him, in fact, a writer (*Etat civil*, pp. 50–51). Margaret Mead, in *Blackberry Winter*, is categoric in her assertion that her grandmother was "the most decisive influence in my life,"[19] while for Molly Weir, in *Shoes Were for Sunday* (1973), it is the grandmother who furnishes the central structural pivot of the whole book. Often indeed it is the death of the grandmother or grandfather which marks the conclusion of the childhood, and consequently the completion of the literary form.

Apart from natural affection, there would appear to be three reasons why the writer *as a writer* should be fascinated by the figure of one or more grandparents. First, there is the fact that, by the operation of the laws of nature, the life of the grandparent rarely extends far into the adult life of the grandchild. In consequence, there is seldom occasion for that disillusionment which often takes place in relation to the parents. As opposed to the relationship with the father, and more especially with the mother, which, as we have seen, involves plotting the graph of continually changing and frequently deteriorating emotional reactions, the relationship with the grandparent is static, and can be conceived of as a totality, thus providing a point of rest, against which the unceasing movement of the remainder of the Childhood can be *measured*. Moreover, because of the correspondence in time between the known life of the grandparent and the duration of the writer's life as a child, there is normally a closer relationship between the two than is the case with any other relative: to write about the grandparent is indirectly to write about the self-as-a-child; and in fact the act of recalling the grandparent often serves as a catalyst in recalling other facts about the self. In the effort to recreate the vision of the world which the writer possessed as a child, the grandparent-figure is invaluable, since it usually incarnates that vision uniquely, to the total

19. Margaret Mead, *Blackberry Winter* (London and Sydney, 1973), 45. *Blackberry Winter* is a "straight" autobiography, rather than a Childhood; nonetheless, its comments on the childhood experience (as one would expect from an anthropologist) are of considerable interest.

exclusion of the later self. The use which Marcel Proust makes of "ma grand'mère" is a perfect illustration of this process.

Proust also furnishes a good example of the second reason for the importance of the grandparent in the writer's work of recreating the past: namely, that "Granny" or "Grandad" is frequently the first and most immediate link with a time preceding his own birth. Children rarely gain a genuine sense of past time before adolescence and, because of the emotional intricacies of the relationship, this sense is even more seldom acquired from their own parents. But the grandparent is at one and the same time a subject of clear perception to the child and the visible incarnation of a past unmistakably more distant than that embodied in its own parents. It is a *living* past, actually surviving into the present and hence an essential part of that child's experience. The contrast between past and present may take the form of dress, or manners, or speech; it may be the subject of deference, or mockery, or moralizing; but it is always there. James Thurber's grandfather is splendidly comic in that he still lives in the days of the American Civil War and, like Sterne's Uncle Toby or Thomas Aldrich's Grandfather Nutter, enriches a prosaic present with the vanished glamour of a rumbustious military adventurousness.[20] Valerie Avery's grandmother represents a past of cleanliness and eau-de-cologne, which contrasts every day more sharply with the dust and disorder of blitz-ruined London.[21] And, in all periods of war, revolution, and social upheaval, we find the grandparent incarnating the "good life" as it was lived before the cataclysm.

The third reason for the significance of the grandparent is in fact consequent on the first two—the comparative stability of the figure remembered, and its contrast with everydayness. Because of these two factors, the grandparent forms the perfect subject for the literary portrait, from delicate vignette to full-length study.[22] And if the survival of past into present reveals itself as a touch of eccentricity, so much the better. However, this quality of providing material for portraits or caricatures is not a property exclusive to grandparents; it belongs even more emphatically to uncles and aunts.

In exploring the particular importance accorded to uncles and aunts in the Childhood genre, it is worth considering Claude Lévi-Strauss's chapter on "Language and Kinship" in his celebrated study *Structural Anthropology*. Lévi-Strauss is dealing basically with primitive societies, whereas our children who are also writers-to-be are by definition comparatively sophisticated; consequently, the arguments of the anthropologist are no more than partially applicable. Nonetheless, there is perhaps enough of the inherited primitive in

---

20. Thomas Bailey Aldrich, *The Story of a Bad Boy*, 41–42. See also James Thurber, *My Life and Hard Times:* "The Night the Ghost got in" and "The Day the Dam broke."

21. Valerie Avery, *London Morning* (London, 1964), especially pp. 18–19.

22. Two good examples of the full-length study can be found in Louis Guilloux, *Le Pain des rêves* (1942) and in Marguerite Yourcenar, *Souvenirs pieux* (1974).

every child to make what Lévi-Strauss termed "the problem of the avunculate" worth referring to. "Language and Kinship" deals primarily with the anthropological status of the *maternal* uncle, and with the distinction between the child's attitude toward this personage in patrilinear, as opposed to matrilinear societies:

> In groups where familiarity characterizes the relationship between father and son [i.e., in matriarchal societies] the relationship between maternal uncle and nephew is one of respect; and where the father stands as the austere representative of family authority, it is the uncle who is treated with familiarity.[23]

Lévi-Strauss then proceeds to subject this analysis (a classic anthropological "structure") to a number of criticisms; but these hardly concern us here. Most of the sophisticated, Europe-oriented societies of the twentieth century, with the half-exception of Indian and perhaps Jewish family groups, are categorically patrilinear, in practice if not by tradition; and so what seems to have happened is that the characteristically primitive relationship of "familiarity" (or even of tolerant contempt) between the boy-child and his mother's brother has been extended and generalized, so as to become that of all children for all aunts and uncles from whatever side of the family. There are occasional "rogue" specimens, such as D. J. Enright's "Uncle Jack"—

> He was the bad-tempered uncle,
> His smoke-stained cottage the ogre's castle
> > (*The Terrible Shears*, p. 18)

—but they are uncommon. Aunts more typically are despotic, especially where, as not infrequently happens, they take over the child's early upbringing from a busy working mother.[24] But, on the whole, the relationship is more than tolerant on both sides. The "avunculate" is the bringer of gifts, whose gifts are *not* feared.

The poets, however, do not have to rely on the anthropologists to explain to them the inner workings of their own minds and sensibilities. André Gide, for instance, is perfectly well aware of the debt he owes to his "adopted Aunt," his mother's erstwhile paid companion, later her closest friend, the Scotswoman Anna Shackleton, who appears not only in *Si le grain ne meurt*, but also in *La Porte étroite*. For him, the "charm" and the significance of Anna is quite clear: she provided for him an engulfing warmth of affection which allowed him to develop more freely than ever he could with his parents, precisely because it was an affection from which the strains and responsibilities of the parental

23. Claude Lévi-Strauss, *Anthropologie structurale* (Paris, 1958), 1:47–52.
24. For example, "Aunt Mary" in Jon and Rumer Godden, *Two under the Indian Sun* (London, 1966).

relationship were absent, an emotional relationship imbued with all the love he was capable of feeling for his mother, but less intense and, above all, less complex. (*Si le grain ne meurt* especially page 32). Surprisingly, however, it is the Moroccan writer, Mouloud Féraoun, in his memorable little book, *Le Fils du pauvre* (1954), who gives an alternative, and even more lucid explanation. Féraoun was on the whole happy with his parents, in spite of his family's extreme poverty and his status as an "enfant colonisé"; but, parallel with this "principal" family, he developed a "secondary" one in the household of two of his aunts, the gentle Nana, and the brusque, exuberant, and unrestrained Khalti. Nana was the artist, the weaver and pot-maker; Khalti the story-teller, the grown-up companion to the six-year-old boy—and the tragic crisis of his childhood was upon him when Nana died in childbirth and Khalti subsequently went crazy with grief.

Mouloud Féraoun's analysis of the psychological background to this division of affections is illuminating, and is borne out again and again from the evidence of other Childhoods:

> As a general rule, the child sets no great store by the love of his parents. It is something he takes for granted, he doesn't even bestow a thought upon it, and, when they spoil him, he just gets bored. What he really covets is the affection of outsiders: he makes advances, tries to secure friends; the ungrateful wretch wants to give his little heart; he is quite ready to betray his mother, to prefer another man to his father, provided only that he can find somebody reliable.[25]

The vital qualification here is "provided only he can find somebody reliable." It is the *trustworthiness* of the aunts or grandmothers, nannies or family retainers, which constitutes their essential quality, at all events in the eyes of the still-young child; but, given this, it is the fact that their affection and interest need to be conquered by his own efforts, that these cannot simply be taken for granted, which represents their supreme attraction, and hence contributes to their ultimate influence.

Without aunts and uncles, the genre might well be rather less fascinating than it is. Not infrequently, their presence is so pervasive that they spill over into the title: Rodolphe Töpffer's *La Bibliothèque de mon oncle*, for instance, or Robin Eakin's *Aunts up the Cross*, or Cecil Beaton's *My Bolivian Aunt*. Their ubiquity, and the significance of their role, both lie in their dual relationship, first to the child, then to the writer. Unlike the parents and, to a lesser degree, the grandparents, there is not usually a powerful emotional bond between child and uncle or child and aunt. They are sufficiently distant to be perceived and remembered objectively, often from a very early age; and yet, since they are frequently in close contact with the family, their presence comes to be

25. Mouloud Féraoun, *Le Fils du pauvre* (Paris, 1954), 74–75.

stamped indelibly on the child's mind. For the adult writer, on the other hand, for the poet who is necessarily concerned with the inner laws of the form he is using, and who must therefore treat the arbitrary with extreme care, the value of aunts and uncles is that they are not contingent: they are an integral and necessary part of the child's central experience, which is that of the family; and therefore they can be lovingly portrayed in all their glorious eccentricity without fear of irrelevance. In brief, they are sufficiently distant to be contemplated with detachment, and sufficiently close to be intrinsically meaningful.

And of course, if by some lucky chance the aunt or uncle concerned happens to be a well-known personality in his or her own right, the portrait can only be the richer for it. Gwen Raverat's Aunt Etty is memorable in any case with her hypochondria—

When there were colds about, she often wore a kind of gas-mask of her own invention. It was an ordinary kitchen strainer stuffed with antiseptic cotton-wool, and tied on like a snout, with elastic over her ears. (*Period Piece*, p. 123)

—and with her extreme skill in the art of hunting stinkhorns. But the effect is all the more dramatic when one realizes that "Aunt Etty" was in reality Henrietta, eldest daughter of Charles Darwin, and that in the stinkhorn-hunting there are distant echoes of *The Origin of Species*. This, however, is only an additional luxury. Ordinary aunts and uncles get by happily without the need of such extra boosts to bring out the full flavor of their oddity: think of Aunts Glegg, Pullett, and Deane in *The Mill on the Floss*, or Aunts Lilla, Mina, Netta, and Anys ("These my Father gleefully referred to as Litter, Titter, Fritter and Anus") in *Aunts up the Cross*. Michel Leiris's Uncle Léon, for instance, son of a senior police official and destined for a career in the *haute bourgeoisie*, flings everything to the four winds and becomes a circus acrobat, fascinating young Michel as he practices in his bedroom (*L'Âge d'homme*, pp. 83–86). V. S. Naipaul's Uncle Bhakcu is a "mechanical genius," who spends his entire life inventing gadgets which don't work.[26] William Saroyan's Uncle Melik, "just about the worst farmer who ever lived," buys up six hundred and eighty acres of cactus-filled desert at the foot of the Sierra Nevada mountains because they look pretty, plants them with pomegranate trees because he likes pomegranates, and is faintly pained and puzzled because they do not grow.[27] Lucky is the child whose uncle is an explorer, with a lifelong habit of turning up unannounced laden with rare, exotic, and wholly impractical gifts: a gibbon, or a twelve-foot palm-tree in a pot, to be housed in some small Paris or Odessa apartment. Francis Jammes had one such, Uncle Ernest, explorer of Mexico (*De l'âge divin à l'âge ingrat*, pp. 46–47). Konstantin

26. V. S. Naipaul, *Miguel Street* (1959; Harmondsworth, 1971), 114–27.
27. William Saroyan, *My Name Is Aram* (1940; reprint, London, 1971), 53–76.

Paustovsky had another, Uncle Yusia, who had been all over Africa, Asia, and Europe, who had fought as a volunteer in the Boer army, and who became a revolutionary in 1905, not out of any ideological conviction, but because he could not stand reading in the papers about the insurgents' incompetence in the handling of their guns:

> He had little understanding of politics . . . but, as an old artilleryman, he had found it unendurable to hear of the wretched marksmanship of the mutineers, and . . . had joined them and taken over command of the battery. (*Povest' o zhizni*, 1:61–62; trans., 1:52)

In the outermost orbit of the family circle are the cousins and even more remotely connected relatives; but these are hardly to be distinguished from strangers, and are valuable for literary portraiture only on the same level as "characters" or eccentrics of other varieties whose oddities in retrospect impress the child and provide incidental material for entertaining the reader. André Gide did eventually marry his Cousin Emmanuèle Rondeaux, and in fact *Si le grain ne meurt* ends on the announcement of his engagement; but this is a unique and exceptional role in cousinhood. Far more typical are William Saroyan's Cousin Dikkan or Cousin Mourad (*My Name Is Aram*, pp. 17–31) or Dylan Thomas's Cousin Gwilym, preaching to an imaginary congregation in a barn:

> I sat on the hay and stared at Gwilym preaching, and heard his voice rise and crack and sink to a whisper and break into singing and Welsh and ring triumphantly and be mild and meek.[28]

These are no more than a source of anecdotal material. Only one other precisely archetypal role falls to the cousin, and that is as the man (or woman) of the world, more experienced, more adept and more richly endowed than the child-self, and therefore apprehended with a mixture of fear and adulation. It is the cousin, with money to jingle in his pocket and a mistress to flaunt in delicious secrecy, who frequently embodies the adolescent's dream of what he himself will be in a few years' time, as soon as he can grow up.

Outside the blood-related family circle there are of course other archetypal figures: the nurse or nannie, the handyman, the holy fool or harmless lunatic, the elderly naturalist (a frequent nineteenth-century grandfather-substitute);[29] and then the tutors, governesses, village schoolmistresses—all manner of teachers, competent and incompetent, tolerant or sadistic, feared, revered, or despised. Among all these, however, there are only two that seem to call for special comment: the friendly servant and (in the wake of uncles,

---

28. Dylan Thomas, *Portrait of the Artist as a Young Dog* (1940; reprint, London, 1956), 13.
29. See, among others, André Gide, Edmund Gosse, Pierre Loti, Charles Nodier, and Konstantin Paustovsky.

aunts, and cousins) the memorable eccentric. It may seem strange—recalling Tolstoy's Natalya Savishna, or Chateaubriand's La Villeneuve, or Christopher Robin's immortal "Nannie"—to omit the nurse-figure from this discussion of significant archetypes; but in fact, either she is lost in the mists and myths of early infancy, or else she merges so completely with the mother-figure that there is nothing to say that has not been said already; or finally, she represents a very special case relating to a particular culture (the English nannie) and must be considered separately.[30] Perhaps the really significant feature of the child/nurse relationship is that it is not static: it follows a pattern of evolution similar to that of the child/mother relationship, but speeded up, condensing perhaps thirty years of changing emotional dependencies and judgments into four or five, and consequently bequeathing to the adult an emotional legacy of disarray, uncertainty, and guilt. Frequently, the writer expresses in terms of the nurse what he cannot or dare not express, or even formulate, in relation to the mother: the sense of bewilderment resulting from a totality of affection freely given, then totally discarded, and perhaps, in the first instance, misplaced and undeserved. The nurse recalled forces the adult writer to contemplate the total emotional irresponsibility of his former self.

Indeed, the nurse and the friendly servant play opposite roles in the development of the child's social consciousness. The Nurse is discovered at some point to be, not a mother but a servant, insignificant in the all-important eyes of the parents, preeminently dismissable; and this discovery is often a profound shock. Chateaubriand, with the inbred social self-confidence of the eighteenth-century aristocrat, can (almost) take it in his stride: "My childish affection for la Villeneuve was rapidly obliterated by another, *a worthier friendship*" (*Mémoires d'outre-tombe*, 1:20; my italics)—this time an enduring one, for his sister Lucile; but even so, his description of the death of la Villeneuve reveals an uneasy conscience (1:103). Drieu la Rochelle is much more outspoken; for him, his nurse was primarily "a woman of the people," and for that there is no redemption:

> Part of each of my days I lived deep-immersed in the populace, among the common people who for so many centuries had gone in fear and trembling, in the company of women of the common people who still live in a state of fear; and so all that time I lived a double life . . . , now in middle or upper class society, now in the proximity of social classes infinitely remote from my own. (*Etat civil*, pp. 25–26)

The difference between the nurse and the friendly servant is that the nurse is imposed; the friendship of the servant, like that of the uncle or cousin, is selected and has to be merited. It is an act of freedom. Moreover, the servant is

---

30. See my essay "Education and the English," in the *Proceedings of the Leeds Philosophical and Literary Society* 19 (1984), part 6, in press.

known from the outset to be a servant, only subsequently discovered to be a friend, whereas the nurse is an illusion: apprehended as a mother, she turns out to be a servant. In other words, while relations with the nurse involve the child in its earliest intimations of social inequalities, injustices, and disillusionments, the friendly servant invites a first awareness of human equality: the man waiting to be discovered beneath the chauffeur's uniform, beneath the lackey's livery, beneath "the long white achkan and pleated turban" of Azad Ali, the Bengali butler of Jon and Rumer Godden's childhood at Narayangunj (*Two under the Indian Sun*, p. 38). After the early death of his mother, the most tragic moment in Stendhal's childhood came when his friend, "the best friend I had," a valet of his grandfather's named Lambert, fell off a ladder while picking fruit from a pear tree and, three days later, died. "I knew suffering for the first time in my life," he recalls. "I thought upon death" (*Vie de Henry Brulard*, 20:215–16). His reaction to his mother's death had been that only of a child; by contrast—

> The grief that came upon me at Lambert's death was grief as I have known it all the rest of my life, a grief that knew itself to be grief, arid, tearless and inconsolable. (20:218)

The death of Lambert was the first step toward Stendhal's maturity.

There is one further point that Stendhal makes in this analysis of his relationship with Lambert, which is that, for the child, the discovery of equality works in two directions at once: not only does the servant reveal his common humanity with the son of his employer; but he is also unique in the child's world of parents, parsons, and teachers in that he alone does not give orders and expect to be obeyed. In his humanity, he is the equal of the child; but the child is equal to him in that both share a common state of subservience. "He had the great advantage," wrote Stendhal elsewhere, "of *not* being my superior. In his company alone I tasted the sweetness of equality and of freedom" (20:179). In a very different society, Sergei Aksakov discovered that same elating sense of equality and liberty in the company of his serf Yevseitch;[31] and the situation is in fact so archetypal that it takes all the self-torturing, masochistic perversity of Jean-Paul Sartre to reverse it:

> I treat inferiors as equals: this is a white lie which I enact for their benefit, and which it is right and proper that they should swallow, up to a certain point. My nursemaid, the postman, my pet bitch—I address them all in the same tones redolent of patience and moderation. (*Les Mots*, p. 23)

Yet again, the question arises: is this the authentic portrait of the child Jean-

---

31. Sergei Aksakov, *Detskiye gody Bagrova-vnuka*, 1:347.

Paul? In view of all our other evidence, it would seem difficult to believe in such precociously cynical sophistication.

Finally, in this procession of childhood archetypes, come the eccentrics: characters who have nothing to do with the family, but who are just . . . eccentric. Considered as elements of the material available to the writer, they are invaluable; in fact, many of the more loosely structured, anecdotic childhoods (such as Fred Archer's *The Distant Scene* [1967] or Gerald Durrell's *My Family and Other Animals* [1956]) consist of little more than a succession of human oddities, portrayed with humor, tolerance, and a pervasive sense of wonder at a world which can contain so many improbable variants of normal behavior. Sometimes there is a situation which seems to invite them—as in nineteenth-century Vancouver Island:

> Strange characters came to little Victoria. It seemed as if people who could not fit in anywhere else arrived here sooner or later until Victoria poked, bulged and hollowed over queer shapes of strange people, as a snake, swallowing its food whole, looks lumpy during digestion.[32]

Sometimes they just happen, unexplained and inexplicable.

Even in the most carefully structured and least humoristically intentioned forms, moreover, they occur with extraordinary frequency. In *Dichtung und Wahrheit*, Goethe gives us a whole array of miscellaneous eccentric misanthropists: von Reineck, for instance, who spends his life damning the human race because somebody once ran away with his daughter, and who quarrels irremediably with von Malapert because the latter *dared* brush with his finger one of von Reineck's prize pinks.[33] Edmund Gosse's almost despairingly serious *Father and Son* contains more than one portrait of Plymouth brothers and sisters—Mr. Dormant, for instance, or the Pagets, or Susan Flood, the shoemaker's daughter who, after a somewhat noisy conversion "with sobs, gasps and gurglings," had run amok in the sculpture gallery of the Crystal Palace, where "her sense of decency had been so grievously affronted, that she had smashed the naked figures with the handle of her parasol" (pp. 177–78)—portraits which, in a more frivolous context, might readily have been labeled as caricatures. Eugène Ionesco's *Journal en miettes*, a book which is fragmentary, but whose high seriousness of purpose is never in doubt, has its père Baptiste and its père Grude (pp. 11–12); while W. H. Hudson's *Far Away and Long Ago* has its Captain Scott the hunter and Mr. Trigg the tutor (pp. 11–13). And so on, and so on. . . .

Two writers whose Childhoods are rich in eccentrics offer tentative expla-

32. Emily Carr, *The Book of Small* (Toronto, 1942), 181.
33. Goethe, *Dichtung und Wahrheit*, in *Goethes Werke*, ed. Truntz and Blumenthal (Hamburg, 1955), 9:160–61.

nations for the frequency of their occurrence and suggestions as to their significance. The first of these, Francis Jammes, offers one of the best-stocked galleries of freaks and oddments in the whole of our literature of childhood; the second, Henry Handel Richardson, is particularly interesting in that she is the earliest writer to exemplify what appears to be a particularly Australian talent for developing a vignette of eccentricity into a full-scale portrait.

In *De l'âge divin à l'âge ingrat*, Jammes offers a unique collection, including the portraits of a rich miser who, in order to save wear and tear on his trousers, used to drop them to his ankles before sitting down; of right-thinking family who were so terrified that their daughter's maidenly modesty might be corrupted by her reading that they solemnly cut out every announcement of a marriage or a birth from each newspaper before she was permitted to look at it; of an inconsolable widower who, in memory of his dear departed, had on display in his sitting room various pots of jam labeled "Very Last Preserves made by My Well-Beloved Victoire" (pp. 171–72, 205–06). Jammes is himself intrigued by the manner in which his remembered childhood appears to be peopled so thickly with fantasticks. He proffers two explanations, which are at once illuminating and puzzling, because it is not quite clear whether they complement or contradict one another. In the first, he claims it is because he is a poet; in the second, because he is a scientist. His sister Marguerite, he comments in the first volume of his *Mémoires*, observed the same phenomena as he did himself, but was unimpressed and immediately forgot what she had seen because her mind and sensibility were not those of the poet:

> I have often noticed that what is so special about the poet is that he will retain for all time a deep impression from something which will produce nothing more than the lightest of evanescent touches upon others. . . . Where others will allow a gesture, a word, a fact to glide past them and vanish, I will hold fast to it. (*De l'âge divin à l'âge ingrat*, p. 53)

There is possibly some truth in this; but it surely requires a very special *kind* of poetic sensibility to retain precisely the more grotesque and idiosyncratic manifestations of human behavior, rather than the sublime, the impressive, or the universal. Jammes's alternative explanation is more convincing: as a naturalist, as a typical nineteenth-century collector of "specimens"—like Goethe, like Gide, indeed like Philip Gosse—his instinct, fashioned by the capturing and labeling of rare lepidoptera, quite automatically applies the same technique to the rarer and more wondrous specimens of humanity, and "pins" them into his collection.[34]

For Henry Handel Richardson, however, there is a simpler explanation. The eccentrics who caught her attention during childhood caught it for good

---

34. Francis Jammes, *L'Amour, les muses et la chasse*, 36.

and all. They caught it because they, much more than the "normal" inhabitants of Maldon, Victoria, where she lived, were fascinating and inexplicable. To explain them, she was forced to try and fathom the secret workings of the human mind; the exercise developed her and, out of this development, the novelist, in due course, was born. The bank official who wore gloves; the baker's intended; the man whose father fought against Napoleon—these were seeds which, in that arid and mindless community somewhere between Castlemaine and Bendigo, "helped to nourish the imagination of the future story-writer."[35]

Archetypal encounters, as we suggested at the beginning of this chapter, are chancy material on which to base an argument, not only because they tend to obviousness and thus, unless reduced to the form of statistical tabulation, are liable to make rather dull reading, but more pertinently, because it is not clear whether they are equally valid for all children, or only for those rather exceptional children who will later grow up to be poets and autobiographers. Our evidence is largely literary; and therefore there is a strong element of preselection from the outset. On the other hand it is worth noting that studies using very different methods and sampling far more representative groups of children suggest no prima facie contradiction.[36] Thus there may well be a significant correlation between the experience of the exceptional and that of the average child.

However, until this is demonstrated, it is as well to keep the possible distinction in mind. And if this is true of the *people* who populate these reconstructed worlds of the child-self, it is even more true of the events and incidents which fill them. The "portrait of the artist surrounded by his family and friends" may well have a degree of general relevance, since families are families everywhere; by contrast, the second chapter in this analysis of archetypes, which explores the artist's childhood activities and inner preoccupations, could well prove to be of less general applicability, since their import lies primarily in their relation to the future creator and manipulator of words, images, and ideas.

35. Henry Handel Richardson, *Myself When Young*, 46.

36. See, for instance: Edith Cobb, *The Ecology of Imagination in Childhood* (1977); Liam Hudson, *Contrary Imaginations: A Psychological Study of the English Schoolboy* (1966); Herbert Kohl, *Thirty-Six Children* (1967); Michael Paffard, *Inglorious Wordsworths: A Study of Some Transcendental Experiences in Childhood and Adolescence* (1973).

5 Portrait of the Artist Accompanied by Allegorical Figures

Over and above the archetypal *personages* of childhood revisited, there are also necessarily the archetypal *experiences*: the experiences of fear and anger and boredom; of holidays, journeys, and festivities; of the joys and miseries of learning; and of the discoveries of language and time. Among these, however, there are five experiences which predominate: all "discoveries," each one of which adds a new dimension to the self—the discovery of evil; the discovery of sex and, often wholly unrelated to it, that of love; the discovery of theater; and finally the discovery of death.

Of these, the most ubiquitous is the first: the discovery of the delights and torments of being *bad*. The poet who subsequently recalls his own childhood in the form of literature was once, by definition, a *mauvais sujet*, a "Little Horror," an *enfant terrible*; he had lived, however provisionally, in the shadow of the Disobedient Angel.

LUCIFER

> *Of man's first disobedience, and the fruit*
> *Of that forbidden tree whose mortal taste*
> *Brought death into the world, and all our woe . . .*
> —John Milton, *Paradise Lost*

"It has always seemed to me," wrote Joyce Cary in *Charley Is My Darling*, "that every child is by nature a delinquent, that the only difference between us as children was the extent of our delinquency, whether we were found out or not

169

and how we were punished for it."[1] Some writers, such as St. Augustine or Paul Chamberland,[2] attribute this to the fact that the grace and knowledge of God are withheld from the unformed infant reason; others, to the observation that, in the child, the id is imperfectly controlled by the ego; others again, to the corrupting pressures of society and to the child's instinctive delight in imitating the vices, rather than the virtues, of its elders. In the context of our literary reminiscences, however, there are two further and more obviously convincing explanations: first, the fact that truancies and misdemeanors, days of disobedience or moments of diabolically inspired sadism, stand out far more sharply in the memory than months or years of docility and obedience; and second, the inescapable truth that these same truancies and wickednesses provide far more interesting material for the reader than any account of gentle devotion to duty. The little girl sitting primly in her spotless starched dress learning her lessons is far less easy to write about than this same little girl driven to such a point of fury by the tedium of a fitting session that she seizes between her teeth the pink cotton frock that was being tried on, and bites it all to pieces. "Another time," recalls Gwen Raverat, "I fairly liquidated a hat" (*Period Piece*, pp. 254–55). And if this is the case with girls, it is even more emphatically so with boys. The title which the American Thomas Bailey Aldrich gave to his Childhood, *The Story of a Bad Boy*, might in fact be applied as subtitle to virtually every book we are considering, with the exception of certain recent examples, such as Georges Perec's *W ou le souvenir d'enfance* (1975), Joy Kogawa's *Obasan* (1981), or Melinda McCracken's *Memories are Made of This* (1975), in which both the tonality and the narrative technique have been modified, either by the objectivized noneventfulness of the *nouveau roman*, or else by the dispassionate approach of the sociologist. But otherwise "badness" is inherent in the genre, from the prodigal son structure which is typical of many early specimens—Antoine de la Sale's *Petit-Jehan de Saintré*, for instance, or Tristan l'Hermite's *Page disgracié*, or Benjamin Constant's *Le Cahier rouge*—to the complex "confessions" of Jean Genet in *Miracle de la rose*, Albert Spaggiari in *Journal d'une truffe*, or Claude Brown in *Manchild in the Promised Land*. In effect, the only wholly "good" children whom we encounter are those who are so impossibly, unshakably, immeasurably good that their very goodness becomes intolerable. "I never cry, I am scarcely alive, I make no noise," observes Jean-Paul Sartre of his four-year-old self; but in that sentence he epitomizes his complete rejection of the calm and right-thinking bourgeoisie to which he once belonged, indicting as a positive evil a society whose noiseless conformism was its major defect. Simone de Beauvoir, in her

1. Joyce Cary, *Charley Is My Darling* (1940; reprint, London, 1959), 5.
2. Paul Chamberland, *L'Inavouable* (Montréal, 1967), 42–43.

Mémoires d'une jeune fille rangée (1958), uses her own early docility to point a similar accusation.

If, as is in fact the case with Sartre or with Simone de Beauvoir, "goodness" in the child-self is condemned and rejected out of hand as evidence of an imposed conformism, it is logically to be expected that the converse will also be maintained: namely, that "badness" is to be taken as the first sign of that independence of mind and spirit which is destined to grow and flourish as the child develops, until eventually he or she becomes that most independent and antisocial of all creatures, the poet. This is, in fact, the explanation most frequently encountered. Balzac, recalling his truancies at the Collège de Vendôme, heads the list of his own and his companions' misdeeds and punishments with the significant words, "Our independence . . . ," which alone suffice to provide ultimate moral justification for all that follows.[3] His contemporary, Stendhal, goes further, giving in effect thanks to destiny for having surrounded him in his earlier years with harshness and injustice. The only words he ever writes in praise of his hated Aunt Séraphie are to the effect that she alone prevented him from becoming a conformist, and thus helped him to retain his independence. Treated justly, reasonably, he argues, such was his character that potentially he could have been molded into any shape desired. "I shudder at the thought of it," he concludes. "If Séraphie had possessed the intelligence and the politeness of her brother, she could have made a Jesuit out of me."[4] And to make the point more clearly, he ends this section of *Henry Brulard* with the description of his wild (and wildly expressed) delight when, at the age of eleven, he learned that two Jesuit priests had been guillotined in his home city of Grenoble (20:242–43).

Stendhal probably *was* an appalling child, much more so than most Stendhalian scholars have been prepared to recognize; and it is not surprising that his habit of picking up revolutionary slogans (much as the modern child picks up TV ads)—*liberté, egalité*, and so forth—and of applying them directly to his own family situation irritated his elders. Moreover, in the years 1794 and 1795, his membership of the "Bataillons de l'Espérance" was not merely irritating, but actively dangerous; and the reactions of his aunt and father to this adherence (20:187) can without distortion be compared in more modern times to the reactions of an anti-Nazi family whose twelve-year-old son became a fanatical member of the *Hitlerjugend*. This would seem to be "independence" with a vengeance.

In fact, however, from Rousseau onward, we find interspersed among

3. Honoré de Balzac, *Louis Lambert* (1832, rev. 1835; Paris, 1968), 60ff.

4. Stendhal, *Vie de Henry Brulard* [written 1835–36], in *Œuvres complètes*, 20:210; see also 20:231 and 21:3–4.

these standard justifications of infant or adolescent awfulness a scattering of others which are both more subtle and more elaborate. If we can trace the source of this new complexity back to Rousseau, it is because Rousseau, in working out his philosophy of childhood, runs headlong into a contradiction which he is unable properly to resolve.

The child for Rousseau, as we know, was "naturally" good—the key word used in the description of his own character up to the age of six or seven is *doux* [= both "gentle" and "docile"]. In such a child, therefore, there cannot be true badness: such "sins" of which it may be guilty are either manifestations of intense activity in mind and body, which may, admittedly, be uncongenial to others (such as Dylan Thomas's habit of riding on the roof of a lorry and aiming apple cores at women on the pavement; *Portrait of the Artist As a Young Dog*, p. 52), but which are, in themselves, perfectly "normal" and "natural"; or else too trivial to merit being classed as "sins" at all—as when Jean-Jacques pees in Mlle Clot's cauldron of soup which she had left simmering on the stove while she went out to church.[5] In the child, then, there is no evil; all evil comes from outside, the product and emanation of an unjustly or irrationally constituted society. Yet at the same time Rousseau argues not only that the "Confession" which he is writing is the absolutely faithful portrait of his "true" and "natural" self, but that its vital interest lies in the fact that it is also a portrait of the "natural" self of any living man—and that this natural self includes *as something intrinsic to it* the shameful, immoral, and antisocial actions to which he is confessing. And as if this contradiction were not already sufficiently baffling, there is the added factor that Rousseau is constantly referring to the "evil" which he had committed, while using a kind of pre-Freudian technique of psychological autoanalysis, in which all moral concepts and categories are totally irrelevant.

Among Rousseau's successors in this analysis of the complexities of motivation in the *enfant terrible*, the most outstanding is Tolstoy. In some ways, indeed, it could be said that this analysis constitutes the central theme of the second volume of his trilogy, the volume entitled *Boyhood*. In the major series of episodes (chapters 11–17), after an introductory scene in which Nikolai deliberately smashes all his brother Volodya's collection of china ornaments,[6] Tolstoy accumulates into "one unfortunate day" a whole series of equally deliberate "evil" actions—Nikolai refuses to learn his lessons; he steals the key of his father's private dispatch case (in which, incidentally, the latter keeps his love-letters from his mistress) and opens it, breaking the key in the process; he

5. Jean-Jacques Rousseau, *Confessions* [1764–70], ed. Michel Launay (Paris, 1968), 1:48.

6. L. N. Tolstoy, *Otrochestvo* [1854], in *Sobraniye Sochineniy*, ed. S. P. Bychkov (Moscow, 1951–53), 1:117; trans. Aylmer Maude, *Childhood, Boyhood and Youth* (1930; reprint, Oxford, 1947), 149.

purposely tears his governess's dress on two separate occasions; he insults his tutor; and finally, dissolving in a welter of tears and tantrums, having been locked up for the night in the lumber room, he proceeds carefully to analyze his motivation.

The outcome of the analysis is a curious mixture of self-castigation, rationalism, and irrationalism; or rather, it is a rationalistic analysis of the irrationality of the child-mind, which, insofar as the narrative is autobiographical, carries overtones of self-castigation. What Tolstoy concludes is that the child-self is neither good nor evil as a *state*, but, while being as a general rule rational and therefore "good," it is subject at times literally to "possession" by a force belonging to the domain of not-self, to invasion by a wholly irrational and inexplicable upsurge of destructive emotions which, in the most absolute and uncompromising sense, can only be termed "evil." At the root of this complex of emotion one feeling predominates, the feeling of *hatred*—the hatred that takes possession of Nikolai, suddenly and without warning, in relation to his tutor Saint-Jérôme:

> Yes, this was a feeling of real hatred . . . , the hatred that inspires you with irresistible aversion for a person who yet deserves your respect, and which causes his hair, his neck, his gait, the sound of his voice, all his limbs and movements to seem repulsive to you, while at the same time some incomprehensible power draws you to him and compels you to follow his slightest action with restless attention. (*Otrochestvo*, 1:149; trans., p. 187)

At bottom, in other words, the irrational behavior of the *enfant terrible* is due to the uninvited presence of an emotion indistinguishable, in all but one of its manifestations, from the emotion of love; it is the negative aspect of love, generating the same obsessions and the same fantasies, the same profound awareness of life and death and God (Nikolai attributes his first religious doubts to that "unfortunate day" and to the subsequent night spent in the lumber room); and, because of this affinity, Tolstoy, with relentless logic, begins to consider whether love itself, or at least passionate, unreasoning, physical love, may not likewise at heart be evil. In the *enfant terrible* lie the seeds of that destruction which, in the end, will annihilate Anna Karenina.

Tolstoy's analysis of this upsurge of "pure evil" which occasionally "takes possession" of the child is very much confirmed by the surprisingly large number of reminiscences which describe acts of quite conscious and deliberate sadism, often committed when the child-self was comparatively young, and almost invariably followed by a violent and lasting reaction. Drieu la Rochelle at length and with a still-vibrant passion of self-disgust tells how he once tortured and finally killed a hen (*Etat civil*, pp. 65–68); Georges Duhamel, how, under similar circumstances, he annihilated a whole colony of tree frogs (*Inventaire de l'abîme*, p. 152). Clara Malraux deliberately and lucidly destroyed all the roses in the garden, and later, at the age of eight, created as her companions an imaginary troupe of dwarves especially so that she might whip and flagellate them (*Apprendre à vivre*, pp. 11, 52–53). Jean-Paul Sartre's juvenile attempts at fiction included a scene in which he pricked out the eyes of a heroine called Daisy, "and I stabbed them just as I would have pulled the wings off a fly" (*Les Mots*, p. 122). Julien Green's very earliest memories are of his delight in causing terror, both in himself and in others;[7] and we have already referred to Marcel Pagnol's ecstasy at the sight of ants devouring a mantis from the inside (*La Gloire de mon père*, pp. 182–88). Robert André, at the age of five, exults in the murder of a rabbit;[8] Jules Renard, scarcely older, revels in the torturing of a mole.[9] All these, it should be noted, are solitary acts of sadism; they are quite different in nature from the situation when a *gang* of boys tortures a cat. Perhaps the most explicit of all these scenes is that described by John Raynor when, at the age of five, he frightened a hen—another hen-victim—to death:

> For a few terrible seconds I tasted, as never before or since, the hateful thrill of complete power. It was orgasmic, and relaxed my limbs in melting, fluid waves of satisfaction and release, I felt weak with delicious fulfillment. I, all alone; *I* had done this; had actually made a chicken die of fright! What excitement! What power!
>
> And then the glow faded; I grew cold and shivered. I began to realise that I had done the unspeakable, the unforgivable. . . . This was beyond tears; it would never be forgiven, not by the grown-ups, but by God and myself. (*A Westminster Childhood*, p. 65)

Here, the link with the Tolstoyan interpretation is even clearer; the irrational onset of sadistic violence is the infantile equivalent of a sexual orgasm, followed by the classic reaction: "Post coitum omne animal triste." It is because of the intensity of the postorgasmic reaction that such episodes remain supremely significant. Jammes maintained until the end of his life a refusal to kill any living creature; Drieu notes that, from the instant of the death of the hen, he could never bring himself again to touch a bird without blanching. So again, in Tolstoyan terms, the rational disorder of the universe may be merely a reflection of its suprarational order. "How ruthless and hard and vile *and right* the young are!"[10]

It is noticeable that many French poets—characteristically, Francis Jammes, whose attitude toward the problem is summed up in the two adjectives "divine" and "ungrateful" which, between them, pinpoint the difference between his earlier and later childhood"[11]—tend to attribute the onset of

---

7. Julian [*sic*] Green, *Memories of Happy Days* (New York, 1942; reprint, London, 1944), 4.

8. Robert André, *L'Enfant miroir* (Paris, 1978), 115–19.

9. Jules Renard, *Poil de carotte* [1894], in *Œuvres*, ed. Léon Guichard (Paris, 1970) 1:675–76.

10. Hal Porter, *The Watcher on the Cast-Iron Balcony*, 88.

11. Francis Jammes, *De l'âge divin à l'âge ingrat* (Paris, 1921). *Ingrat* has additional meanings beside "ungrateful": e.g., "crude," "uncouth," "unprofitable," etc.

serious antisocial activities in themselves as children or adolescents to the loss of that infinitely precious solitude which is suffered when the home is exchanged for the school. The child—and particularly the only child who is the future poet—in his family is docile and contemplative. It is the change of environment which brings about a transformation in mentality; the "I" gives place reluctantly to the "we," and the individual is replaced by the member of the gang. For Jammes, as for Pierre Loti, Raymond Queneau, Drieu la Rochelle, and innumerable others,[12] the school/adolescence period, with all its rebellions and its torments, appears, not as a true and integral part of the development of the self toward maturity, but rather as a violent and unforgivable interruption: the adolescent self is not the real self at all, but is experienced in retrospect as the self (again) "possessed" by some alien spirit.

From the age of twelve to the age of fifteen, I went through a stage of being sulky, foul-mouthed, sneering and rebellious. We were one and all infected by the bug of subversiveness. We despised and we hated the older generation. We were unseeing and we were violent. We thought of nothing but creating a riot. (Drieu la Rochelle, *Etat Civil*, pp. 131–32)

The *enfant terrible* who takes over at this stage and under these circumstances is the enemy, not only of society, but of the poet's own essential reality; and the true self can evade this enemy only by retreating completely into the subconscious, reemerging some five or seven years later, when school and adolescence both are ended and the long-delayed passage into adulthood can be completed.

In total contrast to this is the portrait of the *enfant terrible* as hero—as a kind of Robin Hood adventurer, bold, reckless, in love with danger, the leader of his fellows in their crusade against the obtuse world of adults, a ringleader who, in the course of time maturing and strengthening his character, emerges at last as a true leader of men. Such is Tom Brown, in Thomas Hughes' ever-popular *Tom Brown's Schooldays* (1858), or the other Tom, the Tom Aldrich of *The Story of a Bad Boy* (1869); such are the heroes of *Stalky & Co.* (1899), or of Jules Renard's *Poil de carotte* (1894), or of countless fictions or semifictions, ranging from *Tom Sawyer* and *Huckleberry Finn* to the many-volumed adventures of Richmal Crompton's irrepressible, red-headed *William*. In part, this idealized image of the self as heroically disobedient and disrespectful was (in its earlier versions at least) a straightforward reaction against the sentimentalized portrayal of the child in which the Victorians indulged: Frederic William Farrer's "Eric," from *Eric, or Little by Little* (1858), or Charles Dickens's "Little Nell," from *The Old Curiosity Shop* (1841), or the comtesse de

12. See my essay "Education and the English," in the *Proceedings of the Leeds Philosophical and Literary Society* 19 (1984), part 6 in press.

Ségur's "Torchonnet," from *L'Auberge de l'Ange Gardien* (1863).[13] Aldrich, in particular, was conscious of this motivation and, in later editions of the *Bad Boy*, quoted in his preface an extract from a review which appeared in the *Atlantic Monthly* in January 1870, showing that the reviewer had taken the point: "No-one else seems to have thought of telling the story of a boy's life with so great a desire to show what a boy's life is, and with so little purpose of teaching what it should be."[14] But the point was not so difficult to take; Aldrich himself makes it emphatically enough in his opening passage:

> I call my story the story of a bad boy, partly to distinguish myself from those faultless young gentlemen who generally figure in narratives of this kind and partly because I really was *not* a cherub. . . . I did not want to be an angel and with the angels stand. . . . In short, I was a real human boy. (pp. 1–2)

The distinguishing feature of the earlier examples, at least, among this collection of *enfants terribles*, is that it was the *realism* of the character study which was essential; whatever ideological message the book may have carried (and many indeed *are* the conscious purveyors of a message), the didactic purpose was nonetheless always subordinate to the desire to portray a truth in a field from which contemporary writing in the nineteenth century seemed determined to exclude it. In an oblique way, it was the swing of the pendulum: the revenge of St. Augustine against Jean-Jacques Rousseau. Psychological observation was to kill off the myth of the "Little Angel" as surely as anthropological observation was to kill off the myth of the Noble Savage. And one of the weapons used to exterminate the former was humor. A truth can be told in many ways, and humor is one of them. The specific aim of the "bad boy" subspecies of the Childhood was—and still is—to deflate the more solemn pomposities of other contemporary writings about children and about child psychology.

The rebellious idealism of adolescence is a phenomenon so universal and so universally recognized as to make comment superfluous. Virtually all our Childhoods show the poet passing through a stage, either of revolt or of idealism, or more usually of both combined: sometimes directed against a structure of ethical imperatives, sometimes against a social, political, or religious order, sometimes just simply against parents or family. With Jules Vallès, the target is the entire French educational system; with Maxim Gorky, it is the "vile abominations" of social and economic injustice in czarist Russia; with Jean Genet, it is the bourgeoisie in all its ramifications; with Tolstoy, fired

---

13. See Peter Coveney, *The Image of Childhood* (Harmondsworth, 1967), in particular Chapter 7, "Reduction to Absurdity," for further instances of nineteenth-century sentimentalism in the portrayal of childhood.

14. Thomas B. Aldrich, *The Story of a Bad Boy* (Boston, 1894), Preface, p. vii. The review concerned was by William Dean Howells, himself later the author of a Childhood.

as he was by "an ecstatic adoration of the ideal of virtue," the target was no less than the entire fabric of the moral universe:

> At that time it seemed very possible to improve all men, to destroy all the vices and miseries of mankind, and it seemed very easy and simple to improve oneself, to assimilate all the virtues, and to be happy. (*Otrochestvo*, 1:174; trans., p 219)

Among these innumerable rebellions of adolescence, perhaps the only truly interesting one, from our point of view, is the rebellion against the family, in that it has both changed direction and deepened in intensity since the beginning of the present century. In the earlier Childhoods, the unsatisfactory parent or family was simply ignored, or at worst, quietly abandoned. Stendhal, whose loathing for his father was so profound and all-pervasive, nonetheless made no serious attempt to analyze the reasons for it, either in himself, or in M. Beyle, Senior; he was content with repetitive vituperation. Juliette Adam waits until the very last page of *Le Roman de mon enfance et de ma jeunesse* before she hazards a guess at the motivation behind her mother's sadistic ill-treatment of her as a child, and even then she combines this rather superficial analysis with a dutiful, if unconvincing, expression of forgiveness. But, in the period between 1890 and 1914, there comes a change. The relationship between child and parents comes more and more to be analyzed as a phenomenon in its own right; and where the child rebels, it is ever more likely to be against the relationship itself, and all that it stands for, rather than against particular grievances. The reasons for this change are many and complex: the "liberation" of the 1890s, with its conscious rejection of Victorian pomposity, solemnity, and authoritarianism; the growing democratization of Western societies; the Freudian insistence on the importance of the experiences of early infancy in determining the later character of the adult; the weakening of the Fifth Commandment, "Thou shalt honour thy Father and thy Mother . . . ," a shift in attitude reaching its noisy climax in the slogan of the 1968 student revolts in France—"Papa pue!"

But there are also significant literary influences at work. The impact of Ibsen's *Ghosts*, with its message that parents are *not* to be honored save where that honor is due, went deeper than is perhaps usually suspected, particularly in Protestant communities, where family bonds often reflected more the force of religious injunction than the instinctive clan-ship and overriding blood-loyalties of Latin Catholicism. But three other writers, André Gide in France, together with Edmund Gosse and Samuel Butler in England, all achieved immense popularity among the young on account of their passionate rebellion against the institution of the family as such—and particularly against the very notion of parental authority.

The importance of these works is that they served to crystallize and to rationalize for adolescents the feelings of rebellion against the very concept of the family as a sacrosanct social institution which were certainly present already, but diffuse and unformulated. The novelty of the approach, and its potential revolutionary power, can be gauged from the fact that *Ghosts*, which was written in 1881, was banned in England until 1914; and that Samuel Butler was so daunted by his own extremist audacity in writing *The Way of All Flesh* that he would not allow its publication until after his death.

The paradoxical feature of this antiparental revolt of the twentieth century (which is also strongly reflected in writers such as Beckett, Ionesco, Arrabal, Genet, and other modern dramatists) is that it corresponds in time with a new and more enlightened attitude on the part of parents toward their children. The Victorian parent, by and large, did not attempt to "understand" its young. Obedience and dutiful affection were all that was demanded. The twentieth-century parent, standing (thanks to the virtual disappearance of servants, nannies, tutors, governesses, and other intermediaries) much closer to its children, and influenced by innumerable books, articles, and television programs telling "How to Raise a Brighter [or Healthier, or Happier, or More Integrated] Child," frequently makes efforts to penetrate the mind and sympathize with the reactions of its offspring, efforts which would have appeared to be a ludicrous waste of time to previous generations. Arthur Calder-Marshall grasps the paradox as clearly as anyone. "In retrospect I feel sorry for all parents whose children grew up during the twenties," he writes:

> The curious thing was that the generation which felt the brunt of this infantile attack was the first generation to try earnestly if not always successfully to understand their children. [But] violence grows on what it feeds on. The greater the efforts that parents made to understand their children, the more difficult the children became to understand.[15]

This is probably even more relevant in the 1980s than in 1951 when it was written; as is also Arthur Calder-Marshall's conclusion: "There is little enough that can be done with adolescents whose real grievance is that they are not yet as old as they would like to be."

By and large, from the evidence of our Childhoods, the idealistic rebelliousness of the adolescent against the habits and conventions of the preceding generation has remained a constant from the earliest times. But no generation of adolescents before the 1890s would seem actually to have "rebelled" against the fact that they could not become adult earlier than nature had decreed. Or (and perhaps this lies at the heart of the problem), is the decree exclusively that of nature, or is nature aided and abetted by the rigid,

---

15. Arthur Calder-Marshall, *The Magic of my Youth* (London, 1951), 38–40. For a general survey of adolescent rebelliousness in the context of autobiography, see Patricia Spacks, *The Adolescent Idea: Myths of Youth and the Adolescent Imagination* (New York, 1981).

anti-individualist structure of state-controlled, compulsory education? In contrast to the young of the present age, it would seem that adolescents of the seventeenth, eighteenth, and even the nineteenth century enjoyed a now-vanished freedom to be exactly as old as they wanted to be.

PRIAPUS, EROS, CUPID, AND OTHERS

Whatever sex was, it was another enemy.
—D. J. Enright, *The Terrible Shears*

The savage, primitive, sadistic undercurrents of immaturity that are so vividly portrayed in William Golding's novel *Lord of the Flies* would seem to be an essentially modern feature of the Childhood. Admittedly, Stendhal's earliest recollection is that of biting his cousin, Madame Pison du Galland, hard in the cheek instead of kissing her, as was expected of him (*Vie de Henry Brulard*, 20:35); but there are no moral or metaphysical overtones to accompany the telling of this episode. Nonetheless, and without necessarily drawing any Tolstoyan conclusions, it is impossible to separate those two other archetypal experiences, the discovery of sex and the discovery of love, from the overall self-portrait of the artist as an *enfant terrible.*

In all the literary delineations of the self as a child which we are considering, there is an evident tension between reality and myth. Because of the openly proclaimed autobiographical element, the direct contribution of reality is perhaps higher than in most other literary forms; on the other hand, myth clearly exerts a primary influence on certain ways in which the self is restructured in its literary context. The prodigal son pattern of seventeenth- and eighteenth-century Childhoods, the Robin Hood picture of the nineteenth-century *enfant terrible*, the passage through hell of many modern reminiscences—these are evidently, in a broad sense, myths, in that they reflect the ideas and the ideals relating to childhood which were current when they were conceived. But when we discover a theme which remains virtually unchanged over the centuries, independently of culture, fashion, or literary history, then the probability is that, inasmuch as the literary formulation of a truth can ever correspond absolutely to the truth of experience, we are confronted, not with a myth, but with a reality.

One such reality is this: for the child, the initial discovery of sex is an experience so overwhelming that it can scarcely be expressed, save in terms intrinsically foreign to itself—whether of introspective guilt, religious confession, romanticized euphemism, quasi-naturalistic "objectivity," humoristic self-deprecation, or aggressive pornography. The sexual experience constitutes, quite specifically, a "sixth sense," for which no directly related conceptual language exists. Whether the writer realizes it or not, therefore, the description of this experience constitutes a major literary problem. When Marcel, in *A la recherche du temps perdu*, relegates to one line of a Proustian paragraph the fact that, at Balbec, in the prime of his virile adolescence, he had "fourteen girls in one summer" (2:789) we may be virtually certain that here, at least, Marcel is a fictional rather than an autobiographical character. In authentic reminiscence, early sexual experience, however banal or unrewarding, is never so anodyne. From St. Augustine confessing publicly to God the circumstance in which he had used church as the place, and divine service the time, for his more audacious sexual experiments, to Philip Roth's Alexander Portnoy "squirting his seed into the empty wrapper from a Mounds bar," the evidence is that the early discovery of sexuality is not merely obsessive, but seems to *demand* some kind of confession or expiation. The only question is, to whom? "I lived in a world of matted handkerchiefs and crumpled Kleenex and stained pyjamas," continues Alexander Portnoy (confession this time *not* to God . . . or is it?):

> I moved my raw and swollen penis, perpetually in dread that my loathsomeness would be discovered by someone stealing upon me just as I was in the frenzy of dropping my load. Nevertheless I was wholly incapable of keeping my paws from my dong once it started the climb up my belly. In the middle of a class, I would raise my hand to be excused, rush down the corridor to the lavatory, and with ten or fifteen savage strokes, beat off standing up into a urinal. (*Portnoy's Complaint*, p. 19)

For St. Augustine, this is "madness"; for Alexander Portnoy, it is a neurotic obsession, demanding the services of a psychoanalyst: the same thing, in the long run. In either case—in all cases—the discovery of sex is, once again, a direct experience of that world of "magic," of irrational sensation beyond the bounds of normal logic or facticity, which, at all levels and in all ages, characterizes the literary world of the Childhood.

The problem, for the writer even more acutely than for the average member of the human race, is that the adolescent's discovery of sex embodies an insoluble contradiction: it is, in the fullest sense, one of the "magical" experiences of childhood; yet it is one which neither society nor language is prepared to recognize as such.[16] Hence every description almost necessarily falls wide of the mark. What *does* emerge, however, from this study of our poets, is that the final achievement of sexual maturity involves not one, but at least four stages of self-discovery, each one of which is, in all essentials, quite distinct and

16. Western society, over the last twenty years, has considerably relaxed its grip; but the "new" language of sex remains almost as wide of the mark as the older euphemisms and reticence. From our evidence, the current cult of four letter words, by confining the early experience of sex to its crudest and least "magical" level, seems likely, in the long run, to prove more, rather than less, inhibiting to the future poet in his quest to discover a language with which to convey the incommunicable.

independent. Moreover, they do not necessarily follow each other in the same order. There is the physical discovery of the self as a sexual identity, usually through masturbation. There is the discovery of the *possibility* of sexual contact with another human being. There is the first realization of that contact. And there is the first experience of "falling in love." All four are, or can be, equally traumatic.

Setting aside for the moment the experience—the most acceptable in traditional literary terms—of "falling in love" for the first time, it is interesting to see how our poets handle the other three stages—and worth noting at the outset that there would appear to be no essential difference between men and women. Simone de Beauvoir, Violette Leduc, Kathleen Raine, Gwen Raverat, Henry Handel Richardson, Monique Wittig (the last the most aggressive of lesbians), to name but the frankest and the most outstanding, all, in their basic approach to their analysis of erotic experience, follow paths which, in the last resort, are indistinguishable from those of their male counterparts. And the most striking feature of these paths is their wildly erratic unpredictability.

Whether, with the wider introduction of sexual education in schools, the situation is now different, it is too early to say; but, for the overwhelming majority of the children in our study, brought up for the most part in an atmosphere in which any discussion of sex with either parents or teachers was unthinkable, the reaction to the first stirrings of sensuality was not so much one of confusion—although this was bad enough—as of a failure to make any connection whatsoever between sexual experience, "love," and parenthood. The confusion more often than not betrays itself, in girls as well as in boys, by the primitive and meaningless shouting of obscenities, usually in a gang; for somehow the uttering of forbidden words acts as a kind of fetishistic ritual to propitiate the dark gods:

> My friends and I were fascinated by the taboo words for the organs and acts of sex. We used them all the time, and even shouted them. . . . Shouting things we normally had to whisper had an exhilarating effect on us, and we always ended up laughing giddily and feeling oddly purged. (Byrne, *Memories of a Non-Jewish Childhood*, p. 88)

Sometimes drawing takes the place of verbal incantation. Dylan Thomas and his companions drew "naked girls inaccurately," of which some "were detailed strangely, while others tailed off like mermaids" (*Portrait of the Artist As a Young Dog*, p. 41). Eugene Gant and his friend Otto "amused each other by drawing obscenities in their geographies, bestowing on the representations of tropical natives sagging breasts and huge organs" (Wolfe, *Look Homeward, Angel*, p. 75). But our poets, as we have seen, are essentially solitaries; and, once returned to solitude, the fear of sex is immeasurably greater than the joy or the wonder. It is the same Thomas Wolfe whom we have just seen, as "Eugene Gant," gleefully delineating obscenities in the company of Otto, who later gives the truer picture of what lay beneath that demon-placating act of fetishistic bravado. His teacher, he recalls, one Margaret Leonard, thought that she "knew boys":

> In fact, however, she had little knowledge of them. She would have been stricken with horror if she could have known the wild confusion of adolescence, the sexual nightmares of puberty, the grief, the fear, the shame in which a boy broods over the dark world of his desire. She did not know that every boy, caged in from confession by his fear, is to himself a monster. (p. 254)

But to return to the question of the compartmentalization of the various domains of erotic activity and experience. Not only is there the predictable barrier between the "impurity" of carnal desire, frequently in its crudest form, and the "purity" of platonic affection or intellectual sympathy, but there are others equally insurmountable. Jean-Jacques Bouchard (admittedly something of a phenomenon) recalls "that he began to throw a leg over little girls who used to come and play with his sister" when he was no more than eight years old;[17] and only some four years later did he learn what he was doing. In extreme contrast, John Raynor claims that, in his "Bright Daydream" (as opposed to the sadistic "Dark Daydream" which closed in upon him while he was in the act of assassinating the hen), he already, between the ages of three and six, "knew, in a deep, intuitive way, about love-making." The "Bright Daydream" included a girl to whom he consciously refrained from making love—an act of self-denial, he concludes, which gave him "an ecstasy as sharp and keen as any I have ever felt since" (*A Westminster Childhood*, p. 70). Masturbation is not infrequently something that happens completely in a vacuum, "like nibbling at a biscuit while the mind is on other things"—such is the case with Violette Leduc, whose sexual and emotional life, in all other respects, was fairly eventful. Or else it is assimilated to other realms of activity, having nothing to do with love, procreation, or even—in any strict sense—with sex. Thus Luigi Meneghello, or, at all events, his *compagnia*, or gang, growing up in Malo, near Vicenza, in the 1930s, indulges as a matter of course in masturbation competitions, described in terms more closely allied to bicycle racing or to professional football than to the sport of Eros:

> Masturbation was a wholly different matter within the context of that pagan and amoral institution known as "the gang," where it was transmuted into a collective, pleasurable activity, devoid of any connection with "purity," and becoming, in a word, a straightforward continuation of normal sporting activities.
>
> Those of my companions who remained behind in the village used to foregather on the meadows, or on the slopes beyond the watercourse, and would make a race out of it, lined up for the start, and timed with a stop-watch.[18]

17. Jean-Jacques Bouchard, *Les Confessions* [?1634], ed. Alcide Bonneau (Paris, 1881), 11.
18. Luigi Meneghello, *Libera nos a Malo* (1963; rev. ed., Milan, 1974), 197.

Of course, in assessing the significance of passages such as those I have quoted from Philip Roth, Thomas Wolfe, Robert Byrne, and Luigi Meneghello, we are once again confronted with the problem of language. In the field of sexual experience, more than in any other, the language and the vocabulary available to the writer have changed over the last two decades; and it is not impossible that what appears to be a chasm between the experiences themselves may prove in the end to be a chasm between the emotional overtones of the words used to *describe* those experiences. When Chateaubriand, after accidentally touching the pretty wife of a visitor to his parents' house, writes:

From that instant I glimpsed the truth, that to love and to be loved in a manner as yet unknown to me, was assuredly the loftiest summit of felicity. Had I but done what others commonly do, I would soon have learned both the torments and the delights of that passion whose seeds were already sown within me. (*Mémoires d'outre-tombe*, 1:92)

he is exploring exactly the same area of adolescent frustration, the anguish of intuiting a fulfilled sexuality without the remotest possibility of realizing it, that Robert Byrne expresses rather differently:

Jesus, if only I could have banged somebody in those days! Just once! . . . What a relief it would have been! To have that relentless curiosity satisfied, to be free of that aching desire for a while—my grades would have improved, I know. . . . I would have been more help to Mum around the house, too. (*Memories of a Non-Jewish Childhood*, p. 53)

The language of contemporary literature is actively concerned with the "demystification" of sex—an operation which often carries with it the "depoeticizing" of the experience. *If* the barrier between the two domains in the past was merely one of language, of an "unreal" poetry imposed by prudishness where it had no cause or reason to be, then it is possible that, for the present generation of children, the various domains may coalesce. But if, on the other hand, there *is* an element of inexpressible "magic" in the sexual experience, then present-day children may be even worse handicapped by their inability to conceive of sex in terms of poetry than were their grandparents by the difficulty in talking about male and female in plain terms of sex. Moreover, in this study of the Childhood we are concerned primarily with poets; and the poetic sensibility is rarely satisfied with the purely physical discovery of sex, however traumatic in itself that discovery may be. In the poet (or in any artist), it would appear that the sense of frustration at the unrealized but instinctively apprehended harmony of physical and emotional experience is felt earlier and more acutely than in less exceptional beings, and therefore the gap appears wider. Probably, at bottom, no matter what language may do to try and close it, that gap *does* exist. Hal Porter, who contrives better than any other of our writers to combine sexual realism with pure poetry in his use of language, experiences the frustration as intensely as anyone. But he also records the existence of the gap:

> During the numerous, often elaborate and, to me, increasingly boring, unrewarding and time-wasting sexual interchanges I have in barns, behind hedges and in the Renardi's piano-case with little girls and other little boys, it never enters my head that what we are up to has anything to do with fathers, mothers, babies . . . or me. (*Watcher on the Cast-Iron Balcony*, p. 74)

If the description of adolescent sexual desire and experimentation poses one of the thorniest problems that the poet of the Childhood has to resolve, the reenactment of the experience of first love is rather more straightforward. The very phrase "First Love" has a deliciously poetic ring about it: so much so indeed that many of the writers who have used it as a title for poems or stories have done so with carefully calculated irony.[19] Whatever may, in any period or country, be the current diction of poetry, it is available for the haunting reevocation of what is often the most memorable experience of a childhood. For Tristan's Page, it is the language of preciosity and of *la Carte du tendre* (*Le Page disgracié*, pp. 127–28); for James Joyce, the language of Catholic sensuality and the Litanies of the Virgin Mary: "Tower of Ivory, House of Gold" (*Portrait of the Artist*, p. 43). From the critic's point of view, the interest in this archetypal experience lies, on the one hand, in the way in which it reflects, or responds to, specific cultural backgrounds; and on the other, in those variations from the norm of passing adolescent "crushes" and "calf-loves" which are encountered with surprising frequency among our poets.

Tristan l'Hermite was perhaps fifteen when he fell in love, for the first time in his life, with the unnamed young English girl to whom he addressed the formal galantries recorded in *Le Page disgracié*. But his comments on the episode are especially revealing, as they reflect preoccupations and problems almost wholly foreign to adolescent lovers of later centuries. Our own, post-Romantic vision of emotional euphoria is totally absent. There is a poignant and wistful nostalgia in this memory of a first love; but for the one-time Page, still very much a man of the Renaissance, emotion as such plays little part in his idealized vision of perfected humanity. For him, the ideal of maturity toward which he is progressing is modeled on Baldassare Castiglione's *Courtier*, on the gracious-mannered inhabitants of the Abbaye de Thélème, on Francis Bacon's "full, ready and exact" man, or on Ophelia's dream-image of Hamlet: "Courtier, soldier, scholar, eye, tongue, sword." So, in his analysis of

---

19. Isaak Babel', for instance; or Samuel Beckett; or even (albeit less pointedly) Ivan Turgenyev.

the adventure, the key word is *refinement*, in a quite literal sense. By love, he is refined, as gold is refined. His love is a "fire" which eliminates the dross and the impurity of his erstwhile childish nature: "This fire, subtle and life-giving, awakens souls sunk in the grossest slumber and effortlessly endows the most bestial of sensations with an aery spirituality" (*Le Page disgracié*, p. 129) By this, his first love, he is transformed from a shapeless hunk of boy into the first elegant silhouette of a Cherubino, with all the latter's grace, audacity, precocity, and sublimated sensuality. Nor is the comparison drawn at random; for it is more than probable that Beaumarchais, in fashioning his Chérubin, drew, not only upon the model of Petit-Jehan de Saintré, but also upon that of the Page.[20] Yet, in Tristan, not everything is sublimated. There is realism as well. In the servantless twentieth century, we sometimes forget that the great houses of the past, with their armies of footmen and flocks of chambermaids, for all their luxury and privilege, lacked the one thing which, to adolescent lovers, is part of the everyday heritage of The Laurels, Laburnum Grove: namely, privacy. It is the prying eyes of servants that destroy the idyll of Tristan's first love. Shakespeare's Lover and his Lass were perhaps justifiably cautious in getting well out into the green cornfields to escape the inquisitive espionage of Sir Thomas Lucy's fourth scullion or fifth gamekeeper. And Greasy Joan probably had a sharp eye, too, in her moments off from keeling the pot.

Many of our children, falling in love between the ages of eight and sixteen with women (or men) much older than themselves—Konstantin Paustovsky, aged nine, with his sixteen-year-old cousin Hannah; Henry Handel Richardson, aged fourteen, with the thirty-year-old vicar, Jack Stretch—have no doubt about the overwhelming power of the emotion experienced, but as adults they have difficulty in ascribing it to any commonly recognized category of love. It appears in retrospect to have been neither sensual, nor spiritual, nor sentimental; it was a state of being which, in maturity, has no equivalent, and therefore cannot be described in any precise language. From this point of view, it is the opposite of sexual experience, for which the language, if usable at all, is *too* precise. The twelve-year-old Charles Nodier, in love with his Séraphine, admits frankly that any attempt to find words for the episode defeats him: it was

a love, to which the polish and refinement of our language and of our manners has as yet given no name. Nothing less resembles "love," as men commonly understand it; and yet it is a sentiment wholly distinct from family affection, as indeed it is from school friendships.[21]

20. Chérubin, in his turn, contributed something to Louvet de Couvray's portrait of the Chevalier de Faublas; and Faublas was the principal model used by Hugo von Hofmannsthal for the character of Octavian in *Der Rosenkavalier*.

21. Charles Nodier, *Mémoires de Maxime Odin* [1832], in *Œuvres complètes* (Geneva, Slatkine, 1968), 10:51.

In this respect again, first love, for the poet, is diametrically opposed to first sex. The latter crosses the frontier into a world of "dark magic," in the description of which the normal language of poetry, with its symbols and allusions, is totally inappropriate; the former enters, however timidly, a realm of faerie which, if it remains necessarily inaccessible to any exactness of descriptive analysis, nonetheless *can*, however indirectly, be reincarnated by the recognized processes of poetic evocation. "I loved Séraphine with a simplicity of feeling which was wholly ideal, *wholly poetic*" (pp. 53–54; my italics), concludes Nodier, thus to some extent modifying his earlier conclusion that *no* language was available to describe the experience. Sometimes, indeed, the very attempt to hold fast by this overwhelming, this ineffable vision of first love actually stimulates the first momentous experiments with language in the future poet: such was the case with Goethe evoking his "Gretchen am Spinnrade,"[22] or James Joyce recapturing his Eileen and the moments in which "his heart danced upon her movements like a cork upon a tide" (*Portrait of the Artist*, p. 69). Sometimes, one may suspect, the Poet, in retelling the episode of his first love, reveals rather more than he consciously intended. Nine-year-old Konstantin Georgevich confides to his cousin Hannah that when he grows up, he is determined to become a sailor; "and you," he adds, "will come as my wife."

> Hannah stopped and looked sternly into my face.
> "Will you swear it?" she whispered. "Swear it by your mother's heart?"
> "I swear it," I said, without a moment's hesitation.
> She smiled, her eyes became green as sea-water, and she kissed me hard on the forehead. Her lips were feverishly hot. (Paustovsky, *Povest' o zhizni*, 1:32; trans., 1:28)

It is difficult, outside the context of Russian hothouse emotionalism, to picture a sixteen-year-old girl demanding an eternal vow "on his mother's heart" from a little boy of nine that he will remain for ever faithful to her. Happily, some six months later, Hannah died of consumption, although there is no evidence, in Paustovsky's narrative, that he realized his luck. The world, and literature, were at least spared the devastation of yet one more neurotically impassioned Slavic female.

The most fascinating aspect of these Childhoods, however, is the frequency with which *very* early impressions of love exercise a lifelong influence over the poet. There are legendary figures among the German Romantics who fall in love with a once-glimpsed maiden barely emerging from childhood, and who dedicate the remainder of their lives to the celebration of that vision; but that there should be, among flesh-and-blood poets and novelists, so many whose

---

22. Johann Wolfgang von Goethe, *Dichtung und Wahrheit*, in *Goethes Werke*, ed. Truntz and Blumenthal (Hamburg, 1955), 9:168ff.

basic emotional development follows the same pattern is, to put it mildly, unexpected. It is as though, from the evidence of our Childhoods, the phenomenon which that great naturalist and ecologist, Konrad Lorenz, has described as "imprinting," were almost as common among poets as it is among ravens or greylag geese.

Imprinting is a mental process by which, if the image of a given living creature is stamped on the brain of a bird or animal at one precise moment during its early period of development, that same creature will be sought after for the rest of the "imprinted" victim's life as the ideal sexual partner, however ludicrously inappropriate the subject of the choice may be.

There is no limit to the queer errors that may arise in this connection. A female barnyard goose which I now possess was the only survivor of a brood of six, of which the remainder all succumbed to avian tuberculosis. Consequently she grew up in the company of chickens and in spite of the fact that we bought for her, in good time, a beautiful gander, she fell head over heels in love with our handsome Rhode Island cock, inundated him with proposals, prevented him from making love to his hens and remained absolutely insensible to the attentions of the gander.

Lorenz gives a number of other examples of the phenomenon, including that of "a lovely white peahen" which "fell in love" with one of the giant tortoises from the Galápagos islands in Schönbrunn Zoo. "It is typical of this extraordinary state of fixation of sexual desire on a particular and unnatural object," he concludes, "that it cannot be reversed."[23]

Imprinting is definitive; it is not something from which one recovers, even after years of convalescence. It is a psychological scar which, in goose or poet, is there for life. Henry Handel Richardson took six years to recover from the impact of the Rev. Jack Stretch; but that is not imprinting. By contrast, although Francis Jammes was already seventeen by the time when, wandering around the Quartier des Capucins in Bordeaux, his attention was caught by an unnamed, unknown, unapproached "damsel in a grey dress, with a narrow profile," who sat sewing at a window, this vision in grey was to dominate and direct the rest of his life, both as a man and as a poet:

At that instant there was born, like a grey flower in the silence, my pure, my true first love. . . . She it is who, unknowingly, has presided over every phase of my life. She has known familiarly the *enfant terrible* that I was, the ailing and melancholy young man that I became, the solid patriarch that I am now, here in this house alive with the noise of children. (*L'Amour, les Muses et la chasse*, p. 41)

Observe the stress on the adjective *grey*. It will recur.

In similar fashion, James Kirkup, aged four, is imprinted with the image of "Tom-boy Isa"; Mulk-Rāj Anānd, aged six, with that of twelve-year-old

23. Konrad Lorenz, *King Solomon's Ring* (London, 1952), 133–36.

Rukmani, "with her long black hair in two plaits on her shoulders, matching the colour of her almond-shaped eyes"; Abel Hermant, at the age of seven, with a little girl once glimpsed on a beach; Georges Duhamel, aged eight, with another little girl, name forgotten, for whom his passionate love, some fifty years later, still causes him the intensest of suffering, "as only children know how to suffer."[24]

It is a singular fact—this is offered as an observation, without comment—that in every case where imprinting takes place, frequently among poets and novelists with a vivid and luminous sense of color, the color is absent. Imprinting occurs in halftones, black and white, perhaps ink-blue, above all grey. It happens on a grey beach, from which the sunset colors have faded; by the banks of a grey river; in the grey-blue shadows beneath a cast-iron balcony. In this, as in almost every other aspect of the autobiography of childhood, *The Watcher on the Cast-Iron Balcony* offers the last and the most memorable word. Hal Porter is six years old.

> I fall in love. The expression is absurd, yet there seems no other.
> Now I am in love with a little girl.
> Name?
> Nameless. . . .
> She wears a grey velvet dress with a lace collar spreading over her shoulders. The collar contains an extra hole on the right shoulder that is larger than, and not, a lace-hole. . . . I shall never again see such a carven, tender face, never such ink-blue polished eyes and sooty lashes, never such a circular mole that sits above her lips. It is like a spot from a moth's wing. We walk, and I watch us walk, mildly on out of each other's lives, giving up, as we part, two facsimile wraiths that remain together and continue walking together. (pp. 43–44)

Five years and eighty pages later, she is the "nameless little Kensington girl, who haunts me like Lucy Gray, like all the lost children of ballads and life" (p. 124); and later still she reappears—grey, unforgettable grey ghost or spirit—as "that Kensington child in the grey velvet dress [who] to this day does and to the end of my life will . . . excite me" (p. 170).[25]

This is the point at which literary criticism must, if it is honest, admit that it is out of its depth. If the writers whom we have been discussing are seeking above all to be truthful—and this is a basic criterion of the genre which we have established earlier—then their convergence, from England, from France,

24. James Kirkup, *The Only Child*, 102; Mulk-Rāj Anānd, *Seven Summers*, 163; Abel Hermant, *Confession d'un enfant d'hier*, 36–37; Georges Duhamel, *Inventaire de l'abîme*, 94.

25. The mythological (Orphic and Eurydicean) implications of the recurrent image of the "little grey girl" are discussed in my essay "Myth and Madame Schlésinger; Story and Fable in Flaubert's *Mémoires d'un fou*," in *French Literature Series* (University of South Carolina) 12 (1985), in press.

from India, from Australia (to cite only the instances quoted), upon a particular imagery to illustrate a particular experience *cannot* be the result merely of controlled literary artifice. It might be the result of sheer coincidence. The statistical evidence is insufficient to prove the contrary. Or it may be that, in the Jungian sense, there is a communal subconscious, to which individual artists respond in necessarily identical terms. But, of all the archetypes of childhood, the overall greyness of "das Ewig-Weibliche" apprehended by the poet at the age of six and never forgotten is perhaps the most inexplicable, and certainly the most fascinating.

MOMUS, DIONYSUS, MELPOMENE, THALIA, ET AL.

> *J'allais alors tous les dimanches*
> *au Théâtre municipal*
> *tout seul et j'étais fasciné*
> *par les divettes et chanteurs*
> *d'opérettes franco-viennoises*
>
> —Georges Perros, *Une vie ordinaire*

The essential pattern of childhood recreated is rhythmic, in a sense ritualistic. Everyday acts made automatic and familiar by repetition are themselves subsumed into the regular cycle of the year: Christmas, spring, Easter, summer holidays, harvest, Halloween, winter. Inevitably, country-bred children, particularly in regions where there are marked seasonal differences, are the most profoundly conscious of this rhythm. Anne Treneer in *School House in the Wind* (1944), Alison Uttley in *The Country Child* (1931) and again in *Ambush of Young Days* (1937), Flora Thompson in her classic *Lark Rise to Candleford* (1939–44), Laurie Lee in *Cider with Rosie* (1959)—all these structure a significant part of their reminiscences around the rhythmic repetitions of the changing seasons, with the high points—Christmas, Easter, and High Summer above all—acting as the metronome of the child's life. Birthdays (an arbitrary and individual phenomenon) and name days hardly count. Strangely, however, among all these country children, it is left to a mostly town-bred child, Luigi Meneghello, to analyze the significance of this rhythmic pattern. In the search for a meaning of life to be apprehended amid the apparently arbitrary and meaningless sequence of contingencies which make up an existence, the one common factor of all experience is precisely this "predestined" recurrence of the seasons. "The seasons," he writes, "made more sense, because they were always observed from the same places, suffered in the same houses. It seemed as though even a private, individual life, therefore, assumed more meaning, or at least, took on a fuller meaning" (*Libera nos a Malo*, p. 114). The meaningless triviality of the child's day-to-day existence, in fact, takes on its earliest apprehended pattern from the inescapable pattern of the year.

Across the regular ground bass of repetition, however, come those events which interrupt the rhythm, or which give it a new and more exciting tempo. These may be purely private—a death in the family, a bankruptcy, an emigration—but in many cases (and this is what will concern us here) they will be public: the great ritual spectacles that occur perhaps no more than once or twice in the whole of the child's experience, and remain colorfully and indelibly printed in the memory: the jubilees, the centenaries, the royal parades, the flags and fireworks which happen once and once only, which will never be repeated.

By comparison with the children of earlier generations, the modern child is ill served in this respect. The television broadcast of a procession of khaki-colored tanks through Red Square, Moscow, or a service in Westminster Abbey can exert none of the miraculous fascination of, say, Queen Victoria's Diamond Jubilee in 1897, or even her funeral in 1901, let alone the return of the French fleet to Brest in 1783.[26] It was an epoch which ended in the later 1940s, killed perhaps by a mixture of Hiroshima and television. With their loss of confidence in themselves and in their future, the peoples of Europe, it seems, have lost the ability to celebrate. "Victory Day" in England in 1946 was a stilted and artificial affair compared with the spontaneous scenes which greeted the end of World War I,[27] let alone the relief of Mafeking; and the jubilee of Queen Elizabeth II in 1977 was pathetic and flat compared even with the jubilee of King George V in 1935. Goethe, at the age of fifteen, watched the coronation of Archduke Joseph as Holy Roman Emperor on 27 March 1764, and devoted no less than twenty-five pages of *Dichtung und Wahrheit* (*Werke*, 9:178–202) to a description of the pageantry—in fact, so momentous was the experience for him that it marked the end of his childhood. Nor was this the only comparable event of its time. There had been the earlier coronations of Charles VII and Francis I; and, Goethe comments,

> There was no single inhabitant of Frankfurt, of a given age and upward, who could have failed to count these occasions, and all the circumstances accompanying them, as the very high peak and summit of all his life. (9:21)

The very high peak and summit of a life—to us, the idea is ludicrous. And yet, again and again, our Childhoods confirm it.

Francis Jammes, in provincial Bordeaux, watched the first-ever national celebration of the fall of the Bastille, on the fourteenth of July 1880, and, forty years later, recalled the day, and the fireworks display in particular, as one of

26. See Chateaubriand, *Mémoires d'outre-tombe*, 1:73.
27. See A. L. Rowse, *A Cornish Childhood* (1942; reprint, London, 1975), 7, 206.

the most "beautiful" in his whole life (*De l'âge divin à l'âge ingrat*, p. 203).
Seven years later came Queen Victoria's comparatively unmemorable Golden
Jubilee—and yet the child who was destined to achieve lasting fame as the
illustrator of *Winnie-the-Pooh* could still, sixty years afterward, draw in detail
and from memory the scenes that had remained in his mind.[28] And there is
scarcely a child alive in England at the time who fails to recall the Diamond
Jubilee—perhaps the most memorable exhibition of pomp and circumstance
in the whole history of modern Europe. In Dresden, Erich Kästner watched the
King's Birthday Parade; far away in Delhi, the five-year-old Mulk-Rāj Anānd
watched—or at least tried to watch, being too small to see over the heads of
the milling, cheering crowds—the Royal Durbar of 1910. On Vancouver Island, Emily Carr watched the races held in celebration of the Queen's Birthday—races in which not only did the Royal Navy row their heavy ship's-boats
round Esquimalt Harbour, but Indian tribes came from hundreds of miles up
the coast, and competed in their slender, racing dugout canoes.[29] In Hobart,
even so minor an event as a visit from the Prince of Wales in 1920 "transformed the River Derwent into a fairy-land" for the watching Graham
McInnes.[30] Indeed, how could any child forget a firework display which concluded with "a set piece of the German raider *Emden* burning after being
beached by HMAS *Sydney* on the Cocos-Keeling Islands"?

In an impressive number of instances, it is the color and above all the
"luminosity" of such spectacles which remain imprinted on the child's mind,
and which seem to offer the key to their "magical" quality. Recalling the role
that the experience of "luminosity" and "incandescence" plays in the quasi-
mystical philosophy that emerges from the dramas of Eugène Ionesco, we can
turn to his *Journal en Miettes* to discover whether this same luminosity is also
associated in his memory with the *fêtes* of childhood. And indeed it is. Even
when the real *fêtes* are absent, the child's fantasy supplies imaginary ones to
take their place: "I conjure up in imagination many-lighted merry-go-rounds,
carnival lighting effects, and ladies in lovely dresses, people singing in the
streets, luxurious drawing-rooms" (p. 9). The description sounds like that of a
transformation scene in a masque, or in a traditional English pantomime.[31]

28. Ernest Shepard, *Drawn from Memory* (London, 1957), 73–87.

29. Emily Carr, *The Book of Small* (Toronto, 1942), 178.

30. Graham McInnes, *The Road to Gundagai*, p. 59. By contrast, a State Visit to Brisbane in
1963 by Queen Elizabeth II was greeted by a confrontation, with protesters arguing loudly that
the money spent on a (minimal) display of fireworks had been better employed on improving
the city's (admittedly lamentable) sewerage system. The interest displayed by modern scholars
in the "carnivalesque" elements of the past is perhaps inspired by the total absence of such
colorful ritual in the utilitarian present.

31. See my essay "On Being Very, *Very* Surprised . . . Eugène Ionesco and the Vision of
Childhood," in *The Dream and the Play: Ionesco's Theatrical Quest*, ed. Moshe Lazar (Malibu,
Ca., 1982), 1–19.

And this perhaps is the link with, and the beginning of an explanation for, one of the most persistent, omnipresent, and perhaps least expected of the archetypes of childhood experience: theater.

The word *theater*, of course, is to be taken in a very broad sense, including not only Shakespeare, Racine, Schiller, and the great classics of the literary stage but also opera, ballet, pantomime, and melodrama, together with the circus, marionettes, *guignols*, and plain Punch and Judy shows. And, in earlier or less sophisticated societies, the wandering entertainers, the Christmas mummers—Gwen Raverat can still recall seeing them in Southampton as late as 1899 (*Period Piece*, pp. 179–80)—the solitary *jongleurs*, and the peripatetic hawkers and fairing-sellers of preindustrial Europe, with their packs on their backs, their trays of trinkets, and their hallucinatory patter. The very simplest form of theatricality can and frequently does produce a state of emotional upheaval so violent that the pattern of a life is altered. When Edmund Gosse describes his first encounter, at the age of eight, with Punch and Judy, he adopts the language of Aristotle watching the *Oresteia*:

> All this was solemn and exquisite to me beyond words. I was not amused—I was deeply moved and exhilarated, "purged," as the old phrase hath it, "with pity and terror." (*Father and Son*, p. 59)

For Drieu la Rochelle, it was a first encounter with the circus which produced the impact; and the language—the poetry—which he uses to describe the acrobats seems to antedate by some thirty-five years the thrill of existential anguish felt by Jean Genet at the sight of a tightrope walker:

> Human beings were grasping at the utmost limits of the possible; their gestures shot pain through me. . . . My whole being was shaken to its very foundations. I made an exhibition of myself. (Drieu la Rochelle, *Etat civil*, p. 73)

For Albert Bensoussan, the little Jewish child brought up in the remote Isbilia region of Algeria, the role was played by a solitary *jongleur*, an ex-soldier turned hawker and peripatetic entertainer;[32] for Mulk-Rāj Anānd, it was another Autolychus-figure, the "Dumbri," with his one-man parody of an entire British regiment going through musketry drill (*Seven Summers*, pp. 141–44); for Flora Thompson, it was the "cheap-jack man," with his "continual stream of jokes and anecdotes" and with his songs, which, fifty years later, she could still remember:

> There was a man in his garden walked
> And cut his throat with a piece of chalk;
> His wife, she knew not what she did,
> She strangled herself with a saucepan-lid.
> (*Lark Rise to Candleford*, pp. 134–35)

32. Albert Bensoussan, *La Bréhaigne* (Paris, 1973), 50.

Among these reactions to very primitive types of theatre, the most unexpected development is that worked out by Thomas Hughes in *Tom Brown's Schooldays*. In the early part of the story, before Tom goes to Rugby, there occurs an episode when he is taken to see the mummers "dressed out in ribbons and coloured paper-caps," as they stamp around the Squire's kitchen "repeating in true sing-song vernacular the legend of St. George and his fight" (pp. 23–24). For Hughes, this episode has a double significance: first, because it takes place in the *Squire's* kitchen, before the Squire himself and his family, but with basically the whole village also in attendance; and second, because he believes that the mummers' performance is a last living relic of the "old Middle-Age Mysteries." From this seemingly odd and unpromising starting point, Hughes develops a theory and ideal of popular drama: a drama which is no longer elitist, but classless, appealing equally to all levels of society and education—and one which, in the first instance, might be based on a revival of the medieval mystery plays. In France, we shall see this identical idea being developed by writers such as Charles Péguy, Romain Rolland, Paul Claudel, and Michel de Ghelderode, and by theater directors such as Jacques Copeau, Léon Chancerel, and Firmin Gémier. The latter gradually moved away from the Mystery-Play element, substituting the spectacle of *sport* in its place. It was Gémier who became the founder-director of the Théâtre National Populaire; and so, through many transformations, we can trace a continuous development of ideas from the sort of theater for the masses first intuited by Hughes, to the work of Jean Vilar and Roger Planchon, to Avignon and Villeurbanne.

Hughes himself, however, took a short cut. He moved quickly away from the Mystery-Play basis, while retaining the ideal of a multiclass audience; instead (anticipating Gémier) he began to concentrate on the dramatic and spectacular qualities of sport—hunting, backswording, prizefighting, and, above all, cricket—and so he began gradually to evolve his "socialistic" ideal of a totally integrated society and—in another direction—of the role that sport should play in the English Public-School system. It is highly probable, of course, that the elaboration of this sequence of ideas was far less smooth and continuous than it is shown to be in *Tom Brown's Schooldays*; but there at least he traces the origin of these notions, which have done so much to reshape English society, back to that moment when he was brought down into the kitchen to witness the mummers, "at the mature age of three."

In the majority of cases, it is not the *quality* of the drama or the performance that is important, but its pure theatricality. Stendhal's Virginia Kubly—an early love which fashioned at least one aspect of his personality—was anything but a Rachel or a Mademoiselle Mars, while the famous performance of *Il Matrimonio segreto* which he witnessed in Ivrea and which transformed his whole life and sensibility was given by a third-rate, down-at-heel traveling company, led by a Carolina who had one of her front teeth missing. "Delicious poison sipped from a dirty cup" is Hal Porter's characteristic comment, after seeing his first play, *Uncle Tom's Cabin*, in a one-night-stand in Bairnsdale, Victoria. A. S. Jasper lay awake for weeks in a thrill of terror after watching *The Face at the Window* from a penny seat in the gallery at the Old Britannia Theatre in Hoxton. Ernest Raymond (*The Story of My Days*, London, 1968) was no less overwhelmed by seeing Wilson Barrett and Maude Goodman in *The Sign of the Cross* in 1914 than had been Ernest Shepard by seeing *The Babes in the Wood* at Drury Lane in 1888. Eleanor Farjeon might have been more privileged, since she came from a theatrical family, and most of the great stars of the period were her parents' relatives or friends; nonetheless, the "magic" that began to operate on her when she was four years old and her "first theatre-curtain rolled up after dark"—the spell which was to last a lifetime, "never ceasing to glitter like a star in my memory"—was occasioned by a third-rate, completely forgotten drama called *The Japs*.[33]

True quality in the play or in the performance tends to make its impact at a much later stage in the child's development. Simone de Beauvoir was fourteen before she began to succumb "body and soul to the magic spells of the stage," as a result of seeing *Cyrano de Bergerac*, followed by *Britannicus*, and twenty before she experienced the total and inexpressible dazzlement produced by Diaghilev's *Ballets Russes*; Valerie Avery, sixteen or seventeen before the aggressive vulgarity of her early childhood was suddenly transformed and civilized by the discovery of Shakespeare; Kathleen Raine, probably fourteen before she was finally converted by Rutland Boughton's once overwhelmingly popular *Immortal Hour*. All three of these last examples are drawn from Childhoods written by women, and this is perhaps not wholly coincidental. From our evidence, it would appear that girls (albeit with a fair number of exceptions) are less susceptible than boys, particularly at a very early age, to the unalloyed seduction of the theatrical experience as such. They seem less able to achieve total identification with the characters on the stage; they are more self-conscious as members of the audience, more aware of the barrier of the proscenium arch, and consequently more critical, from the start, of improbable plots, bad acting, or tawdry costumes. Colette was "repelled" by the inadequacies of the second-rate touring companies she saw as a child—the smoking lights, the paint flaking off the decor, the actors "as dismal as caged animals" (*La Maison de Claudine*, p. 116); and even when at last she did see a good company performing, all she gives us is an amusing anecdote of small-town gossip about the effeminate *jeune-premier*. Juliette Adam was a ripe

33. Eleanor Farjeon, *A Nursery in the Nineties* (London, 1935), 325. For other accounts of Childhoods in theatrical families, see Audrey Marshall, *Fishbones into Butterflies: A Kind of Remembering* (London, 1964); Lyn Irvine, *So Much Love, So Little Money* (London, 1957).

fourteen by the time she could confess to being moved by a play; even then, she dismisses the emotion in three lines, and devotes the next two pages to discussing the effect of her new dress on other members of the audience. André Gide could stand fascinated for hours, watching through a crack in the fence the stage of a *café-concert*, "upon which some unpretentious starlet stood uttering inanities" (*Si le grain ne meurt*, p. 17); by contrast, Fredelle Bruser Maynard, culture-hungry in the wilderness of Saskatchewan, recalls, of equally inept live-theater performances by visiting troupes, only the "talcum-powdered limbs in pale mauve tights . . . , striped trousers, twirling canes, much eye-rolling and finger-snapping" (*Raisins and Almonds*, p. 17). For entertainment value, she frankly preferred the cinema. No girl, from present evidence, actually pees in her knickers from sheer emotional exhaustion on first discovering the "miracle" of theater . . . as did Michel Leiris (*L'Age d'homme*, p. 48).

The experience of cinema, and presumably that of television, is totally different from that of theater.[34] Theater *interrupts* a rhythmic, regularly structured pattern of existence; consequently, it offers, however feebly, intuitions of an alternative dimension. The cinema (and, one guesses, even more the television) is an integral part of that everyday pattern:

> Threepence on Saturday afternoons,
> A bench along the side of the hall,

writes D. J. Enright (*The Terrible Shears*, p. 32). Even for children who are not taken regularly, there is a kind of anonymous and humdrum uniformity about the ambiance which is entirely different from the "extra-special" (or "ritualistic," or "ceremonial," or even "sacred") atmosphere of theater. Theater audiences are aware of each other in a way that cinema audiences never are. Sumptuous the cinemas may have been, particularly in the 1930s, that supreme epoch of Metro-Goldwyn-Mayer garishness and the Mighty Wurlitzer. "Its cinemas gave Sydney much of its significance," observes Donald Horne of the period. "The big 'picture-shows' were its true Cathedrals" (*The Education of Young Donald*, p. 125). But the effect of cinema, especially in this period, lay not in its magic, but in its realism. It brought otherness into close (if temporary) contact with everyday reality; it did not transfigure everyday reality with a new radiance. In consequence, where cinema was not merely part of routine, it tended rather to be frightening. "I jumped up and down on my seat shouting

---

34. There is at present too little evidence of the later recollections of children brought up in the omnipresent company of the television screen to draw any clear conclusions about its lasting impact on the sensibility of the future poet. Melinda McCracken, in *Memories Are Made of This* (1975) offers one of the rare exceptions; but this is a Childhood so rigorously sociological and documentary that it is of little help in the present chapter.

'Oh don't let it happen! Don't let it happen!'," recalls Graham McInnes of his first visit to a film show. "The film was a real shock, and for weeks afterwards I had nightmares about it" (*The Road to Gundagai*, pp. 56–57).

Jean-Paul Sartre is among the first of the authors of our Childhoods whose early years were dominated by cinema rather than by theater; he is also the only one who has attempted to analyze the difference between the impact produced by the two different genres. This analysis, while predictably tendentious, nonetheless makes certain valid points. For him, cinema represents democracy, freedom, republicanism; whereas theater embodies all the frustrated aspirations toward nobility of the wealthy nineteenth-century bourgeoisie. "No bourgeois of the last century ever forgot his first evening at the theatre," he writes (*Les Mots*, p. 96); by contrast,

I absolutely defy my contemporaries to give me the date of their first encounter with the cinema. We were entering blindfold into a century which was destined to single itself out from all the others by its bad manners, and the new art, the art of the common people, foreshadowed our barbarity. . . . We adored it, my Mother and I, but we barely wasted a thought on it, and we never spoke about it. (p. 97)

Certainly this may be part of the difference, but it is not all of it by a long chalk. It may help to explain the lack of magic in cinema; it does not explain the total magic of theater. And there is another way in which the theater has the advantage: the child who sees a play can come home and write or direct or act a play of his own; the child who is impressed by a film is confined to the world of fantasy as soon as he seeks the skills of the filmmakers or the photogenic beauty of the stars. Again, it is a matter of the relationship between realism and reality.

Probably as far back as the beginnings of civilized society, certainly as far back as the Renaissance, boys and girls have found delight in acting, writing, and directing dramas of their own—and, as all good educators have realized, have learned an immense amount about literature, people, and themselves in the process. From the twelve-year-old Michel de Montaigne taking leading roles in Latin tragedies at the Collège de Guyenne to thirteen-year-old Molly Weir (*Shoes Were for Sunday*, London, 1970) organizing a backstreet theater in the slums of Glasgow, the tradition flows on unbroken, and the passionate commitment to this, of all art forms the most immediately accessible to the child, unvarying in its intensity. And this, of course, has nothing to do with the social aspirations of the nineteenth-century bourgeoisie.

Let it not be thought that all these productions are great art—or indeed anything but grotesque by Old Vic or Comédie Française standards. Occasionally we encounter a privileged child: Florian, at the age of ten, was allowed a small part in a new play by his Great-Uncle Voltaire, in which he was rehearsed by Mademoiselle Clairon. "On the night, I received much applause," he recalls complacently.[35] Frequently the results are deplorable or disastrous: Thomas Bailey Aldridge producing *Hamlet* and playing the title role at the age of seven, or Henry Handel Richardson obliged to play Juliet, instead of Romeo as she would have preferred, because the rest of the cast—her sister Pin—was unable to climb the tree which represented the balcony.[36] But just as frequently, the experience is a revelation. A. L. Rowse made the definitive discovery of his own mature identity in the course of playing Malvolio, as did Valerie Avery while playing Ophelia—both in school productions.[37] Given the odd fact that amateur theater, and school theater in particular, was virtually extinguished in France from the time of the Revolution, at almost exactly the same time as it began to emerge as a phenomenon of importance in England,[38] it is not surprising that most of these examples are from Anglo-Saxon Childhoods. As an extreme instance, the narrative structure of Joyce Cary's *House of Children* revolves entirely around a series of family productions by himself and his numerous cousins. Nonetheless, the phenomenon is not unknown elsewhere: Erich Kästner recalls a kind of Total-Theater monodrama created by his eight-year-old girlfriend, Hilda Gans; nor should it be forgotten that, in Russia, the great Konstantin Stanislavsky emerged from a joyous background of "family theatricals."

Once again, between cinema and theater, the distinction is one between realism and reality. The cinema—witness everything from *King Kong* to *Star Wars*—can create an extraordinarily effective *impression* that "this is really happening": emotionally, the realism is acceptable; intellectually it is not. In theater, the contrary is true. Because of the presence of a live actor on stage, the wildest of fantasies remains rooted in reality. In Karel Čapek's *Insect Play*, an ichneumon fly drags the corpse of a cricket to its lair, observed indifferently by two beetles and a human tramp. This is far more "unreal" (from one point of view) than *King Kong*, where photography shows pictures of *real* jungles and *real* skyscrapers. But, in the theater, the character named in the program as "the Ichneumon Fly," disguise himself as he may, remains incontrovertibly *there*; whatever fantasies Čapek may have invented for him, he stays anchored within the limitations of what a human being can physically achieve. His "real presence"—to use a theological term—distinguishes him absolutely from the

35. Jean-Pierre Claris de Florian, *Mémoires d'un jeune Espagnol* [1807], in *Œuvres complètes* (Paris, 1810), 24:32.

36. Thomas B. Aldrich, *The Story of a Bad Boy*, 62–64; Henry Handel Richardson, *The Getting of Wisdom*, 15. See also the well-known chapter "A Merry Christmas" in Louisa May Alcott's *Little Women* (1868).

37. A. L. Rowse, *A Cornish Childhood*, 230; Valerie Avery, *London Morning*, 120–24.

38. In France, where the tradition of a school play persisted at all during the nineteenth century, it was mainly in church-controlled institutions. In England, the tradition was established by the Public-Schools, originally with plays in Latin or, as at Winchester, in Greek.

"unreal presence" of the cinematographic image. In this sense, Sir Lawrence Olivier playing Hamlet in the film of Shakespeare's play is closer to Mickey Mouse than any live actor, however incompetent, playing the part of Père Ubu on the stage of any local dramatic society.

The power of theater lies, as does the power of the symbol for Jean Genet, for whom theater is itself the supreme symbol, in the fact that it exists simultaneously in *two* dimensions: that of living, three-dimensional reality, and that of myth, poetry, and magic. In earlier centuries, particularly under the crushing, formalized, bureaucratic autocracies of the seventeenth and eighteenth centuries, the companies of actors themselves represented a kind of freedom, tiny republics at the heart of conformist despotisms, and as such attracted to their ranks numerous men and women of high birth and higher abilities—the intellectual dissenters and dropouts of the period: we see something of this in Tristan l'Hermite, more still in Scarron's novel of theatrical life in the seventeenth century, *Le Roman comique* (1651–57). But, in the more recent, more democratic world of the majority of our Childhoods, the experience of theater represents an escape in a less political, more metaphysical direction. It is an escape from materiality: materiality not rejected, but *transmuted* into something more significant, infinitely more marvelous than itself—and in this sense again, it is magical. For Marcel Jouhandeau, watching a theatrical performance organized by nuns among the girls at his sister's convent-school, the experience was an overwhelming revelation of the dimensions of the divine and the diabolical—to such an extent that he took the name of one of the girl-performers, Joséphine *Chaminadour*,[39] and transformed it into that of an imaginary town—battlefield of God and Satan—which was to form the center of his entire creative work. For Michel Leiris, the theater was "a miraculous dimension-of-Being," and an introduction to the realm of "ritual and tragic gravity," which, for so many contemporary nonreligious thinkers, characterizes that inaccessible domain of the spirit from which the traditional God is absent, yet which continues to haunt and torment the mind of man dissatisfied with materiality.[40] Or, to take the same experience from the opposite point of view: in the course of acting a play, scruffy boys and anemic girls appear transformed "for a space to a grotesque and moving loveliness" (Porter, *Watcher on the Cast-Iron Balcony*, p. 149). Through the reality of theater they become what the reality of life will never allow them to be—themselves. "For one rare moment," records James Joyce of his own Stephen Dedalus, who did not like acting and was required to do it against his will for the Whitsun-

---

39. Marcel Jouhandeau, *Mémorial*, 2:26. "Chaminadour" is in fact Guéret, in the Department of the Creuse.

40. Michel Leiris, *L'Age d'homme*, (1922; reprint, Paris, 1972), 49–50.

tide play at Belvedere School, "he seemed to be clothed in the real apparel of boyhood" (*Portrait of the Artist*, p. 85).

THE DARK ANGEL

> "*Je vas-t-y rien que mourir quand je serai vieille?*"
> —Antonine Maillet, *On a mangé la dune*

Drama, from the most primitive times, has had associations with religion; theaters through the ages have been temples dedicated to whatever may have been the highest ideal of the communities which they served, even if, as in nineteenth-century Europe, that ideal may have risen no higher than a cult of luxury. Possibly, then, it is this much profounder level of the meaning of theater which is unconsciously sensed by the child, and which suggests why it is that, at least for the somewhat exceptional beings who populate our Childhoods, the reaction to theater is so intense and (*pace* M. Jean-Paul Sartre) so otherwise inexplicable. Nor is it a mere coincidence that, in sophisticated cultures, the highest manifestation of theater should take the form of tragedy. From Aeschylus to Beckett, drama has been concerned with mankind's awareness of death.

We have left to the last any discussion of the traumatic effects of the discovery of death on the child because this reaction is the most complex and unpredictable, and perhaps the most subject to variation through the influence of contingent ideas and circumstances. If the underlying theme of the Childhood is the initial groping toward and the eventual consummation of, a complete and individual identity, it is logical to conclude (as certain analysts of the autobiographical mode in literature have concluded) that the discovery that this not-yet-realized identity is inevitably doomed to extinction must necessarily be one of the most tragic crises of childhood experience. To judge from the evidence which we have before us, this *may* be the case; but it is by no means inevitably so.

It is, in fact, quite possible to be so effectively inoculated against the fear of death that the soul-shattering discovery that it applies to oneself, that it is one's *own* identity which is impermanent, is delayed until long after the end of childhood. For centuries, the Christian doctrine of the immortality of the soul taught the child to welcome death rather than to fear it: Michel de Montaigne was probably forty by the time he began to find that doctrine partially insufficient, and to seek a second inoculation in the form of Stoicism. Wordsworth, however, was only nine when he watched the body of a drowned man being pulled out of Lake Esthwaite: "Yet no soul-debasing fear possessed me," he claims,

                      for mine inner eye had seen
              Such sight before, among the shining streams
              Of faëry-land, the forest of romance.   (*The Prelude*, 5:451–55)

Wordsworth, in fact, was inoculated by his reading, his imagination, his love of poetry; by the whole Romantic image of death.[41] Country children were often inured to death by sheer familiarity, frequently seeing their elders slaughter hens and pigs; seacoast children, by the constant discovery of drowned sailors as they played among the rocks and on the beaches. "Scarcely was I born but that I heard talk of death," recalls Chateaubriand.

Almost every year, vessels were wrecked beneath my very eyes, and, as I exercised my limbs in careless play along the seashore, the ocean would throw up at my feet the bodies of foreign men, men who had died far from their homeland. (*Mémoires d'outre-tombe*, 1:33)

Chateaubriand, indeed, is a perfect example of multiple inoculation: Christianity, familiarity, the true Romantic sense of the rich pathos which can be harvested from the passage of time, the pure poetry of *Eheu fugaces.* "I am perhaps the only creature alive who knows that these people existed," he observes, commenting on the death of his grandmother and of her generation:

This impossibility of permanence or of duration in human relationships, the profundity of the oblivion which follows us, the invincible silence which takes possession of our graves and, emanating thence, extends its empire to our house and lineage, recalls me incessantly to the need to live in solitude. (1:24)

These (to us) somewhat unconvincing philosophical generalizations, with their not-over-original conclusion, are typical of the earlier nineteenth century, and survive occasionally into the twentieth. Fred Archer's voluminous memoirs of a Worcestershire farm-laborer are suffused with nostalgia for a rugged generation of rural eccentrics dying off one by one, and to each is added the refrain: "Alas, we shall not see his like again." The tears "streaming down the cheeks" of successful-author Archer hardly redeem the platitudinousness of his philosophy.[42]

Although there are exceptions, it is only as we move toward the twentieth century, and as the inoculating serums lose their power, that the discovery of the great condemnation begins to emerge as a major archetype of childhood experience. Other fears are diminished—the ghosts in the dark corners of the

---

41. It may seem anachronistic to refer to a "Romantic image of death" affecting the nine-year-old William Wordsworth; but Young's *Night Thoughts*, Hervey's *Meditations among the Tombs*, McPherson's *Poems of Ossian*, not to mention Gray's *Elegy in a Country Churchyard*, had profoundly affected the cultural climate of England in the 1770s and 1780s.

42. For example, the funeral of "Shepherd Corbisley." See Fred Archer, *The Distant Scene* (1967; reprint, London, 1973), 57.

staircases which at bedtime terrified earlier generations of children have vanished with the advent of rationalism and electric light; the primitive terrors of cold, likewise, with the spread of well-warmed public transport and central heating. But the child born after the publication of *The Origin of Species* is singularly defenseless against the encounter with the premonition of death.

From the defenses of the past to the vulnerability of the present: there is a fascinating picture of the transition in W. H. Hudson. Hudson was six years old when his "old dog Caesar" died. Probably children through the ages have been similarly depressed and saddened by the death of a creature who, always, had been part of their lives. But we are not concerned with childhood as such, but with childhood recreated, and recreated as literature—that is, in terms of the sensibility of the adult writer. And in the recreated childhood, the death of "old dog Caesar" becomes something quite different. "There is nothing in the past I can remember so well: it was indeed the most important event of my childhood," comments the writer nearing his eightieth year. "It was the first thing in a young life which brought the eternal note of sadness in" (*Far Away and Long Ago*, p. 32). Following the death of the dog, Hudson records two adult comments: a sermon on mortality by his tutor, Mr. Trigg; and a consoling lesson from his mother on the immortality of the soul, of "the Myself, that I am I, which knew and considered things, [and which] would never perish" (p. 36). Mr. Trigg left him dazed. "I had heard something terrible, too terrible to think of, *incredible*"; by contrast, when he left his mother's side, "I wanted to run and jump for joy and cleave the air like a bird." But, in the pitiless, desentimentalized climate of Argentina in the 1850s, with death on all sides, from the brutal killing of cattle in the slaughter-yards of Buenos Aires to the equally brutal killing of men in the various insurrectionary campaigns of the time, the battle between the severe "Old Testament" and the consolatory "New Testament" views could not be reconciled; and gradually it was the Old Testament, the Calvinistic, the Sartrian, the twentieth-century view which triumphed. Hudson was sixteen when he made his final choice:

> I now discovered that in spite of all my strivings after the religious mind, the old dread of annihilation which I had first experienced as a small child was not dead, but still lived and worked in me. This visible world—this paradise of which I had had so far but a fleeting glimpse . . . would have existed in vain, since now it was doomed with my last breath, my last gleam of consciousness, to come to nothing. (pp. 303–04)

Some of these sentences might have been written by Eugène Ionesco in the 1960s. William Henry Hudson was born in 1841; yet in him lie all the seeds of the twentieth-century child's terrifying encounter with the idea of death.

For the post-Darwinian child, the very idea of death is unacceptable—and yet has to be accepted. Here, there is a clear break between earlier and later experience: something fundamental, perhaps, which accounts for "the incomprehensibility of modern young people." It is "an indefinable anguish," "a mysterious anguish."[43] We are plunged straight into the Beckettian world of compelling contradictions, of irreconcilable oppositions: "You must go on, I can't go on, I'll go on." One could argue, in fact, particularly after rereading *Les Mots* and the *Mémoires d'une jeune fille rangée*, that at the back of the whole existentialist mood there lies this newly intensified awareness of death that takes possession of the child, a tormenting enigma at the very center of identity which, unlike other enigmas which beset the immature being, proves progressively less, instead of progressively more capable of solution as maturity approaches. Through the whole of Simone de Beauvoir, the growing awareness of death runs like a dark thread. Protected in early years by her own and her family's traditional Catholicism, she was perhaps fifteen when she had a first glimpse of the reality, and that reality was overwhelming:

> One afternoon, in Paris, I realized that I was condemned to death. There was no one else save myself in the flat, and so I made no attempt to keep my despair within bounds; I howled, I clawed at the red carpeting. (p. 139)

Later, she recalls another moment of inexpressible presentiment:

> Anguish swooped down on me; already, earlier on, I had known what it was to be afraid of death, to the point of dissolving in tears, to the point of screaming; but this time it was worse. Already life had toppled over into the Void; nothing existed any more, save only the immanence of terror, a terror so violent . . . that I retained ever after of this night a memory of being terrified.[44]

The problem here, of course, is to distinguish between the original experience and that experience refashioned in the telling by the adult already trained in a specific form of philosophical expression. The impression that there is at least a firm foundation of authentic experience is strengthened by the manner in which identical reactions are expressed by poets who are anything but existentialist in outlook or in vocabulary: it is the fruitless, the terrifyingly baffling attempt of the animate to "think itself into" the state of the inanimate, the attempt of Being to conceive itself as Not-Being. For Alan Marshall, at the age of six, the realization comes with the sight of "a perfectly good cat" that someone had thrown away (*I Can Jump Puddles*, p. 15); for James Kirkup, at the age of five, by the chance of accidentally touching the "magic bloodstone" in his backyard without first going through the propitiatory ritual of spitting on it:

At that moment in the back yard I knew what death would be like—an unspeakable

---

43. Gide, *Si le grain ne meurt*, 117; Ionesco, *Journal en miettes*, 10.
44. *Mémoires d'une jeune fille rangée*, 204; see also pp. 51 and 214. Cf. Jean-Paul Sartre: "I lived in sheer terror, it was an authentic neurosis" (*Les Mots*, 78).

moment of realization which we can share with no-one, for the shock of knowledge takes us out of ourselves, and puts us faraway, on our own, lonelier than ever, and far beyond the reach even of those we know and love best. (*The Only Child*, p. 73)

And then again, there is Kathleen Raine. In more than one sense, the first sixty-odd pages of *Farewell Happy Fields* constitute a very litany of death: the killing of butterflies, the drowning of kittens, the slaughtering of the pig, the slaughtering of the bull—all culminating, when Kathleen was twelve, in the death of her cousin, an event which was so traumatic that "it put an end to his childhood and, as it seems, to my own," and (many years after) gave rise to one of the profoundest and most moving descriptions of the dawning awareness of mortality in the range of this field of literature. It is something more than just fear. It is, once again, a kind of "possession"; the true self is expelled, its place taken by another, a non-self. It is "an invasion of consciousness by death":

> The horror that took possession of me was, literally, a darkening of the light. The light was filled with blackness, the light itself was emptied of light. . . . For me, the bright Easter sun was dark, shedding blackness; I could see objects about me, and people, but I could not reach them; they and I were in the same physical space, but between them and me there was a great gulf fixed. . . . I remember looking at brilliant golden dandelions in the sun, and their being entirely filled with blackness, emptied of all substantial reality. (pp. 61–62)

It is evidence such as this that may incline us to grant authenticity to Simone de Beauvoir and to Jean-Paul Sartre, and to conclude that this specifically twentieth-century reaction to the first awareness of death is something authentically recalled by the child, and not merely the reflection of a literary or philosophical climate, existentialist or otherwise.

The conclusion which emerges, perhaps rather unexpectedly, from this chapter and the chapter preceding it, is that whereas the archetypal *figures* of childhood are static—even Stone Age children, it may be assumed, lived in the framework of some sort of family surrounded by mothers and fathers, grandparents, aunts, uncles, and cousins—the archetypal *experiences* vary considerably, in intensity if not in essence, from age to age. The experiences all have this in common: in each case, the child who is to be a poet finds itself in contact with something which it can neither explain nor assimilate, with something alien to itself and to normality, which exists, or is felt to exist, in another dimension, which is both wondrous and terrifying, and for which no words can be found, since the child is not yet the poet. It is this quality of "Otherness" that distinguishes the truly archetypal experiences of childhood from those which are common to all or most children—the first day at school, the first friendship, learning to read and learning to write, the boredoms, embarrassments, and *gaucheries* of immaturity—but which remain on the level of day-to-day reality . . . experiences which are social rather than existential.

This being so, it is still strange that there should be such a degree of variation in the intensity with which these archetypal first awarenesses are assimilated. The obvious explanations—first, that every child reaches consciousness in a given moral, intellectual, and religious climate, and will be conditioned by that climate from the moment of its birth; and second, that all our Childhoods are recreated by adult writers who, even more than children, reflect the changing intellectual fashions of their time—these explanations are difficult to refute; but somehow they are not wholly satisfying. For, once again, we are dealing in the main with poets; and the poet, at least in the Romantic definition, is the man or woman who is *not* confined to, nor exclusively conditioned by, the limitations which constrict the awareness of other beings. His "intuition" takes him beyond himself precisely in the direction of that which is other than himself, beyond the present toward the future, beyond Freud toward Jung. And so one is left wondering whether our Childhoods may not, by a devious route, have produced evidence in support of that much-derided notion of Teilhard de Chardin: namely, that when the human race ceased to continue along the Darwinian path of physiological evolution (as it apparently did, for lack of competition, stimulation, or frustration), it began instead to blaze a new trail of spiritual evolution. Not "improvement," or "perfectibility"; but quite literally *evolution*. It is an argument as difficult to confirm as to refute. But certainly—bearing in mind all possible reservations—there does appear to be some evidence of an evolving susceptibility toward "Otherness" in the recreated Childhoods of the later nineteenth and twentieth centuries. It is a field which might be worthwhile exploring further. Meanwhile, however, these unexplored hypotheses reveal something of the immense complexity of ideas, emotions, and intuitions which lie beneath the surface of that supremely banal phrase: "the magic of childhood."

6 Inventories of a Small World

In those days, schools were usually nastier than now. But meals were nicer; and as for sweets, I won't tell you how cheap and good they were.
—C. S. Lewis, *The Magician's Nephew*

Qu'on me pardonne le récit trop minutieux de ces puérilités.
—Robert André, *L'Enfant-Miroir*

The child's world, as we have seen earlier, is a small world, made up of a block or two of mean streets or houses, a few fields or a field-path, an encampment, a village; and yet, as John Masefield comments, "he knows his mile, or at most his two miles, better than the grown-up knows his parish."[1] Sometimes— more often in the case of country than of urban children—this intimate, closely apprehended domain is felt to be linked to a "something" outside it which is mysterious, probably frightening, unknown and maybe unknowable; and at this point, the "link"—it may be a road, a river, a canal—assumes the power of a symbol, often associated in the writer's imagination with other symbols of the inexplicable. It is "the Road," in Anānd, "the Road which dominated my life with its unknown past and its undiscovered future"; in Jon and Rumer Godden, it is the River, which takes on something of the sacred quality that, throughout northern India popular religions attribute to the river and its gods (the Goddess Durga, for instance, whose image is brought down annually to the banks for ceremonial immersion).[2] In Thomas Wolfe, again it is the River, in this case categorically associated with the image of the snake, and with all that that implies (see above, chapter 3):

And he looked upon the huge yellow snake of the river, dreaming of its distant shores, the myriad estuaries lush with tropical growth that fed it, all the romantic life of plantation and canefields that fringed it, of moonlight, of dancing darkies on the levee,

---

1. John Masefield, *Grace before Ploughing* (London, 1966), 1. Emanuel Litvinoff's apt title *Journey through a Small Planet* conveys the scale of the Childhood's world.
2. Jon and Rumer Godden, *Two under the Indian Sun* (London, 1966), 27, 137. Cf. Richard Vaughan, *There Is a River* [= the Usk] (London, 1961).

of slow lights on the gilded river-boat, and the perfumed flesh of black-haired women, musical wraiths below the phantom drooping trees. (*Look Homeward, Angel*, p. 129)

"Escape routes" such as these, however, are the exception rather than the rule, certainly for the very young child. More characteristically, the supreme experience is of a very small place, complete in itself, and perfect in its completeness: "a whole made up of wholes," as Kathleen Raine, with her usual flair for identifying essentials, defines it. And part of the wholeness, the perfection, lies in the name. By naming it—whatever *it* is—the child assimilates it, makes it his own, allows it to sink into the very fibers of his being, into a darkness from which, later, the poet may or may not be able to retrieve it. "It" is "a universe of such tiny things: as soon as they are named, they slip between the fingers" (Chamberland, *L'Inavouable*, p. 43). There is a curious, negative confirmation of this importance of the *names* of things in the configuration of the child's world from two Australian poets, Randolph Stow and Donald Horne; for, in the thinly populated, only recently explored Outback, many, if not most, of the flowers have not yet received familiar names. They are just "that mauve one with three petals," or, "that pink one like the ones Little Red Riding Hood was carrying in the picture book."[3] This namelessness is felt by the poet as a serious, even as a frightening deprivation. He has been robbed of something, part of himself, his very birthright. Is it even *possible* to be a poet with such a gap at the very heart of experience? muses Donald Horne, looking out across a valley filled with anonymous blossoms:

> I wondered how Keats would have described it. I had no way of describing it. I did not know the names of anything I saw. Australia was an inadequate country, not written about in good literature. (*The Education of Young Donald*, p. 195)

There is also, it would seem, a rough correlation between the poverty that accompanies so many of our Childhoods and the intensity of minute and detailed observation in the refashioning of that childhood experience by the adult poet. The wealthier child who is surrounded by a multitude of frequently changed objects, and who travels comfortably and regularly, tends to be less deeply, less "existentially," aware of the tiny but significant details of his surrounding world than is the child of the slum or of the subsistence-level village, unless he is brought to this awareness later and by different, external means: a family bankruptcy, for instance, or a passion for the microscope. There are, of course, exceptions to this, but they are comparatively rare. Poverty, by and large, is a significant element in the genre almost from the earliest times—

> Pauvre je suis de ma jeunesse,
> De pauvre et de petite estrace.

3. Randolph Stow, *The Merry-Go-Round in the Sea* (1965; Harmondsworth, 1970), 260.

> Mon père n'eut oncq grand richesse
> Ne son ayeul, nommé Erace.
> Pauvreté tous nous suyt et trace.[4]

—to all but the most recent. At the very time that Stanley Holloway was making his reputation and his fortune with the comic monodrama *Runcorn Ferry* ("Per tuppence per person per trip"), Helen Forrester and her family were dying of starvation on the wrong side of the Mersey River because the "tuppence" was not available (*Twopence to Cross the Mersey*, 1974). Whether the current age of affluence will alter this aspect of the Childhood can only be surmised. Granted, there *is* poverty in the 1980s; but, as a general rule, in Western Europe at least, it bears little relationship to the poverty of the past. In our Childhoods, particularly those of the nineteenth century and of the Depression, where there is poverty, it reveals a degree of denudation even of the barest necessities, let alone the luxuries, that is barely comprehensible today, save perhaps in the Third World, and not always there. Flora Thompson refers to the inhabitants of Lark Rise, her childhood village of Oxfordshire farm laborers at the end of the nineteenth century, as "the Besieged Generation." "The hamlet was indeed in a state of siege," she writes, "and its assailant was Want" (*Lark Rise to Candleford*, p. 95). "There was never enough of anything, except food" (p. 103)—and, by comparison with other areas of the world, this community was comparatively prosperous. Jean Guéhenno, whose father was an out-of-work cobbler and whose mother was a stocking-maker, the victim of an iniquitous system of exploited cottage labor, discovers that he himself can hardly visualize the degree of deprivation from which he suffered as a child, and finds himself forced to call into question the relevance of his own book. Can such a Childhood mean anything to those who have not endured the experience? What is its status, other than that of a kind of Gothic novel, a tale of distant horrors, of despairs as remote as those occasioned by the fall of Carthage or the Black Death?

> The kind of poverty which I am evoking is assuredly a thing of the past, and it may well be that a book such as this will henceforward have no real immediacy except among those peoples whom we refer to as underdeveloped.[5]

In Guéhenno, this recollection of poverty and exploitation inspires a mood of passionate anger, and lies perhaps at the root of that quest for a rational and humane revolution in social justice which is the hallmark of his career as a reformer and publicist, and as editor and guiding spirit of the review *Europe*;

---

4. François Villon, *Le Grand Testament*, stanza xxxv. "Poor have I been since my first youth, born of a poor and ill-considered line. My father never knew great wealth, nor his father before him, Erace by name. Poverty pursues us, bays at the heels of all of us."
5. Jean Guéhenno, *Changer la vie* (Paris, 1961), 77.

but this, by and large, is exceptional. We can find it in Jean Genet, in Pierre Vallières and some of the Québécois writers, in Maxim Gorky perhaps, and, in muted form, in D. J. Enright. The average child, provided that its home background is secure, is largely unaware of the economic struggles and anguishes that torment its parents, unless, as not infrequently happens, these very struggles give rise to acrimonious accusations and counteraccusations between Mother and Father—in which case the essential element of security is itself endangered. Often, the memory of this very denudation, shared with parents deeply loved or respected, forms an integral part of the "paradise lost" aspect of childhood—its vanished simplicity, its romantic aura. For Ernest Renan, recalling the death of his mother, it was the memory of their shared deprivations which was most poignant to him: "I had been happy with her, I had been *poor* with her."[6] James Kirkup, brought up in a community where "children went barefoot and in rags, begging for coppers in the street" (*The Only Child*, p. 50), is a classic example of the *paradis perdu* variant of the Childhood. Much more characteristic than the bitterness of revolt is simply the longing—"when I'm bigger"—to escape: on ships . . . to the fabulous land of the *Angresi-log* . . . to the world of fantasy, or Hollywood, or make-believe:

> Abdullah the Grocer used to tell me tales of a magnificent King who lived in a realm of lights, and flowers, and perfumes, far away beyond the Seas of Darkness, far away beyond the Great Wall. And it was my longing to make a pact with the Invisible Powers, . . . that they should carry me away, far away beyond the Seas of Darkness, far away beyond the Great Wall, to dwell in this Realm of lights, and perfumes, and flowers. (Séfrioui, *La Boîte à merveilles*, p. 10)

Poverty, in fact, is something from which there is always an escape available.

We have already discussed, from a psychological and metaphysical point of view, the phenomenon of the irrelevance of toys (see above, chapter 3). But toys obtrude their presence also into the contrasting domains of wealth and poverty. The rich have too many, and so they become irrelevant; the destitute have none. In any case, in the Childhood's world of significant triviality, toys are classed in the nether region beneath the memorable—unless, of course, they are self-devised and home-constructed, like Davie Burns's "kero-tin canoe." They are the trivialities beneath triviality. The child—or at least the child-poet, our subject—inhabits a world either of immediate reality or of imagination: the *book* is of desperate importance; the *toy*—that halfway house between the real and the imagined, that mass-produced artifact which is the poorest substitute either for reality or for imagination—vanishes without trace. Indeed, this virtually total silence about toys is unexpected almost to the point of being inexplicable. Just here and there, a "Golly" (Enright, *The*

6. Ernest Renan, *Souvenirs d'enfance et de jeunesse* (1883; Paris, 1960), 103.

Terrible Shears, p. 23), or a "doll called Blondine" (de Beauvoir, *Mémoires*, p. 58), struggles for a line or two to survive, attempting, already half-drowned, to swim on the surface of the sea of memory—"Blondine," in this case, surviving only because she could reason exactly like Simone de Beauvoir and argue back with her owner, because she was the externalized "double" of this owner's emergent identity. But otherwise, hardly a sailboat, a Lionel train, a miniature steam engine, a dollhouse, a F.R.O.G. airplane, a Kiddie-Kar within the whole range of our evidence. Alan Marshall, the newly crippled and bedridden son of a desperately poor family, received his first (and only) Meccano set from a certain Mrs. Carruthers, wife of the local station-holder (the "Lady of the Manor" of the Australian Outback); but his reaction could hardly be called enthusiastic:

> It was valuable, not because it would entertain me—a candlebox on wheels would have pleased me better—but because it was evidence that Mrs Carruthers was aware of my existence. (*I Can Jump Puddles*, p. 47)

The few toys which *do* survive with some regularity in the poet's memory (other than those which are recalled because they evoke a long-past, now wholly vanished epoch, such as "the red box with the black-and-gold label" which housed the more expensive kind of toy soldier)[7] can be reduced to a minute number of categories: marbles (particularly the glass variety: "A small one, of black agate, with a white equator and white tropics");[8] soap bubbles and the clay pipe which went with them; colored chalks and their accompanying blackboard for drawing; kaleidoscopes and (this last an extraordinarily persistent toy archetype) transfers.[9] Add to this, in England between 1920 and 1940, cigarette cards. A curious selection.

If we dare—admittedly, the undertaking is risky in the extreme—draw any conclusions at all from this apparently haphazard collection of "memorable" toys, we can begin with these generalizations. First, all these archetypally significant objects are small, comparatively simple, easily obtained, and

---

7. Ernest Shepard, *Drawn from Memory* (London, 1957), 30.

8. Gide, *Si le grain ne meurt*, 11. For the names given to different species of marbles, see Norman Douglas, *London Street Games* (London, 1916), 110–18. Alan Milberg, in *Street Games* (New York, 1976), provides an illustration of the most characteristic American varieties, but unfortunately not in color (see p. 95).

9. "Burmistrov . . . sold the most wonderful things—fishing-rods, bright-coloured floats, fish-tanks, goldfish, birds, ants'-eggs, *and even transfers*" (Konstantin Paustovsky, *Povest' o zhizni*, 1:67; trans. Harari and Duncan, *Story of a Life*, 1:57). More than one of our children recalls, as the major personal catastrophe of the 1914–18 war, the fact that the supply of German transfers—by far and away the best on the market—dried up, and inferior, locally produced substitutes had to be used instead. Modern "simplified technique" transfers bear not the slightest resemblance to the pre–1939 German-made spellbinders.

above all cheap.[10] Second, all are normally brightly colored. And third, all require the exercise of considerable skill before the fullest satisfaction can be obtained from them. It could be mentioned further that none is in any sense "cuddly"; that marbles and cigarette cards were not merely used in various forms of competitive games and gambling, but were also, in preaffluent days, the common currency of childhood; that the cigarette cards and transfers offered in addition something of the range of encyclopedic visual information now provided by television; and finally, that four out of the six listed—glass marbles, soap bubbles, kaleidoscopes, and transfers—are in some way or another related to the luminous and magical world of "Otherness." The forever inaccessible, strange beauty at the heart of the glass marble; the fragile, irridescent loveliness of the soap bubble; the wonder of the kaleidoscope, transforming arbitrary slivers of colored glass into patterns as meaningful as the stained-glass windows of the Sainte-Chapelle; the enchantment of transfers—greyish, opaque chrysalises, out of which emerge as if by magic the multihued contours of the final image: perhaps, after all, it is not wholly surprising that these, rather than Dinky-Toys or Fischer-Technik building sets, should form part of the jeweled pattern of our Childhoods.

One suspects that, with the coming of the age of affluence and pink plastic, the pattern may change; but not necessarily so, since, with the exception of the transfers and the cigarette cards, all the other toys associated with archetypal experiences are still available. Nonetheless, the contemporary child evolves in a different atmosphere. It is the combination of abundance with expendability, of toys so easy to come by and consequently so little valued, "the ill-assorted mass of gadgets, toys and easily-forgotten objects," as Margaret Mead has put it, which may prove "so difficult to weave into memories";[11] and Luigi Meneghello makes the same point, contrasting the memorable *solidity* of artisan-made objects, difficult to replace, with the easy-come-easy-go fliff of Woolworths, Safeway, Prisunic, Standa, GUM, etc.:

> The very frugality of that way of life made them seem more significant. Even children's playthings [*giochi*] were more serious; there were fewer little cheap plastic toys [*giocattoletti di plastica*]. There was less worthless nonsense [*schiocchezze*]. Everything used to cost more, and was the more highly valued; even the marbles—the proper "heavies"—and the swap-cards were treasures. (*Libera nos a Malo*, p. 114)

Between the words *giochi* and *giocattoletti* lies all the difference between one age and another.

---

10. I exclude sports equipment: footballs, airguns, skates, toboggans, fishing-lines, etc., which are not strictly "toys," inasmuch as they are also employed by adults. Further, since I am dealing with artifacts, I exclude "natural" toys: conkers, sandcastles, snowballs, etc.

11. Margaret Mead, *Blackberry Winter* (London and Sydney, 1973), 12.

The point is, however, that whether in the age of the baroque or in the age of the bomb, the child's existence is compounded of trivialities; and for the writer, one of the most fundamental problems is how to justify the retelling of them, how to give them shape and significance, how to involve the serious reader, soaked through and through with Shakespeare and Dostoyevsky and Kafka, in the joyous but interrogative squeak of the two-year-old encountering an unknown object, or in the traumatic conundrum (spread out over four pages) of the ten-year-old faced with the momentous problem of eating a chicken croquette.[12] In brief, how to weave the utterly inessential into the fabric of an epic. From Rousseau onward, virtually every serious author of a Childhood has had to face up to the question, and has attempted, in one fashion or another, to justify his use of "trivia."

What we shall call *trivia* (as opposed to *curiosa*, which we shall discuss later) are those elements in the autobiography of childhood which are of no intrinsic interest (historical, sociological, psychological, or even anthropological), which can be of no obvious or immediate significance to the reader, and which, even if they seem meaningful to the writer, may be deemed so personal and (seemingly) insignificant that they neither could nor should form the material of literature. Such at least would be the opinion of the classical poets, who considered valid only that which was noble and exceptional, yet universal. The transition from the classical to the existential—from that which is noble, exceptional, yet universal, to that which is ignoble, commonplace, and obstinately individual—can be followed in all its diversity and with all its ramifications through the history of the Childhood, and in particular through the successive justifications for the use of trivia.

1. THE EGOTISTICAL ARGUMENT—not the most prevalent, because it requires a certain amount of courage and aplomb to use it, but nonetheless one of the most persistent over the decades: "I don't care if these details *do* bore the reader, they are important to ME!" This, on the whole, is a justification which works if it is asserted with sufficient conviction—that is, if the writer's personality is strong enough to carry the affronted reader along with him. The effrontery in itself is sufficiently arresting to counteract the potential boredom. Thus Rousseau (pioneer in this as in so many other aspects of the Childhood), states unashamedly: "I am perfectly well aware that the Reader has no great need to learn all this; but *I* need to tell him about it" (*Les Confessions*, 1:59). Implicitly, if not explicitly, this argument is used by many writers whose childhood was predominantly happy. The urge to recapture the insignificant details of a magical *paradis perdu* is endowed with at least a

12. Eugène Ionesco, *Découvertes*, 36. Robert L. Duffus, *Williamstown Branch* (New York, 1958), 163–66.

semblance of logical necessity by the fact that it *was* paradise and the details *were* magical. They are not so much irrelevant, as *irrationally* significant; they are, in Erich Kästner's phrase, "the memories which we always carry around with us like lucky coins" (*Als ich ein kleiner Junge war*, 6:152). Frequently, the underlying irrelevance or insignificance can be disguised by the writer's laying stress on the grotesque, or more especially on the *comic* side of the episode— witness Marcel Pagnol's delightful panegyric (addressed to himself) on the skill with which, at the age of seven, he had learned to simulate most realistically all the *noises* connected with getting washed, without ever actually touching a single drop of water.[13] At the opposite end of the scale, this same underlying egoism can be raised to the status of self-torture leading to self-purification: the emotions—preferably of shame—which result from the recalling of childhood's turpitudes and betrayals generate a fire destined to "purge and refine" the adult writer's moral sensibility, regardless of whether the reader can share in the experience or not. Michel Leiris refers to this objective quite frankly as one of "katharsis," and to the form of his autobiography as being one "able to bring *myself* to a state of exaltation." He would hope, rather perfunctorily, that it might also be one "able to be understood by others," but this is a relatively minor consideration, since he adds immediately afterward, "as much as possible" (*L'Age d'homme*, p. 13). A Leiris is sufficient unto himself; anything he proves, he proves to his *own* satisfaction, not to that of the reader—"A fly that I crush between my hands demonstrates to me my own sadism"—with always the final, supremely egotistical idea of "exaltation" added: "A glass of spirits tossed straight back sets me up on the dizzy heights inhabited by Dostoyevsky's great drunkards" (p. 167).

2. The Total-Truth Argument—in its simplest form, the contention that only by the avowal of the most intimate detail of experience, unknown to anyone save the writer, can the total truth of a unique, living being be reconstituted. The aim, in fact, is a synthesis of truth and triviality, each lending form, meaning, and vitality to the other. This synthesis receives its clearest formulation in Hal Porter's most memorable resolution: "therefore I must try for the truth *which is the blood and breath and nerves of the elaborate and unimportant facts*" (*Watcher on the Cast-Iron Balcony*, p. 10; my italics)

This argument (once again) was first advanced by Rousseau; nonetheless, in spite of the emphasis which he laid upon it, it by no means found immediate acceptance. As late as 1857, Sergei Aksakov, at work on his *Years of Childhood*, could still write to his friend Professor Maksimov of Moscow University: "The life of a child will not be understood by everyone, and the detail of the narrative will seem to many trivial and worthless";[14] and, rather more pompously,

13. Marcel Pagnol, *La Gloire de mon père* [1957], in *Souvenirs d'enfance* (Paris, 1968), 1:59.
14. Quoted by J. D. Duff in his introduction to the English translation of S. T. Aksakov's *Dyetskiye gody Bagrova-Vnuka: Years of Childhood* (Oxford, 1923; reprint, 1951), v.

Ernest Renan, writing round about 1880, claims to have excluded everything which is not directly relevant to his work as a philosopher and as a historian:

> To imagine that the insignificant details concerning one's own life deserve to be fixed on paper is to afford proof of a singular degree of petty vanity. If one records such things, it is only that one may transmit to others that theory of the universe which one carries within oneself. (*Souvenirs d'enfance et de jeunesse*, p. 8)

Perhaps such classical reticence and restraint in the matter of the minutiae of personal experience has something to be said for it. More pertinently, however, this complex synthesis of truth and triviality reveals itself as one of the factors which help to determine the elusive borderline between the Childhood and the novel; for the "Truth" of literature and the "Truth" of self are not necessarily identical, even when the second forms the subject of the first. For the self, it is sufficient that a triviality should be *felt* to be significant; for literature, it is essential that a triviality should be *perceived* to be significant. Thus the greater artists have consistently denied themselves this particular form of self-indulgence, using the "elaborate and unimportant facts" only when they can be demonstrated to be meaningful. Proust is a case in point; but so also is Joyce. Nothing, in the *Portrait of the Artist as a Young Man*, could seem less likely to escape from the domain of intimate triviality than the infant song "O, the green wothe botheth"; yet later when, at the age of ten, Stephen Dedalus makes his first attempt to elaborate an aesthetic, the seemingly pointless "green wothe" suddenly sharpens into focus and, pointless, makes the point: "But you could not have a green rose. But perhaps somewhere in the world you could" (*Portrait of the Artist*, p. 12). The trouble is that this is all too neat; *everything* fits in, everything is part of a pattern. There are no trivialities in Joyce, any more than there are in Proust. Yet, plainly, there *should* be: life is not like that. It is the absence of the arbitrary, the unrelated, and the insignificant which detracts from the "truth-to-Self" of the *Portrait of the Artist*, pushing veritable autobiography over the knife-edge into the alien territory of the novel, transforming the truth of fact into the alternative truth of fiction. The *authentic* narrative of childhood must necessarily contain an element of utterly irredeemable triviality, because this, more than anything else, constitutes the lived experience of the child. On the other hand, a Childhood which consists of nothing but trivialities is a trivial Childhood. There must be a meaning, even in un-meaning. This is the fundamental paradox of the genre.

3. THE "PETIT FAIT VRAI" ARGUMENT. Originally formulated by Stendhal in the 1830s, the notion of the "tiny, true fact" is important in that it leads straight to that unique mixture of realism and symbolism which is characteristic of the best of nearly all subsequent accounts of the earlier self.

In its simplest analysis, the Stendhalian concept of the *petit fait vrai* is this: the art of the writer consists in selecting, from among the infinite variety of material available to him, just that *one* fact or incident which, minute and insignificant as it may be in itself, nonetheless has the quality of alerting the reader into a sudden state of wakefulness by his realization that this is something *absolutely right* and *absolutely true*; and, going beyond this initial conviction of an accurately observed, "natural" truth, to suggest to his mind a whole scene or atmosphere, conjured up again in the total sum of its reality by that unique detail, vibrant with implications and resonances, yet so improbably *right* that it cannot conceivably be the product of a novelist's imagination, but must belong to the domain of observed or historical *fact*.

The technique of the *petit fait vrai* is one that Stendhal uses again and again in his great novels; but, in the *Vie de Henry Brulard*, he adds two further ideas to his basic concept. In the first place he notes that, precisely because the *petits faits vrais* which he is recalling are in themselves minute, they require, in order to be effective, the minutest, most accurate of descriptions—in short, he is prescribing the technique of the "close-up," as it will be used by so many writers of the later nineteenth and of the twentieth centuries. The significant incidents of childhood, he observes, *are* tiny; but "precisely because of their microscopic dimensions, they need to be related with extreme distinctness" (20:29)—otherwise they will prove totally uninteresting. This is fundamental: Trivia can be *made* meaningful by the precision and the detailed, analytical accuracy of their description alone; conversely, the slightest hint of vagueness or of imprecision will immediately destroy any conviction which the reader may hold of their authenticity, and hence of their interest. And in the second place, he suggests that the awareness that "this is *absolutely right* and *absolutely true*" argues a kind of Platonic (or perhaps rather "poetic") Absolute Perfection of experience, of which he himself alone may be aware, but which is so overwhelming in its impact that it constitutes one of those "sublime instants" which, alone and in themselves, serve to justify human existence and to give meaning to an otherwise meaningless universe. Monsieur de Corbeau was fishing for trout. It was winter. There was a bite. M. de Corbeau twitched his line; the twelve-ounce trout flashed through the air and caught across the naked branch of a willow tree. Miracle: a silver fish flashing against the sky, twenty feet in the air above the head of the watching child. "What delight for me!" (20:212). There is no rational explanation of this unadulterated, "miraculous" joy, recalled in all its detail and clarity some forty years later. It is the *petit fait vrai* illuminating the whole of an *inner* landscape.

4. THE EXISTENTIAL ARGUMENT. Under this very broad heading there may be grouped a wide variety of justifications for the use of trivia, all of which have in common the fundamental idea that "existence precedes essence," and that first the child, subsequently the adult, is shaped deterministically by his physical contact with the outside world, and consequently that every sensation encountered, however fleeting, is ultimately of incalculable importance. The

variations include the Lockeian/Wordsworthian proposition, to the effect that every idea in the mind is the direct product of impressions received through the senses (*"Nihil est in intellectu, quod antea non fuerit in sensu"*); the Freudian proposition, that everything essential in the psychological make-up of the adult is fashioned by experiences undergone by the child before the age of five; and, more interestingly, the idea that the "alternative dimension" of childhood can be basically explained by the fact that the child lives in a sort of permanent extension of the Sartrian "pre-reflexive cogito"—a state in which the mind, unalienated from its surroundings, neither observes nor analyzes them, but simply *is* (or "is-with") the phenomena which impinge upon its consciousness, at the same time as it imposes its own pattern and meaning upon them through the fact of its awareness. Thus the impressions stamped by way of the senses on the mind may originate in encounters and experiences trivial in themselves; but there is not—there *cannot* be—such a thing as a trivial sensation. Everything bears its due weight, everything contributes its tiny share to the eventual completeness of maturity. Such is perhaps the most convincing, and the most widespread, justification of this literature of trivialities.

5. THE ARGUMENT FROM POETRY. This is an argument in two parts, the one rooted in the nature of the object itself, the other in the poet's awareness of it. "All knowledge of the intimacy of things immediately becomes a poem," observes Gaston Bachelard,[15] stating the first part of the case: the object-in-itself, divested of its measurable properties and its utilitarian functions, will forever remain inaccessible, a mystery, and hence something beyond the region of rational experience. So here, once again, there *are* no trivial phenomena: every single phenomenon or experience becomes (once it is "known in its intimacy") significant because of its very *lack* of rational significance. That which defies explanation cannot be disregarded: it is either too sublime, or else it is too dangerous. Where the rational intelligence has to admit itself defeated, it cannot simply dismiss with contempt the object—the "Thing"—which has humiliated it. That object-in-itself, considered as a *Ding-an-sich*, belongs to another dimension. And the only human mind which has access to that dimension is that of the poet. "My personal truth has never interested me," concludes Georges Duhamel, "save insofar as I am aware that it transcends me and goes beyond me" (*Inventaire de l'abîme*, pp. 26–27).

The other side of the argument is that which is advanced, perhaps more traditionally, by the poets themselves rather than by the philosophers: namely, that all human truth starts with the insignificant *trivia* of observed behavior, but it is precisely the function of poetry to bestow form, durability, and

15. Gaston Bachelard, *La Terre et la rêverie du repos* (1948; Paris, 1965), 1:11.

significance upon that which, otherwise, would have remained individual, commonplace, and uninteresting. In other terms, great writing about small events and small people transforms them into great events and great people— which, potentially, was what they were anyway, for otherwise the poet could not have accomplished the transformation. In more everyday language, this essentially "classical" approach is precisely that which is recorded by Maxwell E. Perkins in his well-known account of an early interview that he had with Thomas Wolfe. Faced with the ungovernable mass of Wolfe's disordered manuscripts, and interrogating the writer about the content, he received the reply that "these people in it were his people"—that is, trivial, unimportant people.

My face took on a look of alarm, and Tom saw it, and he said, "But, Mr. Perkins, you don't understand. I think these people are *great* people, and that they should be told about!" He was right. He had written a great book.[16]

Whether Mr. Perkins fully grasped all the implications of this argument is not clear; but on analysis it reveals itself as a characteristically twentieth-century mixture of the classical view of the poet as the "universalizer of the particular," and the existentialist, or perhaps even structuralist, view that the ultimate reality in literature is the text, and that everything in the background to that text, including its models, owe their reality *to* that text. A "great" text *creates* a "great" reality. And so, once again, transformed by the genius of the poet, nothing is in itself trivial.

Not even sweets. Throughout this literature of childhood there runs a thin, glittering, translucent vein of pure poetry, a kind of incantation, a chanting of the magical names of candies. From Royal Leamington Spa there come

> Chewy locust, thick strong liquorice sticks,
> Aniseed balls, bull's-eyes and sherbet.
>
> (D. J. Enright, *The Terrible Shears*, p. 33)

and from stricken and decidedly un-Royal South Shields:

Dolly mixture, toffee-apples, "Mixed Shot," liquorice bootlaces, the wrapped lumps in the blue-and-white tins of Farrar's Original Harrogate Toffee . . . , Berwick Cockles, Edinburgh Rock, glacier mints and liquorice Allsorts, sherbet dabs, soda-fountain. . . .

For a ha'penny, we could buy a pipe made of liquorice, its "bowl" sprinkled with bright red hundreds-and-thousands to represent fire. . . . a ha'penny would also buy a drum of "Cut Cavendish," or a gobstopper, or a portion of cinder toffee. (Kirkup, *The Only Child*, pp. 117–18)

In Cornwall, there were

16. Maxwell E. Perkins, Introduction to *Look Homeward, Angel*, p. x.

long sticks of rock, huge oranges . . . liquorice, gingerbreads, comfits and dolly-day-dreams,[17]

and in Kiev there were

oily blocks of vanilla and chocolate halva . . . translucent chunks of sticky pink and lemon Turkish-Delight . . . pyramids of sugared pears, plums and cherries. (Paustov-sky, *Povest' o zhizni*, 1:78; trans., 1:66–67)

Brixton could furnish

clove-sticks, locusts, sugar-candy, coconut-ice, bull's-eyes, bouncers, brandy-balls, Chinese cushions, liquorice-sticks, Chicago caramels, Jap nuggets, Pontefract comfits, crystallised chips, coconut nibstick, popcorn, barley-sugar, colt's-foot-rock, marzipan, burnt almonds.[18]

yet Glasgow offered a more slender selection, including merely

sugar-mice and dolly-mixtures . . . jelly-babies and toffee-balls, sherbet-dabs and sug-arally-straps. (Molly Weir, *Shoes Were for Sunday*, p. 81)

Nor, seemingly, was the antipodean cornucopia less abundant: in Bairnsdale there were

Milk-Kisses, Silver-Sticks, Helen's Babies, Coffee Stars, aniseed balls and tiny glass tubes of Silver Cachous. (Porter, *Watcher on the Cast-Iron Balcony*, p. 150)

and, equidistant from Melbourne but in the opposite direction, the streets of Yuralla were paved, as it were, with

rum-rum-go-goes, Milk Poles, Silver Sticks, Cough Sticks, Sherbet Suckers, Liquorice Straps, Aniseed balls and Snowballs. (Marshall, *I Can Jump Puddles*, p. 63)

And so the tale goes on: not the taste (our children do not appear to have been greedy children), but the colors and, above all, the names. Out of child-hood's addiction to Callard and Bowser's Butterscotch, mint Imperials and humbugs, the true poet can conjure up a vision as "jeweled" as that of King Herod, in Oscar Wilde's drama, as he evokes the image of all the treasures in his palace to bestow upon Salome. "Leçon de choses, de choses!" exclaims Jules Supervielle.[19] Poet, or existential realist, the "lesson of things" is the same. Miracles themselves have their root in triviality.

17. Anne Treneer, *School House in the Wind* (London, 1944), 66.
18. Thomas Burke, *Son of London* (London, 1947), 30.
19. Jules Supervielle, *Boire à la source* (Paris, 1951), 56. This is one of the few occasions on which Supervielle's rather uninteresting Childhood reveals a connection with the preoccupations of contemporary French poetry. For a "leçon de choses," cf. Francis Ponge, *L'Œillet* [ca. 1941], from *La Rage de l'expression*, in *Œuvres* (Paris, 1965), 1:291–304.

In this study of the detailed inventory of the child's world, the last examples we have quoted, from the nostalgic poetry of dolly-day-dreams and sugarally-straps, take us into a different area of experience, posing different literary problems. The trivialities of childhood can be evoked in two ways, and with two distinct purposes: either to entrance and delight the writer himself with a glimpse of that lost paradise which can never be wholly accessible to any other being—Stendhal, and the flash of flickering silver from the trout suspended against the sky—or else to charm the reader back into that vanished country, enticed thither by memories which he must, if he comes from the same region and belongs to the same generation, share with the writer and perhaps with no one else, or, going still further back in time, to fascinate the reader with details about which he may have read in the history books, but to which now, for the first time, he discovers an eyewitness, and a child eyewitness at that. Such events, such phenomena are in this last case not merely "the kinds of accident that affect character and affront human dignity with the importance of their triviality" (Horne, *The Education of Young Donald*, foreword); they belong to a domain which can perhaps best be described as personalized social history. They are no longer *trivia*, but *curiosa*.

The trivia of childhood, by and large, all belong to a single, indivisible category: that of the insignificant. The writer's problem is how to make them significant in spite of all to anyone but himself. The curiosa, by contrast, can virtually be guaranteed to fascinate the reader, for all that he has only the slightest sense of history or the faintest proneness to nostalgia; and they can be subdivided into a number of categories, each with its own particular brand of imaginative appeal.

The first and most widespread of these categories, particularly in Childhoods written since World War II, is what one might call, seeking a pompous-sounding title, *Curiosa nostalgica*: "That's how it was when I was a child."[20] Nostalgia, as we have seen earlier, is rarely, if ever, a strong enough motivation in itself for inspiring a major Childhood, and so it is normally among the minor specimens of the art that this type of "curiosity" tends to flourish. Its primary definition is that the writer is fully conscious of the nature of the material which he is exploiting, and of the sympathetic response which will be evoked in the reader, and above all, perhaps, of the fact that this response will be pleasurable. The minutiae of daily life, familiar to anyone of that generation but now unknown and unrecorded, are details of a manner of existence which was fundamentally acceptable and therefore *right*; and so their passing can inspire nothing but regret.

Serious political and sociological writers of an earlier generation—Cobbett or Howitt, for instance—were already evoking something of the same nostal-

---

20. Cf. the title of Maureen Duffy's Childhood: *That's How It Was* (London, 1962).

gia in relation to the transformation of rural England at the time of the Industrial Revolution; but at the present time, perhaps unexpectedly, it is the changing face of the city rather than of the countryside which seems to evoke the most intense regret. The trams, the barrel organs and the pavement artists; the flower-sellers and the street cries; "the log-man, the muffin-man, the coal-man, the harp-man" (Christopher Robin Milne, *The Enchanted Places*, p. 22); the mechanics of the pawnshop;[21] the ingenious procedures for getting granite from the quarries to the docks in a train without an engine in Boston,[22] or the no less ingenious techniques and skills required to fit a new gas-mantle in Glasgow (Molly Weir, *Shoes Were for Sunday*, p. 60). Eleanor Farjeon (*A Nursery in the Nineties*) recalls getting milk direct from "The Cow" in Hyde Park; Ernest Shepard (*Drawn from Memory*), riding in the "cable-tram" that once climbed Highgate Hill. From Ernest Raymond (*The Story of My Days*), we can learn of the price of beer, matches, and whiskey in London in 1910; from James Kirkup (*The Only Child*), of the routine of washdays and baking days in South Shields; and from Richard Hoggart, of the protocol governing Working Men's Clubs and of the value of aspirin as an alternative to alcohol in Hunslet, both in the 1930s.[23] In the exploitation of this kind of material, the English writers far outstrip any of their contemporaries, with the exception of the Australians. Whether from this it is legitimate to conclude that the awareness of, and nostalgia for, the city is stronger in these two cultures than in any other is perhaps doubtful; yet, without any question, no two other cities evoke the same degree of nostalgia among the children who grew up in them as do London and Melbourne.

The problems arising, from the writer's point of view, out of this type of curiosa stem from the fact that its effect on the reader is somewhat unpredictable. For the reader who has shared the experiences—that, say, of keeping treasures in the miniature biscuit-tins that used to be put out for advertisement by Messrs. Huntley & Palmer, Peeke Freane, Carr and others (Kirkup, *Sorrows, Passions and Alarms*)—the effect may be electric: a "total recall," in the manner of Proust's *madeleine*. On the other hand, it may be *too* familiar, and thus produce no reaction at all. Or again, for the reader who has *not* shared the experience, the recounting of it can refer to the domain only of minor social history—which, of course, will eventually be the case for all readers, once the writer's own generation has disappeared. This has already happened for Childhoods dating back even to the latter years of the nineteenth

21. Mary Rose Liverani, *The Winter Sparrows* (Sydney, 1975). Cf. also A. S. Jasper, *A Hoxton Childhood* (London, 1969).

22. Edward Everett Hale, *A New England Boyhood* (Boston, 1893), 77.

23. Richard Hoggart, *The Uses of Literacy* (1957; Harmondsworth, 1965), passim. Hoggart offers a classic example of the way in which a work which started out as a straightforward Childhood finished up as a major text in the field of grass-roots sociology.

century. All women of *that* period knew what it meant to wear a bustle; but to the average woman of the 1980s, Flora Thompson can only be a "curiosity" in the fullest sense—the surprising revelation of something neither remembered nor forgotten, but simply never known:

> [The bustle was] the most popular fashion ever known in the hamlet, and the one which lasted longest. They cost nothing, as they could be made at home from any piece of old cloth rolled up into a cushion and worked under any frock. Soon all the women, excepting the aged, and all the girls, excepting the tiniest, were peacocking in their bustles, and they wore them so long that Edmund was old enough, in the day of their decline, to say that he had seen the last bustle on earth going round the Rise on a woman with a bucket of pigwash. (*Lark Rise to Candleford*, pp. 102–03)

The second category of curiosa lies in the realm of customs, institutions, and attitudes which are still familiar, but completely *un*acceptable, to the contemporary reader. Here, the reaction is completely different: not nostalgia, but rather a sense of shock that such experiences of primitive barbarity were the common lot of the child not more, perhaps, than fifty years ago. The ever-present darkness, cold, and fear; the little girls who, winter and summer, took it for granted that they had to walk four miles to school and four miles back again;[24] the boredom, drabness, and brutality of those schools once they were reached, and the savage stupidity of schoolteachers, the bullying and the bestiality[25]—or, alternatively, the torture of the *lack* of school for the intelligent child who wanted it but could not get it;[26] the slavery of the factory, the slavery of the home; the iron prison of dullness, good behavior, and compulsory churchgoing that gripped the child on Sundays; the ferocious medicines, the poultices and mustard plasters, the still fish-tasting cod liver oil,[27] the "castor-oil, epsom salts, calomel, magnesia, each and all of [which] have ripped my guts apart and caused me to writhe in discomfort and pain" (McInnes, *The Road to Gundagai*, 61); and the even more ferocious home-devised remedies and panaceas:

> We were put to bed at night with our mouths sealed with adhesive tape to prevent

24. Alison Uttley, *The Country Child* (1931; Harmondsworth 1976), 10–11.

25. See, among innumerable others, Lord Berners, *First Childhood*; Louis-Ferdinand Céline, *Mort à crédit*; Gilbert Cesbron, *Notre prison est un royaume*; Bernard Dadié, *Climbié*; Jean Genet, *Miracle de la rose*; Robert Musil, *Die Verwirrungen des Zöglings Törless*; George Orwell, *Such, Such Were the Joys* . . . etc., etc. By and large, French (and especially French-Canadian) children seem to have suffered from their schooling more than children of any other culture. *Cf.* Claire Martin, *Dans un gant de fer* (Ottawa, 1965–66).

26. Cf. Claude Brown, *Manchild in the Promised Land* (New York, 1965); Helen Forrester; Maxim Gorky; Ezekiel Mphahlele, *Down Second Avenue* (1959; London, 1972); Gabrielle Roy, *La Petite Poule d'eau* (Paris, 1951); Charles Shaw, *When I Was a Child* (1903; Firle, 1977) . . . etc.

27. Marcel Pagnol, *Le Château de ma mère* [1958], in *Souvenirs d'enfance* (Paris, 1968), 2:89.

mouth-breathing. . . . Our pillows were taken away from us; we were given a sulphur-and-molasses Spring tonic, and in the Winter, on Saturdays and Sundays, we were made to stay out three hours in the morning and three in the afternoon, regardless of temperature. We had come from a mild climate in Seattle, and at fifteen, twenty or twenty-four below zero we could not play, even if we had something to play with, and used simply to stand in the snow, crying, and beating sometimes on the window with our frozen mitts, till my Aunt's angry face would appear there and drive us away. (Mary McCarthy, *Memories of a Catholic Girlhood*, pp. 40–41)

These experiences date neither from the Middle Ages, nor even from the period of the Devils of Loudun: both belong to the 1920s and 1930s. It is fashionable to grumble at the failings of the National Health Service, the fumblings of Medicare and Medibank, or the tergivisations of the Sécurité Sociale; but how many of the grumblers recall what the wretched child had to put up with before 1940?

> Putting up with things
> Was a speciality of the age.
> You couldn't change things, and
> Trying would only make you miserable.
> (Enright, *The Terrible Shears*, p. 21)

These last examples of "torture by medicine" lead directly into what is in fact the major role played by curiosa in the structure of the Childhood; namely, that of incidental, minor, but fascinating aspects of social or technological history. The main distinction between this and the aspects discussed so far is that the facts of the past are presented to the reader objectively: no emotional reaction, whether of sympathy, nostalgia, or revulsion is expected; it is a straightforward record of the ways in which the world has changed. Sometimes this effect of objectivity may be accidental, time having removed that generation of readers who *might* have reacted with sympathetic emotionality. But more often than not, it is deliberate; the memorialist is consciously transforming himself into the historian of his own epoch.

And what emerges is a supremely interesting, if utterly disjointed and episodic, picture of the manners, fashions, and habits of past ages—the sort of material which, by the very fact of its triviality, lies well beneath the levels explored, not only by traditional narrational or modern analytical history, but even below that of the broad sweep of social history. Social historians will tell us of the arguments for and against smallpox inoculation;[28] Jean-Pierre de Florian tells us of the steps that the ordinary citizen had to take in order to obtain such inoculation.[29] The *New Cambridge Modern History* is excellent on

28. A medical technique introduced in the early eighteenth century and preceding by nearly a century Jenner's discovery of the principle of vaccination. See Introduction note 21.
29. Jean-Pierre de Florian, *Mémoires d'un jeune Espagnol*, 21–22.

the development of gunnery techniques during the eighteenth century—but the same Florian will give us details of the entrance examination which had to be taken by a sixteen-year-old candidate for a commission in the artillery: an examination which took place at Bapaume, and at which there were a hundred candidates for forty places (p. 71). Benjamin Constant, traveling in England at the age of nineteen in 1787, affords us a most curious picture of the way in which, already in the eighteenth century, the big business houses of London arranged long-term contracts with hotels and inns all over the country, so that their commercial travelers could be assured of a meal and a bed of a guaranteed standard and at a fixed price.[30] From Sergei Aksakov, we can learn how Russian peasants built a rye-straw rick at approximately the same date. Thomas de Quincey informs us how the system of registered mail and of money orders worked some forty years before the introduction of the modern mail system, and appends to this picture a summary of the progress and problems of the tourist industry in North Wales in the year 1802. If we turn either to Juliette Adam or to Gwen Raverat, we can learn something about what normal intercity traveling was like in the nineteenth century, before the invention of the suitcase. The suitcase is so obvious and so necessary an accompaniment to modern life that it seems inconceivable that civilized travelers could ever have done without it—yet, until the later years of Mr. Gladstone, such had in fact been the situation. Juliette Adam's family would transport their luggage in a multitude of hand-sewn parcels, "for in those days, in my Grandmother's household, suitcases were unknown, as also were trunks";[31] by Gwen Raverat's day, half a century later, "trunks and portmanteaux" at least existed, but they were so massive that they required no less than two strong men to carry them, and so there grew up a race of "cab-runners," who would attach themselves to the London four-wheeler "and hope to get a tip for carrying luggage upstairs."[32] And in case anyone is seriously seduced by the romantic, Georgette Heyer picture of the sheer beauty of horse-and-carriage transport, there is Gwen Raverat again to shatter the illusion: "I used to think that it would almost have been easier to put The Horses into the carriage and push them ourselves" (p. 174). And both De Quincey and Stendhal give an idea of the cost!

This substratum of minutiae, of the unremembered details of social and technological history, continues right through the nineteenth and twentieth

30. Benjamin Constant, *Le Cahier rouge* [written 1811], in *Œuvres de Constant* (Paris, 1957), 121.

31. Juliette Adam, *Le Roman de mon enfance et de ma jeunesse*, 80. The reference is to a journey made circa 1840.

32. Gwen Raverat, *Period Piece*, 128. When Humpty Dumpty coined the expression "a portmanteau word," his creator, Lewis Carroll, was cashing in on a very recent, and hence fashionable, innovation.

centuries. Even the austere Goethe deems it worthwhile to record the extraordinary difference that occurred in people's daily lives when the old, circular, bottle-glass windows were replaced by the square, modern, perfectly transparent panes, and the genuine "revelation" of the world that resulted from this "perfection of brightness," when for the first time ever houses were flooded suddenly with light (*Dichtung und Wahrheit*, 9:29). The first encounter with the bicycle has a special place of its own, as does the first encounter with the cinematograph (still referred to by my own father as the *Kye-nee-ma*) or with the tomato. We have forgotten now that in 1900 there were bicycling schools, exactly as today there are driving schools, and that sober, middle-aged people might be observed in every city in Europe

> learning to manage bicycles: their eyes staring, their jaws clenched, they would of a sudden shoot away from their instructor, rocket across the broad-walk, vanish into a clump of bushes, and reappear later with their machine around their neck. (Pagnol, *La Gloire de mon père*, 1:43)

Or that, in 1904, the bicycle was the fastest vehicle on the road of any country and, thanks to this fact, bred a race of irresponsible adolescent riders in precisely the same manner as the motorcycle does today.[33]

The story of the early cinema is, of course, by now well documented, although the histories of science and technology tend perhaps to stress cinema's achievements rather than dwell upon its inefficiencies. To the goggling child in the audience, it was perhaps the latter rather than the former which stamped themselves upon the memory; for example:

> A wet sheet was stretched across the stage. Then the chandeliers were put out, an ominous vivid light played on the sheet, and black spots scurried about on it. A smoky shaft pierced the darkness just above our heads, sizzling alarmingly as if a whole boar was being roasted behind our backs. (Paustovsky, *Povest' o zhizni*, 1:77; trans., 1:66)

This was in Kiev; but even in sophisticated Paris, the picture (or rather, the non-picture) was identical; only the similes used differ slightly:

> Newspaper had been pinned up over the windows. The screen was an ordinary sheet hung on a rope. Presently M. Nicole extinguished the gas chandelier, and we were plunged in Egyptian darkness. . . . Then a noise was heard which sounded like grains of sand striking a pane of glass, and a rather uncertain light was cast on the screen. . . . I opened my eyes as wide as I could, but all I could discern on the screen was something that looked like rain. (Green, *Memories of Happy Days*, p. 60)

It was, in fact, the very uncertainty of the early cinema as an effective means of entertainment which made it memorable to the child in the au-

---

33. Richard Church, *Over the Bridge*, 173. The symbolic role which the bicycle occupies in Proust's account of his (and Albertine's) early life needs to be seen in this perspective.

dience. As soon as the technology improved, as it had done by the 1920s, the child's interest waned and, as we have seen earlier, the movies became just an integral part of the commonplace, daily round, in no way competing with the ever-renewed "magic" of the theater.

Nor, to us, does it seem conceivable that, as late as the 1880s, the tomato was a virtually unknown, exotic, and frankly scarifying vegetable. Flora Thompson records her first, distinctly dubious, sight of one, "flatter in shape then than now, and deeply grooved and indented from the stem, giving it an almost star-like appearance" (Lark Rise to Candleford, p. 122); and from German-occupied Alsace, in a surprisingly dull Childhood of which this episode constitutes one of the few bright pages, Albert Schweitzer recalls how his mother received her first gift of "some of those red things" and, in high embarrassment at having not the faintest idea of what to do with them, eventually threw them away, to the satisfaction of the remainder of her family.[34]

We could continue this submerged history of social life and technology almost indefinitely, for, within the structures of the genre, it represents one of the essential means, always ready to hand, of sustaining the reader's interest through a world of trivialities. We could learn of the problems of running a butcher's shop in the days before refrigeration and, from more than one child-observed source, of adventures in the hairdressing-trade. We could learn of the very different problems, for a woman and a mother, of trying to climb aboard a moving electric tram in a hobble skirt. We could learn of the first introduction of electric light, of running tapwater, or of margarine—margarine, known in England circa 1880 as butterine, regarded with awe and suspicion by a generation of farm laborers who could rarely afford to eat the butter they themselves produced . . . margarine, circa 1940, banned by law in Québec Province, and, in Montréal, sold only in a surreptitious and clandestine manner, along with cocaine and other dangerous but desirable substances.[35] We could learn finally (since an end must be made) of the splendidly baroque elaboration bestowed upon lavatories by the French provincial nobility in the early days of the Third Republic, in whose châteaux, "in the remotest retreat, the Seat offered ten or more apertures, each of a different diameter, running from the adult to the smallest of small babies." (Jammes, L'Amour, les muses et la chasse, pp. 66–67). Clearly, there is fascination even for "The Specialist" in the vast fabric of curiosa which forms the backdrop to so many of our Childhoods.

Two further categories of curiosa are those which we might label the folkloric and the exotic. Both are much less widely exploited than the categories which we have examined so far; but, where they do occur, they are usually

34. Albert Schweitzer, Aus meiner Kindheit und Jugendzeit [1925], trans. C. T. Campion, My Childhood and Youth (1924; London, 1960), 26.

35. Mordecai Richler, The Street (1969; London, 1972), 66–67.

treated in considerable detail. The first is rooted basically in the community life of children—in what Richard Church calls their "tribal activities" (*Over the Bridge*, p. 123)—street games, skipping songs, nonsense songs, daring-rhymes, counting-out rhymes, and so on: the kind of material which has been so lovingly collected and analyzed by Norman Douglas in his pioneering *London Street Games* (1916), by the Opies in their *Lore and Language of School-children*, by Alan Milberg in *Street Games*, and, although with a rather different emphasis, by Kornyei Chukovsky in *From Two to Five*. Intriguing as some of this material is, it is only fair to say that this is an area where the preoccupations of the adult take over so completely from the direct experiences of the child that it barely concerns us in the present study.

Curiosa exotica are a different matter altogether. The "Exotic" first began to exercise its fascination over the European sensibility in the period 1780–1820, with tales of romance and adventure in far-distant lands, such as may be found in Bernardin de Saint-Pierre's *Paul et Virginie*, Chateaubriand's *Atala* or Tom Moore's *Lalla Rookh*. However, during the entire nineteenth century, no single Childhood would appear to have been published by a writer who had grown up outside Europe or the United States; and it is not until the year 1900 that we encounter the first specimen: the poet Louis-Honoré Fréchette's *Mémoires intimes*, describing his boyhood (circa 1840) in the Wilderness of Québec Province. Thereafter, however, examples multiply: Charles A. East-man or, by his Sioux name, Ohiyesa, in 1902; Saint-John Perse, from Guade-loupe, in 1910; W. H. Hudson, from Argentina, in 1918 . . . and so on, gradu-ally building up to the steady stream of African, West Indian, and Chinese contributions in the present era.

Childhoods whose narrative material is substantially colored by the exotic may be divided very roughly into three overlapping categories: the didactic; the interpretative; and the schizophrenic—and of these, only the first uses the element of curiosa for its traditional, or "Romantic" purpose. In the two other categories, the exotic is rarely if ever exploited for its own sake, but is employed only as a means for penetrating to the heart of much more serious problems. In all three categories, however, the difficulty which faces the writer is that phenomena and experiences familiar to the child itself in the country or in the ethnic community where it grew up must be assumed to be totally unfamiliar to the reader, so that no built-in response or recognition may be expected.

1. The Exotic-Didactic Childhood. In the vast majority of cases, the authors in this category were European children growing up, through some fortuitous concatenation of circumstances, in non-European surroundings: Edgar Austin Mittelholzer (*A Swarthy Boy*, 1963) in British Guyana, or Jules Supervielle (*Boire à la source*, 1951) in Uruguay. Exceptionally, the direction can be reversed: thus Julien Green's description of his Parisian upbringing in *Memories of Happy Days* (1942) is fundamentally different from any other

Parisian Childhood, in that it is destined for American instead of French readers and therefore consistently treats as *curiosa exotica* incidents which, in France itself, would be no more than the trivia of common experience. But in all cases, the writer's main concern is to *describe*: to provide, in palatable and curiosity-provoking form, information about landscape and living conditions, flora and fauna, manners and customs, with which the reader has no first-hand acquaintance. Frequently one learns a lot: Jade Snow Wong (Chinese ethnic community, San Francisco) has four pages of details on the best ways of selecting and preparing rice in Chinese home-cookery (*Fifth Chinese Daughter*, pp. 72–76); Mary Elwyn Patchett (inland New South Wales) is instructive concerning the customs and beliefs of the Myall group of Aborigines living on the fringes of the Sturt and Simpson deserts, knowledgeable about the unpleasant habits of black-snakes and the rather pleasanter ones of platypuses, and a positive mine of information on a whole variety of living creatures ranging from bull-ants to swagmen.[36] Flame trees (Elspeth Huxley), ombù trees (W. H. Hudson, Jules Supervielle), bombax trees (Camara Laye), tea plantations, coffee plantations, cocoa plantations (Bernard Dadié)—all these make their dutiful appearance and are displayed for the stay-at-home inhabitant of Bourg-la-Reine, Peckham, or Newark, New Jersey, accustomed principally to the idea that coffee and cocoa grow in tins and tea in packets. In this area, the exotic Childhood plays the part of an illustrated home encyclopedia.

2. THE EXOTIC-INTERPRETATIVE CHILDHOOD. Of far greater interest, poetically, sociologically, and often politically, this category represents an attempt by writers from newly independent national groups (India, Nigeria, the West Indies, the Malinké communities of Upper Guinea, and so forth) to make their former colonial masters aware, through the experience of their own childhood under an alien administration, that the culture of that anonymous, faceless mass of Wogs, or Nigs, or Slit-Eyes, which Europe for so many generations had treated as merely "pagan" or "primitive," was in fact as rich, as profound, and as complex as their own—if not, indeed, superior to it. There are problems, of course, and the first of these is that, by definition, in order to communicate with a European readership, the indigenous writer must use a language (and a literary form) foreign to his own heritage. He must write in English or French, or (more rarely) in Spanish or Portuguese or Dutch—thereby acknowledging that he has to some extent betrayed his own national and cultural authenticity and accepted the superior idiom of his colonizer. A second problem is that, if he is to assert the value of his own culture, he must almost of necessity portray his childhood as a happy and satisfying experience, *even* though it was spent

---

36. Mary Elwyn Patchett, *Ajax the Warrior* (1953; Harmondsworth, 1974), 63–67, 90–101, and passim.

under an "intolerable" foreign domination; and this, inevitably, will bring him into conflict with the more vituperative nationalist agitators and propagandists of his own country, whose "party line" is that any experience endured by the *enfant colonisé* must ipso facto be intolerable.[37] In practice, the poets would seem to have held out against the politicians; no more than the minutest fraction of the numerous Childhoods written by poets who grew to maturity under colonial administration contains so much as a hint of political vindictiveness.

Rather, it is the *positive* side of the non-European culture which comes to the fore—the warmth, the richness, the frequently baffling intricacy of clan relationships and clan loyalties, as opposed to what seems to be the sterile aridity of the European-patterned "nuclear" family; or else the unforgettable rituals and ceremonies which have been systematically obliterated in the childhood experience of the rationalistic West, leaving a void which needs to be supplied by sex, or drugs, or violence. Camara Laye, in *L'Enfant noir* (1953; trans. *The African Child*, 1979)—the first major work by an African writer to attract international attention—devotes the central and most memorable section of his narrative to the ceremonies and rituals of circumcision and initiation (*The African Child*, pp. 111–35); the significance of this being, not only that it constituted the climax and culmination of his own progress from childhood to adolescence, but that the public, celebratory, and *communal* recognition of the pains and responsibilities of awakening sexuality offer an alternative to the misery and the self-torturing isolation which so often afflict the European adolescent at a similar stage of development. Even in the far more Westernized, already Protestant, background of Wole Soyinka, whose father was a headmaster and whose mother ("Wild Christian") was a founder-organizer of the women's movement in Abeokuta, Southwest Nigeria—even here, the traditional ritual has its vital part to play. "There is more to the world than the world of Christians, or books," his grandfather tells the nine-and-a-half-year-old Wole, the evening before the painful initiation rites of ankle-and-wrist-cutting[38]—and once the operation has been endured, then most of the torturing complexes and insecurities of adolescence are discarded along with the oil-soaked bandages which temporarily protect the scars. These experiences are not just something "exotic" and alien to the Western tradition;

37. Cf., for instance, Alexandre Biyidi [pseud. Mongo Beti], "Afrique noire, littérature rose," in *Présence africaine*, n.s. nos. 1–2 (April–July 1955), 133–45. See Adèle King, *The Writings of Camara Laye* (London, n.d. [ca. 1981]), 98–101. Paradoxically (from our evidence) the only children who consider themselves positively to have suffered as the victims of colonization are the Québécois: see Pierre Vallières, *Nègres blancs d'Amérique* (1968); see also Albert Memmi, *Portrait du colonisé, précédé du portrait du colonisateur* (Paris, 1957), and in particular the section entitled "L'enfant colonisé."

38. Wole Soyinka, *Aké: The Years of Childhood* (London, 1981), 143.

they offer an alternative psychology—a tried science, like that of herbal medicine—until recently despised, but now due for belated recognition, as a reme-
dy to arrest the seemingly irrevocable slide toward emotional bankruptcy in
the West.

And closely associated with this concept of ritual, and at the very heart of
these "exotic-interpretative" Childhoods, is the experience of "magic." Not in
the individualistic, secretive, or symbolic sense in which we have discussed it
to this point, but in the sense of a quite literal, "real world" experience,
acknowledged as part of the normal routine of existence by the community as
a whole, much as the efficacity of Communion or of the laying-on of hands is
recognized by the average Roman Catholic. Camara Laye's father has "a little
black snake with a strikingly marked body," which sleeps in his bed and which
is his "familiar," his "guiding spirit," as it had been that of all his Malinké
ancestors; and almost the first lesson that the boy learns is that this creature is
"sacred" and must not be harmed (*The African Child*, p. 22). Similarly, his
mother possesses "strange powers":

> I hestitate to say what these powers were, and I do not wish to describe them all. I
> know that what I will say will be greeted with skeptical smiles. And today, now that I
> come to remember them, even I hardly know how I should regard them. They seem to
> be unbelievable; they *are* unbelievable. Nevertheless I can only tell you what I saw with
> my own eyes. How can I disown the testimony of my own eyes? Those unbelievable
> things. I saw them. I see them again as I saw them then. Are there not things around us,
> everywhere, which are inexplicable? In our country there were mysteries without
> number, and my mother was familiar with them all. (pp. 69–70)

Once again, the significance of these episodes is *not* that they are "exotic,"
but that they are *normal*. For the European child, the experience of Otherness
is haphazard and chancy; for the African child, it is institutionalized.

3. THE EXOTIC-SCHIZOPHRENIC CHILDHOOD—the narration of an experience
of the past self, in which two incompatible cultural backgrounds clash so
violently that the eventual writing of the autobiography becomes something of
an exercise in psychotherapy, an attempt to rescue the adult self from the void
to which contradictory, self-canceling forces have consigned it. Evidence of
this "divided self" may be discerned, albeit in minor and muted key, in the
Childhoods of many Jewish writers, where the inherited religious and cultural
traditions of the race come into fierce collision with the alternative standards
of an adopted country: in Judah Waten, for instance; or in Albert Bensoussan,
now a lecturer in the progressive Université de Rennes, but still for all that the
child who used to participate in moonlit rituals with his father on the roof of
his house in the Maghreb:

> For we would dance, you remember, within the sacred circle, linking our hands

mingled in the prayer of the father and of the son, rhythmically shaking our bodies inside the moonlit ring, in the Mosaic observance of the *Birkat*—blessèd be—*Ha-lébana*—the Moon.[39]

By and large, however, the Jews, with some three thousand years of exile and hence of potential cultural schizophrenia behind them, are relatively experienced in dealing with such problems. Not so the innumerable exiles and emigrants of the twentieth century—the Icelandic child suddenly transplanted to Winnipeg, the Italian child to Sydney.[40] In particular, the schizophrenic trauma is liable to occur (to judge from our evidence) among second-generation emigrant children, themselves born and brought up in the new country, but their parents and families still ineradicably held by the old. The situation is brilliantly portrayed from the parents' point of view by Vladimir Nabokov in *Pnin*, in the episode where the American-born children of émigré parents gape with hilarious disbelief while their progenitors wallow in rich steam-baths of pre-Revolutionary Russian emotionalism; but the most impressive analysis of this aspect of the exotic from the child's point of view is to be found in Maxine Hong Kingston's *The Woman Warrior* (1976).

The subtitle of *The Woman Warrior* is "Memoirs of a Girlhood among Ghosts"—a revealing and accurate description of the "exotic," when its effect on the child is that each of the different elements in its background is felt, not merely as "foreign," but as actively *hostile* to the others, so that, eventually, they cancel each other out, "killing" each other, and leaving nothing but voids or "ghosts" for the child to clutch at in its quest for an authentic foundation to its own existence. On the one hand, peasant China, with its millennial traditions, its family bondings and intimacies—with its "magic" no less than in Africa, and its rituals, but also with its superstition and its inhumanity, its merciless and murderous cruelties, its enslavement of women, its child prostitution, its brutal persecutions "explained" socioeconomically in terms of bad harvests and political turmoil. On the other, get-rich-quick California, the "Mountain of Gold," with its liberty and its philistinism, its opportunity and its blind materialism, its round-eyed, fair-skinned, semihuman natives who, in the awareness of the Chinese immigrants, have no solidity, no rooted reality, no meaning, no life . . . they are just ghosts. *All* ghosts. At San Francisco International Airport there are crowds of soldiers and sailors awaiting transport to Vietnam; "They were Army and Navy Ghosts." At Ellis Island there had been "an Alien Office Ghost." There are "Suitcase-Inspector Ghosts" and Ghosts who stamp papers:

We were regularly visited by the Mail Ghost, Meter Reader Ghost, Garbage Ghost.

39. Albert Bensoussan, *La Bréhaigne* (Paris, 1973), 44.
40. Laura Goodman Salverson, *Confessions of an Immigrant's Daughter* (1939; reprint, Toronto, 1981); Silvana Gardner, *When Sunday Comes* (St. Lucia, Queensland, 1982).

Staying off the streets did no good. They came nosing at windows—Social Worker Ghosts; Public Health Nurse Ghosts; Factory Ghosts recruiting workers during the war . . . ; two Jesus Ghosts who had formerly worked in China. We hid directly under the windows, pressed against the baseboard until the ghost, calling us in the ghost language so that we'd almost answer to stop its voice, gave up. They did not try to break in, except for a few Burglar Ghosts. The Hobo Ghosts and Wino Ghosts took peaches off our trees and drank from the hose when nobody answered their knocks.[41]

On the other hand, if the New Country, hollow and transparent in its unreality, is dead, the Old Country is no less so. What is China, to the Chinese child born in America? Not so much a promise as a kind of threat, a persistent force dragging it in an unwelcome, unknown direction, undermining even that minimum of security which the child has established, if only by its acquired familiarity with the ways of American Ghosts. But Chinese Ghosts? "I am to return to China, where I have never been" (p. 76). China is even less of a reality than America, not only because it is seven thousand miles distant, not only because it has been abandoned, but because it has, quite literally, ceased to exist. Chairman Mao's New China has swept like a hurricane across the Old and annihilated it. The half-starved peasants of the family memories have now been branded as "former landowners" and massacred; the "uncles" have been executed, "kneeling on broken glass," by people who have other plans for the land. And yet, in the New China, there is no more enslavement of women, no more child prostitution. Where is the truth?

I continue to sort out what's just my childhood, just my imagination, just my family, just the village, just movies, just living.

Soon I want to go to China and find out who's lying. (p. 205)

So, almost with a cry of despair, concludes Maxine Hong Kingston, robbed by the "exotic"—that is, by the alternative possibilities of existence engaged in a perpetual mental and spiritual struggle for survival—even of that subsistence-level minimum of certainty and security without which the human child, or adult for that matter, can barely exist. For the grown-up reader, the "exotic" may well be merely "romantic"; for the child who experiences it, it can be anything from daydream leading, by way of "magic," to plain nightmare.

The final category of curiosa which pervades the literature of the Child-hood is that which may be termed *Curiosa historica*: the reactions of the child to those events, large or small, which the reader may recall from his history books, or may, if he is that way inclined, look up in the daily press of fifty, a hundred, or a hundred and fifty years ago—or perhaps, indeed, learn about for the first time, and then find himself tempted to verify afterward. This is the

41. Maxine Hong Kingston, *The Woman Warrior. Memoirs of a Girlhood among Ghosts* (New York, 1976), 98.

basic material of history observed from "below-stairs": as Hitler's Viennese-born vegetarian cook, Fräulein Manzialy, might have observed her employer's historic meeting with Chamberlain and Daladier at Munich; or (to take an example from fiction), as the little peasant girl Malasha looks on at, and interprets in her own terms, the debates of the Russian Higher Command after the Battle of Borodino.[42]

Again, perhaps, this type of curiosa belongs to the domain of memoirs rather than to that of autobiography proper: memoirs of public events, memoirs—the first intimation we have had so far—of awarenesses of the greater world intruding on the small world of the child. There is a child's-eye view of the great Sydney dock strike (Waten, *Alien Son*, pp. 144–55), and one of the railway engine which fell from the high-level platform of the Gare Mont-parnasse in Paris straight down into the street below (Duhamel, *Inventaire de l'abîme*, p. 114). Svetlana Alliluyeva recalls the domestic arrangements and the polite table talk which accompanied her father's first formal meeting with Winston Churchill.[43] There are innumerable recollections of the Paris Interna-tional Exhibition in 1900. Occasionally we encounter a Childhood almost entirely composed of reminiscences relating to such nine days' wonders. The comtesse de Pange, for instance, great-granddaughter of Madame de Staël and scion, from another strain, of the historic de Broglie family, moved even from her infancy in circles both socially and intellectually so exalted that virtually every event of which she has any recollection at all hit the headlines of the press for a day or two at least.[44] Sometimes the scale of events is bigger, but the reaction still equally circumscribed. For Stendhal, the French Revolution was a glorious game of cops and robbers, significant only because the whole strength of revolutionary France now appeared to be in alliance with *him* (aged eleven) against the father and aunt whom he hated. For Goethe, the Lisbon earth-quake was memorable, but mainly because, in himself as in so many others, it occasioned the first doubts as to the all-embracing benevolence of God (*Dicht-ung und Wahrheit*, 9:30). For Valerie Avery, the Blitz on London is reduced to the dimensions of a single air-raid shelter, with her mother "the last to come in, clutching her insurance policies in one hand, candles and matches in the other" (*London Morning*, p. 10); for Pascal Jardin, the lasting image of total war is formed when a German fighter plane crashes at the back of his house. It is a late spring evening; and, when the alarm is over, he walks through the orchard down to the river:

But suddenly, the water grows murky, changes color, becomes suffused with red

42. L. N. Tolstoy, *War and Peace*, Bk. 3, ch. 4.
43. Svetlana Alliluyeva, *Dvadtsat' pisem k drugu* (New York, 1968), 160–61; trans. Priscilla Johnson, *Twenty Letters to a Friend* (Harmondsworth, 1968), 150–51.
44. See Comtesse de Pange, *Souvenirs*, 3 vols. (Paris, 1962–68), particularly vol. 1, *Comment j'ai vu Paris 1900*.

dye, then turns blood-red. And then bits of human beings start floating down. Assortments to suit everyone's taste there are, on the surface of that shifting display-counter, feet naked or shod, heads, hands, bundles of intestines, viscera shaped like jellyfish, trunks all entangled in clumps of watercress. The bits which are still clothed are encased in green cloth. . . . Down drifts, all on its own, a helmet, a singular little boat, spinning round like a top in the whirlpool hollows.[45]

To observe that the child has, and always has had, the ability to reduce the most momentous events of history to its own scale can be nothing but a platitude. What would appear to be a more fruitful conclusion to draw from this rapid survey of the various categories of curiosa, and of their use as the material of literature, is that, in one important sense at least, they are "padding." The greater the writer, the less, as a general rule, the intrusion of curiosa. There are few in Stendhal, virtually none in Tolstoy or in Gide, none at all in Bely or in Joyce. Joyce, again, in this respect as in so many others, offers a perfect illustration of the way in which historical contingency can be integrated into the higher structure of an artistic concept. Here and there, the *Portrait of the Artist* seems, at first sight, to let fall a careless specimen or two of *Curiosa historica*: the description of the horse-drawn trams, for instance, in Dublin circa 1890, or of the Highland sentries pacing up and down outside the railway stations or the Bank of Ireland. But, as was the case with Joyce's trivia, these are curiosa only in appearance. They are in fact completely functional, and fully used for significant effect. In subsequent developments, the horse-trams will be used by Stephen Dedalus as an illustration of "realism" as opposed to "romanticism" in poetry (p. 71); and, nearly a hundred pages after their original appearance, the sentries will be revealed in their true light as pure symbols: "The University! So he had passed beyond the challenge of the sentries who had stood as guardians of his boyhood" (p. 165).[46]

Save in rare and exceptional cases, curiosa do not add significantly to our understanding, either of the child, or of childhood. Only when they are wholly assimilated, via one or more of their details, into the inner consciousness do they become significant. On the other hand, they serve as a useful counter-weight. If, as we have argued, the poet's recollection of his own childhood is again and again apprehended as something magical, as an experience relating to a dimension altogether alien to that of everyday, adult life, the curiosa serve to set this preoccupation with the irrational and the transcendental in its proper perspective. *Parts* of childhood may be magical; but clearly not all of it. Other parts remain irremediably rooted in commonplace reality. There may be "magic" in the child's first experience of theater; there is clearly none whatsoever in its first glimpse of a tomato, an air-raid shelter, or a bicycle.

45. Pascal Jardin, *La Guerre à neuf ans* (Paris, 1971), 159.
46. Cf. pp. 87 and 96.

The child is virtually immune from the greater world; the adolescent, by contrast, is not. In fact, a significant part of the evolution toward maturity could be described as a process by which the Greater World slowly intrudes upon, then eventually usurps the place of, the Small World, so that the latter remains only as a distant memory, to be resuscitated later, with industry and effort, by the adult.

In the present epoch, two concepts above all have to be mastered, and mastered with difficulty, before the child emerges through adolescence into the adult: the concept of class and the concept of politics. Both, but especially the first, are totally alien to the child. Class is something that cannot be apprehended in itself; it can only be grasped in relation to something that the self is not; it is, in Sartrian terms, the *Others* who designate one as "lower," "middle," or "upper" class. The child knows only that it is happy or unhappy; its sense of class can only be imposed artificially, by adult indoctrination. ("Peer group" indoctrination, of course, merely reflects a prior indoctrination of the peers by other adults.) More often than not, this takes the form of snobbery, direct or inverted[47]—but equally parrotlike and fundamentally meaningless in both cases. The child may be, in the long run, "determined" by its class background; but this is not something of which it can be aware *as a child*. When D. J. Enright comments:

> I can't help it, I still get mad
> When people say that "class" doesn't mean
> A thing.   (*The Terrible Shears*, p. 64)

he is expressing an entirely adult point of view. This is especially true, of course, among our atypical children who, future poets, are by definition intelligent, and who, in consequence, feel their intelligence as a far greater barrier between themselves and others than any conceivable division between squire and laborer, millowner and charge-hand, *barin* and peasant. "Mit der Dummheit kämpfen Götter selbst vergebens"[48]—the ultimate class barrier is one of intellect, and our Childhood poets from the outset have been the first to realize this. Nothing is more striking, among the evidence which we have

---

47. Tom Sawyer and Huck Finn, with their inexpressible contempt for children who wear shoes, are classic examples of "inverted snobbery" in action. All in all, the sociologists confirm our independent conclusion, that the normal (young) child may feel "unhappy," but does not, without adult prompting, feel itself to be "underprivileged." The Harlem kids described by Herbert Kohl in his *36 Children* (1967; reprint Harmondsworth, 1972) dislike their own environment and long to improve it (pp. 47–53); but, as Mr. Kohl found, they dislike other (materially better) environments even more (p. 107). The sense of "familiarity" and of "home" far outweighed any sense of "underprivilege" or of "class."

48. "Against stupidity the Gods themselves / Do fight in vain"; Schiller, *Die Jungfrau von Orleans*.

surveyed, than the almost total absence of *any* sense of class other than taboos quite clearly inspired by adults. The nearest that the child itself gets to a sense of class superiority is the highly personal, often nanny-encouraged doctrine "*We're* better than those awful children in the next-street-but-three." The awareness of *racial* distinctions raises rather different problems; but that is an issue which goes beyond the present study.[49]

The early awareness of politics is more complex, responding far more directly to the tensions of a given situation than does the consciousness of class. Two factors above all may affect the child: a general threat of impending disaster, often acutely intuited rather than openly expressed, which can oppress a whole community—that "dread of war," for instance, which, as James Kirkup recalls, "hung round us all the time and grew greater as the Thirties advanced" (*Sorrows, Passions and Alarms*, p. 64); or else particular political dissensions which can cause rifts, disharmonies, and quarrels within the family itself. The rare cases of "politicized" Childhoods result invariably from this split-family background: Stendhal, Juliette Adam, Mulk-Rāj Anānd, James Joyce—Ireland at all times, India on the brink of liberation, France in her reiterated moments of revolution.

James Joyce gives most of the political background to the *Portrait of the Artist* without comment until his concluding sections, when Stephen Dedalus is already an undergraduate and able to discuss the issues from an adult point of view. By contrast, in *Le Roman de mon enfance et de ma jeunesse*, perhaps the first and still the most impressive example of a wholly politicized Childhood, Juliette Adam has her direct and personal introduction to political issues when, at the age of four, she is forcibly abducted by her Royalist-Catholic mother, and aggressively baptized, against the wishes of her left-wing, anti-clerical father. With each year that passes, the political tensions that divide the family increase. Her grandmother (her mother's mother) *loathed* Juliette's father—

"My son-in-law is a dangerous maniac, with those social-democratic ideas of his! Godless, my God! Ideas like his, they're the end of everything, the end of religion, the end of the family, the end of property, the end of . . . the end of the World, they are!" (p. 88)

—she herself being an *Orléaniste*, a supporter of the current (1830–48) dynasty of Louis-Philippe, and therefore at daggers drawn with the *Légitimiste* supporters of the displaced Bourbons—including her own daughter, Juliette's

---

49. This is the reason why highly significant texts such as Claude Brown's *Manchild in the Promised Land*, Sheikh Hamidou Kane's *Aventure ambiguë*, N'Gugi wa Thiong'o's *The River Between*, or Richard Wright's *Black Boy* have not received the attention which they merit in the present essay.

mother. She was also barely on speaking terms with her own husband, who, as though deliberately to aggravate matters, had declared himself an impassioned *Bonapartiste*. Given the French love of symmetry, in war as much as in peace, it therefore became inevitable, under all these pressures, for Juliette's father to swing progressively further and further to the Left, abandoning the comparatively tame regions of free-thinking radicalism for the orgiastic intoxication of syndicalism, socialism, and—eventually—communism. By the time Juliette was six, both her grandparents were separately taking her aside and indoctrinating her, first one, then the other, with their mutually hostile ideologies; by the time she was eight, her father was giving her advanced courses on the political theories of Robespierre, Saint-Just, Louis Blanc, Pierre Leroux, Proudhon, and Ledru-Rollin. It was the quarrels, of course, that stuck chiefly in her memory:

> It is impossible to conceive the scenes that took place. I can recall my terror when they first started; I used to scream at the top of my voice, or burst into sobs, but nobody even heard me. (pp. 89–90)

Nor is it surprising that, before long, she had a nervous breakdown, during which, at the height of her delirium, "I could babble of nothing but politics, and socialism" (p. 124; see also pp. 111–12). Eventually she had to be sent away to some nonpolitical aunts in the country for a kind of ideological convalescence.

The unusual, almost the unique feature of Juliette's case, however, is that from a very early age, as a result of all these pressures, she actually began to *think* about the political issues for herself. The scenes, the quarrels, the ideological confrontations, she notes, "penetrated deep into my memory, *and even deeper into my thought*" (p. 88; my italics). By the age of ten, she was reading with critical attention writers such as Proudhon, Fourier, and Victor Considérant, and by the end of 1847, when she was eleven and a half, she had a fully formed political ideology of her own, to which, she adds, she was destined to cling for a further thirty-five years before finally discarding it as unrealizable. Politics, practical as well as theoretical, seem to have run in the family. Not only did the name of Saint-Just appear in the family tree, but it was her own godmother, Camille, who had organized Prince Louis-Napoléon's escape from the fortress of Ham in 1846, where he had been imprisoned in consequence of his unsuccessful attempt to carry out a *coup d'état* in 1840. It is not to be wondered at, therefore, that in February 1848, when the Revolution broke out, Juliette, still not yet twelve, led a classroom insurrection and became the dominating figure in her school *phalanstères* [cooperative work-groups] and the guiding spirit of its turbulent attempts at social reform. For a while, she recalls, the teachers were genuinely frightened of her; clearly, with her lucid mind, her impassioned ideological convictions, and her powers of leadership, she had inherited something more than simple blood kinship with Saint-Just. 1848 was the high-point of her childhood:

The men of 1848 were Apostles, they were Saints. Never, in any epoch, had there been more honesty, more virtue, more noble simplicity. They were not politicians, they were spirits in love with the Ideal. (p. 293)

Throughout the spring and early summer of 1848, this state of euphoria persisted; but by June, the tide had turned. The "National Workshops," in which she was so passionately interested, were being disbanded—one of the saddest moments of disillusionment in French ideological history—and, with this incontrovertible evidence that the Revolution, at least as far as its *social* aims were concerned, had failed, the authorities in Juliette's boarding school began to recover their self-confidence, and she was expelled. In rapid succession she passed through stages of aggressive frustration, disillusioned boredom, and, finally, self-criticism. "I reached the verdict that I was pretentious, unbearable, and I resolved within myself that I was going to be somebody quite different" (p. 324). It was, in fact, the end of her childhood proper, although politics, albeit of a less ardent variety, were to continue to preoccupy her for the remainder of her life.

Unique in so many ways, Juliette Adam's political involvement between the ages of ten and twelve is especially so in that it is spontaneous; that is, thanks to the fact that she was indoctrinated in so many different directions at once, she had acquired by the age of ten a capacity for independent political reasoning which normally is not achieved until late adolescence, if at all. From the first, politics, for her, involved real issues, directly affecting her own life and that of her family, instead of being the mere parrot-repetition of slogans. She was active in her search for an ideology capable of transforming the world, whereas ninety-nine children out of a hundred, even when they have glimpses of this particular aspect of the greater world outside, remain passive.

As contrasting examples of politicized Childhoods—examples which strikingly illuminate this characteristic passivity—we have two narratives of children brought up in Italy under Fascism: Susanna Agnelli and Luigi Meneghello. Of these two, Susanna Agnelli's experience was probably less than typical, primarily because of the fact that her grandfather was the millionaire founder-owner of the Fiat industrial empire, and thus was able to maintain the family's independence against virtually any regime, but also because of the fact that her upbringing was cosmopolitan, including French and English schools and a much-revered English governess. Nonetheless, the patterns of political indoctrination to which she was subjected in no way conflict with those imposed upon Luigi Meneghello; it is simply that their hold upon her was much weaker.

Born in the early 1920s, Meneghello was brought up during the decade or so when Mussolini was at the height of his power; and an important aspect of his regime (and one which Hitler borrowed from him) consisted in the *total* indoctrination of the younger generation. The skill with which this was undertaken emerges clearly, both from *Libera nos a Malo* (1963) and from the later *Pomo Pero* (1974). The process is the opposite of that which we have examined in the case of Juliette Adam: not the presentation of conflicting ideologies, which can have the undesirable consequence of making the child think for itself, but the subtle and imperceptible permeation of all the most normal preoccupations and delights of childhood by one specific ideology: to use our own terms, the penetration of the small world by ideas drawn from the greater world, without allowing the small world to lose any of its comfortable and accessible smallness.

All children, for instance, hear nursery rhymes; little Luigi hears *fascist* nursery rhymes. All children sing songs; Luigi sings *fascist* songs. Most children learn hymns; Luigi learns *fascist* hymns, more often than not without understanding a word, so that, for instance, "Vibra l'anima nel petto" becomes "Vibralani! Mane al petto!";[50] while

> Freme, o Italia, il gagliardetto
> E nei fremiti sei tu!

is transmogrified into

> Freni Italia al gagliardetto
> E nei freni ti sei tu![51]

Libera nos a Malo, in fact, opens with the glimpse of a very small Luigi bouncing on the parental double bed to the joyous accompaniment (in his own local dialect) of anticommunist slogans:

> The surface is elastic, you can't stay upright, you try to keep your balance, dancing from side to side: you sink down and bounce up again with legs widespread, what fun! They laugh, and I laugh with them, balancing and singing, *Get yer guns, boys, we're the Fassists, we'll bash the cummunistists!*
> What a lovely game, how little the difference between falling down and standing up: the morning is all bright gold. *And we compose the cadres of FASSISM!* What delightful words! I wonder what they might mean. (pp. 7–8)

For the Italian child, the Feast of the Epiphany (Twelfth Night) is a major event in the cycle of the year, inseparable from the receiving of presents and from

---

50. *Libera nos a Malo*, 9, 299. The original phrase means "The Soul stirs in the Breast"; the child-version is delicious nonsense.

51. The original phrase could be translated, "The pennant, O Italy, is a-tremble, /And in its quiverings, Thou art found"; the child's version retains memories of the brakes on its bicycle [*freni*].

other long-anticipated delights, much as Christmas is to the German or English child, or New Year and St. Nicolas's Day are to the French. For Luigi too there was a "Befana"; but it was no longer Christian, or at least not wholly so; it was the "Befana fascista":

The first days of the year, a time above all others instinct with poetry, filled with goodwill toward men, situated in the unreal atmosphere of holiday and in the curious, clear brilliance which the cold weather and the wintry sun, the multiple Confessions and Holy Communions, impart to the emotions:

> The Fascist Befana in the sun
> Showers sparks of Love and Faith on everyone.   (pp. 55–56)[52]

It is, in fact, this fusion of naive childhood Catholicism with a perhaps naive childhood Fascism which sets the tone of Meneghello's experience from the very opening pages of Libera nos a Malo, and which necessarily distinguishes it from the specifically anti-Christian indoctrinations of the Soviet Union and (presumably) of Nazi Germany. The powerful subconscious links which exist in the Catholic child's mind between God-the-Father and his own human father, between Mary-Mother-of-God and the woman he knows as Mother-of-Himself, are subtly altered, so that, while the God/Father identification is allowed to subsist, the Mary/Mother is doubled by a nationalistic equivalent, that of Country/Mother: "Ama la Patria, o fanciullo. Essa è come tua madre."[53] Thus the political indoctrination works simultaneously on two levels: that of natural family affection, and that of an all-pervasive, colorful, sensual religious ambiance.

Inevitably, the child Luigi (and even the child Susanna)[54] grew up as convinced little Fascists—up to a certain point. To what point exactly, had outside events not intervened, will never be known. Both Susanna Agnelli and Luigi Meneghello belonged to exactly the same generation: that which had reached the age of twenty when the first cracks began to appear in the Fascist edifice, followed within a few months by collapse, shame, and agony, and the ideological void and turmoil which followed Hitler's Machiavellian takeover of Italy, and his cynical reinstatement of the fallen Duce as a puppet-Quisling. In the third volume of his Childhood, Fiori italiani, Luigi Meneghello describes the traumatic effect of his discovery that there might be such a thing as "anti-

52. "La Befana" (a popular corruption of the word Epifania) is symbolically portrayed as a very old woman carrying on her back a wicker basket full of toys.
53. Quoted from an Italian primary-school reading book dated 1951—that is, well after the Mussolini period. "Love thy Fatherland, O [male] child; it is as thy Mother." Concerning some of the implications of this patriotico-symbolico-androgynous mix-up, see my essay "Mother Russia and the Russian Mother," in Proceedings of the Leeds Philosophical and Literary Society 19 (1984), part 6, in press.
54. Susanna Agnelli, Vestivamo alla marinara (Milan, 1975).

Fascist" ideas;[55] his conversion was complete within a few weeks, and he finally realized his mature identity—and the "end of his childhood"—as an anti-Fascist partisan fighter. But let us imagine that Mussolini's Italy had *not* collapsed. . . . The tone of both *Libera nos a Malo* and *Pomo pero* is oddly impersonal; the very humor of the books seems to act as a kind of defense mechanism, guarding against self-revelations or self-examinations which might be decidedly uncomfortable. The politicized, indoctrinated child-self is neither pitied nor criticized; it is accepted as a fact: "That's how it was." Perhaps the most disturbing feature of this kind of manipulation of the small world by the greater is that it leaves the child no point of reference outside itself. "Whatever is, is right"—necessarily so, since there is no known alternative.

Thus if, in some cases, the small World and the greater World interact, it is only to a very limited degree. In the vast majority of our Childhoods, the small world predominates absolutely, and the first intellectual preoccupation of the child is to establish its inventory. In this sense again, Rousseau's assertion that the mind of the child is totally distinct from, and inaccessible to, the mind of the adult, is confirmed. But the writer encounters yet another problem, since the act of writing for a public belongs irremediably to the greater world, and thus cannot fail to distort the picture of a world which, in its authentic reality, was entirely small. In terms of the inner structures of the genre, this is perhaps a further significance of the distinction which we have established between trivia and curiosa, and of the balance which major writers maintain so carefully between them. It is the *trivia* which constitute the authenticity of the small world, the *curiosa* which link this same small world with the greater. Insofar as the writer is concerned at all times to distinguish the self-that-was from the self-that-is, and yet at the same time to establish and define the link between the two, the first a unique and isolated identity, the second a sociopolitical animal, it is the trivia which incarnate and symbolize "pure childhood" as an autonomous mode of being, while it is the curiosa which represent the link between the child's experience and the alien world of adults to which, eventually, he or she is doomed to accede. Thus, if social and political history may, at first sight, appear to be unhappy constituent elements of the Childhood, they have nonetheless specific functions to fulfill.

55. Luigi Meneghello, *Fiori italiani* (Milan: Rizzoli, 1976). I have not located the authentic narrative of a non-Jewish child growing up inside Nazi Germany.

7   Puer Ludens:
An Excursion into Theory

Early childhood is surely the metaphysical age.
        —Romilly John, *The Seventh Child*

A mesure que le ciel se dépeuple, le sacré reflue sur la terre.
—René Girard, *Mensonge romantique et vérité romanesque*

In his excellent, all-too-brief essay on the pastoral as a mode of literary expression and of cultural sensibility, Peter Marinelli puts forward the idea that there is a direct connection between the decline of the pastoral in the closing years of the eighteenth century, killed by utilitarianism and industrialization, and the rise of the Childhood during the same period. The second, in fact, is a continuation, in a different mode, of the first. "If the pastoral lives for us at all at the present time," he argues,

it lives by a capacity to move out of its old haunts in the Arcadian pastures, and to inhabit the ordinary wintry landscape of the modern world, daily contracted by the encroachment of civilisation and as a consequence, daily more precious as a projection of our desires for simplicity. . . . We have begun to transfer the aspects of the pastoral Golden Age into the time of innocence that every individual can remember and to speak of a pastoral of Childhood.[1]

Marinelli supports this argument with a number of very valid parallels between the two genres: the ubiquity of the "garden" image, for instance; the discovery of a "voluptuous and pagan sexuality"; the myth of an original innocence still "trailing clouds of glory" on its first appearance in the world, only to be destroyed by the "Fall" of adolescence and maturity; and the need for the writer to distance himself from his vision, either by the perspective of history, or by that of adult status (pp. 75–80). He concludes that the true descendant of the "pure" pastoral is the modern narrative of childhood and adolescence: "The youth of mankind finds a parallel in the youth of each man" (p. 21).

Unfortunately, the instances of the modern Childhood adduced in support

1. Peter Marinelli, *The Pastoral* (London, 1971), 3–4.

of this argument—Laurie Lee's *Cider with Rosie*, Thomas Wolfe's *Look Homeward, Angel*, and Richard Llewellyn's *How Green Was My Valley*—are inadequate in themselves to substantiate it. Childhood seen as a *paradis perdu* would appear to be (marginally) the exception rather than the rule among the narratives which we have been considering; there are just too many tyrannical fathers and sadistic mothers, there is just too much poverty and brutality, for us to be able to accept without qualification the equation: Childhood = Arcadia. In spite of this, however, there is an important sense in which Marinelli is absolutely right in his argument. Unquestionably, the Childhood does continue and replace the pastoral, but on a rather deeper level than the one suggested.

What has emerged from our analysis so far is that the experiences of childhood take place in a dimension, whether material, spiritual, or linguistic, *different* from that of the adult. It is, in a sense, irrelevant whether these experiences in themselves are pleasant or unpleasant, glorious or fearful, for their remoteness and their "Otherness" constitute their unique role. It is this clearly sensed, yet rarely analyzed awareness of a wholly different mode of being in the world that is so frequently referred to by the all-embracing term *magic*.[2] It would seem to be possible, by following up a particular current of ideas developed over the last half-century by a number of philosophers, psychologists, and sociologists, to circumscribe this common notion of "magic" still more closely, and to see the undoubted parallelism between the pastoral and the Childhood as something perhaps more fundamental, and certainly of wider application, than their common roots in nostalgia for the simplicities of a vanished Garden of Eden.

The argument—one of the more significant contributions which the present century has made toward an understanding of the human condition—runs briefly as follows: All human experience can be divided into one or the other of two categories: a "real" dimension, in which acts produce *useful* consequences, and are evaluated in terms of their practical, material contribution to the well-being of the performer; and a "play" dimension, where acts are wholly gratuitous, and generate no direct consequences which affect in any way the well-being of the performer in the "real" world, but which are nevertheless felt to be at least as valuable and in every sense as serious as their counterparts in the dimension of "reality." The "real" dimension is that by which man sustains his existence as an animal, having needs in common with all other animals. The "play" dimension is that in which he asserts his uniqueness as a human being; it is the foundation of all culture, all art, and all

2. It is worth recalling that the Magician is one of the stock characters of the pastoral. Cf., for instance, Polistène in Racan's *Les Bergeries* (1619).

religion; and the standard by which it is evaluated is, in a very broad sense, the *aesthetic*.

Certain of the foundations of this concept were established in the late nineteenth century by the sociologist Emile Durkheim and by the anthropologist and folklore scholar Sir James Frazer, whose monumental study of the relationships among myth, ritual, magic, and religion, *The Golden Bough*, began to appear in 1890. However, the crucial essay in which hitherto scattered notions began to be brought together was a comparatively late paper by Sigmund Freud, *Beyond the Pleasure Principle* (1920), in the course of which his thinking started to move away from his earlier, more or less exclusive preoccupation with the psychology of the individual toward a consideration of the problems of "culture" as a whole.

Freud's argument, reduced to its most elementary terms, is as follows: the human mind prefers a state of "pleasure" or "harmony" to one of discordancy or "un-pleasure"; consequently, all mental activities will be stimulated in the first instance by a sensation of unpleasure, and will aim at resolving this disquiet in order to return in the end to a state of harmony. Where the disquieting sensation is actually *present*, the mental activities will be directed toward removing its immediate cause,[3] but where the immediate cause cannot be removed—for instance, where the unpleasure is caused by an idea, or, more particularly, by the memory of a *past* sensation which was unpleasant—then the mind has two alternatives: either to bury this memory deeply in the subconscious (the classic Freudian doctrine of repression), or else to *reenact* the past circumstances of the unpleasure consciously and repetitively, in such a way that, although the discord is not resolved into harmony, it will be transferred into another dimension of mental experience. The unpleasure will not cease to be felt, but the sufferer will have endowed it with a different structure, and thus will have made it acceptable, for all that it will never cease entirely to be disquieting. Thus the mind can learn boldly to confront, instead of retreating from, the more anguishing experiences of life, and to transmute them into values which are "higher" than those determined by the rudimentary "principle of pleasure." The mind "gets used to" an unpleasant memory, emotion, or concept by converting it into a "game."

The initial case history that Freud analyzed to demonstrate the operation of this mental mechanism is the now-celebrated instance of a "game" invented by an eighteen-month-old child whose mother was obliged periodically to go away and leave it. The child's first, instinctive reaction was to howl in protest; after a while, however, it succeeded in controlling this reaction, and

---

3. This is, at bottom, an argument carried over from the pre-Freudian, "rationalist" psychology of the eighteenth century, and was familiar to most thinkers of that period, from Hobbes and Locke down to Helvétius and Condillac.

the effort involved in exercising this control is described by Freud as an "instinctual renunciation" which was "the child's first great cultural achievement" (the adjective *cultural* here is, of course, of the highest significance). But this did not mean that it was less attached to its mother, or that it felt her absence any less as a state of tension and mental unpleasure. To cope with it, the child invented a "game": it proceeded to reenact, over and over again, its mother's departure and its own misery; and by repeating this game, *which it had itself invented*, it transformed its own status from that of being merely a passive sufferer to that of being an active creator who, by his creativity, could dominate, even though he could not eliminate, his own suffering. The eighteen-month-old child had discovered for itself the "play-structure" which we know as tragedy.[4]

This summary covers only a small section of the extraordinary wealth of ideas propounded in the sixty-odd pages of *Beyond the Pleasure Principle*, but it gives what will prove to be essential in constructing a theory which may help us to understand and to interpret the literary form which we have called the Childhood. The next major step, oddly enough, appears to have been taken by a scholar who was ignorant of Freud's paper, yet who reached similar conclusions independently: Johan Huizinga, who, from 1915 to 1941, was professor of history in the University of Leyden, and whose supremely influential *Homo Ludens: A Study of the Play Element in Culture* appeared in 1938. It is perhaps not an exaggeration to claim that Huizinga, just as much as the linguisticians Roman Jakobson and Leo Spitzer, can be sensed in the background to much of the contemporary theory of structuralism.

Freud stressed the value of play—in itself a nonfunctional activity—as being nonetheless functional, under certain circumstances, in relation to the psyche. Huizinga, by contrast, begins by refuting certain widely accepted notions of play as being of utilitarian value to the body: the theory, for instance, which holds that the kitten playing with a ball of wool is instinctively training itself for its future survival as a catcher of rapidly moving animals—birds or mice. These deterministic explanations omit the essential characteristic of play—namely, that it is "fun":

> Now this last-named element, the *fun* of playing, resists all analysis, all logical interpretation. As a concept, it cannot be reduced to any other mental category.[5]

And once (he argues) one starts to think seriously about the sheer fun of

4. See Freud, *Beyond the Pleasure Principle*, in *The Complete Psychological Works of Sigmund Freud*, trans. James Strachey, Anna Freud et al. (London, 1955–74), 18:3–65, esp. 7–17.

5. Johan Huizinga, *Homo Ludens: A Study of the Play Element in Culture*, trans. by Huizinga himself (1949; reprint, London, 1970), 21. The English word *fun* is used in Huizinga's original Dutch text.

playing—the passionate, emotional, and (in a particular sense) the desperately *serious* involvement of the player in the game, then its gratuitousness becomes apparent:

> In acknowledging play you acknowledge mind, for whatever else play is, it is not matter. . . . From the point of view of a world wholly operated by blind forces, play would be altogether superfluous. Play only becomes possible, thinkable and understandable when an influx of *mind* breaks down the absolute determinism of the Cosmos. The very existence of play continually confirms the supra-logical nature of the human situation. (pp. 21–22)

Play, in fact, is not merely evidence of, but actually takes place within, a dimension which is "different from 'ordinary' life." It has its own "significant form." It creates "a second, poetic world alongside the world of nature" (p. 23). It is a "freedom"—play undertaken under compulsion (except in the special case of ritual) is no longer play at all. For the adult, its characteristic is that it is temporary: the football match, the night at the opera, the mountaineering holiday, the midnight mass are brief glimpses of an alternative reality, whose fascination is emphasized by the fact that its existence is circumscribed by exact limits in time. Where those limits fail, the result is unspeakable frustration and anguish—as in those unfinished and unfinishable games of chess which figure so symbolically in the Godot-less universe of Samuel Beckett. The alternative reality of play is also—and this is still more significant—circumscribed in space. For adult and for child alike,

> all play moves and has its being within a playground marked off beforehand either materially or ideally, deliberately or as a matter of course. Just as there is no formal difference between play and ritual, so the "consecrated spot" cannot be formally distinguished from the playground. The arena, the card-table, the magic circle, the temple, the stage, the screen, the tennis-court, the court of justice, etc., are all in form and function playgrounds, i.e. forbidden spots, isolated, hedged round, hallowed, within which special rules obtain. (pp. 28–29)

And here Huizinga comes to the key section of his argument: within this "sacred" area, this "privileged" playground, circumscribed equally rigidly by place and time, a special order reigns: an "absolute and peculiar" order. Play has its rules, which are *not* those of the "real" world. One footballer may not move even a few inches ahead of another at a certain instant specifically designated by the rules; otherwise he is "offside" and is penalized accordingly—whereas the same two individuals, not more than ninety minutes later, can take up any positions they like in relation to each other without anyone caring a hoot. Play, in fact, "creates order, *is* order. Into an imperfect world and into the confusion of life, it brings a temporary, a limited perfection" (p. 29). Play is a kind of porthole in the ironclad walls of ordinary life, a "magic casement" opening, not—or not at first sight at least—on the foam of perilous seas, but rather on "faery lands" where form and order reign as they reign nowhere else in this imperfect world.

Moreover—so continues Huizinga's argument—any *group* of players in any game will be bound together by the fact that they are isolated by their own "rules" from the rest of the world. "Inside the circle of the game the laws and customs of ordinary life no longer count. We are different and do things differently" (p. 31). This applies as much to religious sects and secret societies as it does to footballers or kids from the same street-gang. Quakers and Freemasons, Old Rugbeians, and Old Orielenses are as closely bonded by the unsharable experience of a "temporary abolition of the ordinary world" as are the survivors of Buchenwald or Mauthausen or Hiroshima[6]—or as are the members of the cast of any theatrical production. For in theater, in particular, the extra-ordinary nature of play reaches its climax:

> The disguised or masked individual "plays" another part, another being. The terrors of childhood, open-hearted gaiety, mystic fantasy and sacred awe are all entangled in this strange business of masks and disguises. (p. 32)

And from theater to religious ritual is but the shortest of steps. The "feast-day," or day of high ceremonial, marks a similar hiatus in the time-flow of ordinary life. The religious precinct is as clearly marked off from the surrounding world as is the center court at Wimbledon or the test-wicket at Lords. The costumes of the celebrants are as far removed from day-to-day jeans and sweatshirts as are the costumes of actors in Sheridan or Marivaux. And the seriousness of the communicant is not markedly different from the seriousness of the chess player—or of the child "being" its current hero, whether Superman or Astérix, Captain Nemo or Long John Silver. The difference, above all, is one of degree. The player *looks at* an alternative world through the porthole in the side of his ship, but knows (as normally the child "pretending" knows, in his heart of hearts) that he is not *of* it. But in the rituals of primitive religion and—perhaps—even in the highest forms of sophisticated religious experience, so long as some kind of ritual, albeit only that of a reiterated mental discipline, remains in operation, the "magic casement" may open just that little bit wider, and the worshipper actually participate in, and be fused with, the otherness of the "perfect" yet at the same time frightening world beyond.[7]

Huizinga's argument, then, leads us toward three conclusions, all interre-

6. This "bonding" of the survivors of catastrophe (a "gratuitous" dimension *par excellence*) forms the principal material of many of the best plays of Armand Gatti. Cf. *L'Enfant-Rat, La Deuxième Existence du camp de Tatenberg, La Cigogne*, etc. For other examples of "bonding," see Claude Simon's *La Route des Flandres* (1960), or Jorge Semprun's *Le Grand Voyage* (1963); see also Mary McCarthy's *The Group* (1963).

7. See Huizinga, pp. 38–46.

lated, and all relevant to this analysis of the Childhood. It implies (i) that all the "gratuitous" activities of childhood—that is, the play activities—are not satisfactorily explainable in terms of any deterministic theory of the world, but represent an autonomous mode of being which, in certain circumstances, persists into adult life; (ii) that the "small world" of the child is not simply the result of a limited experience, but that it has its own satisfying structure of "perfection" and "order" which is significantly different from that of adult reality; and (iii) that the games and rituals which characterize the child's mode of being in the world can open up onto a dimension of experience which is not only different from but of a higher order than that of everyday routine. Many criticisms of detail have been leveled against *Homo Ludens*, but none of any serious import against the basic structure of the argument, which seems strong enough to have withstood the better part of forty years of anthropological research and philosophical speculation. Nor is it necessary to go along with *all* Huizinga's conclusions. If we accept the essence of his contention, namely, that the "play-structure" of certain areas of human activity constitutes a positive "alternative dimension" *outside* the range of material determinism and positivistic rationalism—a dimension above all which is a "freedom" as opposed to the inexorable "given" conditions of the rest of life—then for our purposes this is sufficient. With one important qualification: for the adult, the "game" is known to be a *temporary* suspension of the "real" laws of existence; for the child, this is not necessarily so. It may well feel (or believe in retrospect that it *had* felt) not only that the "other dimension" is freer and more perfect than its ordinary dimension of existence, but, even in a literal sense, that it is more permanent. In which case, the recollected "magic" of childhood experience is not all that far removed from the religious or mystic experience of the adult.

The central sections of *Homo Ludens* analyze various aspects of language, law, literature, philosophy, and art in terms of the play concept, and demonstrate that, as Freud had suggested, the gratuitousness of an "alternative mental level of response" lies at the root of all the higher forms of culture. Only one other aspect of Huizinga's argument need detain us here, and that lies in his resolutely pessimistic conclusion. In the chapter entitled "Western Civilisation *sub specie ludi*," he suggests that European culture reached its highest peak of perfection in the baroque and rococo arts and life-styles of the eighteenth century, with its wigs and knee-breeches, Sheraton furniture and ormolu clocks, Dresden shepherdesses and Mozart sonatas, with the flippancy of its wits rivaled only by the polished irresponsibility of its politicians—in fact, in that period when culture achieved its supreme degree of *artificiality* in a "play-dimension" as remote as possible from that of "real" life.[8] Thereafter,

8. The most vituperative criticism of Huizinga's thesis, as may be surmised from this aspect

the play element entered into a decline—and culture declined along with it. In the nineteenth century, he observes caustically, "all Europe donned the boiler-suit":

> Even in the eighteenth century utilitarianism, prosaic efficiency, and the bourgeois ideal of social welfare—all fatal to the Baroque—had bitten deep into society. . . . Henceforward the dominants of civilisation were to be social consciousness, educational aspirations, and scientific judgement. . . . (p. 218)

And "Culture" as such, but above all as an all-pervasive style of living, was inexorably doomed: yet another version of the "Decline of the West," as Oswald Spengler had analyzed it. If this view needs confirmation, we have only to turn to Stendhal, uncomfortably astride the two Europes, nostalgic for the elegance, the artificiality, and the "graces" of the eighteenth century, but feeling ever more threatened by that diabolic English invention, the steam engine, and by the impending "massive seriousness" of the nineteenth.[9] However, the significant fact that emerges is that it is, once again, precisely during this period that the social play-dimension of the pastoral gives way to the individual play-dimension of the Childhood. To return to our starting point: if the pastoral yielded to the Childhood after 1789, it was not simply because one particular cultural artifact, which had flourished from the age of Theocritus to the age of Marie-Antoinette, suddenly proved unacceptable to the "boiler-suited generations" of post-Revolutionary Europe; but rather because a fundamental attitude toward life—one which is summarized in the notion that a "gentleman" did not *work*—was found wanting, judged to be incompatible with the earnestness of adult preoccupations, and relegated to those secret recesses of mind and memory whence it had originated in the first place. The Child began to be treated seriously, when the Man was forced to stop finding the same kind of delight in the world as he had done when a child; that is, when all men save the poets were forbidden to shape any save the most marginal fragments of their adult lives around the "other-dimensionality" of childhood.

Johan Huizinga was by training a medieval historian; and this background is the reason for certain limitations in his manner of sustaining his initial argument; he is more familiar with the Norse sagas than with Proust, with the court of Henry the Fowler than with that of the Empress Josephine. By contrast, Roger Caillois, whose equally influential essay, *L'Homme et le sacré*, was published in the same year as *Homo Ludens*, was by training a sociologist and

---

of his argument, comes from the Marxist Left. However, ideological objection to the *conclusion* of an argument does not necessarily invalidate the data on which that argument is based.

9. See my article "From Correggio to Class Warfare: Notes on Stendhal's Ideal of 'la grâce,'" in *Balzac and the Nineteenth Century*, ed. D. G. Charlton, J. Gaudon, and A. R. Pugh (Leicester, 1972), 239–54.

anthropologist, and as such was able to contribute yet a further element to the general stream of ideas. At the time of writing *L'Homme et le sacré*, Caillois was unaware of *Homo Ludens*; however, when he came to revise his essay for republication in 1950, he added a significant appendix, entitled "Jeu et sacré," in which he recognized the weight of support provided by Huizinga to his own rather different arguments; and in 1958 he further acknowledged his debt to the earlier scholar in a book entitled *Les Jeux et les hommes*—at the same time submitting Huizinga's thesis to a certain number of pertinent criticisms.

In the last analysis, both Caillois and Huizinga are twentieth-century humanists, seeking new evidence for free will, responsibility, and self-determination in the face of the crude doctrines of materialistic determinism which, ultimately, were the bequest of nineteenth-century scientism to Mussolini, to Stalin, and (with a strong admixture of arbitrary irrationalism) to Hitler. In this, both the Frenchman and the Dutchman belong to that ever-growing contingent of contemporary philosophers, still perhaps dominated by the shadow of Jean-Paul Sartre, who, accepting the discipline of science even when untrained in its specific techniques, insist on the fact that any "science" concerning itself with human behavior which excludes the irrational is by definition unscientific, since it is excluding part of the evidence.

Thus, where the more traditionalist historian Huizinga had been content to distinguish between "utilitarian" and "gratuitous" activities, the socioanthropologist Caillois is decidedly bolder and less conventional in his choice of terms (as is his contemporary and colleague, Georges Bataille), and marks out a far more emphatic boundary between the different modes of human experience, calling them respectively the "profane" and the "sacred." In its simplest formulation, Caillois's argument is that "religious" experience—the experience of *le sacré*—is not something to be written off by the rationalistic inquirer as so much imaginative nonsense. Such experience is virtually universal among the innumerable races and tribes of Homo sapiens, and consequently must be accounted for. This is not a revival of the "proof of God by universal consent," as expounded by the Jesuits of the sixteenth century. To take cognizance of the ubiquity of a religious sense does not, for Caillois or Bataille any more than it did for Jung, imply affirming the existence of a god, or gods, in any traditional sense. What, for want of a better term, we shall have to call the "religious experience," is a phenomenon rooted *in*, not *outside*, the human mind. It is a response to something beyond its normal habits of rationalization, that is all. And the absolute, arbitrary, and inexplicable existence of, say, a stone or a tree is as far beyond these normal limits as that of a god. Consequently, the anthropologist—scientist or philosopher—can talk about the dimensions of "sacred" or "religious" experience, as opposed to "profane" or "utilitarian" experience, without thereby proclaiming his adherence, even by the remotest of implications, to any church, faith, sect, or doctrine whatsoever.

The most striking feature of the Caillois/Bataille argument is that it reverses the normal relationships between the "serious" and the "gratuitous" activities or experiences of life. For Huizinga, as we have seen, play was *as* serious as work; for Caillois (as, in a different way, for the later Freud), play— the nonutilitarian dimension of *le sacré*—is *more* serious than the rational, day-to-day experiences of *le profane*. This reversed relationship is taken as a starting point in the very first paragraph of *L'Homme et le sacré*; but at the same time, Caillois also reverses Huizinga's identification of "determinism" with "work" and of "freedom" with "play":

> The distinction between the sacred and the profane sets two worlds in opposition: one in which the Believer goes freely about his daily occupations, engaging in activities which entail no consequences for his salvation, and the other in which he is paralysed alternately by fear and by hope, and in which, as though he stood on the brink of an abyss, the slightest deviation in the slightest of gestures could set the seal on his irremediable perdition.[10]

Here, the freely accepted "inviolability" of the "rules of the game" has been replaced by the unchallengeable discipline of a ritual; nor can the authority which imposes this demand for stark obedience be reduced in terms of rational analysis. The domains of the sacred and the profane

> can only be defined the one strictly in terms of the other. They are mutually exclusive, yet necessarily complementary. Any attempt to reduce their opposition to any other terms would be futile: it is experienced as an absolute phenomenon of consciousness [*une donnée immédiate de la conscience*]. It can be described, broken down into its component elements, elaborated as a theory. But it no more lies within the scope of language to define its ultimate essence than it does to encompass in words the essence of a pure sensation. Thus the Sacred is to be apprehended as a basic category of sensibility. (p. 18)

Significantly, the phrase at the heart of this quotation, "une donnée immédiate de la conscience," is a positive and unmistakable reference to Bergson,[11] and to the concept of the "intuitive" as opposed to the "rationalizing" aspects of the human mental processes. Bergson showed, and Caillois accepts, that there are two complementary processes by which the mind "knows" phenomena outside itself: a *distancing*, rationalizing process, by which the object

10. Roger Caillois, *L'Homme et le sacré* (1939, rev. 1949; Paris, 1972), 17.

11. Henri Bergson's epoch-making philosophical essay, *Des Données immédiates de la conscience* (1889), is one of the all-pervasive influences in virtually every branch of modern French philosophy.

is apprehended, not as itself, but as the sum of its abstract properties, which can then be "broken down" mathematically, thus providing the kind of data about the world which, in the long run, will lead to the formulations and achievements of modern science and technology; and a *direct*, intuiting process, by which the object is apprehended in and for itself, as an irreducible totality-of-being, situated in a time-continuum [*dans la durée*], which cannot be abstracted or broken down, any more than can any of the other "awarenesses" of the object, without the reality of the phenomenon being distorted and the immediacy of the mind's intercourse with it (the "être-avec," or "being-with" of Gabriel Marcel's analysis) being destroyed irrevocably.

The domain of the sacred is more than merely irrational: it is arbitrary, unjust, violent; it creates life but also it decrees death; and the violence of sexuality—the primary act of creation—is inseparable in its metaphysical essence from the violence of rape, death, and destruction.[12] In the origins of the human race, the instinctual world of *le sacré* was dominant, virtually to the exclusion of the profane; by contrast, the slow process of civilization and of culture has gradually restricted and delimited the effective areas of operation and of contact with the terrifying domain, in the interests originally of "order"—ultimately of knowledge and perhaps, simply, of comfort. But, while it can be repressed, the domain of the sacred can never be entirely eliminated. It survives in the primitive mythological subconscious of the individual and of the race; it breaks out in wars, or potlatches, or other orgies of sexuality and destruction; it is a force which the human race has constantly sensed as needing to be placated (the rituals of sacrifice, etc.). Above all, from our point of view, it is an area of experience for which allowance must be made, for, if denied absolutely, it is liable to prove explosive. In other words, from the most primitive to the most modern times, generations of men have felt that, every so often, the rational order of existence must be interrupted *for a limited, strictly circumscribed period in time and usually in a limited and preestablished ritual or sacred area*, for the individual or the group to reestablish contact with these forces greater than the self and more powerful than its reason. These "privileged moments" may take the form of religious ritual, culminating in the ecstatic, mystic experiences of a St. Theresa of Avila; they may manifest themselves as permitted orgies of sexuality, or of destruction; or they may be incarnated in the comparatively innocuous form of festivities and games. But in all cases, the underlying principle is identical: the dimension of experience is *different* from that of "profane" or ordinary life; an element of ritual is involved; and the contact with the "alternative dimension" acts at the very lowest as a kind of safety valve for the subconscious (the

12. See, e.g., Georges Bataille, especially *L'Erotisme* (1957) and his essay on de Sade in *La Littérature et le mal* (1957).

Freudian id), at the highest as the induction into a mode of being different from, and superior to, that which is normally acceptable.

For Roger Caillois, as for Georges Bataille, the supreme moment of the breakthrough, the crack or fissure (*la fêlure*, to use Jean Genet's significant term) in rational life which allows a moment of participation in, and possession by, the other dimension, is that of *la fête*—Dionysiac orgy, religious ceremony, pop festival, Black Orpheus carnival, or April Fool's Day escapade.[13] *La fête*: perhaps symbolically, there is no equivalent word in modern English; English rationalism, utilitarianism, and scientism have relegated the very concept to the domain of childhood, outlawed it from the reasonable regularities, the "steady careers," of adult life.[14] Yet the concept survives, in echo at least, in spite of all:

> In opposition to the monotony of the daily round, fully occupied with the routine of work, peaceful, imprisoned in a grid of do's-and-don'ts, wholly gripped in patterns of precautionary measures, and in which the maxim *Quieta non movere* keeps the world spinning firmly upon its axis—in opposition to this is set the effervescence of the orgy [*la fête*]. . . . The orgy implies a vast concourse of excited and noisy people. . . . Even nowadays, when our impoverished "festivities" barely emerge from the dull-grey background constituted by the monotony of daily existence, and make their appearance in forms which are scattered and fragmentary, hardly dragging their feet above the bog, nonetheless, here and there, they give glimpses of a few wretched remnants of that former communal letting-the-hair-down which once upon a time characterized more primitive bacchanalia.[15]

The occasion of *la fête* is a moment of total release, when a community as a whole assumes the license to shatter the framework of order and civilization, to defy its laws and to resume contact with the alternative dimension which controls, rather more effectively than the local registration office, the irreducible pattern of birth, copulation, and death. In primitive societies, *la fête* involved a deliberate and conscious defiance of taboos, a breaking of the frail boundaries which culture had erected against ancient Chaos.[16] In modern societies, it tends to be a collective, albeit somewhat shamefaced and self-

13. April Fool's Day escapades play a much smaller role than might have been predicted in our Childhoods. There is a description of some rather anodyne traditions in William Dean Howells's *A Boy's Town* (New York, 1890), 114–15.

14. André Gide: "Que les carrières honorables abêtissent!"

15. Caillois, *L'Homme et le sacré*, 123–24. The recent proliferation of "pornography" has, to a certain extent, given the liberating concept of the "orgy" a new lease of life. (Cf. "Anatomy of an Orgy," by Michael Walsh, in *Club International*, vol. 4, no. 12 (1976), pp. 20–22, 78)—but this is very much *res privata* rather than *res publica*.

16. This association of *la fête* with violence and taboo-smashing is central to Fernando Arrabal's program for a "théâtre panique." The replacement of the concept of "evil" by that of "desecration" is a major factor in contemporary ethical speculation.

conscious violation of the accepted conventions of "decency," "communal responsibility," and "respect for the rights of others." In its latter form, however, it is becoming rarer and rarer; and in Western European society, even one of the few survivals—noted as characteristic both by Caillois and by Huizinga—the "students' rag-day" has, over the last decade or so, been forced out of existence by the unimaginative earnestness of left-wing do-gooders. But the alternative dimension, with the best will in the world, cannot be suppressed or contained altogether; and, banished from the surface of day-to-day existence, deprived, in fact, of its safety valve, it reasserts itself in other forms: in desperate appeals to the psychiatrist; in outbreaks of hooliganism, bomb-throwing, violence, strike mania, football fury, or "demos"; or, finally, in an ever-growing recourse to the *paradis perdu* of childhood. "There is no God! I can't bear to grow up!"[17]

The various related theories which we have discussed here have four factors clearly in common: each recognizes an "alternative" or "play" dimension of experience, opposed to that of the rationally constituted, utilitarian dimension of everyday adult life; each acknowledges that that experience is "serious" and "dynamic," although they differ as to whether this dynamism needs to be repressed or encouraged in the interests of civilization and culture; each agrees that its communal, spontaneous manifestations are curtailed, if not completely suppressed, by the dreary, automobile-and-deep-freeze-oriented pragmatism of modern life; and each refers ultimately to the experience of the presocial being—the primitive or the child—as an example of the human mind more closely attuned to the sacred dimension of existence than is the adult. "Play," in fact, is the most supremely serious of all human activities, because it alone either constructs (Freud), reveals (Huizinga), or refers back to (Caillois) a system of values which transcends the drab and stultifying restrictiveness of deterministic utilitarianism. The child alone (other than the near-extinct savage of the Amazon Basin) escapes from Marx, escapes from Bentham and Kinsey, escapes even from Chairman Mao. Behind every published Childhood lies a vision of the experience of childhood as such, as Henry Vaughan's absolute alternative:

> I cannot reach it; and my striving eye
> Dazzles at it, as at eternity.

---

17. A scream first heard from a group of hysterical students, naked, driving in an open car round and round the "dandelion-puff" fountain of King's Cross, Sydney, on the night of the "Cuba crisis" (27 October 1962). The impression produced on the writer by this incident was one of the starting points of the present study.

Relever le défi des choses au langage.

—Francis Ponge, *Le Parti-pris des choses*

Henry Vaughan's categoric "I *cannot* reach it" reflects both the spiritual and the literary limitations of the seventeenth century. In the background to most of the more serious Childhoods of the last 150 years lies some sort of determination to reconstruct, at least in terms of poetry, the otherwise inaccessible experience of immediate openness to that alternative dimension. And, first and foremost, in terms of language.

For the writer, the paradox is an obvious one. More than any other factor in human experience, it is the use of rational language which destroys the child's "intuitive" relationship with the world. Language creates distance between the self and the object; language generalizes, transforming a unique perception into a common one; language transmutes realities into abstractions, replacing the "being-there" [*Dasein*] of the phenomenon by its measurable properties. On the other hand, the writer has no tool other than language at his disposal—hence the tendency, which we have referred to earlier, to use language to a greater or lesser degree *irrationally*, to prefer where possible poetry to prose, to break down overlogical linguistic structures into impressionistic, at times frankly incomprehensible, word-groupings—as in Marc Cholodenko, say, or Arthur Rimbaud,[18] Andrei Bely or Paul Chamberland—which rely on overtones, free associations, and images rather than on the formal patterns of grammar.

In the light of these arguments, the problem of prelinguistic memory takes on a new significance. If we accept, reluctantly or enthusiastically, the Wittgensteinian argument that *all* conceptualization is consequent upon the possession of language, this would mean that writers such as Miles Franklin, James Kirkup, or Eugène Ionesco, who claim to have a clear recollection, not only of incidents which took place before they could speak, but of the *fact* of not being able to speak forming an ingredient of those incidents, are either romancing or else misremembering. Unless—and this would seem to be a possible alternative—the state of being "without language" means in fact the state of having a language *different* from that of the adult, more individualized, less rational in structure, each word more immediately and directly related to specific phenomena than will be the case later on. That such private languages persist in weakened form through later childhood and adolescence is obvious; most groups of children use "secret" languages among them-

---

18. Marc Cholodenko, *Le Prince. Portrait de l'artiste en enfant* (Paris, 1974). Arthur Rimbaud, *Enfance* [ca. 1873], in *Œuvres*, ed. Suzanne Bernard (Paris, 1960), 255–60.

selves,[19] whose apparent raison d'être is to bind the group together and to make its inner world impenetrable to the unwelcome curiosity and interference of grown-ups, but which may also refer back to an earlier stage when, for each child, the individual language was more significant than the common one. Inasmuch as most of our children are poets, Eugène Ionesco's argument becomes of major significance: the poet is he who, *as a child,* begins by imposing *his* meaning on language, rather than by accepting passively the second-hand significance of words which others bequeath to him. And this meaning can only reflect the intuited "real presence" of a world not yet alienated from the self by rational conceptualization.

Ionesco, writing in 1969, was well aware that his conviction that the evidence of his memory implied the existence of a wealth of prelinguistic material was "virtually heresy." Yet his arguments, shorn of their ingenious and captivating rhetoric, are in the last analysis beautifully simple. Homo sapiens, he proposes, is descended from the higher apes; the higher apes do not have language; therefore, reasons Ionesco, at some stage in the evolutionary process Homo sapiens did not possess language; therefore he must have invented it. But no invention—or at least, no invention as revolutionary and as complex as language—is made unless the need for it is felt, and the feeling of a *need* for language can only have been a need for expressing concepts. For expressing the simpler emotions such as fear and hunger, "animal noises" would have sufficed. Language is the logical outcome of a desire to communicate concepts; therefore concepts preceded language in the human race and, logically again therefore, will continue to do so in some at least, if not in all, individual members of that race. When the infant starts to *create* language out of prelinguistic concepts, it is a poet; when it abandons this creativity, contenting itself with words dictated to it by others, then it ceases to be one. As simple as that.

> Thus inventive or creative language—and my baby-language was essentially just that—is the attempt, the *successful* attempt, to encompass, to appropriate, to express, to integrate, to communicate something uncommunicable or hitherto uncommunicated, whereas language given by others is a noninventive language, necessarily so, since it is given, it is ready-made. It makes life a lot easier, obviously, but it is not a creative act. Sometimes, indeed, it has to be dismantled, or thinned out, so that the world can be seen through it, in all its original strangeness; and this is precisely what the poet does, destroying words or creating them.[20]

Ionesco's conviction, however, that thought precedes language, and consequently that the adult *can* retain memories of a prelinguistic existence, is by no

19. See Iona and Peter Opie, *The Lore and Language of Schoolchildren* (1959); Alan Milberg, *Street Games* (New York, 1976), 78–81; etc.

20. Eugène Ionesco, *Découvertes* (Geneva, 1969), 35–36.

means unique, and we can discover similar ideas expressed with the same conviction, and indeed with considerably more intellectual subtlety, almost exactly three centuries earlier, in the poetry of Thomas Traherne. And, for the seventeenth-century poet as for the contemporary poet, the distinction between "creative" and "noncreative" languages is that the former only develop in *solitude.* "To create speech, one needs to be alone" (Ionesco, *Découvertes*, p. 36).

More categorically than any other Childhood in our collection, Traherne's *Divine Reflections on the Native Objects of an Infant-Ey* (written circa 1670) not only affirms the fact of prelinguistic memory, but asserts its superiority over all other varieties of remembered experience. For Traherne, the essential "Paradise" of infancy is not only purely sensual (mainly visual) in itself, but is actually destroyed by the acquisition of language. "When I began to speak and go"[21]—the theme is reiterated in prose and poetry alike—the Divine Vision was banished. The rationality of language is accorded the same role as the Serpent in the Garden of Eden:

> . . . this was my blessed case;
> For nothing spake to me but the fair Face
> Of Hev'n and Earth, when yet I could not Speak:
> *I did my Bliss, when I did Silence, break.*[22]

Taken in its most obvious and literal sense, this means that Traherne's childhood experience of the privileged dimension owed its ecstatic quality, not only to the "Otherness" of that experience in itself (although this was overwhelming enough), but also to his own absolute and literal uniqueness as an identity. In the absence of language, the vision was unshared and unsharable with any other being. Objects "spake" to him in their own language, through his senses—"and ev'ry Sense / Was in the like to som Intelligence" ("Nature," *Divine Reflections*, p. 154)—and they "spake" to him *alone*:

> Then did I dwell within a World of Light
> Retir'd and separat from all mens sight;
> Where I did feel strange Thoughts, and Secrets see
> That were (or seem'd) only revealed to Me.
> There I saw all the World enjoy'd by One;
> There All Things seem'd to end in Me alone.
> ("Dumness," *Divine Reflections*, p. 159)

Then, gradually, as he learned the common language of others, this unique identity was destroyed, its sovereignty invaded and usurped—as happened

---

21. Thomas Traherne, *Centuries of Meditations* [1670–74], ed. Hilda Vaughan (Leighton Buzzard, 1975), 115 (*Meditation* III, x).

22. Traherne, *Divine Reflections on the Native Objects of an Infant-Ey* [ca. 1670], ed. Burney, Wade, and Dobell, in *The Poetical Works of Thomas Traherne* (1903; reprint, London 1932), 158 ("Dumness"). The poet's own italics.

with Samuel Beckett's *Unnamable*—and the self was lost in the clamorous mindlessness of the mass.

It is worth spending a little time on Traherne's *Divine Reflections*, not only because he is in himself a very great poet, but because his experience casts light on all our other texts which lay claim to prelinguistic memory. There are in fact four possible interpretations of Traherne's claim that "simple sense / Is Lord of all created Excellence" ("The Praeparative," *Divine Reflections*, p. 108), and of his deep-rooted belief that language, as an indispensable prerequisite of cognition and recollection, is superfluous.

The first of these interpretations—the logico-positivistic or Wittgensteinian argument—has already been mentioned. It is the proposition which would deny emphatically that any true cognition, any conceptualization, and hence, of necessity, any memory, is even thinkable without language. Thus many modern psycholinguists, as well as theorists of cognitive development, would agree wholeheartedly with Leonard Bloomfield when he asserts that "concepts" as such have no existence, save as that which is signified by language.[23] In the Beginning, in fact, was the Word, and before the Word, there was just . . . Nothing. An unexpectedly biblical view of the situation, and one which is, or perhaps rather *was*, until the disruptive advent of Noam Chomsky, widely held among Anglo-American linguistic philosophers. In this interpretation, Traherne's prelinguistic vision is non-sense. It is, in any literal interpretation, impossible. It is just poetic license, on a par with visions of mermaids and unicorns—but nonetheless attractively "poetic" for all that.

A second interpretation, while still accepting the Wittgenstein/Bloomfield premise of the inevitable precedence of language over concepts, would nevertheless concede a greater degree of veracity to the poet. If we look carefully at Traherne's affirmations, it would seem that the "evil contagion" brought about by the language of others, while it may in part lie in the actual sharing of a common vocabulary, consists principally in the "thoughts" which that common language conveys; and by "thoughts," it may be surmised that Traherne was envisaging, very characteristically in the context of his milieu, his century, and his known preoccupations as an ordained minister of the church, a scale of moral values. What the "Others" taught him was not simply the *names* for objects or concepts, but rather a value hierarchy which esteemed rarity above intrinsic beauty, monetary worth above aesthetic quality, and in general art and artifice above nature. Traherne evidently resisted this "worldly" (rather than simply "verbal") pressure as best he could:

> It was difficult to persuade me that the tinsell'd ware upon a hobby-horse was a fine thing. . . . Natural things are glorious, and to know them glorious. Nature knows no such riches, but art and error make them. (*Meditations*, pp. 114–15)

23. See Leonard Bloomfield, *Language* (1914; rev. ed., New York, 1933).

But in the end he succumbed; and in the *Meditations*, more transparently than in the *Divine Reflections*, he reveals that it was "thoughts" rather than mere "words" which corrupted him, and which destroyed, not his ontological, but his *moral* integrity:

> Thoughts are the most present things to thoughts, and of the most powerful influence. My Soul was only apt and disposed to great things; but souls to souls are like apples, one being rotten rots another. When I began to speak and go, nothing began to be present in me but what was present to me in their thoughts. The glass of the imagination was the only mirror wherein any thing was represented or appeared to me. (p. 115)

This is, of course, close to the language and the metaphysic of Traherne's exact contemporary John Bunyan, and may indeed represent the true limit of his thought. Nonetheless, there is sufficient ambiguity to encourage us to consider other possible interpretations, and to continue to think of him as perhaps the earliest poet to confront the problems of language as such in a form, if not with a vocabulary, which is strikingly "modern"—and thus to account for the enthusiasm with which he has been rediscovered by poets of the twentieth century.[24]

The third interpretation is one which rests on the conclusions that recent psychological experimenters, working along lines suggested by Jean Piaget,[25] have drawn from their studies of cognitive development. Piaget's argument (based to some extent at least on the observation of his own children, which was clearly *not* the case with Wittgenstein) is that language does not simply "happen" in the three-year-old child "out of the blue"; and that to maintain that the eighteen-month-old child, because it has no recognizable means of precise linguistic communication with adults, is therefore devoid of concepts or unaware of an urge to communicate, is a patent absurdity. That it should have taken a Piaget to formulate this idea, which would have been the most obvious of platitudes to any practicing mother or nanny, is due to the absolute preeminence of status accorded to "formal" language, both in the educational systems and in the cultural hierarchies of all Western (and indeed of most Oriental) communities until the general revision of accepted cultural values which began with the aftermath of World War I. Piaget argues that, in the normal child, and in particular between the ages of eight months and two years, there is a sensori-motor stage of conceptual development, in which undoubtedly clear concepts develop out of direct contact with, and willed action in respect of, objects in the outer world, without the need of a linguistic intermediary. This is obviously not the place to go into the details of the

24. For one instance among many, see Edwin Muir, *The Story and the Fable* (London, 1940), 215.

25. See Jean Piaget, *The Origins of Intelligence in Children* (1936); *The Construction of Reality in the Child* (1937); and *Play, Dreams and Imitation* (1945).

evidence collected by Piaget and his successors;[26] the point at issue is that research over the last few years has provided educational theorists with ample evidence of the very young child's ability to conceptualize, at least in a simple manner, long before it has either a linguistic mechanism or a vocabulary in which these concepts may be expressed.[27]

The problem here, however, is that these investigations can give us no idea how complex the sensori-motor conceptualization can become. For the obvious reason: the investigator is observing from the *outside*; therefore he can only identify those concepts which the child can reveal without the help of language—namely, the very simplest ones of all, each normally involving the relationship between *one* object and the self. What can never be discovered by the outside observer is whether the concept communicated represents the totality of prelinguistic conceptualization, or whether it is merely the tip of the iceberg, the child in fact having realized a far more complex pattern of concepts and interrelationships which, precisely because it does *not* possess a syntactically viable language, must remain forever shut away within itself. Unless, of course, years later, when it *does* have a language at its disposal, it can recall these concepts and recreate them. Which is the third possible interpretation of Traherne—and a possible function of the Childhood as source material for the psycholinguist.

The fourth interpretation is very closely related to the third, save for the fact that it presupposes that the child has mastered a fairly dense and complex word/concept/phenomenon relationship (still basically sensori-motor), but lacks any rational syntactic structure to give these relationships a "generalized" significance, so that each remains individualized, and hence, in its own way, inexplicable, mysterious, and "magic." In simpler terms, we may postulate the existence, at a certain stage, of a kind of "secret" language, wholly intelligible to its possessor, but virtually useless for the purposes of communication with the world at large. And at this point, however reluctantly, we must leave Traherne and look for evidence elsewhere.

This postulated existence of a "secret" language, and its relationship to intuitive, irrational, or "privileged" experience, is discussed and analyzed by

26. See, for instance, Harry McGurk, *Growing and Changing: A Primer of Developmental Psychology* (London, 1975), especially 33–41; Joanna Turner, *Cognitive Development* (London, 1975), especially 86–116; Roger Brown, *A First Language: The Early Stages* (London, 1973), especially 198–201; Andrew Wilkinson, *Language and Education* (Oxford, 1975), especially 49–66.

27. Valerie Minogue, in a skillful analysis of the child-narrator's language in Nathalie Sarraute's novel, *Portrait d'un inconnu* (1947), refers to it as "a language barely separable from sensation, an imagery drawn from our first experience of the world, from physical pleasure or disgust, or recollections of childhood games" ("The Imagery of Childhood in *Portrait d'un Inconnu*," in *French Studies* 27 (1973): 117–26). It may be that it is this kind of language, "barely separable from sensation," that Traherne refers to as silence.

numerous writers, of whom three may serve as examples—again, the three being chosen from totally different cultural and linguistic traditions. The first of these—first, not in time, but in the uncomplicated directness of his approach, is Gavino Ledda, whose *Padre padrone: l'educazione di un pastore* [Dad as Boss: The Education of a Shepherd] appeared in 1975, and was promptly made into a highly effective film. The interest of Ledda's narrative lies not only in the fact that the accidents of his upbringing resulted in an unusually contrastive juxtaposition of two languages, one secret, the other public, but that this onetime shepherd boy, now university lecturer, simultaneously appreciates and rejects the special qualities of his unique and secret language.

Gavino Ledda was born in 1938 in the town of Siligo in Sardinia, of illiterate parents who spoke only a Sardinian dialect, incomprehensible to a mainland Italian. Shortly before he reached his sixth birthday, he was sent to school, where the emphasis was on learning the "correct" (that is, "public" or "common") language of Italy; but for economic reasons he was removed by his father after a few months, and taken off to a remote area in the mountains, where he had almost no contact with any other human being, and where he effectively developed a unique language of relationships with animals and natural objects, satisfying to himself, but meaningless to anyone else.

In Ledda we find exteriorized and consciously analyzed the formative process of a "privileged" language which, in the majority of writers, because of its uselessness as a means of communication with others, is later forgotten, so that the memories which it records can, without inaccuracy, be classed as prelinguistic. From the first, this language has "magic" (that is, animistic) properties, in that each tree, animal, or stone receives a unique and personal name, applicable to itself alone. At the outset, it is his father who teaches him some of these names:

> "Look at that big oak-tree, over there, right away over: he's called *s'avure manna* [the big tree]. Our valley here, that's called *su addiju de su palone* [the valley of the tall post]. . . .
>
> I listened spellbound . . . , in a kind of ecstasy, as if his mouth were a forge transforming names into realities. My father appeared to me like the Creator of this world which his words were bringing into being before my very eyes.[28]

At a later stage, Ledda continues the process by inventing his own language, transferring names and epithets half-remembered from the remote world of Siligo to the natural landscape which surrounds him, and thereby giving each phenomenon a "personality" with which he can communicate directly. "In consequence of my solitude," he recalls, "nature became my one

28. Gavino Ledda, *Padre padrone* (Milan, 1975), 15–16.

intimate acquaintance, yet indefinitely extended; my *only* friend, the one being I could talk to without shame or embarrassment" (p. 51).[29] Over and above the actual imaginative process of language creation, however, two other factors emerge from Ledda's analysis: the first, that the area defined in terms of this "secret" language reserved for the high pastures is in every respect a "privileged" area, a unique experience contrasting with, and liable to be destroyed by, the everyday, utilitarian reality of life "down there" in the flatlands: it is a "play situation," with its own rules and codes, its own "dimension of Otherness," which is *not* that of rationality. And secondly, and even more significantly, that this language is "a language of silence": a silence in which (as happens in Traherne) objects "speak" directly through the senses, rather than through any process of transformation into concepts:

> This private language between nature and myself, in a word this language of silence, had become as natural and as familiar to me, as though nature were for all time silence, and objects *were* its language. (p. 51)

To the concept of silence—or at least, to that of the silence of rational language—as one of the most revealing features of the privileged dimension, we shall return shortly; but, as will be apparent from the argument in this section, it is logical and necessary that this should be so. The magic objects of childhood (and this *is* their magic) communicate directly, without the intermediate stage of rational conceptualization. Or such, at least, is the poet's interpretation of his experience. The unhappy childhood is not only the result of brutality, brainwashing, or neglect; at a profounder level, its unhappiness is caused by the fact that the child, in pure self-defense, is forced to develop its rationalizing faculties earlier than need be, thus losing, perhaps for ever, the possibility of bypassing rational language and of communicating directly with the world of pure phenomena.

The ambiguities of this type of fundamental childhood experience, however, are also clearly brought out by Ledda. The "play-dimension," more clearly in the context of *Padre padrone* than in any other of our texts, is *gratuitous*; that is, it is wholly divorced from the utilitarian activities of earning a living or contributing in any way to the structure of an adult community. Exceptionally rich in substance for the poet, it is worse than useless for the radio operator, as Ledda discovers when he volunteers for the army. Gradually the perspective changes, and with the attainment of his maturity, Ledda sees his father, not as the "Creator of a World," but as a petty boss of the capitalist-exploiter class who has condemned his family to the status of second-rate citizens, if not of

---

29. There is the usual problem in this passage of translating the "tu-" form into English. The literal translation of the first sentence of this quotation is "nature became for me an indefinite *thou*."

slaves, by deliberately excluding them from the privileges of literacy and education—in fact, of participation in the common domain of rational, useful, and "normal" communication. Here again, politics and childhood appear, not merely as incompatible, but as mutually exclusive. It is the same conclusion—typical of the twentieth century—that we find at the end of Jean Genet's long pilgrimage from *Our Lady of the Flowers* to *The Screens*: the poet must *choose* between poetry and politics, for he cannot truly practice both. Gavino Ledda opts (or at least seems to opt) in the end for politics, and in a final scene, not merely terminates, but denies, his childhood by knocking his father down. But enough memory of the earlier magic subsists for him to be able to give us a unique picture of the linguistic mechanism by which it was created.

Ledda's experience is quite exceptional among our Childhoods, in that he was initiated—or perhaps *re*initiated—into what would appear to be a characteristic secret-animistic language of infancy at an age when most children are in the process of forgetting it. On the other hand, Ledda, *because* of the fact that he was older, does not combine, as most children do, half-dimmed memories of that earlier language with the equally characteristic memory of an alternative angle of vision as something essential to the privileged space in which he evolved—memories of a world in which, once again, "the grass was taller," and the proportions of everything different from those which confront the adult: the sense of being "magically close to things," since "his eyes are only two or three feet above the ground, instead of being five or six."[30] The interest of our second example, which is taken from Philip Toynbee's *Pantaloon* (1961) is that, in however self-conscious and artificial a manner, it combines *both* these most characteristic features of the adult's attempt to recapture a former experience of the alternative dimension: alienation through language, and alienation through height. Children, argues Toynbee, actually "possess" land and water by being literally close to them; adults, "grown upright and stalking the land like cameras on tripods" and "murmuring approbations," are literally "dispossessed":

> Lament for the days before the Word divided us;
> Words; words without end.
> The Word is the beginning of our division.
> Words part us from the world and from ourselves,
> And are worshipped at last for themselves alone,
> The symbols of objects which have long ago been lost behind them.[31]

Toynbee, surprisingly, puts the age at which the magic world is finally

---

30. Edwin Muir, *The Story and the Fable*, 20.
31. Philip Toynbee, *Pantaloon, or The Valediction* (London, 1961), 59.

abandoned as late as fifteen, perhaps because, in spite of the emphatic stress on the alienation through language in the last quotation, he is far more directly aware of the effect of alienation through height. The main point at issue, however, is that the experience and its interpretation are identical, whether the child was the son of an eminent English academic or the son of an illiterate Sardinian sheep-farmer and olive-grower.

Our third example is by far the most elaborate and the most intricate—if only because the later Michel Leiris would seem to have read far more modern psychophilosophy, including Bergson, Proust, Freud, Jung, Huizinga, Caillois, Bataille, and innumerable others, than did either Ledda or Toynbee. In fact, the early chapters of *Biffures* (1948), in particular " 'reusement," "Chansons," "Habillé-en-cour," and "Alphabet," contain speculations as abstruse, and yet as penetrating, as anything we have considered so far on the relationship between language and the alternative dimension of childhood experience. With this significant difference, however: for Leiris the poet, the structures of *rational* language are as much an autonomous play-dimension as the structures of prelinguistic consciousness. In other words, he (like Ionesco) approaches the problem, not merely as a kind of amateur structural linguistician, but also, and above all, as a *poet*, who, because he is using language *creatively*, is as far beyond mere rationalistic utilitarianism on the one side as the three-year-old child is on the other. At one point indeed he refers to his immense, four-volume *Summa* of early experience, *La Règle du jeu* (1948–76),[32] to which *Biffures* is no more than an introduction, as his *Art poétique*. Child and poet meet, as Baudelaire said they must, in a remote and rarified stratosphere far above the heads of ordinary mortals; and the link between the two is to be sought in those myriad, wholly irrational resonances which language awakens in the labyrinths of the subconscious.

Perhaps the simplest approach to the complexities of *Biffures* is to begin exactly where Leiris himself does: namely, with the supremely trivial incident when a toy soldier with which he is playing falls off the table, but "luck'ly" [*'reusement*] doesn't get broken. Taking the concept-grouping "my / toy / soldier," the third element, on analysis, proved the least important: at the age of (roughly) three, the notion of a "soldier" was virtually meaningless; "it awoke no definite resonance in me."[33] The first element, the "my," referred back (although the point is not insisted on) to that "possession of the world" which we have just been discussing. By contrast, the second element, that of the "toy," revealed itself to be essential. In the fullest Huizinga-sense, "toy" evoked

32. "The Rule of the Game": the use of the word *game* in this title is quite deliberate, in a precise Huizinga/Caillois context.

33. Michel Leiris, *Biffures*, vol. 1 of *La Règle du jeu* (Paris, 1948). All quotations in this section are taken from *Biffures*, 1:10–13.

the alternative dimension in its totality, a "closed world" whose laws and structures are imperative and meaningful in as much as they *are different from* the laws and structures of reality: "A world . . . whose components, by their forms, their colours, stood in stark contrast to the real world." So far, this is well within the tonality of *Homo Ludens*. But immediately, within the space of these two or three opening pages, Leiris leaps out far beyond the comparatively decorous "Otherness" of Huizinga's "alternative dimension" in the direction, first of Caillois, and then of a whole range of other poetico-metaphysical visionaries—Rimbaud, Claudel, Genet among others. For the "closed world of toys" is not merely *different from* the real world, but it intensifies the fascination of that otherness by being at the same time exactly *parallel to* that real world: a miniature reduction of it, and hence—being itself, and yet existing in a different dimension both of size and of experience, controllable instead of being out of control—it is a *symbol* of the real world, and a symbol which "represents" it "perhaps at the highest pitch of intensity." In other words, the effect of the *contrast* between two alternative dimensions is intensified many times over—a point which Huizinga did not make—when the *appearances* of the two worlds are identical: it is Stilitano the Beggar's "fake sore which exactly reproduces the real sore beneath it";[34] it is Sartre's *pour-soi* which "*is* what it *is-not*"; it is Claudel's God, "who *is-not* all that the universe is"; it is living beings on the stage of a theater pretending to be . . . living beings. This, for Leiris, as for Genet and for Caillois, is not merely "magical" (although Leiris uses the word repeatedly), but something far more powerful, perhaps more terrifying—the word he uses (as does Genet for similar experiences verging on the purely mystical) is "miraculous" [*prestigieux*]: emanating from the dark worlds of myths and demigods, "weighed down with the sadness and the solemnity of twilight."[35] And then, by a sudden reversal of imagery, this same aura of solemnity, awe, and myth-born grandeur is transferred to those other natural phenomena which, within the apartness and the immediacy of the child's space-dimension, are endowed with overpowering, language-defying significance, belonging to a

world apart, over and above that of daily life . . . , an intense world, the parallel of all those things which, in nature, incarnate the domain of *ceremony and circumstance*: butterflies, poppies in the cornfields, seashells, stars in the sky, and even the mosses

34. Jean Genet, *Journal du voleur* (Paris, 1949), 57. Cf. Lord David Cecil, *Max, A Biography* (Boston, 1965), 61–63, in which the author describes an occasion on which Max Beerbohm attended a fancy-dress ball wearing a mask which exactly reproduced his own features hidden underneath.
35. Jean Genet, "Lettre à Pauvert sur *les Bonnes*," in *Les Bonnes: Les deux versions précédées d'une lettre de l'auteur* (Sceaux, 1954), 147–48.

and the lichens with which rocks and tree-trunks appear to have been decked out for gala occasions. (*Biffures*, p. 11)[36]

But this is not the end of the speculations and "resonances" of this extraordinary little four-page essay, which is simultaneously childhood vignette, prose-poem, psycholinguistic casebook, and metaphysical disquisition. When the toy soldier falls and yet remains miraculously unbroken, the child exclaims " 'reusement," and is promptly corrected by a disembodied adult voice of reproof: not " 'reusement," but "*heu*reusement" [not "luck'ly," but "luck*i*ly"]. For the child-Leiris, " 'reusement" was not "rational" language; it belonged in fact to the domain of prelinguistic language which we have attempted to analyze above: incantation, animal noise, symbolic-animistíc identification, sensori-motor protoconceptualization, poetic creativity, call it what you will—a confused, instinctive, or intuitive (in Bergson's sense) formulation of emotion, "still close to my entrails, like laughter or crying"—but *unique*. Not, as was the case with Ledda, unique in its relationship to the phenomenon which it designated, but unique in relation to himself: it was *his* cry, as much an integral part of *his* being as *his* tongue or *his* lips, "magic" in its arbitrary isolation, undefiled by the vulgar noises of the many. And then, suddenly, thanks to that adult intervention, the word was wrenched out of the private domain and became common property. The unique, visceral " 'reusement" was revealed as forming part of the general morphological and syntactic structure of the total heritage of classical French: "*heu*reusement." It became "something shared or—if you prefer it—something *socialised*." And we expect the same plunge into the abyss of disillusionment as we found in Traherne.

But Leiris's experience is utterly different. For Leiris, language is not merely a pragmatic device concerned to reduce the splendors of the sensual world to a series of useful and manipulable formulas; it is in itself an alternative dimension in its own right, the most wondrous, delicate, and complex of all the games that the human mind has ever invented. The magic of a unique protolanguage is transmuted into the even more spectacular magic of a game structure involving some seventy-odd million individuals, relating Latin-past to Parisian-present, the here and now to the faraway, dream to poetry:

36. Edwin Muir likewise recalls the "rough grey stones spotted with lichen" as one of the more symbolic evidences of the child's relationship to objects in a reduced dimension of space (see *The Story and the Fable*, 20). All the other elements in Leiris's vision of the components of the "magic dimension" of childhood are archetypal, and have been discussed elsewhere. For the "poppies in the cornfields," see my essay "On Being Very, *Very* Surprised . . . Eugène Ionesco and the Vision of Childhood," in *The Dream and the Play: Ionesco's Theatrical Quest*, ed. Moshe Lazar (Malibu, Ca., 1982), 1–19, especially 14–15. For the "seashells," cf. Heather Cooper's well-known painting *Sarah on the Beach* (1974).

This word, which hitherto I had used without the slightest awareness of its real meaning, but simply as an interjection, revealed all of a sudden its links with *heureux*, and *thanks to the magical quality inherent in such a relationship*, promptly assumed its place within a whole structured series of precise significances. (*Biffures*, p. 12; emphasis added)

It is not that Leiris is inherently more optimistic than Traherne or Ionesco in his interpretation of the stupidity and cupidity of the human race in general; it is rather that, imbued with the special French tradition of linguistic awareness,[37] trained by Rimbaud and Mallarmé, Breton and the surrealists, Caillois and the socioanthropologists, Artaud, Jakobson, Bataille et al., he is able to conceive of language—even of adult language—as a system of signs which, while *apparently* rooted in an unalterable and permanent relationship to phenomena or concepts, in fact has a dynamic life of its own, sending out innumerable filaments ["un tissu arachnéen"] in all directions, linking one word, one sound, one concept with another, and creating a vast, a universe-embracing complex in the face of which even the adult-self feels dwarfed and insignificant. Moreover, to return to the child as such: at the same time as it becomes aware of the aesthetically beautiful "patterns" of language as an autonomous structure, it is equally fascinated by what it does *not* understand. Out of the perfect-in-itself aesthetic lacework of pure logico-linguistic concepts there will occasionally drop stray threads which, once grasped, will lead the mind onward to yet another structure of ideas or concepts, even more remote, this time, from the dull utilitarianism of the dreary pragmatists, scintillating with the rainbow-shimmers of iridescent absurdity: the patterns, radiating from a "magic" void of meaning, which Alice, plunging in pursuit of the White Rabbit, might have found if, at the bottom of the bottomless well, she had landed in the dimensionless center of one of Belacqua's "Beethoven-pauses" in a Beckettian symphony.

The *Cahiers* (later, the *Dossiers*) *du Collège de 'Pataphysique*, that pioneering publication ostensibly dedicated to preserving the pious memory of Alfred Jarry, but in fact concerned above all with offering a joyous alternative dimension of language in answer to the sterile conventions of adult (and above all academic) linguistic rationalism which had defeated both Traherne and Wordsworth, has devoted more than one of its issues to a study of what can happen "in the interstices of language."[38] For Leiris likewise, the "childhood magic" of language can be recaptured at any time through its malapropisms and misunderstandings, its inappropriate cross-references effected in the subconscious, its voluntary puns with their involuntary but revealing symbolism.

37. See my essay "First Encounters with the French Language," in *Proceedings of the Leeds Philosophical and Literary Society* 19 (1984), part 6, in press.

38. *Dossiers du Collège de 'Pataphysique*, no. 17, dated "22 Sable 89 E.P." [=1962]: "Exercices de littérature potentielle."

And at the root of all is a *void*; for, were it not so, the pattern of language would be rooted in facticity, and its magic would again be lost. "Adieu notre petite table" [Farewell, our little table], sings Manon Lescaut, struggling with that most irremediably prosaic of linguistic obstacles, the French operatic mute *e*. "Adieu notre petit *té*table," hears the child-listener; and out of this simple misunderstanding there grows a vast panorama, a wholly new structure-pattern of concept and imagery, whose magic is rooted in the fact that it bears no relationship whatsoever to pedestrian linguistic fact:

> Doubtless the word *tétable* derives its magic, does it not, from the fact that, while it retains elements of the notion of "table," and while at the same time it emits a creaking sound, like faldstools being shifted and grating over the flagstones, in actual fact it designates nothing, at the same time as it appears to designate something, *remaining a label attached to a pure Void*, or else that of some object destined until the end of time to remain beyond the range of understanding? It is to be surmised that there will always be some traces of *Ding-an-sich* hanging on to the coattails of words such as these, words which appear to correspond to this or that reality, but which, in the last analysis, are devoid of any meaning whatsoever. This is the source of their aura of revelation, for they are by definition formulas embodying that which is the most obstinately recalcitrant to all form, they are the proper names of phantasmagorical creatures populating a world that lies wholly outside our own laws. (p. 22; emphasis added)

The significance of Michel Leiris, apart from his status as the creator of one of the most monumental and influential Childhoods since Joyce's *Portrait of the Artist*, lies in the fact that he has shown that, for the poet at least, the prelinguistic image/word associations which incarnate the alternative dimension of infancy, and which imbue it, in adult recollection, with magic, are not necessarily relegated to an irretrievable past, but that something at least of the adventurous autonomy of prelinguistic immediacy of apprehension can be extended into adult life. *Puer ludens* is linguistically the father of *Homo ludens*; but it is up to *Homo ludens* to make the effort and restore the contact.

If so far, in this attempt to elucidate and to illustrate some of the more influential theories underlying the Childhood, we have dwelt particularly upon the linguistic aspects, it is because both for the child and for the poet the acquisition and the use of language are the unrivaled imperatives of life: language distinguishes the human child from the infant chimpanzee, language distinguishes the poet from the grocer, and language links the poet-who-was-a-child to the child-who-will-be-a-poet. However, the "alternative dimension" theories which we have analyzed may serve equally to illuminate other archetypal features of the Childhood. The obsessive manner in which early displays of tantrums, so easily explainable in the rationalistic language of the psychologist, continue to haunt the adult poet with a sense of having been "possessed" by a spirit or an identity not his own can also be interpreted in

Caillois's terms as a temporary triumph of the more primitive and violent "sacred" aspect of human consciousness over the "civilising" structures of the "profane." The unforgettable impressions left on virtually every child of a pre-1939 era by fairgrounds and fireworks, by the feast-days and high festivals of the church year, or by the massed colors and the massed bands, the pomp and the flamboyant circumstance of durbars and jubilees, clearly incarnate a last dying echo in the modern age of the orgiastic license of the pagan *fête*. But if there is one other area of archetypal childhood experience where the impression of magic is most immediately explicable in terms of its "other-dimensionality," that area is theater.

The most pertinent of all the criticisms which have been made of Huizinga's argument in *Homo Ludens* is that the Dutch historian fails to make sufficient distinction between play as games and play as theater. Games involve the *passive*, albeit free, acceptance of a code of rules and a dimension of behavior distinct from those of ordinary life; theater consists in *actively* creating an alternative dimension of the self and of the human situation. That the two are closely related is obvious, if only from the fact that words such as *play*, *jeu*, *jouer*, *spielen*, играть, and so forth apply both to the stage and to the sports field. There is nonetheless a significant difference.[39] The bridge player, the badminton champion, the baseball star—all these retain their identities intact and unchanged, whether they are on their ground, court, or other privileged area, or off it; or if, like the extrovert boxer, Muhammad Ali, they do "put on an act," it is specifically to entertain an audience, and thus introduces an alien element of "theater" into the domain of the "game." In theater, by contrast, the identity of the self is altered, or at least threatened with alteration, by being absorbed into the alternative dimension, forming an integral part of it: whether by actually "playing" a part, or as spectator, by identifying the self with the actors in the "otherness" of their stage existence.

It would be logical to expect, then, that the juxtaposition of reality with an alternative dimension which actually includes and transforms the self would be a more powerful experience than one in which the self retains the full awareness of its identity unchanged; and this, in effect, is exactly what we find in the Childhoods. Save in the very special circumstances of a unique type of school life, where the school itself constitutes a privileged area, sharply divided from the rest of the world, sports and games rarely constitute a significant element of experience in the recreation of childhood. If they are recalled at all, it is generally under the rubric of curiosa, as minor data for the social historian: "*these* were the kind of games we played in (say) Winesburg, Ohio, circa 1885, or in Williamstown, Massachusetts, circa 1910":

There were many games of ball. Two-cornered cat was played by four boys: two to

39. See the appendix.

bat and two behind the batters to catch and pitch. Three-cornered cat was, I believe, the game which has since grown into baseball . . . etc., etc., etc.[40]

Or in London circa 1890, or in Toronto circa 1930. . . . Whereas, as we have already seen, contact with the self-transforming dimension of theater is a "magic" experience, whose power is almost universally acknowledged throughout the whole range of our Childhoods. What is at first sight slightly less expected, although it is in fact again quite logical, is that *watching* theater is not only a completely different but frequently a more vital and vivifying experience than actually performing it. Among the innumerable accounts of taking part in a play, while the feeling recalled is frequently one of intense excitement, it is rarely one of "magic"—save, again, in special circumstances, such as may arise when the fact of performing a part may afford the child his first contact with a great poet, most frequently with Shakespeare. Also quite commonly, the play performed offers the future poet the first opportunity to prove himself (and to show off to others) as a creative writer, and to take part in his own creation. But the actor, even the child-actor, retains beneath the role he plays an awareness of his own identity; his self can never be obliterated, nor lose itself totally in the other dimension, in the way that the spectator may. Consequently, the reminiscences record the fiascos of performance more often than the triumphs and the "magic." Only in the very rarest of instances does some pale reflection of the otherwise irresistible spell of theater survive, despite the amateurishness and the misadventures; and even then, it is only indirectly brought about by theater as such, as Hal Porter, recalling school performances of plays as disparate as *The Pirate's Daughter*, *The Mikado*, and *Twelfth Night*, records in another of his memorable paragraphs:

> If ever I am nostalgically moved by High School it is in recollection of those moments when foul-mouthed boys with boils on their necks, and girls with bandy legs and false teeth, disguised in glittering rubbish, painted like beautiful idols, and flirting their spangled fans or brandishing wooden cutlasses, raise their clear coarse voices in song and dialogue, transforming themselves for a space to a grotesque and moving loveliness—for a little space, before life transforms them to the burdened and confused, the mean and bitter, the defeated and destroyed, the dead. (*Watcher on the Cast-Iron Balcony*, p. 149)

There is a further point: the impact of theater increases, its magic is felt more powerfully, exactly in proportion to the degree of its remoteness from everyday reality. Opera makes a deeper impression than "straight" theater, pantomime more than *Toad of Toad Hall*, and *Toad of Toad Hall* more than

---

40. William Dean Howells, *A Boy's Town* [basically Hamilton, Ohio] (New York, 1890), 83. Cf. also Norman Douglas, *London Street Games* (London, 1916); James Kenward, *Prep School* (London, 1958), 110–20; etc.

dramatized versions of *Uncle Tom's Cabin* or *Little Women*. And this is strikingly true, not only of set, decor, and plot, but above all of language. Naturalism leaves the child—even the late-adolescent—completely cold; it brings the theater dimension too close to reality. The supreme experiences are those in which the language of theater differs as radically as possible from that of home or school: the language of poetry, the language of music, or the language of silence. Particularly the last—and this brings us back immediately to the "silent languages" of Traherne and Ledda. The same is true of cinema: the silent films, particularly of the Wild West variety, retain some traces of other-dimensionality and magic; the "talkies," virtually none. In all the six-hundred-odd Childhoods which we are considering, a fair proportion of which cover the sound-film epoch after 1930, only one talkie is recalled with any frequency, and that, significantly, is the explicitly other-dimensional *King Kong*. The sound film in relation to the silent film, and still more in relation to theater, is as the fresco in relation to the studio painting: the first is a *continuation* of real space, the second its *condensation* into an alternative dimension.

But the supreme instance of this other-dimensionality is—or rather was—that now-moribund genre, the Circus. In the circus, the dimensions of reality and play are not merely juxtaposed, they overlap and penetrate each other. It is *impossible*—no real woman could steer a path uphill balanced on top of a diamond-sparkling rubber ball, no real man could turn his body seemingly inside-out while suspended by one hand from a trapeze thirty feet above the ring—the "Magic Ring" which last week was, and next week will be again, the ordinary, everyday, dog-and-lover-haunted grass of some dreary Victoria Park. And yet it happens. It is there. The performers, in the most advanced Brechtian tradition, are at once disguised, and yet unquestionably themselves. The high-wire artists, the lion-tamers, are absolute Otherness; and yet they incarnate, in their very presence, the child's fascination with danger, and his recent discovery of death. The circus is supreme or absolute theater in the way that nothing else is, except perhaps the bullfight; for if the hero should fail, he will not be present to repeat his failure on the following evening: he is more likely to be in the casualty ward or in the mortuary. The circus, in Caillois's sense, is an immediate confrontation with *le sacré*, as Jean Genet (in *Le Funambule*) and Fernando Arrabal, among others, have realized, the latter exploiting the circus fusion of "real" and "play" dimensions, in *Sur le fil* (1974), by requiring his actor literally to walk a tightrope twenty feet above the stage. Finally, and most significantly, the circus is silent—or, at all events, makes no use of rational language; and if circus dies, it will be because it forgets that rule, the very condition of its miraculous otherness. The clown who is silent is an archetype, a myth incarnate—as all great modern clowns have realized: Grock and Charlie Chaplin, Jacques Tati and Harpo Marx. The talking clown is no more than a third-rate music hall comedian. He destroys the otherness of the dimension created by his fellow artists.

It is not surprising, then, that the experience of circus is among the supreme experiences of the Childhood. "I do not know how boys live through the wonder and the glory of such a sight," exclaims the sober, sociohistorically minded American William Dean Howells, writing in 1890 (*A Boy's Town*, p. 96); and, in the same decade, but from the other side of the Atlantic, "We're-goin'-to-the-circus," sings Harold, in the revealingly entitled episode "The Magic Ring" of Kenneth Grahame's *Dream Days* (1898):

> With shrill voice uplifted in solemn chant, he sang the great spheral circus-song, and the undying glory of the Ring. Of its timeless beginning he sang, of its fashioning by cosmic forces, and of its harmony with the stellar plan. Of horses he sang, of their strength, their swiftness, and their docility as to tricks. Of clowns again, of glory, of knavery, and of the eternal type that shall endure. . . . At least, he doubtless sang of all these things and more; though all that was distinguishable was, "We're-goin'-to-the-circus" and then, once more, "We're-goin'-to-the-circus."[41]

Some forty years before Huizinga, Kenneth Grahame was extolling childhood as a totally *closed* world, a privileged area, complete in itself, abiding by its own rules which are *not* those of "real" (that is, adult) life, utterly inaccessible to those "Olympians," who could control it without ever in the least understanding it, and open only to other "closed" or "sacred" worlds, such as that of the circus. One such alternative "closed world" he created himself in the masterly tale which we know as *The Wind in the Willows*.[42]

In the circus, the various characteristics of otherness which we have analyzed from the writings of a number of philosophers all coincide: it is a "drama" rehearsing and repeating the supreme moments of life—triumphs or failures—in a play-dimension; it is gratuitous; with its scarlet-uniformed

41. Kenneth Grahame, *Dream Days* (1898; reprint, London, 1945), 64–65.

42. We shall not, in this study, have the space to consider the characteristics of the preferred reading matter of the child/future-poet. It may be noted, however, that *The Wind in the Willows* ranks high among the most frequently mentioned "Great Books" of childhood, along with the Bible, *Robinson Crusoe, Tom Sawyer, Huckleberry Finn, Ivanhoe, Bevis, The Last of the Mohicans, Little Women*, and various novels by Jules Verne and Jack London—and not only among English-speaking children. It may be noted also that all these are *long*; long enough, that is, to create a full and satisfying "alternative dimension" parallel to reality. It is to be guessed that Richard Hughes's *High Wind in Jamaica*, Richard Adams's *Watership Down*, and above all J. R. R. Tolkien's *Lord of the Rings* may be destined to join this select list. By contrast, Lewis Carroll's *Alice* books are seldom mentioned, no more than are A. A. Milne's "Christopher Robin" series. However much these last two may appeal to adults, the episodic structure which characterizes them nullifies their appeal to children; it denies to the worlds which the authors have created the consistency, the detail, and the abundance which are required if these worlds are to stand in parallel to the world of reality.

band, its garish lights, and its massed audience, it is a *fête*; it is erotic and it is dangerous, permeated more deeply than the gravest of tragedies with ever-present reminders of death; it is *sacré*; it is pagan and primitive, yet at the same time highly sophisticated; it is "real" and yet it transmutes reality into something more perfect, more luminous, and more abundant than itself. It is the epitome of all that is ultimately "magic" in childhood, in that it is beyond reason and beyond words. It is, in Artaud's phrase, "the poetry *behind* the poetry." "Who," concludes Kenneth Grahame (p. 64), "shall depict this and live?"

We have argued that childhood is a "closed" world, an "alternative dimension" or "play area," separated by its essential gratuitousness from the "functional" or "transactional" world of adults; and that the Childhood as a literary form is autonomous, with its own inherent structural laws distinguishing it from any other. It remains, to conclude this excursion into theory, to determine whether this form, in the precise, contemporary use of the word, can be considered as a "structure," and thus can legitimately constitute the subject of structural analysis independently of larger, fully autonomous structures such as the novel, the epic, or the more traditional forms of autobiography.

According to the definition proposed by Jean Piaget in his remarkably lucid little introductory handbook, *Le Structuralisme*, a "structure," to merit definition as such, must have three characteristic properties.[43] In the first place, it must be a "totality," in which the laws governing the whole are superior to, and different from, the laws governing the elements which compose it, "conferring on the totality as such overall properties distinct from those of its components." In the second place, it must be "transformational"—in other words, dynamic rather than static (although not necessarily within a system of temporality: both mathematics and logic, for instance, are atemporal in their transformations, whereas in genetics or linguistics, the transformations operate within a pattern of time), the component elements within the structure perpetually combining and recombining in such a way as to form *new* patterns, albeit still regulated by the general laws of the totality. Thus, in mathematics, $1 + 1 + 1 + 1 = 4$: 4 being a "new" concept, having properties of its own distinct from the properties of the single units of which it is composed—"transformational," in this case, being opposed to merely "cumulative." And finally, a structure must be "self-regulating"—that is, all new subpatterns created within the structure of the totality will remain strictly within its frontiers, and will perpetuate [*conserver*] its general laws. This does not mean, continues Piaget, that the closed nature of a structure makes it inconceivable for it to form the subordinate part of another structure larger than itself; but it

43. Jean Piaget, *Le Structuralisme* (Paris, 1974), 8–14.

implies that "this extension of general boundaries does not abolish the original ones; it is not a case of annexation, but of confederation, and the laws governing the substructure are not degraded, but maintained, so that the alteration of status constitutes an enrichment."

Now, while we have based this entire study on the notion that the Childhood, considered as a literary form, effectively constitutes a totality in its own right, rather than being merely an accidental variant of the wider genre of autobiography in its traditional patterns, distinguishable only by its incompleteness, that is, by its imperfection in relation to an ideally perfect totality, we would not wish to press this argument too far. That it *is* a totality, and thus satisfies the first required definition of a structure, is demonstrated by the history of its development over the last two hundred years, from the eighteenth century when it first appeared (as in Rousseau or Goethe) as an unusually extended introduction to an autobiography which otherwise followed a conventional pattern, to the mid-twentieth century, when nine Childhoods out of ten are conceived from the outset as independent narrative forms, complete in themselves and ending with the end of adolescence. It is also unquestionable that the genre is transformational or dynamic: in every case, the basic materials of which the Childhood is compounded (the experiential archetypes) are combined in new and original patterns. But whether it is self-regulating, in the sense in which Piaget uses this term, is perhaps more open to doubt.

The difficulty is not so much that it is threatened by absorption into structures larger than itself (here the Piaget metaphor of "confederation rather than annexation" would seem to be admirably appropriate), but rather that it tends consistently to assimilate into itself elements having other laws than its own, which elements are forever threatening to shatter the frontiers that enclose its structure as "literature." If it were possible to respect these boundaries absolutely—as in fact the structuralist literary critic does, when he argues that what he has in front of him is a *text*, that is, a sequence of pages with printed signs on them, and *nothing else*—then there might be less of a problem. Undoubtedly, moreover, it is possible to take this attitude, just as it is possible to consider, say, a textbook on aircraft engineering as a complex series of linguistic sign-symbols, bearing no relationship whatsoever to the alien laws of aerodynamics. But in either case, the attitude would seem to be slightly unreal. In the case of the aircraft manual, *unless* the written symbols bear a rigidly subordinate relationship of accuracy to the physical laws which govern the flying of aircraft, the manual, whatever its semiological interest, is a *non-text*; it fails to fulfill the function for which it was created, and thus is simply meaningless. The same applies to the Childhood. Where the writer specifically declares, as our poets do over and over again, that the only reason for writing the book at all was to tell the truth about his own life and experience, this categoric affirmation necessarily obliges the reader to establish relationships between the literary/textual structure and other structures (biological, psychological, genetic, etc.) alien to itself. As soon as we admit the author's *life* to be an integral factor in any evaluation of the text, the Childhood ceases to be self-regulating; it bulges and eventually bursts out of its enclosing frontiers, and falls immediately under the aegis of other structures and disciplines alien to it—of sociology, say, or of social history, of perception theory or behaviorism, or metaphysics. This, admittedly, is not a problem confined to the Childhood; it affects also the wider genre of autobiography as such. But this does not alter the fact that, in the strictest sense of the terminology, it may be unwise to class the Childhood as an autonomous "structure" without some profounder consideration of the issues. It has most of the required characteristics, but not, without some distortion of the real issues, all of them.

> Art is not life and cannot be,
> A handmaid to society.

The Childhood attempts to reverse the situation, making Society (or "Life") into a handmaid of its own. But the result is no less equivocal. The handmaid is unruly, boisterous, independent, constantly upsetting the neat and ordered structure of her master's house. And so, while we must allow the childhood the fullest possible autonomy as a significant literary genre, it may be premature to affirm too boldly its status as a "self-regulating" structure.

Conclusion:
Childhood as Mythology and as Poetry

My childhood was nearly over—and it's too bad that only the grown-ups know how nice it was to be a child.
                                        —Konstantin Paustovsky, *Story of a Life*

During the period which has elapsed since World War II, Childhood autobiographies have proliferated on an unprecedented scale; and, during the last decade or so, critical studies of autobiography as a literary genre have similarly multiplied. The two phenomena are clearly not unconnected. Both reflect that unparalleled upsurge of individualism which, paradoxically, is the by-product of socialistic leveling. As the clan, the family, the tribe, and the dynasty are dissolved, one after the other, into the equalitarian community, so the individual attains a new consciousness of his autonomy; as servants and retainers disappear, the self, in ever-increasing loneliness and isolation, becomes more acutely aware of its never-to-be-repeated identity. Add to this a nostalgia, all over the globe, for unique traditions and isolated cultures doomed to extinction by the motel and the airport, and there is created a climate in which the experience of the child-self appears to be of incalculable value. "The era of individual destinies is over and done with," observes Sheikh Hamidou Kane, in a phrase even more ambiguous than the title he chose for his own work.[1] For if, on the one hand, the unique and precious qualities of life in Tregonissey, Cornwall, or on Great Blasket Island, County Kerry; among the high sand-dunes commanding the inlet of Buctouche, New Brunswick, or on the precipitous ridges overlooking Siriana, Kenya; in the industrial suburbs of Nizhni-Novgorod (now renamed "Gorky"), U.S.S.R., or in the central square of Illiers

---

1. Sheikh Hamidou Kane, *L'Aventure ambiguë* (1961; Paris, 1972), 92.

(now renamed "Illiers-Combray"), France[2]—if these have already been lost for ever, the consciousness of the self who once recorded these experiences is sharper than ever before in the history of man.

Probably something similar is reflected in the new critical attention being paid to autobiography. The literary critic, after all, is only human, and cannot help but be aware of the trends of thought and feeling around him—and in addition, he has a further motivation. "Qu'est-ce que le moi?" asked Pascal over three centuries ago. "Je est un autre," replied Rimbaud, two and a half hesitant centuries later. "L'Homme est tel qu'il se conçoit"—for a while, Jean-Paul Sartre seemed to have put a full stop to the questions, until Samuel Beckett stepped in with the rejoinder: "Where now? Who now? When now? Unquestioning. I, say I. Unbelieving." The problem of identity has become undeniably one of the most obsessively unanswerable questions in Western metaphysics; and the childhood quest for the self has suddenly assumed, in consequence, a significance which few thinkers of an earlier generation would have seen fit to accord to it.

And underneath these already entangled self-questionings in which the Western intellect has embroiled itself lies a deeper one still: what is it, in heredity, in environment, in education, or in experience, that will transform one human being into a poet and his brother into a real estate salesman? Here, the dreaded specter of inequality rears its Medusa-head; for the poet can tell us something about himself, whereas the real estate salesman cannot. It may be, therefore, in all fairness, that we should discount the verbiage of the poet, and listen only to the silence of his brother. Yet, if we *could* find out by what processes life is transmuted into language, and particularly into the language of poetry, this might be one of the most fascinating discoveries that the combined efforts of psychologists and critics, researchers in cognitive development, linguisticians, and neurosurgeons might make to the sum of significant human knowledge.

While the present study can make no claim to any such contribution, its conclusions have proved to be rather different from those which might have been anticipated at the outset. In fact, most of the presuppositions with which I started out, or which were suggested to me by friends and colleagues, have proved hopelessly wrong. For instance, it has emerged that there is no characteristic *age* at which writers turn back toward their childhood experience: at

2. Anne Treneer, *School House in the Wind* (London, 1944); Maurice O'Sullivan, *Twenty Years A-Growing* (1933; Oxford, 1953); Antonine Maillet, *On a mangé la dune* (Montréal, 1962); N'Gugi wa Thiong'o, *The River Between* (London, 1965); Maxim Gorky, *Detstvo* [*Childhood*, 1913]; Marcel Proust, *Combray* [1914].

most, there are clusters in the middle-thirties and in the middle-fifties; but the exceptions are too numerous to render these clusters impressive. The age at which the writer produces his or her Childhood ranges from not quite sixteen (Gustave Flaubert) to ninety-three (Helen Corke).[3] Nor is there any revealing difference between men and women. So utterly minimal is the role of toys in the recreation of the past self, that the appearance of a doll here, a Meccano-set there, leaves nothing to get hold of. It is tempting to suggest that a man usually recalls his past self directly, whereas a woman will tend to check the uncertain memories of early impressions and reactions by reference to the minute and detailed observation of her own children, as is the case, say, with Eleanor Acland, or Juliette Adam, or Colette, or Flora Groult, or Vera Panova[4]—until one recalls that the undoubtedly male Anatole France does exactly the same thing in the second section of *Le Livre de mon ami*, which he entitles "Le Livre de Suzanne,"[5] and that Alan Marshall checked every angle of vision recorded in *I Can Jump Puddles* from the eye-level of his three-year-old granddaughter.

Again, it might have been anticipated either that the experiences of child-hood would prove to be absolutely universal, as Chateaubriand supposed, or else substantially affected and determined by the political, social, religious, economic, and environmental conditions surrounding the early life. Neither presupposition, in the event, is borne out in any clear-cut fashion. There is a slight predominance (at least after 1900) of writers who grew up in im-poverished homes over those whose families lived in easy circumstances; but, in effect, the genre covers the whole social scale, from the fabulous wealth of a Susanna Agnelli or an Anne Bernays (*Growing Up Rich*, Boston, 1975) to the destitution and near-starvation of their exact contemporary Helen Forrester— incidentally, compared to the latter (daughter of a middle-class English fam-ily ruined by the Great Depression), most Third World and even Harlem chil-dren would seem to have fed copiously.

And on the surface, the most striking national differences tend to be negative. Why is it, for instance, that while Russian literature is rich in Child-hoods, the other Slav-speaking peoples would appear to have produced vir-tually none?[6] Or why is the genre so little practiced among the Mediterra-

3. Gustave Flaubert, *Mémoires d'un fou*, written in November 1838; Helen Corke, *In Our Infancy* (Cambridge, Eng., 1975).

4. Eleanor Acland, *Goodbye for the Present* (London, 1935); Juliette Adam, *Le Roman de mon enfance et de ma jeunesse* (Paris, 1902); Colette, *La Maison de Claudine* (1922; Paris, 1929); Flora Groult, *Mémoires de moi* (Paris, 1975); Vera Panova, *Seryozha* [1955], in *Sobraniye Sochinenii* (Leningrad, 1969), 199–292. *Seryozha* is a novel rather than autobiography.

5. Anatole France, *Le Livre de mon ami* (Paris, 1885).

6. In a recent conversation with an eminent Czech professor of literature, I inquired whether

nean-Latin peoples—notably by the Italians and by the Spaniards? Spain has given us one great example in Ramón Sender's *Crónica del alba* (1942), and a minor but interesting one in Manuel Azaña's *El Jardin de los frailes* (1921); but little or nothing else.[7] Italy offers one splendid but generally neglected specimen in Bruno Cicognani's *L'Età favolosa* (1940); but this is completely exceptional and uncharacteristic. For the rest, there are Luigi Meneghello and Susanna Agnelli (both of whom live, or have lived for lengthy periods, in English-speaking countries), and, from Sardinia, Gavino Ledda. Compared with France, this is a lamentably meager collection. Moreover, with the half-exception of Manuel Azaña, it is worth noting that all are fairly modern. It might be suggested that the close-knit patterns of family relationships in these Catholic Latin countries, persisting as they do right through adult life, make it difficult, perhaps impossible, for the writer to consider his child-self as something markedly distinct from his adult-self. If this *were* the explanation, however, we should expect to find the same difficulty among Jewish writers, who in most cases have a similarly intense background of religious family intimacy; but this, clearly, is not the case. But then again (in support of the theory), there is the remarkable fact that all Spanish and Italian authors of Childhoods mentioned above, with the unique exception of Cicognani, *did* have the normal patterns of family life irrevocably broken, and all ties shattered, whether by the Spanish Civil War, by the Second World War, or by some other circumstance. It may be that, in these cultures, some such traumatic break with the family (or rather, with the clan) is a necessary precondition, the only one which can afford the perspective required for observing and recording the autonomous life of the child-self.

In spite of these predominantly negative conclusions, however, it *is* possible to observe certain more positive distinctions between Childhoods deriving from different cultures. These, for want of a better term, are perhaps most appropriately described as "Myths"—vague, almost indefinable social or cultural emphases, which might well pass unperceived in any individual writer, and which become noticeable only through their cumulative effect.

A *myth*, in its modern, post-Jungian acceptance, and as the term is used by

---

this widely-read scholar could refer me to any texts, classic or contemporary, in Czech or Slovak, so that I might hunt them up. After a great deal of thought, he was unable to name a single one. See, however, Bozena Nemčova, *Babička* [1855], trans. E. Pargeter, *Granny* (Prague, 1962).

7. Carmen Laforet's *Nada* (1944), while it clearly contains autobiographical elements (life in Barcelona in the aftermath of the Spanish Civil War), is first and foremost a novel; and in any case, like Arthur Calder-Marshall's *The Magic of My Youth*, or Beverley Nichols's *Twenty-Five*, it deals with the university years only.

contemporary structural anthropologists such as Michel Foucault and Claude Lévi-Strauss, is the symbolic embodiment of a truth often buried too deep to be apprehended by the conscious mind. Product of a racial, or perhaps of a cultural, subconscious, often engendered in the first place by popular imagination, but sometimes by the intuition of the individual poet, a myth is handed down from generation to generation, its very longevity an indication of its profound and continuing relevance. By studying the myths that recur most frequently and most emphatically in any given culture (or indeed, that are held in common by a number of different cultures), one can learn something important, not so much about man as an individual, as about man as a psychological, intellectual, and spiritual "social animal."

The myths that emerge from our Childhoods do not possess quite this fully matured socioanthropological status. To begin with, they are not quite ancient enough. The Oedipus myth is probably three thousand years old, if not more; the myths of the Childhood have grown up only over the last three centuries. Further, they came into being when society was (on the surface at least) highly sophisticated, literate, and self-conscious; there is no primitive oral tradition behind them, lost in the mists of prehistory. Nonetheless, they do reveal something; in many cases, perhaps, far more than the individual writer intended. And they have this in common with the more orthodox type of myth—namely, that when they reach us in the form of literature, they are the result of the poet "listening" to the faint echoes of a vanished and seemingly legendary past. Whether that past lies in the self or in the community is of no particular consequence. Every child, in its own way, is a "primitive."

This does not mean that the kind of myths that can be detected in the Childhood bear *no* relationship to the particular social and cultural climate in which the writer grew up. Of course they do. The child who grew up in Mussolini's Italy (for example, Susanna Agnelli or Luigi Meneghello) will necessarily have had experiences distinct from those of the child who grew up in Roosevelt's America.[8] Similarly, a child from North-Central Manitoba, where the temperature is well below zero for eight months of the year, will have a tale to tell very different from that of his contemporary in tropical or subtropical Brisbane or Peshawar, Kouroussa or Buenos Aires.[9] The blind or crippled child[10] will recount facts having little in common with those recalled

8. For example, Peter Davison, *Half Remembered* (New York, 1973).

9. For example, Gabrielle Roy, *La Petite Poule d'eau* (Paris, 1951); Jack Lindsay, *Life Rarely Tells* (London, 1958) and David Malouf, *Johnno* (St. Lucia, Queensland, 1975); Mulk Rāj Anānd, *Seven Summers* (Delhi, 1972); Camara Laye, *L'Enfant noir* (Paris, 1953); W. H. Hudson, *Far Away and Long Ago* (London, 1918).

10. For example, Christy Brown, *My Left Foot* (London, 1954); Karl Bjarnhof, *Stjernerne blegner* [The stars grow pale] (Copenhagen, 1956); Alan Marshall, *I Can Jump Puddles* (Melbourne, 1955).

by the young athlete such as Erich Kästner. Schools vary from country to country, as do churches, farms or seaside-resorts. Jules Michelet (father = bankrupt printer under Napoleon I) will recall incidents well separated, if only by thirty or forty years of political change and technological progress, from those recollected by Alphonse Daudet (father = bankrupt silk manufacturer under Napoleon III).[11] And so on. Interesting as these details may be, they remain on the level of curiosa. They are not in themselves of the essence.

The true myths (or "obsessions") are of a different nature altogether. They are betrayed in the manner in which not one or two, but a statistically viable number of Childhoods, originating in the same culture but stemming from completely different social and economic backgrounds, reveal a preoccupation with identical aspects of the experience; not, certainly, to the exclusion of all others, but with sufficient reiteration to command the reader's attention.

Thus the English child (or rather, once again, the writer, or poet, recreating an intimate yet alien past self) is obsessed with the processes of its own education—from dame's school, sunday school, or nannie, via rural elementary, governess, or prep school, to grammar school or Public School and so eventually to university. The French child, by contrast, who as a general rule loathes its lycée more than any other child in the world detests its educational institutions, is fascinated by language, and by the whole process of learning and assimilating the fundamental means of communication. The Russian child characteristically has a different problem altogether: "Lies my mother told me"—so that the whole range of Russian Childhoods, from Sergei Aksakov to Andrei Bely and Konstantin Paustovsky, are at bottom little but innumerable and infinitely subtle variants on the theme of the "Portrait of the Artist Astounded by His Mother." The North American child (U.S. or English-Canadian) appears fascinated over and over again, not by its own past self, but rather by that self's relation to the community: not the "I," but the community framework in which it developed is the essential. Thus William Dean Howells's A Boy's Town and Robert Luther Duffus's Impersonal Memories of a Vermont Boyhood; thus Robert T. Allen's When Toronto Was for Kids, or even Mordecai Richler's The Street, are titles that reveal, in a manner which clearly the authors themselves did not envisage, the underlying mythology of a whole culture. Hal Borland is no master of style; but he reveals his subconscious affinity with other children who grew up on the North American continent when he introduces his Country Editor's Boy:

This is a story of youth—the transition years of a boy, of a town, of the culture of an area. Because I happened to be the boy, it is autobiography; but because the area was

11. Jules Michelet, Ma jeunesse (Paris, 1884); Alphonse Daudet, Le Petit Chose [1868], reprinted as vol. 2 in Œuvres complètes illustrées (Paris, 1930).

the High Plains of eastern Colorado and the time was those years when the Old West was passing and the New West was emerging, it partakes of social history.[12]

The Australian child is inspired to reconstruct his past self by his frustration at the memory of growing up in an overriding love-hate relationship with a cultural vacuum;[13] Jewish, Irish, and French-Canadian children grow up inebriated with the history which they learned, not at school but at home—the history of the calamities attendant upon the races to which, respectively, they belong—and their Childhoods are inseparable from the shadows cast by those calamities.[14] And the children of the Third World—and this includes the Black children of the West Indies and of the United States—are unable to dissociate any aspect of their past selves from the visible or invisible factor of the White Presence.

This analysis could be pursued further,[15] and carried over into any cultural group which has produced a sufficient number of Childhood texts to enable us to get beyond the individual and to perceive the myth that pervades the common perspective. And it is at this point, perhaps, that the application of the methods of comparative literature becomes rewarding. From its inception in the earlier years of the present century, the discipline of comparative literature has tended to dwell on those elements which may be discovered *in common* between different cultural traditions. But it is perhaps even more informative to concentrate on the *distinctions* between one tradition and another. Most cultures and most literatures are sufficient unto themselves— that is, they simply take for granted that the common assumptions made *within* their own closed fields are universal. Not out of arrogance or chauvinism, but simply because there is no incentive to prompt anyone to ask the question. Set against the equally "universal" assumptions of another culture, those of the first may suddenly be revealed as unique, idiosyncratic, or, in extreme cases, demonstrably unjustifiable. And if the comparative method can awaken this kind of critical self-awareness, then it will have justified its existence.

Leaving aside these controversial issues, what *has* emerged from the present study is something about the nature of poetry.

Beginning with the wholly unexpected discovery that something between fifty and sixty percent of the authors of those six-hundred-odd Childhoods

---

12. Hal Borland, *Country Editor's Boy* (Philadelphia, 1970), 7 (opening phrases).

13. See my essay "Portrait of the Artist as a Young Australian," *Southerly* 41, no. 2, 126–62.

14. See my essay "Childhood in the Shadows," *Comparison* 13:3–67.

15. See my study "Introduction to a Comparative Mythology of Childhood," in the *Proceedings of the Leeds Philosophical and Literary Society* 19 (1984), part 6, in press.

which we have located have turned out either to have written and published poetry, or else to be such consummate masters of prose style (Babel', Proust, Stendhal, Tolstoy) that formal versification becomes, as it were, an unnecessary luxury, it would appear to follow that the Childhood (as distinct from all other forms of autobiography, and even more so, of memoirs) is fundamentally a *poet's* form of expression. But since, at the same time, it is a method of self-analysis, it would seem that it *may* be possible to discover, from a careful reading of the Childhood, something which specifically characterizes the early experience of children who, later, are to develop as poets. The nature of that "something" is necessarily elusive: certainly it is nothing so elementary as books which happen to be read, or essays written for the school magazine, although, obviously, it has something to do with language. Not infrequently, a Childhood will end with the discovery that "words are good enough to eat." "Something happened to me about that time," concludes Emanuel Litvinoff in the final sentence of his *Journey through a Small Planet*:

> Suddenly I wrote a poem. The words came unexpectedly to me one day during dinner break at work. I found a crumpled piece of paper in my pocket and wrote them down. "Farewell O Queen of the Night, dark mistress of my cosmic dreams." It was a strange thing to write and I wondered what it meant. But if I failed to understand how the words came, I knew with extraordinary elation that they were a message from inner space. Things would never be the same again.[16]

Certainly this feeling, that "things would never be the same again," after a first contact with poetry, is not uncommon; but it is, in a sense, a final stage, placed by Litvinoff where it properly belongs, at the point of transition into maturity, rather than as an inherent phenomenon of childhood proper.

The notion that the Childhood is specifically "a poet's form of expression" can be interpreted in three distinct ways: (1) the literal use of a verse structure to recreate the past experience; (2) the elaboration, by a poet, of the potentialities of prose to create an impressionistic panorama of the childhood vision; and (3) the refashioning, again by a poet, of a straightforward chronological narrative in such a way as to bring out its peculiar quality of strangeness or otherness.

1. The poetic idiom of the nineteenth century—the poetry of Wordsworth, Lamartine, or Nekrasov, as we saw in the introduction to this study—was totally unsuited to any revelation of the momentous triviality, of the *inconsequence* above all, of the childhood vision. But the far freer, symbolist or quasi-surrealist idiom of poets such as Rimbaud (*Enfance*, circa 1876), Saint-John

16. Emanuel Litvinoff, *Journey through a Small Planet* (London, 1972; reprint, Harmondsworth, 1976), 138.

Perse (*Pour fêter une enfance*, 1910), or Andrei Bely (*Kotik Letaev*, 1916) suddenly transformed the whole relationship between the child-self and its subsequent recreation in verse form, so that, over the last fifty years, the Childhood in verse has become, if not exactly common, at least a far less infrequent occurrence than had been the case earlier. This is not a question of short, isolated lyrics, which have existed since the seventeenth century, but of fully-fledged narrational Childhoods written in the idiom of poetry, sometimes ironical (Raymond Queneau, *Chêne et chien*, 1937), sometimes humorous (John Betjeman, *Summoned by Bells*, 1960), sometimes epic (Philip Toynbee, *Pantaloon*, 1961), sometimes fragmented (Silvana Gardner, *When Sunday Comes*, 1982), but sometimes quite straightforward. Thus in *Another Life* (1973) Derek Walcott, reliving his childhood spent in St. Lucia, West Indies, finds no difficulty in reconciling the use of poetry with an episode as humdrum and as trivial as learning history out of an imperialistically oriented English textbook:

> In the child's mind
> dead fellaheen were heaped in piles of laundry,
> and the converted starched with light and sweetness,
> white angels flocking round Gordon's golden palms,
> the nodding plumes, I SERVE,
> resurrected horsemen choiring from the horizon
> from the sepia washes of the *Illustrated London News*,
> and the child, like a ribbed mongrel
> trailing the fading legions,
> singing in his grandfather's company.
> Peccavi. I have Sind.[17]

Or thus also, albeit rather more hermetically, Marc Cholodenko, in *Le Prince: Portrait de l'artiste en enfant* (1974), evoking rich, Renaissance-splendored recollections of his former self as it evolved among the Palazzi—mirrors and picture galleries—of a starlit Venice where he was born:

> Le rose
> du noeud
> où son poignet
> repose
> est la couleur calmée
> du sang qui le remue
>   et le geste
>   qui l'enlève
> répand

17. Derek Walcott, *Another Life* (New York, 1973), 72.

> au ciel
> le flot
> d'une exsangue
> blessure
> la moire
> perpétue
> à ses pieds
> le vert
> des prés
> stellaires
>   et sa marche
>   y ordonne la danse
>   rapportée de ses rêves
> ainsi
> celé
> au coeur sans lieu
> de son palais
> de glaces
> le Prince grandit
> en toute pureté
> car en telle grammaire
> que peut lire le monde?[18]

"Poésie verticale" of this order does not make for easy reading, but in some ways it is reminiscent of Thomas Traherne in the sense of dream and wonderment which it conveys.

2. The prose idiom, as used by a poet, is frequently diverted from its normal linear structure in such a way as to create a pattern of purely verbal impressions. Most typically, this process resolves itself into a series of vignettes, and at the heart of each lies a kind of child's game with pure language. Thus Sheila Wingfield, riding home from a fox-hunt in the course of her Irish adolescence, reveals her interest in foxes as such, or in hunting, as nil, but her fascination with the changing colors of the landscape as unforgettable.

During the day, these colours had been in turn:

Lichenous	glaucous	rusted
glassy	smoky	sedge
pigeon	ashen	straw

18. Marc Cholodenko, *Le Prince: Portrait de l'artiste en enfant* (Paris, 1974), 58–59. Literal translation: "The pink of the ribbon-bow where his wrist reposes is the color grown calm of the blood which stirs him / and the gesture which sweeps it upward spreads the sky with the flood of a wound drained of blood / the watered silk at his feet eternalizes the green of the fields of the stars / and thereon his steps pattern the dance born of his dreams / thus concealed in the locationless heart of his palace of mirrors the Prince grows up in ineffable purity for in a grammar-book such as this what can the world read?

celadon	flint	mossy
stone	iron	dun
cindered	plaster	oat
slaty	leaden	loam
brick	copper	madder
maroon	lezardous [sic]	plum
leather	verdigris	clay. . . .[19]

This is an extreme instance; nonetheless, prose-poetry of one sort or another is one of the most frequently encountered languages of the Childhood.

3. The poet, even when narrating his childhood experiences in straightforward prose, is liable to dwell more on the dream-world than on the world of everydayness, more on the oddities and eccentricities of factuality, which served to furnish his mind with a sense of wonder at the freakishness of "ordinary" experience, than with the normal and the familiar. In this category, both Francis Jammes and Henry Handel Richardson are typical; but perhaps a better instance—if only because its author is the greater poet—is W. B. Yeats's *Reveries over Childhood and Youth* (1914). Nor is it without significance in the evolution of the genre that Yeats, Joyce, Andrei Bely, Robert Musil, and Alain-Fournier (to mention only the most outstanding) should all have been writing similar prose-poetic fact-fantasies within the same decade.

The *Reveries over Childhood and Youth* are as complex a mixture as one could wish to find of poetic meditation and plain reminiscence—not least, because both Yeats's father, John Butler Yeats, and his brother, Jack Yeats, were painters. In the definitive 1927 edition of the *Reveries*, the text is accompanied by drawings and paintings of a gracious, faery-like quality, and these already influence the tone of the narrative. Every figure, every episode (but particularly in the earlier sections) takes on something of this eccentric-fantastic quality, from the painter Nettleship, who, "that he might not be tempted from his work by Society . . . , had made a rent in the tail of his coat,"[20] to the black, hairy dog who had no tail, "because it had been sheared off, if I had been told the truth, by a railway train" (p. 15). Like virtually all our poet-autobiographers of childhood, Yeats was fascinated by colors and by language, by beetles and sea urchins and sweets (in particular, by a "cutter yacht made of sugar," which was displayed in the window of a shop), by imagery— "My thoughts were a great excitement to me, but when I tried to do anything with them, it was like trying to pack a balloon into a shed in a high wind" (p. 50)—by mystery and by folktales, by poetry and by incongruity, by sex and by solitude:

As I look backward, I seem to discover that my passions, my loves and my despairs,

19. Sheila Wingfield, *Real People* (London, 1952), 45.
20. W. B. Yeats, *Reveries over Childhood and Youth* (1914; reprint, London, 1927), 54.

instead of being my enemies, a disturbance and an attack, became so beautiful that I had to be alone to give them my whole attention. I notice that now, for the first time, what I saw when I was alone is more vivid in my memory than what I did or saw in company. (p. 77)

It would be an exaggeration to claim that the *Reveries* is among the best of the poetically inspired Childhoods; but it is certainly among the most archetypal. It possesses, albeit in a minor and muted key, something of the three categories of childhood experience which would appear to characterize the future poet. Not that every child who has these experiences will necessarily become a poet, let alone a good one; but *unless* he has them, then poetry is likely to be closed to him. These are the related experiences which we have attempted to describe as those of the *alternative dimension*, of *magic*, and of *abundance*.

The alternative dimension is, in the first instance, perhaps simply an angle of vision different from that of the adult recreating his past self. But, in the process of recreation, it becomes symbolic of a much broader experience—the experience of life in a dimension specifically *other* than that of the adult, a *Homo ludens* dimension, with its own rules, its own logic, its own rituals, and its own sensualities; a world from which the adults—the "Olympians"—are forever excluded; the world that Konstantin Paustovsky, in those words which have suggested the title of this study, describes as one in which

everything was different. Everything was more vivid—the sun brighter, the smell of the fields sharper, the thunder was louder, the rain more abundant and the grass taller. (*Povest' o zhizni*, 1:99; trans., 1:85)

It is this sensing of the world as *different* from that of the adult self which provides the poet with the first, instinctive intimation of that alternative apprehension of reality which is the beginning of poetry. This is perhaps the secret of that baffling quality of poetry—Antonin Artaud's "poetry *behind* the poetry"—which totally eludes the rationalistic critic. For the poet is aware of a different way of "being-in" or "being-with" his surroundings. A way in which, while not entirely to be identified with that of his child-self, nonetheless has its roots in that earlier stage of existence.

Similarly, the much-abused word *magic* can be seen as an attempt to express something very much more profound than mere nostalgia for a care-free past, a lost innocence. It may take various forms, from a simple state of exaltation beyond language—yet for which, since it is an experience so momentous, eventually a language must be found—to curious and inexplicable occurrences (such as Thomas Wolfe's serpent in the sewerage), which logically *cannot* have occurred, and yet which are *known* to have happened. Sometimes, albeit rarely, these occurrences are specifically religious, as in the extraordinary episode recalled by Richard Church when he first discovered his ability to levitate:

I drew my breath again, I scorned the laws of space and time, I took the presence of Christ into my hollow, featherweight bones, and I floated down the staircase without touching either tread or bannister. (*Over the Bridge*, p. 164)

More often it is a sense of mystic exaltation, bereft of the imagery and framework of any conventional religion, but nonetheless, in the deepest sense, religious for all that. It is a sense of being at one with the totality; it is a vision of beauty so miraculous that it goes wholly beyond the surface of reality into the very essence of being. This was, three centuries ago, the experience of Thomas Traherne, and, in more recent contexts, the experience of literally scores of other child-poets—among the most notable, Bernard Berenson, R. D. Burns, Eleanor Farjeon, Francis Jammes, Eugène Ionesco, Hal Porter, Kathleen Raine, Saint-John Perse—the sense of being wonderfully, marvelously "immersed in *Itness*."

Nor is the evidence of this type of experience drawn only from our subjective, autobiographical sources. Michael Paffard, in his fascinating survey *Inglorious Wordsworths*, has shown, using methods derived directly from the science of sociology, that a considerable proportion of the adolescents whom he sampled had had experience of this kind of inexplicable "exaltation," although on the one hand they were hopelessly embarrassed if called upon to discuss it, and on the other, they were completely baffled when it came to establishing any relationship between this kind of homespun transcendency, which was undoubtedly real to them, and "religion," which the majority of them actively rejected.[21]

There is no point in trying to make this evidence carry more weight than it will bear; what does appear certain, however, is that the poet, almost invariably, can encounter some aspect of this "magic" in his past self, and that the recollection of this experience has a great deal, eventually, to do with his compulsive need to express himself through poetry—or, for that matter, through music, painting, sculpture, or any other of the arts. The Ancients talked about the Muses. It might seem, perhaps, that these delightful but vaporous Ladies who inspire the artist are not as totally mythical as nineteenth-century materialism had assured us. To be a poet, or a creative artist of any sort, involves a plunge, temporarily at least, into a *different* apprehension of reality from that of everydayness; and this sense of contact, however fleeting, with an inexplicable and irrational "suprareality" would appear to have its roots in the strange and magical exaltations of childhood.

The third and last of these related experiences is that which we have described as "abundance." This is not necessarily the mere material abundance of a well-stocked larder; children from poverty-stricken families are as

21. Michael Paffard, *Inglorious Wordsworths* (London, 1973). See also Edith Cobb, *The Ecology of Imagination in Childhood* (New York, 1977).

frequently aware of it as are those from prosperous, middle-class homes. It is the sense—again we find it in Traherne—of moving and existing in a universe which is *full*; of being crowded in on all sides by sounds and colors, by flowers, butterflies, and grasses, by streetlamps and fireworks and transfers and sweets with marvelous names in many-colored wrappers. One of the reasons, perhaps, why Christmas plays such an important part in childhood reminiscence is that it marks one of the climaxes of this awareness of abundance. The house, the town, the shops are fuller at that time than at any other season of the year, save perhaps, in the country, at the height of summer, which is the other culminating point of abundance. The truly unhappy Christmases are not so much those at which the child receives no toys—although of course those also, in their very multiplicity, are symbols of abundance, and at bottom, like Ahmed Séfrioui's "Box of Miracles," more valued for this, probably, than for their own intrinsic value—as those at which a sensation of emptiness and isolation prevails. "Christmas came and I had but one orange," recalls Richard Wright. "I was hurt and would not go out and play with the neighbourhood children who were blowing horns and shooting firecrackers. I nursed my orange all Christmas Day."[22] And from the other side of the Atlantic, roughly in the same year, comes the echo of the same misery from Frank O'Connor: the loneliness, the empty house, the single gift, "the end of the season of imagination" (*An Only Child*, p. 107). The gaudy cornucopias of cheap and useless toys which predatory manufacturers create for the ready-filled Christmas stocking have, one suspects, a profound psychological meaning. They are a symbol of the phenomenon of abundance—a constituent element of that exaltation which is the most vivid of all experiences, perhaps for most children, certainly for the future poet.

The fact, moreover, that *poets* above all have developed and exploited the Childhood may, perhaps, help to answer a further question which was posed at the outset: namely, can the literary form "Reminiscences of Childhood and Adolescence" truly be considered as an autonomous subgenre of autobiography; or is the distinction purely artificial, leaving the Childhood to merge with no perceptible dividing lines into traditional autobiography on the one hand, and into the novel on the other?

Unquestionably, as we demonstrated in the introduction, the Childhood is a comparatively new genre—but then so is autobiography itself, arising in the Renaissance at the same time as the self-portrait in painting, and both perhaps owing something to the invention of the Venetian-glass mirror to replace the inadequate and inaccurate reflections offered by the polished-silver mirrors of earlier times.[23] The Childhood has flourished only over the last century and a

---

22. Richard Wright, *Black Boy* (1937; London, 1970), 87.
23. See Georges Gusdorf, "Conditions et limites de l'autobiographie," in *Formen der*

half. But all new genres in literature are at bottom responses to significant social, cultural, and technological changes in the community for which they are destined; and, given the vast transformations which have taken place in Western Europe and elsewhere since the French Revolution, it is not surprising that we find new genres evolving to match them. The opposite would be stranger.

In the course of this study, we have attempted to define the genre and, more important, to determine its inner structures, which are quite different from those of traditional autobiography. If there is an awkward category which seems to defy the "rules," it is perhaps that which we might call the "multi-storeyed Childhood"—that is, autobiographies of enormous length and (originally at least) in several volumes each published separately, of which the first one, two, or more volumes, each complete in itself, deal specifically with childhood and adolescence, but are followed by later volumes concerning themselves with adult life. Among these exasperating hybrids we may include George Sand's *Histoire de ma vie* (four volumes of prechildhood and childhood material out of a total of five); Compton Mackenzie's *Octaves* (two and one-half volumes out of four); Osbert Sitwell's *Left Hand, Right Hand* (three out of five volumes); Marcel Jouhandeau's *Mémorial* (seven volumes out of eight); Augustus Hare's *The Story of My Life* (in six volumes), together with Simone de Beauvoir's four volumes of recollections, of which, in both cases, only the first volume is properly a Childhood . . . and others.

The answer of this objection is that in all these, with the half-exception of the interminable Jouhandeau, the stress is on outer rather than on inner experience; they are in fact memoirs rather than autobiography; and even where, as in the case of Simone de Beauvoir, the first volume is truly auto-biographical, the later volumes are recollections of others rather than of the self. To maintain the intensity of self-observation required by the authentic autobiographer, particularly in relation to his early years, for the space of more than one volume without the use of anecdotal or other extraneous material, is difficult; and although there are a number of trilogies of the "Childhood–Boyhood–Youth" pattern, these tend either to come from the pens of *very* major writers (such as Tolstoy and Gorky) or else to prove rather thin and superficial.

Still, the most convincing argument for the autonomy of the genre considered as a form of literature would seem to be, yet again, the way in which, once stripped of its memoir content, it has been evolved and used by poets. It would appear to offer to the poet the means of expressing an essential part of his or her experience which cannot easily find a place in the more traditional auto-biographical forms. For the poet, the vital step in self-knowledge is not what he did, felt, or thought *while* he was writing his poetry—all that matters from

---

Selbstdarstellung, ed. Reichencron and Waase (Berlin, 1956), especially 108–09.

that point of view has been better expressed in the poetry itself—but rather *how* he came to discover and start writing poetry in the first instance. And it was to satisfy this need above all others that, seemingly, the Childhood was evolved. Wordsworth's subtitle to *The Prelude*, "The Growth of a Poet's Mind" ceases, if we accept this explanation, to be the enigma which it has proved to some critics; it is part of the fundamental definition of the genre itself.

As to the future of this genre, everything would seem to point to proliferation on an unprecedented scale. Radio and television, with ever-increasing regularity, are inviting public figures to talk about their early years. "Grassroots" historians and sociologists are insatiable in their demand for intimate childhood reminiscences of undistinguished people: thus, in *Obasan* (1981), Joy Kogawa employs a variant of the Childhood to analyze the effect of the restrictive edicts issued by the Canadian Commonwealth Government against its own Japanese ethnic minorities during World War II; thus *A Memoir of Robert Blincoe* (1832) has been republished after a century and a half, only to conjure up a modern equivalent in Robert Roberts's *Growing Up in the Classic Slum* (1976). Even politicians and trade-union leaders—the last stronghold of the memoir tradition—are beginning to find their infancy as intriguing as their adult lives—witness Jim Bullock's *Bowers Row* (1976). Indeed, over the past two decades in particular, it would seem that, to the traditional "poetic" manifestation of the Childhood, there has been added another, subsidiary form—a "pop" variant, in more or less the same sense as one talks about "pop" music. Like pop music, the pop Childhood appears to be aimed primarily at a teenage or nonintellectual market. It is the occasion for well-known national figures to demystify and democratize their public image by affording glimpses of their preaffluent selves in those early days before their features had become familiar to millions from the television screen. To this category we may assign, for instance, Harry J. Boyle's *Memories of a Catholic Boyhood* (1973)—Mr. Boyle being, among other things, Vice-Chairman of the Canadian Radio-Television Commission. Given the type of readership at which such Childhoods are aimed, the episodes are journalistically resolved into clear, easily assimilable outlines, metaphysical speculation is reduced to a minimum, and illustration—most frequently in the form of caricatural or semicomic line drawings—takes on an added importance. James Krüss's *My Great-Grandfather and I* (1960)—to select one example among many—contains over two hundred line drawings in Thurberesque style, better suited to a sophisticated juvenile market than to normal autobiography. But it also contains a great deal of poetry. For, even in these frequently uninspired specimens of the genre, the poetic element is by no means missing altogether; but it is the poetry of a culture in which Georges Brassens, Mick Jagger, and the Beatles are accepted as serious poets.[24]

24. Two other contemporary "pop" or best-seller variants of the Childhood have made a

At the opposite end of the spectrum, however, it is worth recording the fact that the Childhood is clearly exerting an unexpected influence over some of the more avant-garde manifestations of the contemporary novel—and even of drama. Monique Wittig, in *L'Opoponax* (1964), Steven Millhauser, in *Edwin Mullhouse* (1972), Georges Perec, in *W ou le souvenir d'enfance* (1975)—all these use the structures of the Childhood for sophisticated and abstruse purposes of their own. And in 1976, Jean-Claude Penchenat, producing a dramatized version of *David Copperfield* with the combined companies of the Théâtre du Campagnol and the Théâtre du Soleil, handled his actors so that they worked, "not only on David Copperfield's memories, but also on their own . . . , infusing their improvisations with their own childhood memories and private reminiscences."[25] Nonetheless, and in spite of these offshoots in various directions, the mainstream which we have been studying rolls on unabated. All the old inhibitions have vanished. We are no longer afraid that the triviality of our unimportant selves will be boring to others, nor are we ashamed to confess publicly our past awkwardnesses, awfulnesses, and misdeeds. Our desire for immortality has not abandoned us with the collapse of religious faith; and our passion to understand ourselves has been intensified by Proust, Sartre, and Beckett as much as it has been by Freud and Jung. Finally,

---

niche for themselves in the paperback section of the supermarket:

(i) The semifictionalized "saga" or "series," originating in the 1930s with writers such as Alison Uttley (*The Country Child*, 1931 . . . etc., etc., etc.) and Laura Ingalls Wilder (*The Little House on the Prairie*, 1935 . . . etc., etc., etc.), and continuing through to the present with writers such as Ralph Moody (*Little Britches*, 1950 . . . etc., etc., etc.) and Fred Archer (*The Distant Scene*, 1967, etc., etc., etc.). The apparently inexhaustible public appetite for this variant of childhood autobiography would seem to suggest a most profitable alliance between the saga form of historical romance and the anecdotic/curiosa elements from the Childhood proper.

(ii) The "New Yorker-type" Childhood—i.e., incidents from child-experience (invariably in whimsical, semihumorous, self-deprecating form), destined *first* for publication in periodicals such as *Harper's Bazaar* or *The New Yorker*, but also preshaped for a subsequent circulating-library, hardback market, with a readership guaranteed in advance through the publicity of the periodicals. Perhaps the classic instance of this type of Childhood best-seller is Laurie Lee's *Cider with Rosie*; but there are numerous other examples including James Thurber's *My Life and Hard Times* (1933); Edward Dahlberg, *Because I Was Flesh* (1959); Dorothy Livesay, *A Winnipeg Childhood* (1975); Andrew Ward, *Fits and Starts* (1978); Clive James, *Unreliable Memories* (1980) . . . etc., etc.

In both the above categories, the authors belong exclusively to the English-language group. A recent development, rather more sophisticated but equally popular, among French-language writers, consists in juxtaposing incidents from childhood with incidents from adult, or even from old-age, experience, so that the time-element is destroyed, and a new metaphysical being, the total-self, emerges. Examples include Paul Chamberland, *L'Inavouable* (1967); Alain Bosquet, *Une mère russe* (n.d.); Marcel Béalu, *Le Chapeau magique* (1980–83); Marcel Arland, *Lumière du soir* (1983); Christine Arnothy, *Jeux de mémoire* (1983), etc., etc.

25. See Judith Graves Miller, "From Novel to Theatre: Contemporary Adaptations of Narrative to the French Stage," *Theatre Journal* 33 (December 1981): 431–52.

in a century whose advanced minds, at least, are as disillusioned with materialism as their grandfathers and great-grandfathers were with Christianity, the obscure sense—which we have been trying to analyze here—that there *may* be another dimension, and that Traherne and Blake, Wordsworth and Baudelaire, John Raynor and Richard Church were right when they pointed to their childhood as the period of life when this "other dimension" might the most clearly be apprehended, is likely to inspire ever more passionate inquiry into that past self and into those "early dayes"

> When on some *Guilded Cloud*, or flowre
> My gazing soul would dwell an houre,
> And in those weaker glories spy
> Some shadows of eternity.[26]

26. Henry Vaughan, "The Retreate" (ca. 1650).

Appendix:
A Note on the Concept of "Play"

Essential to the argument of the present study is the contention that the Childhood differs from standard autobiography in that it is not so much an attempt to "tell the story of a life," as to recreate an autonomous, now-vanished self which formerly existed in an alternative dimension: a "magical" or "play" dimension, controlled by concepts and rules, not necessarily incompatible with, but nonetheless essentially *different* from those which dominate the more rational and pragmatically oriented life of the adult.

In this context, an exact definition of the idea of "play" is obviously of the first importance; and it is the major achievement of Johan Huizinga that he was the first to attempt such a definition. Nevertheless, this definition is by no means as precise as it might be; in particular, it fails to make the vital distinction between "play" = "games" and "play" = "theatre"—the first involving a *passive*, albeit free, acceptance of a code of rules and a dimension of behavior wholly distinct from those of ordinary life; the second postulating a conscious and *active* creation of an alternative dimension of the self and of the human situation.

The concept of play needed further clarification; and it was the distinction of Roger Caillois, in *Les Jeux et les hommes* (Paris, 1958), to have proposed a breakdown of the general notion of play into four precisely defined subcategories. These he defines (using quasi-scientific Greek terms, not always immediately comprehensible to the average reader) as (1) *agôn* [competition], (2) *alea* [chance], (3) *mimesis* [theater], and (4) *ilinx* [vertigo]. Moreover, both among these subcategories, and within each one separately, Caillois perceives a progression from the most "regulated" to the most "turbulent" forms of play activity: thus *agôn* is the most regulated, *ilinx* the most turbulent among the subcategories themselves (see his schematic table in *Les Jeux et les hommes*, p. 66).

The first three of these subcategories, with some minor modifications, I accept; but I am not convinced the *ilinx*, whose objective, according to Caillois, is to exploit the physicality of the body in such a way as momentarily to disturb the accuracy of perception, and thus to "inflict on the lucidity of consciousness a sort of voluptuous panic" (p. 45), constitutes a truly independent category of its own. However, the most singular feature of this analysis, and one which brings out with unexpected clarity the distinction between the traditional historian and the modern social anthropologist, is that Caillois omits completely from his table of categories the one variety of play which, for Huizinga, had been the most important of all: namely, "play" = "art" or "style"—the imposing of a gratuitous, or aesthetic, dimension on the basic material of a utilitarian substance or of a functional activity.

Thus, for the purposes of the present study, I would prefer to delineate the subcategories rather differently, beginning with that in which the identity of the participant is most secure and self-assertive, and ending with that in which it is effectively confronted by absorption into something other than itself.

CATEGORY I. "Play" = *Sport/Contest* (football, chess, etc.). The characteristics of this type of play are (i) that the real identity of the participant is maintained intact throughout; (ii) that there is a predominant element of competition, always against a human opponent, deemed equal in strength and skill to the participant; (iii) *because* of this, one section of the "rules" is imposed in order to minimize the element of danger (e.g., in boxing); and (iv) the remainder of the "rules" are totally different from the rules of "reality." Lines may not be crossed, moves may not be made, where, outside the limits of the "privileged area," there is no conceivable reason why they should not be.

CATEGORY II. "Play" = *Challenge* (mountaineering, hunting, gambling, etc.). The characteristics of this type of play are (i) that the real identity of the participant is maintained throughout intact and, incidentally, that it is assumed (as opposed to Categories I, III, and V) that there will *not* be spectators. (ii) There is a strong element of contest, but never against a human opponent, other than the self. The opponent may be the self (testing one's skill and endurance to the limit); or an animal (hunting); or an inanimate object (mountaineering); or the laws of probability (gambling). (iii) There is inevitably an element of risk or danger, without which this kind of play would lose its attraction. And (iv) the "rules" are minimal, and identical with those of reality; they are, in fact, no more than elementary safety precautions. (Caillois's *ilinx* might be accepted as a variant within this category.)

CATEGORY III. "Play" = *Ritual* (religion, parades, etc.). The characteristics of this type of play are (i) that the real identity of both participants and spectators is lost in, or threatened with absorption into, a supra-individual identity greater than itself. (ii) There is a strong element of confrontation, but always with a nonhuman opponent so infinitely more powerful than the self that there is no possibility of challenge or contest, but only of obedience, submission, or propitiation, whether the greater presence be the god, the state, the embodied idea of justice, liberty, etc. (iii) Failing such submission or propitiation, there is the supreme danger of annihilation or spiritual perdition. And (iv) the "rules" are wholly different from those of "real" life. In this category of play, the loss of individual identity is frequently symbolized by the wearing of uniforms, robes or vestments, sometimes even of masks. Moreover, since the confrontation is with a symbolic figure (the Eternal God, or the Eternal Principles of Justice), the ritual is liable to involve the participant in a situation which is simultaneously circumscribed in time, and timeless.

CATEGORY IV. "Play" = *Pattern-Making* (the creation of art, style, fashion, or culture in any area of human activity). The characteristics of this type of play are (i) that the identity of the participant—in this case, of the creator—is outwardly maintained intact, but inwardly transformed, or "inspired" or "possessed," by a "vision," a unique and higher awareness. It may be assumed that there will normally be no spectators for the play activity itself, but as many as possible for the resultant artifact. In this category alone, the play activity is not self-sufficient, but is valued in terms of the product which results from it. (ii) There is a strong, *but normally concealed*, element of confrontation, the "adversary" being found in the recalcitrance of the material ("Vers, marbre, onyx, émail . . .") which the artist is striving to refashion into something other than its natural contours. (iii) There is normally no element of danger. And (iv) the "rules" are (a) wholly different from those of "real" life, yet still compatible with them, or even imitated from them ("Art imitates Nature"); and (b) deemed to be infinitely superior to those of "real" life and, frequently, to owe their authority directly to some transcendental, essential, or irrational dimension of experience, thus being considered "eternal" or "timeless."

CATEGORY V. "Play = *Theater*. The characteristics of this type of play are (i) that the identity of the participant, whether as actor or, through the force of dramatic illusion, as spectator, is temporily subsumed into the play-dimension of the drama. (ii) There is no element of contest or (iii) of danger. And (iv) the "rules" *seem* to be identical with those of "reality," but in fact are not; they are a mimicry of those rules, or, in other terms, the mask which exactly reproduces the face beneath it.

Taking this analysis in conjunction with our general argument, it will be apparent that the most powerful and "magical" moments of childhood-recreated stem from categories III, IV, and V, all of which involve to a greater or lesser extent the transmutation or absorption of the individual identity into something other, or greater, than itself. "Magical" experiences drawn from category II are not uncommon, particularly in the areas of hunting, fishing, or mountaineering, but principally for the reason that, in the course of these activities, the child finds itself again in the presence of something greater than itself, thus forming a link with categories III and IV. "Magical" experiences from category I (with the half-exception of *Tom Brown's School-days*) are virtually nonexistent.

It is perhaps worth adding that contemporary "games theory," as developed by an important school of psychologists and psychotherapists led by Eric Berne (*Games People Play*, 1964), and as applied to literary analysis by critics such as René Girard (*Deceit, Desire and the Novel*, 1965), does not demand any categories of play additional to those outlined above. The entirely adult "games" which are described by Berne consist exclusively of the techniques of Category V (psychological self-dramatization), supplemented with the motivation of Category I ("Contest," or, as Stephen Potter—one of our children—so quintessentially diagnosed it, "One-Upmanship").

A Bibliographical Note

I. PRIMARY SOURCES

A survey of the primary sources on which this study is based will be found in the checklist appended to my extended essay "Introduction to a Comparative Mythology of Childhood," in the *Proceedings of the Leeds Philosophical and Literary Society* 19 (1984), part 6. Included are not only many Childhoods to which there was no occasion to refer in this book, but also a number which came to my attention only after the present manuscript had been passed for press. The Leeds checklist, in addition to standard bibliographical information, records also (1) details of any illustrative material employed; and (2) details of extracts published in reviews or periodicals prior to the appearance of the definitive Childhood.

The only other listing of similar material is that found in the bibliographical appendix to Edith Cobb, *The Ecology of Imagination in Childhood* (New York, 1976). The late Dr. Cobb, anthropologist and educationist, spent the better part of her career assembling material connected with the childhood experience; her private collection is now housed in the library of the Institute of Education at Columbia University. This collection, although inspired by motives quite distinct from my own, is nonetheless of great value in relation to the present study. It is particularly rich in minor English-language Childhoods published between 1920 and 1960. Many of these I have not thought it worthwhile to duplicate in my own checklist; therefore, for the fullest coverage of the material, the two checklists should be used in conjunction.

II. STUDIES COMPLEMENTARY TO THE PRESENT TEXT

Various aspects of the subject, particularly in the comparative field, have been no more than indicated in rough outline in the present study, but have been explored by me in greater detail elsewhere. These include:

(i) Stendhal's *Vie de Henry Brulard*, considered as the first "perfect" example of the Childhood: "Stendhal, Rousseau and the Search for Self," *Australian Journal of French Studies* 16 (1979): 27–47.

(ii) The Childhood and the contemporary theater: "On Being Very, *Very* Surprised . . . Eugène Ionesco and the Vision of Childhood," in *The Dream and the Play: Ionesco's Theatrical Quest*, ed. Moshe Lazar (Malibu, Ca., 1982), 1–19.

(iii) First-love "imprinting" and the "lost little grey girl": "Myth and Madame Schlésinger: Story and Fable in Flaubert's *Mémoires d'un fou*," *French Literature Series* (University of South Carolina) 12 (1985), in press.

(iv) The comparative aspect—the Australian Childhood: "Portrait of the Artist as a Young Australian: Childhood, Literature and Myth," *Southerly* 41, no. 2 (1981): 126–62.

(v) The comparative aspect—the Jewish, Irish, and Québécois Childhood: "Childhood in the Shadows: The Myth of the Unhappy Child in Jewish, Irish and French-Canadian Autobiography," in *Comparison* 13 (1982): 3–67.

(vi) The comparative aspect—the English, French, and Russian Childhood: "Introduction to a Comparative Mythology of Childhood," in the *Proceedings of the Leeds Philosophical and Literary Society*, 19 (1984), part 6, in press.

(vii) Wordsworth's *Prelude* and the subsequent development of the Childhood in verse: "Lyric and Epic in the Autobiographical Mode: Poetry and the Experience of Childhood," *Neohelicon* (University of Budapest) 12, no. 1 (1985).

To these should be added a remarkably perceptive study by Thomas Tausky, " 'A Passion to Live in This Splendid Past': Canadian and Australian Autobiographies of Childhood," originally given as a paper at the ACQL Conference *"Je est un autre*—The Art of Autobiography," held at the University of British Columbia, Vancouver, May 30–June 1, 1983.

III. SECONDARY SOURCES

All the secondary sources which are specifically relevant have been indicated in the notes to the text. A valuable recent updating of general studies of autobiograpy will be found in Philippe Lejeune, "Le Pacte autobiographique (bis)," *Poétique* 56 (November 1983), especially 431–34. A useful source, not mentioned by Lejeune, is the newsletter of the Institute for Modern Biography, published by the Griffith University, Queensland, Australia.

Index

In this index, Childhoods and closely related texts are listed both under author and under title. All other texts are listed under author only. Any reference to a given page includes the footnotes to that page.